Since 1974, more than thirty countries around the world have democratized. The fall of dictators on both sides of the Cold War divide was triggered by regional economic crises and compounded by different political problems: the death of a dictator; defeat in war; or popular protest. The civilians who replaced dictators, juntas, and one-party regimes extended power to people long excluded from politics. They also set about restoring civil society and reviving moribund economies. *Power to the People*, after documenting the emergence of a new interstate system and the Cold War that divided it in the postwar period, examines the factors that led to the process of democratization in countries around the world.

Power to the People

POWER
TO THE
PEOPLE

Democratization
Around the World

Robert K. Schaeffer

WestviewPress
A Division of HarperCollinsPublishers

For Torry, Jazz, and Jeffree

Copyright © 1997 by Westview Press, A Division of HarperCollins Publishers, Inc.

Published in 1997 in the United States of America by Westview Press, 5500 Central Avenue, Boulder, Colorado 80301-2877, and in the United Kingdom by Westview Press, 12 Hid's Copse Road, Cumnor Hill, Oxford OX2 9JJ

Library of Congress Cataloging-in-Publication Data
Schaeffer, Robert K.
   Power to the people : democratization around the world / Robert K. Schaeffer.
      p. cm.
   Includes bibliographical references and index.
   ISBN 0-8133-2338-X
   1. Democracy.   2. Post-communism.   I. Title.
JC 421.S33   1997
320.9'045—dc21   97-16969
                                                                                CIP

The paper used in this publication meets the requirements of the American National Standard for Permanence of Paper for Printed Library Materials Z39.48-1984.

10   9   8   7   6   5   4   3   2   1

CONTENTS

11 Democracy and Development

ACKNOWLEDGMENTS

Torry Dickinson was central to the intellectual development of this project. Her keen understanding of sociology and appreciation of history helped shape the conceptual framework for the book. Her compassion for people around the world kept its attention focused on the human causes and consequences of democratization. She has my respect, admiration, and love.

At San Jose State I have enjoyed the warm and enthusiastic support of my colleagues. Bob Gliner, the department chair, has assisted this project by providing me with efficient class schedules and money to travel to conferences, like the one where I first presented an outline of this work. Joan Block, the university's most effective secretary, marshaled valuable resources and provided essential services, making it possible to write with logistical dispatch. The rest of the sociology faculty believes in and insists on academic freedom, which has made it possible for me to explore contemporary global problems without impediment or restraint. I am extremely fortunate to work in this department, whose members I appreciate and respect.

The students in all my classes, but particularly those in "Global Society," deserve my thanks because they have tested many of the ideas and findings presented here with their astute questions and comments. This research also benefited from grants provided by the San Jose State University Foundation, the California State University, the Lottery Grants fund, and a sabbatical, all of which were awarded by my colleagues from the faculty at large, the dean, and the administration. The library at San Jose State is not large, but it is ably staffed by Shirley Miguel, Cathy Perez, and Hjordis Madsen in Inter-Library Loan. Their efficient collection of books from all over the United States made the university's modest library grow large.

Valerie Bunce at Cornell University invited me to participate in a National Endowment for the Humanities summer seminar on democratization in Southern and Eastern Europe. I am grateful for her able direction and for the contributions made by all the seminar participants, Laura Edles and Paul Manuel in particular. They all provided a congenial setting in which I could discuss the ideas contained in this book. Barbara Yale was kind enough to rent us her house and pool and helped make the summer in Ithaca a memorable experience for my family.

The book also benefited from the work of other scholars. Benedict Anderson read and commented on early drafts and met with me to discuss the project when I was in Ithaca. His formidable ideas and his efforts on my behalf over the years have informed this book and helped secure my career. Bill Friedland also deserves my thanks for his contributions to my work over the years. Ravi Palat invited me to the Political Economy of the World-System conference in Hawaii, where I first presented this material, and he edited an early version for publication in his own book. Political scientist Constantine Danopolous shared his work on Greece, Spain, and Portugal, while Manuel Moreira in Portugal and Ludolfo Paramio in Spain shared their ideas and recollections about democratization. Manuel was a generous host in Lisbon. Giovanni Arrighi has been an enthusiastic critic and supporter for many years. Immanuel Wallerstein encouraged me to think about large problems.

Metta Spencer introduced me to Pugwash Conferences on Science and World Affairs, which in 1995 received the Nobel Peace Prize. She has always been generous with her time and her ideas. The meetings of the ethnic conflict working group at the conferences have provided me with an opportunity to explore issues related to this book with scholars from around the world. Joseph Rotblat, Giovanni Brenciaglia, Francesco Colagero, and Metta Spencer have my thanks for sharing with me their intellectual interests and their passion for peace.

Jill Rothenberg at Westview Press brought her interest and enthusiasm to this project, providing important counsel that helped shape the book. She tightened the presentation and gave free rein to its ideas. I could not ask more of an editor. Lisa Wigutoff, Melanie Stafford, and Jennifer Barrett all helped speed the production of the book. And Dean Birkenkamp deserves credit for his early interest in the project.

To all of you, my deepest thanks.

Robert K. Schaeffer
Manhattan, Kansas

"Amandla! Ngawethu!" ("Power! It is ours!")
—South Africa, 1994

INTRODUCTION

Where dictators fell, civilian democrats came to power. The democratization of political power, which occurred in more than thirty countries around the world since 1974, was a welcome and remarkable achievement. But political change on both sides of the Cold War divide did not come easily. It was triggered by regional economic crises and propelled by political problems in individual states. The civilians who replaced dictators, juntas, and one-party regimes extended power to people who had long been excluded from politics. They rewrote constitutions and held multiparty elections to restore civil society. Then they sold state assets, opened markets, and downsized armies to revive moribund economies. It is not clear, however, that the uniform economic policies adopted in democratizing states the world over can solve problems that have such different regional origins. If the democrats who assumed power are unable to solve their separate economic problems, the dramatic political gains made in recent years may be lost.

To appreciate these developments, it is necessary first to examine the origins of dictatorships in postwar republics. This account of contemporary democratization begins with the emergence of a new interstate system in the postwar period.

During and after World War II the United States and the Soviet Union designed a new interstate system based on developmentalist republican states. They advanced this new "republican" system over the objections of their European allies because they believed that the old "imperial" system was responsible for world war and the Great Depression. Chapter 1 examines the architecture of the new system and the construction of its two central political and economic institutions: the United Nations and Bretton Woods.

Although they agreed on the architecture of the new system, the United States and the Soviet Union reserved spheres of influence for themselves, a development that led to a series of disagreements and conflicts known collectively as the Cold War. As a result, the growing republican interstate system was also divided by the two great republics, a process examined in Chapter 2.

The division of the world into superpower spheres had two consequences. First, some of the new postcolonial republics rejected Cold War assignments and organized the nonaligned movement to create a more autonomous political space, which they described as the Third World. Second, the superpowers moved to expand, defend, and consolidate their spheres of influence. This contributed to the rise of dictatorships in new republics on both sides of the Cold War divide. Chapter 3 traces both developments, examining how the Cold War contributed to dictatorships around the world. It was in this context that contemporary democratization occurred.

The crisis for dictatorships in both the U.S. and Soviet spheres began in Southern Europe in the early 1970s. The 1973 oil embargo triggered a common economic crisis for dictatorships in Portugal, Greece, and Spain. Chapter 4 explains how a shared economic crisis was compounded in Portugal and Greece by the political problems associated with defeat in war and in Spain by the death of Franco. These developments led to the collapse of anti-republican regimes and the rise of socialist parties in republican states.

Dictatorships in Latin America withstood the impact of rising oil prices in the early 1970s by borrowing heavily. But they would not survive the subsequent debt crisis, which raged across Latin America and the Philippines in the early 1980s. Chapter 5 examines the causes and consequences of the debt crisis. Chapter 6 shows how this shared economic crisis was exacerbated in different countries by domestic insurgency, changed U.S. policy, and defeat in elections or war. While Latin American dictators fell—on average, one every year for more than a decade—dictatorships in Mexico and Cuba survived. Chapter 6 concludes by examining the Mexican and Cuban exceptions to the general rule, explaining why these dictatorships survived despite serious economic difficulties.

Unlike their contemporaries, dictators in South Korea and Taiwan witnessed high rates of growth in their countries and were undaunted either by oil embargoes or debt crises. But social problems associated with rapid economic change and a more competitive global environment in the mid-1980s persuaded them to democratize. Although it seemed at the time that China might follow their lead, China did not democratize, nor did Communist regimes in North Korea and Vietnam. Chapter 7 seeks to explain why East Asian capitalist dictatorships democratized and Communist regimes in the region did not.

Throughout the 1970s and 1980s Communist regimes in the Soviet Union and Eastern Europe struggled with stagnant economies, inflation, and mounting debt. The deaths in rapid succession of aging Soviet leaders brought Mikhail Gorbachev to power in 1985. His attempts to address the Soviet Union's multiple economic crises are examined in Chapter 8. Soviet efforts to reduce military spending and to reform the economy triggered a crisis for client dictators in Eastern Europe. Because Communist regimes were linked by shared economic, political, and military institutions, crisis for one (the Soviet Union) became crisis for all in 1989. Chapter 9 examines the collapse of regimes and the process of democratization in Eastern Europe and then in the Soviet Union itself.

In South Africa the economic problems related to debt and divestment and the political problems caused by ongoing black protest created a crisis for the white regime in the late 1980s. Chapter 10 examines developments that led to black majority rule in South Africa by 1994.

Although democratization was everywhere a welcome development, it did not always produce dramatic political change. Chapter 11 examines the different meanings of democracy in various settings and highlights the uniform economic strategies that democrats adopted to develop their economies. Democrats around the world sold state assets, opened markets, and downsized armies. This chapter explains why this common approach has had only mixed success and why the failure to address separate economic problems can jeopardize democratization's gains. The book concludes with an assessment of the prospects and problems of democratizing states.

Focusing on the twenty years between 1974 and 1994, this study examines the relation between economic crises and political change in dozens of countries around the world. But although the relation between economics and politics is important, it is a contingent one. Economic crisis did not always lead to political change. In Latin America, for example, dictatorships in Mexico and Cuba survived despite serious economic problems in each country. I will argue throughout this book that economic crisis and political change have a contingent, not a deterministic, relation.

Still, the fact that economic crisis contributed to political change and democratization is remarkable because it differs from the interwar experience, when economic crisis and the Great Depression led to the collapse of democratic government. In the contemporary period economic crisis was inversely related to political change, leading to democratization, not dictatorship. This development was remarkable, too, because it affected both capitalist and Communist regimes alike, sweeping dictators in both the U.S. and Soviet spheres out of power, the Soviet regime among them. This suggests that the regimes in the two spheres had more in common than is usually assumed.

Although this work examines democratization around the world, it does not analyze economic and political relations everywhere. It is not about the entire world, only about parts of it. And although any theory of change should try to explain as much as possible, there are real-world limits to explanation. Thus the findings here about economic crisis and political change do not have universal application. There are many countries, indeed whole regions of the world, to which this analysis does not usefully apply. It is a work of global sociology because it is concerned about the different social consequences of economic crisis and political change.

Of course, many political scientists and some economists have argued that contemporary democratization in different states or regions *cannot* be usefully compared. They maintain that global or even mid-range accounts facilitate "conceptual stretching" and exceed the boundaries of useful explanation.[1] This view, I think, is rooted in Cold War assumptions that dictatorships in the U.S. and Soviet spheres were fundamentally different, a view I do not share. It is also a product of intellectual investments made in specific countries or regions. Many scholars invest themselves heavily in individual states, training in a particular discipline to study a particular country and learning its language(s). Although these investments have generated valuable returns, producing the close and careful studies that I mined for this book, they have also prevented some scholars from exploring or appreciating comparative studies. As Nancy Bermeo has written, "While concern over 'conceptual stretching' is legitimate and must be kept in mind, 'conceptual constriction' that ultimately reduces all phenomena to exclusive sets of single, unique entities should be of equal concern."[2] The present work finds that important and useful comparisons can be drawn between states located in different regions and across Cold War divides. By providing a narrative account of democratization in countries around the world, this work is meant to repay, in comparative coin, the debt it owes to specialists everywhere.

The reader will also note that considerable attention is paid to some countries—a whole chapter is devoted to South Africa alone—whereas other countries receive only brief mention. This is done because some countries were more important in the democratization process than were others. The consequences of democratization in Argentina were greater than they were in Ecuador, for example, and events in Poland were more significant than were those in Bulgaria. This observation, however, is not meant to slight the importance of democratization to those people living in any of these countries. The demise of dictatorships that imprisoned and tortured their own citizens, bankrupted economies, and mortgaged their inhabitants' futures was a welcome and significant achievement wherever it occurred.

one

THE NEW
INTERSTATE SYSTEM

During World War II U.S. leaders identified recurrent world war and the Great Depression as the two most important problems of the era. They believed that the roots of both political conflict and economic crisis could be traced to a single source, what they called either "colonialism" or "imperialism." Because President Franklin D. Roosevelt believed that competition for colonies had led European and Asian empires into successive world wars, he argued that "the colonial system means war."[1] And on the eve of the U.S. entry into the war, he told British Prime Minister Winston Churchill, "I can't believe that we can fight a war against fascist slavery and at the same time not work to free people all over the world from a backward colonial policy."[2]

For U.S. officials, the problems associated with colonial competition were compounded by imperial economic policy. They argued that the exclusionary trade and monetary policies of the European and Asian empires had contributed to global economic crisis, which in turn had led to conflict and war.[3] Equating "high tariffs, trade barriers and unfair economic competition with war," U.S. Secretary of State Cordell Hull argued that "economic dissatisfaction . . . breeds war."[4]

U.S. policymakers sought to eliminate the political and economic causes of conflict by fundamentally reshaping relations among the states of the world.[5] U.S. officials adamantly opposed a return to the prewar states system, which Roosevelt described as "the system of unilateral action, exclusive alliances, and spheres of influence, and balances of power, and all the other expedients which have been tried for centuries and have always failed."[6]

Rather than allow a small group of European and Asian empires to define and dominate interstate relations, U.S. officials wanted to expand the number of independent states, particularly "republics" like the United States, and to build a new interstate system around them.[7] U.S. policymakers argued that the victors "must assure the sovereign equality of peoples throughout the world [and abolish] discrimination between peoples" and declared that "the age of imperialism has ended."[8]

U.S. officials proposed that independent republics join together to form a collective security structure as protection against predatory states and to formulate trade and monetary polices that would promote global economic growth and advance the development of individual states. To achieve this, U.S. officials organized the United Nations (U.N.) as a global political institution. The United Nations initially consisted of states, most of them Latin American republics, that subscribed to the 1941 Atlantic Charter. U.S. officials then used the Atlantic Charter as a template for the subsequent organization of the United Nations and the Bretton Woods agreement.[9]

The United Nations was designed to solve political problems that had contributed to world war, whereas Bretton Woods was created to avert the economic problems that had led to global economic crisis. Together they would form the two institutional pillars for a new interstate system, which redefined political and economic relations among states around the world. This new system was to be composed of independent *republics,* not empires, and committed to the economic *development* of all states, not just the imperial powers.

The new republican and developmentalist interstate system was created by the two great republics: the United States and the Soviet Union.[10] Like the United States, the Union of Soviet Socialist Republics also opposed imperialism and promoted the creation of a republican interstate system, signing the Atlantic Charter and helping U.S. officials organize the United Nations and Bretton Woods. Together the United States and Soviet Union established a new interstate system over the objections of their imperial European allies, led by Great Britain and France. "Mr. President," Churchill complained to Roosevelt at their 1941 summit meeting, "I believe you are trying to do away with the British Empire. Every idea you entertain about the structure of the postwar world demonstrates it."[11] He was right. But there was little Churchill could do. Britain, like France, would be forced to abandon the old system as the price for its wartime rescue by the great republics.

During World War II surprise attacks on the Soviet Union by Germany in June 1941 and on the United States by Japan six months later revived Roosevelt's and Stalin's latent anticolonialism, which had laid dormant during the interwar period. They began pressing for an end to empire and for the creation of independent states based on the principle of self-determination. As Roosevelt explained, "There are 1,100,000,000 brown people. In many

Eastern countries, they are ruled by a handful of whites and they resent it. Our goal must be to help them achieve independence."[12]

Although U.S. leaders argued for independence and for the creation of republican states, they did not believe that many colonies were ready for independence or that independent republics would soon become democracies. As Secretary Hull explained, "At no time did we press Britain, France or the Netherlands for an immediate grant of self-government to their colonies. Our thought was that it would come after an adequate number of years, short or long, depending on the state of development of respective colonial peoples, during which these peoples would be trained to govern themselves."[13] At the time U.S. officials insisted only that a republic should be synonymous with independence. Only later would they argue that it also should be associated with democracy.[14]

During World War II the United States and Soviet Union collaborated on the construction of a new interstate system. Their cooperation was based on their common identity as "republics," on their opposition to empire and antirepublican dictatorship, and on their determination to create independent republics in the colonies. In this sense U.S. and Soviet republicanism was defined by the opposition of the two countries to the old interstate system, not by an agreed-upon model of the new.[15] They could agree on the need for dissolving the old imperial system, expanding the number of independent states, and using the nation-state republic as the constituent element of a new interstate system. But they did not agree on, or much discuss, the political character of the constituent republics—"democracy" rarely came up—or how they might develop economically. Later this would lead the two superpowers to disagreement and conflict. For the remainder of the war, however, they deferred discussion of the political and economic character of these new constituent republics and concentrated instead on how to create a republican interstate system.

The Superpowers and the United Nations

To address the problems presented by recurrent world war and depression, U.S. officials first assumed global constitutional powers, inviting leaders of Great Britain, the Soviet Union, and sometimes China and France to participate in deliberations about the constitution of the new interstate system. The next task was to create institutions that would dissolve the old system and establish the new.[16]

Even before the United States entered the war, U.S. officials had already decided that the United States and the other "great powers," described variously as the "Four Policemen," the "Big Four," the "Big Three," and, after 1944, the "superpowers," would assume plenipotentiary or supersovereign powers.[17] Each of the "great powers" recognized the supersovereign authority of the others at a series of summit meetings held during the war. In August 1941 Roosevelt and Churchill first met on a ship off the coast of Newfoundland, where they drafted the Atlantic Charter and invited other states to become members of the United Nations. Roosevelt, Churchill, and the Chinese President Chiang Kai-shek met in Cairo on November 26, 1943. Roosevelt and Churchill met with Stalin in Teheran a week later, and the Big Three reassembled in the Black Sea port of Yalta in February 1945.[18]

These exclusive summits effectively served as the constitutional conventions of the new interstate system. The discussions reached by these executive committees would subsequently be ratified by states invited by the superpowers to join the first general meeting of the United Nations in San Francisco in June 1945. In their capacity as superpowers, the United States, the Soviet Union, and Great Britain were the only states that could grant or deny sovereignty to others. Only they could invite other states to participate in the new system. They also defined the meaning of sovereignty for member states, while reserving for themselves important rights not available to others. Delegates to the U.N. conference in San Francisco objected to the veto powers of the three countries. After one U.S. delegate noted that there would be no U.N. Charter without this provision, he then "sweepingly ripped the charter draft . . . to shreds and flung the scraps upon the table."[19] This dramatic display underscored the point that delegates had been invited to approve, not to question, decisions already reached by prior superpower agreement. When asked to consider a general assembly "in which all would be represented and in which [member states] could make their complaints known," Roosevelt said he would not object to "ostensible" participation by small countries.[20]

Of course, it was an act of considerable hubris to assert, as U.S. leaders did, that "in this global war there is literally no question, political or military, in which the United States is *not* interested," or to insist, as Stalin did, "that the large powers must dictate to the small."[21]

To a large extent, wartime developments forced the United States, the Soviet Union, and Great Britain into supersovereign roles. The collapse and occupation of European empires by Axis armies made it necessary for the still-standing great powers to act on behalf of European empires. For example, U.S. officials first announced that they would not permit Axis states to take control of the Latin American colonies of occupied European empires, then took control of Iceland. Britain took control of French colonies in the Middle East.[22] U.S., Soviet, and British officials also assumed great power authority because they wanted to expand or defend their political power, and the war gave them the opportunity to do so.

But although leaders in the United States, the Soviet Union, and Great Britain shared a common hubris as superpower partners, their collaboration was not an equal partnership.²³ It was dominated from the outset by the United States, which possessed three important advantages in negotiations with its associates.

First, except for Japanese attacks on distant archipelagos—Hawaii, Guam, the Philippines, and the Aleutians—the United States escaped Axis invasion. Its allies, however, did not. Great Britain was subjected to intense German bombing, and German submarine warfare resulted in widespread deprivation and hunger throughout the country. The Soviet Union was invaded by Axis armies, its population suffered huge losses, and important agricultural regions and industrial cities were occupied and devastated by the invaders. Because the United States escaped direct assault and was not as militarily and economically pressed as were its allies, it could view events with greater political detachment and exercise patience, usually an advantage in diplomacy.

Second, the United States possessed enormous economic advantages. Historian Eric Hobsbawm noted that "by 1913, the USA had already become the largest economy in the world, producing over one-third of its industrial output—just under the combined total for Germany, Great Britain and France. . . . [I]n 1929 it produced over 42 percent of the total world output, as against just under 28 percent for the three European industrial powers," and output grew to 50 percent by the end of the war.²⁴ As a result, the United States became the primary provider of food, industrial goods, and military supplies to its allies, a development that put the Soviet Union and Great Britain in its debt.

And third, the United States possessed military advantages that grew over time. Already the world's first naval power before the war, it developed the world's only two-ocean navy during the conflict and became the world's most formidable air power, largely because it could produce huge quantities of aluminum and the electric power necessary to smelt it. Its capacity to marshal scientific expertise from around the world and spend billions of dollars on the development of nuclear technologies enabled it to become by war's end the world's only nuclear power. The use of nuclear weapons to destroy Hiroshima and Nagasaki punctuated the military preeminence of the United States.

Its ability to break military and diplomatic codes also gave it an advantage over wartime enemies and postwar allies alike. During the war U.S. cryptographers broke both German and Japanese military codes. And by intercepting the diplomatic messages of its allies at the U.N. conference in San Francisco, U.S. negotiators were able to "control the debate, to pressure nations to agree to its positions and to write the U.N. Charter mostly according to its own blueprint." U.S. historians have recently discovered that "the intercepts played a major role in enabling America to fashion the United Nations into the organization it wished."²⁵

These growing political, economic, and military advantages helped U.S. officials dominate the great power partnership. Although all members of the partnership collectively assumed superpower rights, the United States presided over joint deliberations as de facto chair.

Having assumed global constitutional powers, the United States and its superpower partners created institutions and adopted policies designed to solve problems associated with recurrent world war and depression. The United Nations was the central political institution designed to prevent war. Bretton Woods was the chief economic institution designed to prevent economic depression. Although small at the outset, these two institutions were significant nonetheless. As an organization, the United Nations could be compared to the government of a small country; the World Bank, which began with $10 billion in capital in 1945, was the size of a large New York bank. Although they were small institutions, the United Nations and World Bank should be regarded as tips of the new systemic "iceberg." This metaphor was first used by Ronald Robinson and John Gallagher to describe the nineteenth-century system of British imperialism:

> The empire, as a set of colonies and other dependencies, was just the tip of the iceberg that made up the British world system as a whole, a system of influences as well as power which, indeed preferred to work through informal methods of influence where possible, and through formal methods of rule only when necessary. . . . The conventional interpretation of the 19th century empire continues to rest on the study of formal empire alone, which is rather like judging the size and character of icebergs solely from the parts above the water line.[26]

In the postwar context the United Nations and Bretton Woods were the visible peaks of the new systemic iceberg, floated by below-the-waterline political agreements reached by the superpowers at Yalta and Potsdam and by economic programs such as the Lend-Lease Act, postwar loans, and the Marshall Plan.

During the war the United States and other superpowers fashioned summit agreements and created the United Nations to provide collective security and prevent world war.[27] U.S. and Soviet officials thought this could best be done by dissolving empires and creating independent republics in their place. Invitations to sign the Atlantic Charter and later to become charter members of the United Nations were issued only to "self-governing" independent states. As a result, the United States was able from the outset to lay the basis for the predominance of republican states in the United Nations. There were, of course, some exceptions. The United States and the Soviet Union allowed some British colonies, then called "dominions," to attend as independent states. Thus Australia, Canada, Egypt, India, New Zealand, and South Africa were able to attend, despite the fact that they were not wholly sovereign or, in the cases of India and Egypt, were still colonies. The United States and Great Britain also allowed Byelorussia and Ukraine to send their own delegations to the United Nations, despite the fact that they were constituent republics of the Soviet Union.[28] But by limiting membership, more or less, to independent states and controlling the admission process, U.S. officials created a U.N. membership in which the United States and its republican allies outnumbered imperial states and their allies by a two-to-one margin.[29] Of the fifty governments represented in San Francisco, thirty-three could be counted as republics, sixteen as governments representing European empires and colonies, and the rest as independent monarchies such as Luxembourg and Saudi Arabia.

The domination of republican states, which provided the United States with a working majority, grew stronger over time because this group was able to press collectively for the breakup of colonial empires and the admission of newly independent states to the United Nations.[30] By 1960 membership in the United Nations had doubled, and the vast majority of new entrants were independent republics.[31] As French leader Charles de Gaulle complained, "Roosevelt expected that the crowd of small nations would assault the position of the colonial powers and assure the United States an enormous political and economic clientele."[32] And Churchill complained that U.S. insistence on the extension of a permanent seat on the U.N. Security Council to China amounted to the creation of a "faggot vote" because the Chinese republic would side with the United States "in an attempt to liquidate the British overseas empire."[33]

De Gaulle and Churchill correctly assessed the temper and direction of U.S. and Soviet policy, which was to break up empires and establish independent republics as the constituent political units of the new interstate system. But the new interstate system was not created overnight. Decolonization, first of Axis empires and then of European empires, proceeded slowly between 1945 and the early 1960s. Likewise, the creation of multilateral developmentalist economic policies as signaled by Bretton Woods also took shape slowly between 1945 and the late 1950s. Bretton Woods and its related economic programs were developed by U.S. officials, with British assistance, to prevent global economic catastrophes such as the Great Depression.

Bretton Woods and Economic Development

During the depression it was extremely difficult to conduct trade or make foreign investments because exchange rates changed rapidly. Governments used monetary policies to change the value of their currencies, often only in relation to some but not to all other currencies, in a desperate effort to obtain trade advantages. They also curbed capital flight by establishing controls on currency imports and exports. Under these rapidly changing and often arbitrary conditions, it was difficult for businesses to determine whether they could profit safely from foreign trade or from investment in foreign countries, uncertainties which discouraged such foreign investment and trade. As one U.S. official observed, because governments "staged [the] rise and fall of the different moneys of the world . . . with world money markets the subject of economic warfare, anyone trading on the world market never could tell, from one moment to the next, where his business was."[34]

To eliminate the uncertainties created by rapidly changing exchange rates and currency controls, U.S. officials proposed the creation of a new monetary system and invited delegates from forty-five allied countries to Bretton Woods, New Hampshire, to hammer out an agreement in July 1944. At Bretton Woods U.S. officials made a number of related proposals. First, they suggested that other countries adopt the U.S. dollar as the world's monetary standard. U.S. delegate Harry Dexter White urged the adoption of this proposal because "the dollar is the one great currency in whose strength there is universal confidence," a confidence inspired by the fact that the "United States holds a great part of the world's resources of gold and foreign exchange," in 1945 amounting to nearly two-thirds of the world's total.[35]

As a monetary standard, the dollar could be used as a value against which other currencies could be measured. British officials shared this desire for a monetary standard. "We want an orderly and agreed upon method of determining the value of national currency units, to eliminate unilateral action and the danger which it involves that each nation will seek to restore its competitive position by exchange depreciation."[36] The advantages of such a standard measure were clear. If the value of other currencies could be fixed in stable relation to the dollar, it would be easier to trade and invest with confidence. Moreover, if currency controls were removed so that currencies could be freely traded and converted, businesses could invest in other countries knowing they could take out their profits or liquidate their assets.

U.S. officials proposed the creation of an International Monetary Fund (IMF) to lessen the effects of trade deficits and exhausted cash resources, problems that undermine confidence in a currency and often force governments to consider its devaluation. The fund would use the contributions of wealthy subscribers to provide emergency funds to pay debts and avoid a currency depreciation. The idea was to avert cash-shortage crises and manage any changes in exchange rates by requiring governments to obtain IMF approval before altering the value of their currencies.[37] U.S. officials also proposed creating a World Bank, which would provide loans to ease cash shortages and avert trade deficits before they appeared. "We are not in this thing for charity," White said of the proposed World Bank. "We feel that the more loans that can be made, providing they are sound loans, the better for the world and the better for us. It means more trade, more productivity. It means less unemployment."[38]

U.S. officials volunteered to provide the lion's share of initial funds, provided that other member countries agreed to locate the new institution in Washington, D.C., and allowed the U.S. government to name its executives.[39] They agreed to the U.S. proposal, despite the fulminations of the economist John Maynard Keynes, the chief British negotiator and prime mover behind many of these proposals, who complained, "I went to . . . meet the world and all I met was a [U.S.] tyrant."[40]

Given the weakness of the British economy during the war and the reliance of other countries on U.S. material and economic assistance, delegates at Bretton Woods had little room to maneuver. According to White, the U.S. delegation "dictated the essential terms of the Bretton Woods arrangements."[41]

As a third and final step, U.S. officials proposed creating an institution that would reduce and eventually eliminate trade barriers, settle disputes between trading partners, and require member states to treat other members equally, making it difficult for countries to seek or obtain preferential treatment. The International Trade Organization, as it was originally called, was designed to end ruinous trade competition, break up trade blocs, and open U.S. access to European colonies. "In order to create conditions favorable for the fullest possible expansion of international trade," U.S. officials wrote, "it will be necessary for nations to turn away from the trade-restricting and trade-diverting practices of the interwar period and to cooperate in bringing about a reduction of barriers to trade erected by governments during that period."[42] But because U.S. officials could not persuade Congress to approve a global trade organization, they settled for adoption of the General Agreement on Tariffs and Trade (GATT). Starting in 1947, members of GATT met in bargaining rounds where they agreed to greatly reduce, though not eliminate, tariffs on most manufactured goods during the next forty years.[43]

The sum of these U.S. initiatives, which can be gathered under the rubric of "Bretton Woods," was "multilateral developmentalism."[44] It was developmentalist insofar as these initiatives created the conditions for expanded trade, investment, and economic growth in the postwar period. It was multilateral insofar as it solved economic problems and provided economic opportunities not just for the United States, which sponsored these proposals, but for other countries as well. Of course, multilateralism was not universally extended. The Soviet Union participated in Bretton Woods but did not join the IMF, the World Bank, or the GATT. Nor was development realized by all the states that subscribed to the Bretton Woods initiatives and participated in its institutions.[45] But Bretton Woods, like its political counterpart, the United Nations, shaped a new set of economic relations around the world. The simultaneous creation of the United Nations and Bretton Woods marked the advent of a new republican and developmentalist interstate system.

Decolonization

The new interstate system, which found institutional expression in the United Nations and Bretton Woods, was built on the wreckage of the old imperial interstate system.[46] The new supplanted the old because military defeat and internal economic weakness made it impossible for European empires to sustain the old system, forcing them to transfer military and economic responsibilities for some colonies to new global institutions or to the United States. It also emerged because the United States and the Soviet Union took steps to dissolve the old imperial system from above.

U.S. and Soviet officials moved first to break up the empires of their wartime enemies. They detached Austria and Czechoslovakia from Germany; Tunisia, Libya, Somalia, Eritrea, and Ethiopia from Italy; and Taiwan, Manchuria, and Korea from Japan. U.S. and Soviet officials did so because they viewed the colonies as anathema to a new system based on independent republics. At wartime summits Great Britain agreed to decolonize Axis empires because it viewed them as competitors.[47] But U.S. and Soviet policy toward Axis empires was soon directed toward allied empires as well. U.S. and Soviet diplomats used the newly created United Nations to promote "decolonization," authorizing special commissions to investigate colonial conditions.[48] Petitions from indigenous populations were submitted to the General Assembly, forcing empires to submit political information and fixing timetables for eventual independence.[49]

When they had signed the U.N. Charter, the European imperial powers had agreed in Article 73 only to promise eventual "self-government," not "independence." But the anticolonial block in the United Nations soon shifted the emphasis from self-government to independence, their numbers enabling them to execute a significant linguistic coup.[50] Officials of the European powers had long assumed that responsible self-government—something less than independence—would take "centuries." British Colonial Minister Malcolm MacDonald had argued in 1938, "The great purpose of the British empire is the *gradual* spread of freedom. . . . It may take generations, or even *centuries,* for the peoples in some parts of the Colonial Empire to achieve self-government." (emphasis added)[51] But the United Nations insisted they deliver full independence in a matter of years, even months.[52]

In addition to U.N. decolonization campaigns, the United States also used economic policies to promote decolonization. U.S. officials offered loans and military aid to European states as an incentive to shift military and economic authority to others. They also used embargoes and threats to withdraw loans as a way to force compliance with decolonization.

Finally, a new interstate system emerged because independence movements in the colonies agitated from below against imperial rule for many
years. Independence movements in the colonies were first organized in the
late nineteenth and early twentieth centuries. The Indian National Congress was founded in 1885, the Zionist movement in 1896, Ireland's Sinn
Fein in 1905, the Arab National Congress in 1913, a variety of Korean independence movements in 1919, the Chinese Communist Party in 1921,
the Chinese Nationalist Party in 1922, and the Vietnamese Communist
Party in 1925–30.[53] Leaders of these movements drew their ideas from diverse republican intellectual traditions and relied on international organizations, particularly on the socialist and communist internationals, for support. Ho Chi Minh, for example, attributed his ideas to Abraham Lincoln,
Woodrow Wilson, and V. I. Lenin, and consorted during his long sojourns
abroad with Fabians, Socialists, Nationalists, and Communists.[54] Republican independence movements in European colonies convened congresses
and elected delegates who debated strategies for change.[55] They also relied
on international republican organizations for training, assistance, and
refuge. For example, the Communist International, formed by the Soviet
Union after World War I, helped organize both the Chinese Communist
and Chinese Nationalist Parties during the 1920s and provided forums in
which leaders of independence movements could meet and share ideas.[56]

To assuage demands for independence, or at least demands for reform
(movements in the colonies demanded different degrees of political change),
British and later French imperial leaders promised greater "self-rule" in
some colonies and proposed reforms designed to increase indigenous participation in government without conceding central imperial authority.

But the efforts of imperial powers to reform their empires sharpened the
opposition of independence movements to colonial rule and clarified their
understanding of self-determination. The deferral of home rule reforms in
Ireland during World War I, for example, convinced Irish republicans to
launch the 1916 Easter Rebellion. Later, the British governor-general's unilateral declaration of war against Germany on India's behalf, made without
consulting Indian representatives, persuaded Indian National Congress
leaders to launch a "noncooperation" campaign during the war.

Although wartime rebellion and opposition to colonial rule did not immediately result in the surrender of imperial power, independence movements demonstrated that they could impose serious costs on imperial government. The Easter Rebellion in Ireland; wartime noncooperation and
postwar "direct action" in India, which provoked widespread violence; the
assassination of British minister of state Lord Moyne by Zionist irregulars
in 1944 and the bombing of the King David Hotel in Palestine in 1946; the
guerrilla uprising by the Viet Minh in Vietnam; and the Indonesian uprising
in 1945 demonstrated that independence movements could make serious

trouble for European empires.[57] As Muslim League leader Ali Jinnah said of direct action, "We have forged a pistol and are in a position to use it."[58] Although many movements did not fire their "pistols" in the postwar period, colonial authorities regarded independence movements everywhere as armed and dangerous.

Independence was granted by European empires first to those colonies where the experience and threat of violence was most acute: British Ireland after World War I, British India in 1947 and Burma and Ceylon in 1948, British Palestine in 1948, Dutch Indonesia in 1949, and French Indochina in 1954. Independence for these colonies contributed to pressure for independence elsewhere, with leaders in India, Vietnam, and Indonesia playing particularly important roles in collective efforts to promote independence and, later, nonalignment.

Imperial military defeat and economic weakness, U.S. and Soviet pressure for decolonization, and the demands of republican movements for independence led in the postwar period to the dissolution of the old imperial interstate system and the emergence of a new republican system. As John Darwin argued,

> It is tempting . . . to suggest that, while decolonization was the product of changes at the international, metropolitan and colonial levels, and can only be explained in terms of change at all these levels, it may be that changes at the international level—in particular the Second World War and its after effects— served as the trigger for an infinite series of transformations that cumulatively destroyed the old pre-war relations of the imperial powers with regions of colonial rule and semi-colonial domination.[59]

The new republican interstate system differed in important respects from its imperial predecessor.[60] First, it encouraged a dramatic increase in the number of constituent states. From fifty-one in 1945, the number of constituent states doubled by 1960, tripled by 1990, and nearly quadrupled a few years later. Second, more than fifty years after the war, the constituent units of the new system are now much more homogeneous than their predecessors. Most of the states in the system regard themselves as "republics," adopting constitutions, holding elections, and sending delegates to congresses, in which they insist on their republican identities.[61] Third, member states have almost universally adopted "developmentalist" economic policies, and even the wealthy and powerful states promote the economic development of poor and peripheral states. This does not mean that economic relations between states are equal or that "development" actually improves the economic status of poor states. But the premise of postwar economic relations is that development is mutually advantageous, and the great powers and global institutions have devoted considerable economic resources to this end. Finally, the republican-developmentalist interstate system discouraged unilateral political and economic behavior, promoting instead collective security and economic interdependence. Taken together, the political and economic features of the new republican interstate system distinguish it quite markedly from the imperial system that preceded it.

Collaboration and Conflict

During World War II U.S. and Soviet allies *jointly* created a new republican and developmentalist interstate system. Construction of this system *preceded* the Cold War. These institutions expanded during the Cold War, and they survived the end of the Cold War. Since the end of the Cold War in 1989–90, the number of states in the interstate system has continued to grow, the majority assuming a republican and developmentalist orientation. The political expressions of the system, such as the United Nations, and particularly the economic expressions—the IMF, the World Bank, and the GATT—have become stronger and more important, not less.

The republican interstate system has proved a durable system, surviving even the dissolution of the Soviet Union. But it was compromised from the outset by U.S. and Soviet insistence on the creation of separate U.S. and Soviet spheres of influence. Only by agreeing to recognize each other's spheres of influence could U.S. and Soviet officials collaborate on construction of the new interstate system. Indeed, the project would have been stillborn if the two superpowers had not reserved separate spheres for each other. But the creation of spheres also led to a series of disagreements and conflicts over the boundaries and character of these spheres. These disputes became known collectively as the Cold War. Even as the new interstate system became more deeply ingrained, it would be internally divided by Cold War conflicts during the years after World War II.

two

COLD WAR

The foundations of the republican interstate system were laid by U.S. and Soviet leaders during World War II. In the years that followed a new edifice of republican states was built on the institutional pillars provided by the United Nations and Bretton Woods. Construction of this system was possible only because its U.S. and Soviet architects collaborated on the design. But at wartime summits they agreed to cooperate only on the condition that they recognize and reserve important prerogatives for each other, recognizing spheres of influence and reserving the right to veto resolutions in the U.N. Security Council.[1]

At first U.S. officials argued that they would not recognize spheres of influence. U.S. Secretary of State Cordell Hull insisted in 1943 that "there will no longer be need for spheres of influence, for alliances, for balance of power, or any other of the special arrangements through which, in the unhappy past, the nations strove to safeguard their security or to promote their interests."[2] As Roosevelt told Churchill, "We must be careful to make it clear that we are not establishing any postwar spheres of influence."[3]

But although U.S. and Soviet officials avoided sphere-of-influence language in the agreements they reached at wartime summits, the same agreements allowed them to exercise exclusive rights in areas occupied by their military forces at war's end, effectively creating spheres of influence for each. Roosevelt told Archbishop Francis Spellman that "the European people will simply have to endure" the Soviet domination in Eastern Europe and admitted that "the world will be divided into spheres of influence."[4] And one State Department official said, "So we knew [Yalta] was going to [grant the Soviet Union] a sphere of interest [in Eastern Europe], but we did hope, or think, that if Russia could be got to cooperate generally . . . in the United Nation's scheme of things, she would behave better in defending her interests in Eastern Europe."[5]

U.S. and Soviet leaders both wanted to reserve spheres of influence, though for different reasons. U.S. officials hoped other nations would continue to recognize the 1823 Monroe Doctrine, designed to permit U.S. intervention in Latin America but prevent intervention in the region by European colonial powers. Recalling that Congress had blocked U.S. participation in the League of Nations after World War I—in large part because the nascent organization did not explicitly permit the United States to exercise its Monroe Doctrine privileges—U.S. officials worried that failure to preserve the doctrine in the postwar period would derail passage of the U.N. Charter in Congress.[6] Yet administration officials insisted on preserving Monroe Doctrine prerogatives because they viewed the doctrine as a cornerstone of American foreign policy.

At wartime summits U.S. leaders argued that the Monroe Doctrine should be recognized and its principles extended to Western Europe and Japan. In return for Soviet recognition of this wider, but not yet global, U.S. sphere, U.S. diplomats were willing to recognize a Soviet sphere in Eastern Europe. They realized, too, that the Soviet occupation of Eastern Europe at the war's end gave the Soviet Union prerogatives that Soviet diplomacy alone could not hope to provide, privileges that U.S. diplomats could not deny. As Stalin told Milovan Djilas, a Yugoslavian Communist leader, in 1944, "This war is not as in the past. Whoever occupies a territory also imposes on it his own social system" as far "as his army can reach."[7]

For their part, Soviet leaders were willing to concede U.S. prerogatives in Latin America, a region they viewed as peripheral to their strategic interests, and to recognize a U.S. sphere in Western Europe, Japan, and in areas occupied by U.S. and British military forces during the war. By giving the United States a free hand in the administration of Italy and other occupied European countries during the war, the Soviets were able to secure a free hand in Poland and much of Eastern Europe after the war. Historian T. E. Vadney argued that "Stalin shrewdly compared Soviet hegemony in Eastern Europe to Western dominance in Italy, France, Greece and . . . Japan. Because Italy had surrendered first, in September 1943, the occupation and administration of the south provided the precedents for Stalin's position [on Poland and Eastern Europe] at Yalta."[8]

The British also wanted to secure a sphere of influence. At a bilateral meeting with the Soviets in 1944, Churchill persuaded Stalin to recognize a British sphere in Greece, while conceding a Soviet sphere in Romania and Bulgaria. Fearing U.S. reaction, however, Churchill warned Stalin to describe the agreement "in diplomatic terms and not . . . use the phrase 'dividing into spheres,' because the Americans might be shocked."[9]

Some Americans were shocked and did complain. "Our boys do not want to fight to rule the world," Representative Hamilton Fish argued, "or to divide into three parts, like ancient Gaul, between Great Britain, Russia and the United States."[10] But the British sphere in Greece and Turkey did not survive long. When Britain could no longer afford to support the Greek government during the civil war that erupted after World War II, it surrendered its prerogatives in Greece and Turkey to the United States in 1947, thereby widening the U.S. sphere in the Mediterranean and the Middle East.[11]

U.S. officials followed up on wartime summit agreements securing great power spheres of influence, moving to guarantee recognition of these spheres in the U.N. Charter. At the U.N.'s inaugural conference, Senator Arthur Vandenberg and a young assistant secretary of state for Latin American affairs, Nelson Rockefeller, drafted articles that preserved the Monroe Doctrine and permitted the creation of political and military blocs outside the United Nations.[12] "We have preserved the Monroe Doctrine and the Inter-American system," Senator Vandenberg explained.[13] The adoption of Articles 51, 52, and 53 effectively recognized superpower spheres of influence and allowed the United States and the Soviet Union to organize a series of regional military and economic alliances designed to maintain these spheres.

The United States subsequently used rights given by these provisions to establish the Rio Pact, the North Atlantic Treaty Organization (NATO), the Central Treaty Organization (CENTO), the Southeast Asia Treaty Organization (SEATO), and the Anzus Treaty. The Soviets responded by creating the Warsaw Pact.[14] Political scientist John Ruggie argued that Senator Vandenberg drafted the North Atlantic Treaty "to ensure that the Treaty would be compatible with [Article 51 of the U.N. Charter]. That accomplishment allowed the United States to operate 'within the Charter, but outside the [Soviet] veto,' as the Senator liked to say."[15]

The decision to provide for spheres of influence made it possible for U.S. and Soviet leaders to collaborate on the design of a new interstate system, and it allowed U.S. leaders to obtain congressional approval for U.S. participation in the United Nations, no small matter after the U.S. experience with the League of Nations. But although mutual recognition of spheres made U.S.-Soviet collaboration possible, provision for spheres also laid the basis for postwar U.S.-Soviet disputes. U.S. and Soviet leaders agreed in principle to establish spheres of influence at wartime summits and secured recognition of these principles in the U.N. Charter. But they did not carefully delineate the boundaries or specify the character of these spheres in practical terms. The scope of summit agreements was limited and the meaning of these agreements was often ambiguous. This was due in part to the fluid and indeterminate character of the war and to a widely shared belief that wartime allies could subsequently iron out the details as postwar friends. It was understood that the two superpowers would extend the scope and define the meaning of spheres after the war. But they would do so as antagonists, not as allies.

Postwar disagreements would have important global consequences. But although U.S.-Soviet differences were serious, leading both antagonists to the verge of direct military conflict, these differences did not disturb the fundamental agreements that the two countries had reached as allies. Both superpowers continued to promote the expansion of the new republican interstate system and observed wartime agreements to establish spheres of influence, though this proved more difficult to do in practice than in principle. Moreover, the central Cold War disputes over the boundaries of U.S. and Soviet spheres lasted only a decade, from 1946–1956, making the Cold War increasingly irrelevant.[16] By this time the United States and the Soviet Union had settled most of their outstanding sphere-of-influence disputes, and numerous countries had begun to object to the U.S.-Soviet division of the world and to reject their assignment to either the U.S. or Soviet sphere. As a result, the bipolar world created by U.S.-Soviet antagonisms dissolved, and a heterodox world consisting of multiple political and economic worlds emerged.

But although the Cold War lost meaning as a global conflict after 1956, it had important consequences for many countries assigned to the U.S. and Soviet spheres. In a number of states the Soviet Union and United States allowed old dictatorships to survive or encouraged new ones to emerge because these regimes recognized and supported superpower prerogatives, thereby buttressing superpower claims to spheres of influence in different regions. The legacy of the U.S.-Soviet bipolar order was the spread of dictatorships in many of the new republics.

Disagreement and Division

After World War II ended, U.S. and Soviet officials wrestled with a series of unresolved economic, political, and military issues. The abrupt termination of U.S. lend-lease aid to the Soviet Union and Great Britain and the U.S. decision to offer only a modest, $1 billion loan to rebuild the devastated Soviet economy—far less than the $6 billion the Soviets had requested—greatly antagonized Soviet leaders, just as U.S. loan proposals disappointed British officials.[17] U.S. unwillingness to share nuclear secrets with the Soviet Union also angered Soviet leaders, who worried that the U.S. nuclear monopoly would give the United States an enormous military advantage and allow it to exact political concessions from the Soviet Union.[18] Meanwhile, the reluctant Soviet withdrawal of its military forces from northern Iran and the Soviet decision to deny the Polish government in exile a meaningful political role in postwar Poland greatly disturbed U.S. and British leaders, who regarded Soviet behavior as a violation of the spirit, though not the letter, of agreements made at the Yalta summit.[19]

Disputes over these and other issues led to "declarations" of Cold War. Stalin made the first declaration in a February 9, 1946, speech, in which he announced that the Soviet Union must prepare again for world war. Churchill followed with his March 5, 1946, "Iron Curtain" speech, in which he argued that the Soviets desired "the fruits of war and the indefinite expansion of their power and doctrines."[20] One year later, in March 1947, Truman announced that the United States would "support free peoples who are resisting attempted subjugation by armed minorities or by outside pressures" in Greece and Turkey.[21]

Superpower disagreements about crucial problems in Germany, Korea, China, and Vietnam animated the Cold War during the next decade. During World War II the U.S. and Soviet governments assumed authority over the countries occupied by their armed forces in Europe and Asia. In a few countries that had been occupied both by U.S. and Soviet armies, the superpowers agreed to share responsibility for their occupations and eventually "devolve," or transfer power, to indigenous governments.

They agreed to occupy different parts of Germany, assigning sections to the Soviet Union, the United States, Great Britain, and, later, France. Authority over Berlin, located deep in the Soviet zone, was shared by all. A similar arrangement was adopted for Austria and its capital, Vienna. After Japan surrendered, the two powers agreed to divide Korea into U.S. and Soviet occupation zones at the thirty-eighth parallel. On the night of August 10–11, 1945, Colonels C. H. Bonesteel III and Dean Rusk, who would later serve as secretary of state under Presidents Kennedy and Johnson, took out a map and drew a line across Korea at the thirty-eighth parallel, choosing this latitude because it divided the country roughly in half and placed the Korean capital of Seoul in the U.S. zone.[22] Truman later recalled that the "38th parallel . . . was not debated over nor bargained for by either side."[23]

At Potsdam in 1945 the United States and Soviet Union both recognized Chiang Kai-shek's Nationalist government in China. Both superpowers sent their military forces—the Soviets into Manchuria and northern China and the Americans into central and western China—to help the Nationalists recover areas occupied by the Japanese, despite the fact that Chinese Communist armies controlled some of these regions. U.S. officials persuaded the Soviets to recognize the Nationalist government in return for leases on some Chinese ports, railway concessions, and the creation of an independent Outer Mongolia.[24] As Soviet foreign minister Vyacheslav Molotov told U.S. officials in late 1945, "It was without question that we all agreed to support Chiang Kai-shek and that the Soviet Union had embodied this in writing [at Potsdam]."[25]

At Potsdam the superpowers also assigned responsibility for occupying Vietnam, then still under Japanese control, to Chinese and British forces. They agreed to divide occupation zones at the sixteenth parallel and then to transfer power to French authority, despite Ho Chi Minh's August 1945 declaration of independence.[26]

Although the superpowers agreed to share responsibility for the postwar occupation of these countries, the actual devolution of power to indigenous governments presented serious problems, partly because the superpowers disagreed about how this transfer could best be effected and partly because indigenous forces took matters into their own hands.

The "German problem" became apparent early on. The occupying Allies disagreed about how to devolve power and how to prevent Germany from once again threatening its European neighbors and world peace. During the war the Allies had discussed the possibility of dismembering Germany and dividing it into as many as five separate states, then closing its mines and dismantling "all industrial plants and equipment" so that the residual states would become "primarily agricultural and pastoral in character."[27] As Roosevelt told British Foreign Secretary Anthony Eden, "Dismemberment [was] the only wholly satisfactory solution" to the German problem.[28]

But after the war superpower views changed, and U.S. and Soviet interests diverged. U.S. officials decided that they needed to revive, not destroy, the German economy so that it could help reconstruct other countries in Western Europe. "To talk about the recovery of Europe and to oppose the recovery of Germany is nonsense," policy planner George Kennan argued. "People can have both or they can have neither."[29] U.S. officials realized that Germany could provide coal and industrial goods, then in short supply throughout Europe, in exchange for food, which was scarce in Germany. The Soviets, meanwhile, wanted some $10 billion in reparations from Germany (a sum agreed upon by the other Allies), which the Germans would provide in the form of industrial equipment or raw materials.[30]

U.S. officials opposed using Germany to aid Soviet economic recovery because they believed such a policy would forestall the recovery of other war-battered European economies and perhaps make them more susceptible to the growth of Communist movements. Unless these economies recovered, the United States might find itself subsidizing Germany and Europe— with much of the aid going to the Soviet Union—without laying the basis for long-term recovery. Thus U.S. officials began taking unilateral steps to prevent the Soviet Union from exacting reparations from western Germany. In the fall of 1946 the United States moved to unify the three western occupation zones in Germany into a single economic unit to provide the basis for economic recovery and on June 20, 1948, introduced a single currency for the western zone. The newly integrated western zone then received generous assistance in the form of the Marshall Plan.[31] The Soviets responded by introducing a separate currency in the eastern zone and by blockading Allied access to Berlin.

The growing division of German economic life, a product of diverging U.S. and Soviet approaches to the role of the postwar German economy, was followed by an increasing separation of political life. After the currency reform U.S. officials instructed the minister-presidents of the states in the western zone to convene a constituent assembly and to draw up a

"Basic Law" to guide the development of new political institutions and the devolution of Allied occupation authority to indigenous German government. According to the U.S. State Department, this would mean reconstituting western Germany "as a political entity capable of participating in and contributing to the reconstruction of Europe."[32] The Basic Law was approved by the constituent assembly in May 1949 and soon ratified by the individual German states and by U.S., British, and French occupation authorities.[33] The Soviets responded by establishing a People's Congress in the eastern zone, which ratified a constitution in March 1949 and established a new government on October 7.[34] Reciprocating superpower policies thus left Germany economically and politically divided. With their attention in Europe focused on Germany, the superpowers paid little attention to Austria, which they regarded as a peripheral, residual problem. Austria was jointly occupied but not formally divided during this period.

The problem in Korea was rather different. There the superpowers were eager to transfer power to a single indigenous government and withdraw their occupation armies. But both powers were interested, too, in transferring power to friendly political parties who would presumably play a prominent role in the new state. Discussions of the joint four-power commission stalled because neither the United States nor the Soviet Union wanted to approve a power transfer that might disadvantage their indigenous allies.[35] U.S. occupation forces promoted rightist parties, particularly the party led by Syngman Rhee, and suppressed leftist parties that called strikes and protests in the south.[36] The Soviets, meanwhile, suppressed non-Communist parties in the north.[37]

Because the two powers could not agree, the United States asked the United Nations to supervise the election of a national assembly that would establish a single indigenous government.[38] The Soviets and the Korean Communist Party in the northern zone refused to participate, so the May 10, 1948, election resulted in the creation of an assembly in the southern zone. It convened on May 31, adopted a constitution on July 12, elected Rhee as its first president on July 20, and established the Republic of Korea on August 15.[39] The Soviets responded by convening an assembly in the north, which ratified its own constitution on September 3 and elected Kim Il Sung as the premier of the Democratic People's Republic of Korea. The Soviets officially recognized the new country on September 10, 1948.[40]

For the United States and the Soviet Union, the partition of Korea in 1948 settled *their* differences, and they withdrew occupation forces from the peninsula. But partition did not settle disputes between the newly established Korean governments. Civil war and urban unrest, which predated partition, and then border clashes at the thirty-eighth parallel intensified after partition.[41] Syngman Rhee and Kim Il Sung both vowed to reunify the country by force in the period between partition in 1948 and North Korea's invasion of South Korea on June 25, 1950.[42] The outbreak of indigenous war then triggered a series of developments that compounded existing problems for the superpowers in China, Vietnam, and Germany.[43]

Before the outbreak of war in Korea the superpowers had decided to return power in China to the Nationalists and power in Vietnam to the French. But this did not settle matters. In both countries Communist movements fought for power, leading to civil war in China and insurrection in Vietnam.

In China Communist forces destroyed Nationalist armies in 1947 and 1948, and the battered remnants—400,000 troops and another 1.5 million civilians—fled to the island of Taiwan, the Japanese colony (Formosa) that was returned to China after the war. Chiang Kai-shek imposed military rule on the island's indigenous inhabitants and crushed their attempts to reform Nationalist rule, killing between ten thousand and twenty thousand demonstrators in February and March 1947.[44]

The consolidation of the Communist government on the mainland and Nationalist government on Taiwan created difficulties for both superpowers. The Soviets, who tried to persuade Mao Tse-tung not to initiate civil war and who maintained relations with the Nationalist Kuomintang until the very end, recognized the Chinese Communist government only in October 1949.[45] Having already reached agreements with the Nationalists during the war, the Soviets were reluctant to embrace the Chinese Communists. They also feared that China would pursue an independent course, as it did when Mao Tse-tung rejected Stalin's advice and renewed the Communists' civil war against the Nationalists.

The Nationalist rout, which occurred despite considerable U.S. economic and military assistance, shredded U.S. hopes that Nationalist China could play a role as one of the "Four Policemen" and participate as a great power in the U.N. Security Council. Dismayed by Nationalist misrule in Taiwan, U.S. policymakers even briefly considered supporting the Taiwanese independence movement's claims for autonomy from both Communist and Nationalist rule.[46] U.S. disenchantment grew so deep that on January 5, 1950, President Truman, regarding a Communist invasion of Taiwan as inevitable, announced that the United States would no longer defend Nationalist claims to Taiwan. "The United States," he said, "does [not] have any intention of utilizing its armed forces to interfere in the present situation . . . [and] will not pursue a course that will lead to involvement in the civil conflict in China."[47]

As in China, the outbreak of Communist insurrection in Vietnam posed serious problems for the United States. U.S. officials regarded French colonialism with distaste. "France has had [Indochina] . . . for nearly one hundred years, and the people are worse off than they were at the beginning," Secretary of State Hull said during the war. "The people of Indochina are entitled to something better."[48] But for the United States, Vietnamese communism was not "something better." The State Department recommended neither "full support for French imperialism" nor "unlimited support of militant nationalism," urging instead that the United States "should attempt to have the French transfer sovereignty in Indochina to a non-communist indigenous regime."[49]

But U.S. hopes for a noncolonial, non-Communist government in Indochina were dashed by the return of French forces; their assault on cities held by the Communists; the March 1949 creation of a French-controlled government led by Bao Dai, the Vietnamese emperor who had abdicated in 1945 after Ho Chi Minh declared independence from French colonial rule; and the outbreak of full-scale rebellion. The use of French forces to fight Communists in Indochina also meant that France could not fulfill its military obligations to NATO, which had been established on April 4, 1949, to defend demilitarized Germany and Western Europe from Soviet invasion.[50] U.S. officials warned that the French preoccupation with war in Vietnam would weaken the newly created military alliance in Europe. A 1952 intelligence report noted that the "financial and manpower drain" of the French war in Vietnam "seriously reduce[d] France's ability to meet its NATO obligations."[51]

It was against the backdrop of civil war in China and insurrection in Vietnam that the Korean War erupted in June 1950. Although the U.S. Secretary of State Dean Acheson had said on January 12, 1950, that Korea, Taiwan, and Indochina lay outside the "defensive perimeter" of the United States and that "it must be clear that no person can guarantee these areas against military attack," the initial defeat and retreat of South Korean armies prompted U.S. and U.N. military intervention on South Korea's behalf.[52] Events in Korea also triggered U.S. intervention on behalf of the Nationalists in Taiwan and the French in Vietnam. On June 27, 1950, the day that Truman obtained U.N. approval for the use of military force in Korea, he also ordered the Seventh Fleet into the Taiwan Strait "to prevent any attack on Formosa [by Communist China]."[53] And the next day he ordered that U.S. aid to the French in Vietnam be accelerated, sending military assistance even before legislation providing such aid was drafted or approved by Congress.[54] The administration announced in July that "the United States does not intend to permit further extension of Communist domination on the continent of Asia or in the Southeast Asian area."[55]

The war began with South Korean, U.S., and U.N. forces retreating before the North Korean advance. But a successful amphibious assault behind North Korean lines near Seoul forced the North Korean army to withdraw above the thirty-eighth parallel. General Douglas MacArthur, the commander of U.S. and U.N. forces who believed that the thirty-eighth parallel was a "barrier [that] must and will be torn down," drove north across the border and in November launched an "end-the-war" offensive designed to eliminate North Korean resistance up to the Yalu River, Korea's border with China.[56] At this point China entered the war, and Communist armies drove U.N. forces out of North Korea and back across the thirty-eighth parallel.

Ironically, Chinese Communist intervention in the Korean war was made possible by the U.S. decision to protect Taiwan. Before the Korean War, Chinese Communist troops were preparing to invade Taiwan. The arrival of the U.S. Seventh Fleet in the straits between the Chinese mainland and Taiwan prevented Communist forces from assaulting the island. Then, as MacArthur's armies approached China's border with Korea, the Communist government decided to use its troops to invade Korea instead of Taiwan. Because the Communist leadership was more eager to unify China than it was to unify Korea, by all accounts this was a difficult decision for Mao Tse-tung to make.[57] Chinese intervention in Korea also strengthened U.S. and U.N. support for Taiwan, resulting in the continued partition of China.

Chinese intervention snatched victory from the grasp of U.S. and U.N. forces in Korea, led to a military stalemate for three more years, and brought an end to the war in 1953 with an agreement to divide Korea along the thirty-eighth parallel, where the war began.

The Korean War also had important consequences in Vietnam. There U.S. officials discarded long-standing reservations about French colonialism and after 1950 moved to provide substantial economic and military aid. By 1954 the United States was subsidizing about one-third of the annual cost of the French war effort.[58] With U.S. assistance the French embarked on a major military campaign to defeat the Vietminh, drawing them into battle in a remote valley where they expected to use artillery and air power to destroy Communist forces. But they underestimated their enemy. On May 7, 1954, Communist forces overwhelmed the French garrison at Dienbenphu, setting the stage for the French withdrawal from Indochina.[59]

U.S. officials were resigned to the French withdrawal and to the creation of a Communist regime in the north. But they were not prepared to abandon the idea of creating an indigenous, non-Communist government in the south. On July 20, 1954, at the Geneva peace conference, the great powers agreed to create three states in French Indochina—Laos, Cambodia, and Vietnam—and to divide the latter at the seventeenth parallel, pending reunification elections in the north and south after two years. U.S. officials then moved quickly to establish a viable non-Communist government in the south. They persuaded Bao Dai to retire to Paris after appointing Ngo Dinh Diem as prime minister, organized SEATO to provide defense for South Vietnam, and supplied military advisers and financial assistance to the new government, amounting to $15 billion between 1955 and 1960.[60] Diem preempted countrywide unification elections by holding a south-only referendum at the end of 1955, which resulted in Diem's election as president and further deepened partition.[61]

Developments in Vietnam in turn created problems for the United States in Europe, particularly in Germany. Originally, U.S. officials had hoped that France would hand over power to a viable non-Communist government in Vietnam and return its troops to Europe, where they could be used to defend a disarmed Germany. Defeat in Vietnam allowed France to return its forces to Europe. But by assuming the economic and military burden associated with supporting a non-Communist government in South Vietnam while also maintaining a large army in South Korea, the United States found its resources stretched in Europe, despite the return of French troops. To shore up its position in Europe, U.S. officials proposed that West Germany be rearmed and that its military forces join NATO in the defense of Germany and Western Europe.

Because France had agreed to join NATO only on the condition that Germany remain disarmed and excluded from the alliance, France maintained its opposition to German rearmament and NATO admission, as had the Soviet Union.[62] But by 1954 the French could not easily refuse U.S. proposals, particularly after the United States had taken over for them in Vietnam. Like the British in Greece, the French transferred authority in their traditional sphere of influence to the United States because they could no longer bear the economic and military costs of defending it. In December 1954 French Prime Minister Mendes France persuaded the French assembly to permit West Germany to rearm and join NATO, which it did in May 1955.[63]

Of course, West German rearmament greatly antagonized the Soviet Union. In response, the Soviets organized those Eastern European states under its control into the Warsaw Pact on May 14, 1955, just nine days after West Germany's admission to NATO. U.S. and Soviet differences over economic, political, and now military developments in Germany resulted first in the partition and then in the rearmament of two separate German states.

The U.S. and Soviet solution to problems in Germany, Korea, China, and Vietnam was the partition of these countries into Communist and capitalist republics and their incorporation into expanding U.S. and Soviet spheres of influence. In 1945 superpower spheres had been regionally limited. The U.S. sphere included Latin America, Western Europe, and Japan. The Soviet sphere included Eastern Europe. But the British soon conceded Greece and Turkey to the United States, and France later transferred its authority in Indochina to the United States as well. Meanwhile, North Korea, North Vietnam, and, for a time, China joined a widening Soviet sphere. Developments in Germany, Korea, China, and Vietnam expanded and delineated U.S. and Soviet spheres. Although problems in these regions led to open conflict in Korea, China, and Vietnam and to confrontation, but not war, in Germany, between 1953 and 1955 the United States and the Soviet Union moved to end these conflicts and settle their outstanding differences.

In 1953 an armistice was signed in Korea, ending the war. It left both North and South Korean governments intact and committed each to respective Soviet and U.S. spheres. The conclusion of the Korean War also ended Chinese participation, though it also implicitly confirmed the continued separation of Taiwan from China. The 1954 Geneva Conference brought French colonial rule in Indochina to a close, which suited both the United States and the Soviet Union, and divided the country, assigning North and South Vietnam to separate superpower spheres.

Some disputes remained, such as the shelling of the Nationalist-occupied islands of Quemoy and Matsu by the Chinese Communists. But negotiations aimed at resolving these problems began in 1955, when the Communist government initiated talks with the United States at the Bandung Conference.[64] Another dispute—the admission of the two rearmed Germanys into U.S. and Soviet military blocs—deepened the division of Germany. But it also settled most of the unresolved issues associated with the disposition of postwar Germany. Only Berlin remained a contentious issue. Another conflict subsequently emerged in the early 1960s about immigration from East to West Germany through Berlin, resulting in the construction of the Berlin Wall on August 13, 1961. But the U.S. and Soviet decision to settle most of their outstanding problems in Germany by 1955 made it possible to reach a settlement on Austria. They agreed on May 15, 1955, to withdraw their military forces from Austria and transfer power to an indigenous, non-Communist government at the end of 1955, though they also insisted that Austria remain neutral, joining neither NATO nor the Warsaw Pact.[65]

Several important developments made it easier for the United States and the Soviet Union to resolve their disputes in this period. The death of Stalin on March 5, 1953, made it easier for the Soviet leadership to settle postwar accounts. The acquisition of atomic and then thermonuclear weapons, first by the United States and thereafter by the Soviet Union, was a sobering development for leaders in both countries. As President Dwight D. Eisenhower acknowledged in 1954, "For the first time . . . the United States . . . was no longer immune from [Soviet nuclear] attack."[66] He told his advisers to "withdraw into a quiet room and contemplate . . . the real nature of a future thermonuclear war. . . . The destruction might be such that we might ultimately have to go back to bows and arrows."[67]

The U.S. willingness to settle disputes with the Soviet Union was also motivated by a determination to reduce, or at least contain, defense spending, which by 1955 consumed 60 percent of the federal budget.[68] Agreements with the Soviets allowed the United States to reduce the share of federal resources devoted to military expenditures, which fell by more than half between 1955 and 1986.[69] By initiating military spending cuts, Eisenhower could permit "a substantial growth of federal spending for civilian purposes without regular fiscal deficits."[70]

The partition of Germany, China, Korea, and Vietnam and the neutralization of Austria expanded and delineated superpower spheres of influence in much of the world. By establishing boundaries and recognizing each other's regional interests throughout much—though not all—of the world, by 1955 the United States and the Soviet Union were able to settle most of the disputes that had animated the Cold War.

A World Divided

The U.S.-Soviet division of the world into mutually recognized spheres of influence created what could be described as a modern version of the 1494 Treaty of Tordesillas. The Iberian "discoveries" of overseas worlds—Portuguese explorations in Africa, India, and Indonesia and the Spanish conquest of the Americas and the Philippines—led to conflict between the two Catholic kingdoms. To prevent the outbreak of war over rival territorial claims, Pope Alexander IV confirmed Spanish claims to the West Indies and issued *Inter Caetera,* a papal bull drawing "an imaginary boundary from north to south a few hundred leagues west of the Azores and Cape Verde islands," which assigned territory west of this line to Spain and areas east to Portugal.[71] Using this bull as the basis for negotiation, Portugal asked that the line be moved 270 leagues further west. Spain agreed, and in 1494 the two countries signed the Treaty of Tordesillas, which divided the non-European world between them.[72]

Although they agreed to recognize each other's hemispheres of influence, they could not agree where the line fell, both because they had no accurate means of determining longitude at sea and because they had not yet fully explored the overseas world.[73] Portuguese and Spanish disputes over the boundaries of their spheres in Brazil, the Philippines, and Indonesia led to "a state of more or less open war" for many years.[74] The 1529 Treaty of Saragossa finally settled outstanding disputes created by Iberian exploration, divided the world into two great hemispheres of influence and control, and brought the thirty-five-year "cold war" between Spain and Portugal to a close.

But although Portugal and Spain, with papal assistance, divided the world between them, the Treaties of Tordesillas and Saragossa would soon be dead letters. As J. H. Parry explained, "Neither the bulls nor the treaties in this long diplomatic contest could be held to bind third parties, and the search for the western passage was to be carried on by other nations." Indeed, other nations disregarded Iberian treaties and aggressively explored and claimed overseas territories.[75] As soon as Portugal and Spain divided the early modern world, the hemispheres of influence they created were eclipsed.

Like early modern Iberian monarchies, the great republics of the mid-twentieth century could agree to establish spheres of influence and divide the world between them. And like the Iberians, the United States and Soviet Union found it difficult to determine exactly where their boundaries fell. As U.S. Secretary of State John Foster Dulles explained to Congress in 1955,

There is a great attraction to this idea that we draw a line and say, 'If you cross this line, you get hit.' Well, we found that it was almost impossible to draw a line in terms of concrete, specific named places, and to say 'this is it' and nothing else is it. . . . [I]f you say 'nothing else is it,' then all you do is let the enemy run around the lines that you have indicated. And even to say 'this is it' is not easy.[76]

The indeterminate character of postwar spheres of influence gave rise to apprehension and conflict between the United States and Soviet Union, just as it had for Portugal and Spain. So that the contemporary superpower *could* say "this is it and nothing else is it," the United States and Soviet Union drew lines around the world, right through Germany, Korea, China, and Vietnam. This was a difficult process, not just for the superpowers but for the peoples divided by them, just as it was for peoples in the Americas and Asia when the Iberians drew their lines. The drawing of boundaries and demarcation of superpower spheres took some years to complete. The conclusion of U.S. and Soviet boundary-drawing by 1955 simultaneously settled superpower disputes in these regions *and* created disputes between newly divided states, which gave rise to continuing indigenous conflict and war in these regions.[77] But by resolving the major superpower disagreements that emerged after World War II, the settlements of 1953–55 in Korea, China, Vietnam, Germany, and Austria largely defined the boundaries of U.S.-Soviet spheres of influence, and superpower disputes began to recede.

During the height of the Cold War relations between the superpowers were acrimonious, though disputes did not lead to open war. As soon as they divided the world between them, however, their global spheres of influence began to dissolve. They dissolved because other states refused to recognize superpower boundaries or accept their assignment to superpower spheres. The division of the world was also undermined by the superpowers themselves. Both superpowers took steps that revealed them to be self-interested, sectarian states rather than ecumenical great powers. This promoted widespread cynicism about the putative merits of belonging to either sphere. Over time the credibility and meaning of superpower claims to Cold War spheres eroded. Of course, the superpowers never abandoned their spheres or their bilateral competition for the allegiance of states in each other's spheres. In fact, during the 1940s, 1950s, and 1960s the United States and the Soviet Union would make considerable efforts to shore up their eroding spheres, using dictatorships to buttress superpower authority and police sphere boundaries.

three

SUPERPOWER SPHERES AND DICTATORSHIPS

Growing opposition to Cold War division threatened to undo the spheres that had been so painstakingly constructed by the United States and the Soviet Union and to erode their authority within these spheres. The fact that superpower spheres had been drawn without the participation or consent of the states they encompassed and that assignment to a sphere was generally inimical to the interests of these states persuaded first a few and then many of them to contest the existence and extension of superpower spheres.

To secure their spheres of influence and to prevent dissident states from abandoning their assigned places, both superpowers imposed, supported, or encouraged dictatorships in many postwar republics. These dictatorships would survive until democratization forced them from power, dissolved superpower spheres, and ended the Cold War.

Opposition to the Cold War and superpower spheres emerged early on. Yugoslavia, India, and Egypt were the first group of states to contest Cold War spheres successfully, though they did so in different ways. Yugoslavia, led by Communist leader Josip Broz Tito, was the first Communist country to break with the Soviet Union and "de-align" from the newly created Soviet sphere in Eastern Europe. Having led the most effective guerrilla resistance movement in Nazi-occupied Europe and attained power without the aid of the Soviet military, Tito and the Communist Party emerged from the war with considerable political prestige and credible military skills. Determined to keep Soviet power at a distance, after the war Tito pursued economic and political policies that departed from Stalinist norms.[1] After Stalin tried and failed to remove Tito from power, Tito broke with the Soviets. In 1948 the Soviets expelled Yugoslavia from membership in the Communist International and imposed an economic blockade on the country.[2] Tito was able to withstand Soviet pressure and depart from its sphere because the battle-tested Yugoslavian army made Soviet military intervention problematic; because Tito's regime enjoyed considerable domestic support, unlike other Eastern European Communist governments; and because the United States and Britain provided economic and military aid that enabled Yugoslavia to survive Soviet economic sanctions.[3] U.S. and British leaders helped Yugoslavia de-align in order to weaken Soviet power. "The possibility of defection from Moscow," policy analyst George Kennan argued, "which has hitherto been unthinkable for foreign communist leaders, will from now on be present in one form or another in the mind of every one of them."[4] Or, as U.S. Secretary of State Dean Acheson explained, Tito was a "son-of-a-bitch," but he is "our son-of-a-bitch," a sentiment echoed by British Foreign Secretary Ernest Bevin: "Although [Tito] was a scoundrel, [he] was our scoundrel."[5]

At about the same time, India began pursuing a policy of "nonalignment," refusing to join either the U.S. or the Soviet sphere. After India finally won its independence from Great Britain in 1947, a process that divided British India into the two states of India and Pakistan, Indian prime minister Jawaharlal Nehru announced that "we will not attach ourselves to any particular [superpower] group." He later rejected "trying to align ourselves with this great power or that and becoming its camp followers in the hope that some crumbs might fall from their table."[6] In the 1950s Nehru asked other small countries to adopt his five principles of nonintervention, what he called *Panchsheel,* and helped organize the 1955 Asian-African conference in Bandung, Indonesia, and later the first Nonaligned Conference, which was held in Belgrade, Yugoslavia, in 1961.[7]

Nehru was able to develop a nonaligned foreign policy because India had escaped assignment to either of the superpower spheres that were then being constructed in Europe and East Asia. The United States and Soviet Union would compete for India with offers of economic aid and military assistance and later would attempt to draw the two states on the subcontinent into their spheres—the Soviet Union favored India, and the United States supported Pakistan. But India kept both at arm's length, pursuing its own mix of capitalist and socialist domestic economic policies and an independent, nonaligned foreign policy.[8]

Like Yugoslavia and India, Egypt in the mid-1950s struggled against assignment to a superpower sphere. Held as a British colony but nominally ruled by a domestic monarchy, Egypt experienced a change of regime in 1952 when nationalist military officers overthrew King Farouk and established a non-Communist regime. Led by Gamal Abdel Nasser, the new government stressed the need for *al-istiqlal al-watani,* or independence—"a complex notion [like *Panchsheel*] that involves state power, assertion of national sovereignty, a search for dignity and equality for small countries."[9] Nasser realigned Egypt during the next four years, moving from the British to the U.S. sphere before joining the Soviet sphere. Even while developing ties to the Soviets, however, Nasser maintained considerable autonomy in the relationship with the Soviet Union.

Egypt's realignment was propelled by several developments. After taking power, Nasser asked Britain and the United States to finance construction of the Aswan Dam on the Nile, which would increase the amount of irrigated land and help feed Egypt's burgeoning population.[10] British and U.S. officials were initially enthusiastic about the project. But they grew unhappy with Nasser's foreign policy. They saw his participation in the 1955 Bandung Conference as evidence of growing independence and were dismayed by his plan to acquire Soviet arms from Czechoslovakia.

Nasser wanted arms to rebuild the Egyptian army, which had been destroyed during the disastrous 1948 war with Israel that followed the partition of Palestine. The Egyptian army also fared poorly in subsequent battles.[11] An Israeli raid on Egypt on January 15, 1955, killed thirty-eight Egyptian soldiers and "exposed [Egypt's] military vulnerability."[12] Fearing a Middle East arms race, British and U.S. officials refused to arm Egypt. Nasser then turned to the Soviets for military assistance.[13] But Nasser's September 1955 deal with the Soviets infuriated British and American officials, as did his subsequent recognition of China in May 1956.[14] "The Arabs," U.S. officials complained, are "absorbing major consignments of arms from the Soviets, [and] are daily growing more arrogant and disregarding the interests of Western Europe and of the U.S. in the Middle East Region."[15] Accordingly, they decided to withdraw their support for the Aswan Dam. "The primary purpose" of such a step, U.S. Secretary of State Dulles wrote,

> would be to let Colonel Nasser realize that he cannot cooperate as he is doing with the Soviet Union and at the same time enjoy most favored nation treatment from the United States. We would want for the time being to avoid any open break, which would throw Nasser irrevocably into a Soviet satellite status and we would want to leave Nasser a bridge back to good relations with the west if he so desires.[16]

On July 26, 1956, one week after Dulles told the Egyptians that the United States would not provide financing for the dam, Nasser nationalized the Suez Canal, which was built and owned by the British and the French. Seizure of the canal enabled Nasser "to redress his wounded prestige and also procure financial assets that would make possible the building of the Aswan Dam."[17] The $25 million annual profit from the canal would be used to help pay for the dam.[18]

Stunned by this unexpected development, the British began making plans to invade Egypt, seize the canal, and overthrow Nasser. "Operation Musketeer," as the British called it, initially involved British and French forces. But Britain and France soon enlisted Israel. Together the Musketeers, now three, devised a plan.[19] Israel would attack Egypt across the Sinai, using its long-running disputes with Egypt as a pretext for war. The British and French would then invade Egypt and seize the Suez Canal to "protect" it from the outbreak of Israeli-Egyptian war. The Israeli and then Anglo-French attacks, which began on October 29, 1956, triggered a series of developments that drove Egypt and later France out of the U.S. sphere. [20] As we will see, the 1956 Suez crisis, together with the 1956 revolt in Hungary, would impact heavily upon the stability of both the U.S. and Soviet spheres of influence, marking the beginning of their eventual dissolution.

The ability of Yugoslavia to de-align, of India to nonalign, and of Egypt to realign successfully demonstrated that the superpowers' division of the world was not immutable. Through the collective efforts of these countries, others were more able to break with Cold War exigencies.

The political orientation of leaders in Yugoslavia, India, and Egypt differed. Tito, a Communist, was moving away from the Soviet Union. Nasser, a non-Communist, was moving toward it. And Nehru, a bourgeois socialist, kept a friendly distance from the Soviet Union. But all three shared a common affinity as ardent nationalists and a common antagonism to military blocs: "Egypt was opposed to the [U.S.-sponsored] Baghdad Pact; India was opposed to the Baghdad Pact and to [the U.S.-organized] South East Asia Treaty Organization; while Yugoslavia was opposed to the [Soviet's] Warsaw Pact."[21]

Based on these shared affinities and animosities, Tito, Nehru, and Nasser began to collaborate. Tito and Nehru met before the 1955 Bandung Conference, Nehru and Nasser met at the conference, and the three leaders met together for the first time in Brione, Yugoslavia, in July 1956. Their collective efforts at these anti-superpower summits lay the basis for the emergence of what came to be called the "Third World," which found institutional expression at the Bandung Conference and in the nonaligned movement.[22]

The term "Third World" was coined in 1952 by Alfred Sauvy, a French journalist who used it "to describe countries that were not part of the industrial world or the Communist bloc."[23] Originally, "Third World" had a political meaning, describing countries that identified themselves as nonaligned or independent from U.S. or Soviet "worlds." Over time, however, this political emphasis has given way to an economic interpretation, and today it primarily describes countries that are poor. But in the 1950s and 1960s the term described the emergence of states like Yugoslavia, India, and Egypt and their attempts to define a political space, or "world," outside the worlds created by the U.S.-Soviet Cold War. The 1955 Afro-Asian Conference in Bandung, which brought together twenty-nine states from

Africa and Asia, was the first institutional expression of their efforts to demarcate and widen this alternative world.[24]

Subsequent meetings of the nonaligned movement, which grew from "25 members in 1961 to 47 in 1964, 53 in 1970 and 85 in 1976," built on the foundations laid in Bandung.[25] Although few of the countries that attended Bandung or subsequent nonaligned summits could actually be regarded as fully independent of superpower spheres—most found it extremely difficult to pursue their own foreign and domestic policies freely—these meetings helped them exercise greater independence.

The superpowers did not welcome the emergence of a Third World, the convening of Bandung and nonaligned summits, or the pursuit of de-alignment, realignment, or nonalignment by individual states, particularly when these pursuits challenged the political legitimacy or military purpose of superpower blocs. U.S. officials regarded Nehru's position—that "existing military blocs . . . by the logic and nature of their mutual relations, necessarily provoke periodical aggravations of international relations"—as anathema.[26] A year after Bandung, Secretary of State Dulles denounced Indian "neutralism," as he called nonalignment, arguing that it "pretends that a nation can best gain safety for itself by being indifferent to the fate of others. This has increasingly become an obsolete conception and, except under very exceptional circumstances, it is an immoral and short-sighted conception."[27] The Soviets agreed: "Neutralism, or the idea that these new states could be a 'third force' between the two sides, was a 'rotten idea' that only served the interests of imperialism."[28]

Given U.S. insistence on its own neutrality during the War of 1812 and at the onset of the two world wars, the U.S. attack on nonalignment was ironic. More recently, in 1955, the United States had allowed Austria to become an independent and neutral state.[29] Referring to Austria, Dulles had argued that "a neutral status is an honorable status if it is voluntarily chosen by a nation."[30] But neutrality in Austria was more a product of necessity than of choice, and nonalignment in India was more a choice than a necessity. U.S. officials were willing to concede neutrality in Austria as a pragmatic matter—they could not persuade the Soviets to withdraw without agreeing to Austrian neutrality—but they were not willing to concede nonalignment as a global principle because it would undermine the spheres that they had so painstakingly constructed between 1945 and 1955. For its part, the Soviet Union also conceded Austrian neutralism; indeed, the Soviets insisted on it as the price for their withdrawal. But they did so because they could easily reoccupy Austria in the event of conflict and because a neutral Austria created a geographical wedge between rearmed Germany and Italy.

But although the Soviets were willing to permit Austrian neutrality and allow the Yugoslavs to follow their own road to socialism in 1956, they were not willing to adopt either course as a *general* principle. On June 20,

1956, Khrushchev agreed with Tito that "the roads and condition of social-ist development are different in different countries. . . . any tendency to im-pose one's own views in determining the roads and forms of socialism [is] alien to both sides."[31] But a few months later the Soviets would crush Hun-garian efforts to follow in Austria's footsteps in declaring neutrality and to follow Yugoslavia's lead in withdrawing from the Soviet sphere.

Suez, Hungary, and Eroding Superpower Spheres

At the 1955 Bandung Conference Third World states signaled their opposi-tion to the recent division of the world into superpower spheres of influ-ence. Successful Yugoslavian, Indian, and Egyptian initiatives, which con-tested sphere of influence boundaries and tested Cold War assignments, encouraged others to emulate them. But events in 1955 alone did not per-suade states to adopt independent foreign policies or to join the nonaligned movement. They were also pushed in this direction by the superpowers, who "betrayed" their own allies during the 1956 Suez Crisis and the revolt in Hungary. These betrayals called into question the putative merits of Cold War spheres. U.S. and Soviet leaders had justified their two distinct spheres by claiming that the two superpowers were themselves fundamentally dif-ferent, possessing radically different ideologies, economic practices, and be-haviors. But during the twin 1956 crises the two countries acted in much the same way. The widespread perception that the superpowers behaved similarly during the crises eroded their justification for maintaining sepa-rate spheres.

The 1955 Bandung Conference symbolized the first breach in Cold War spheres of influence. The simultaneous outbreak of the Suez crisis and the Hungarian revolt in the fall of 1956 widened the breach and began eroding the Cold War edifice.

On October 4, 1956, the British, French and Israelis reached a secret agreement at Sevres, France, to seize the Suez Canal from Egypt and topple Nasser.[32] The British decided on military action because they did not want British power "to perish gracefully"; the French because they believed Nasser's defeat would send a negative message to nationalist rebels battling French power in Algeria; and Israel because it wanted to wage a preemptive war against Nasser, who was regarded as the primary threat to Israel's secu-rity.[33] Five days later, at the onset of Operation Musketeer, Israeli forces at-tacked Egyptian forces in the Sinai. Using the Israeli invasion as a pretext, the British and French then warned that if the fighting did not cease, they would intervene to "protect" the canal. The "musketeers" had agreed at Sevres that Israeli forces would not stop fighting until they had reached the military objectives the three countries had set out in advance. Because Is-raeli-Egyptian fighting continued, as the British and French knew it would, the two other "musketeers" then attacked Egyptian airfields on October 31, dropped paratroops in the canal zone on November 5, and landed an invasion force at Port Said the following day.[34]

Even though Great Britain and France relied on U.S. military and economic aid—they had to use U.S. military equipment supplied through NATO to wage their campaign—and were part of the U.S. sphere, they believed they could still exercise independent military power. They hoped that swift action would present U.S. leaders with a fait accompli and that Eisenhower, then wrapping up his presidential campaign for a second term in office, would, in British Foreign Secretary Harold Macmillan's words, "lie doggo until after the election."[35] They could not have been more wrong. British prime minister Anthony Eden apparently forgot Churchill's admonition: "Always remember that there are various large matters in which we cannot go further than the United States [is] willing to go."[36]

As soon as the three "musketeers"—Great Britain, France, and Israel—swung into action, U.S. officials mounted a furious campaign to end the fighting and to force them to withdraw. President Eisenhower told Secretary of State Dulles to send a scathing message to Israeli prime minister David Ben-Gurion: "You'll tell 'em, god damn it, we're going to apply sanctions, we're going to the United Nations, we're going to do everything that there is so we can stop this thing."[37]

Meanwhile, the Soviet Union, Egypt's new ally, threatened to intervene on Egypt's behalf and joined the United States in a U.N. resolution calling for an immediate cease-fire and the withdrawal of Israeli, French, and British forces.[38]

The United States turned on its allies in this way for a variety of reasons. U.S. officials believed that Egypt was within its legal rights when it nationalized the Suez Canal, as Egypt was a major shareholder in the Anglo-French company that operated the canal and was simply exercising its right to buy out its partners.[39] But the United States was upset that its allies, the three "musketeers," had violated NATO agreements by using U.S.-supplied weapons intended for the defense of Europe against Egypt and that the Suez crisis diverted attention from Soviet intervention in Hungary. Dulles said it was "nothing less than tragic that at this very time when we are on the point of winning an immense and long-hoped-for victory over Soviet colonialism in Eastern Europe, we should be forced to choose between following in the footsteps of Anglo-French colonialism in Asia and Africa, or splitting our course away from their course."[40]

U.S. officials were angry that they had not been consulted in advance about the activities of their allies and furious that their allies would violate the U.N. Charter by waging a unilateral colonial war of aggression. Eisenhower told Eden that "such a violation of the U.N. Charter would jeopardize the organization" and threaten the interstate system then under construction.[41] U.S. officials also worried that their inaction would result in the loss of "the whole Arab world and maybe Africa. It could be a major disaster comparable to the loss of China."[42] Dulles noted that although the British and French may have assumed the United States would side with them, "in these circumstances . . . we cannot be bound by our traditional alliances."[43]

U.S. officials then used every means at their disposal to force their allies to decamp. They lobbied hard at the United Nations for a genuine cease-fire and withdrawal and refused to stem the collapse of British finances until the British complied with their demands. The U.S. refusal to provide the British with new loans was an extremely important economic weapon because the war had closed the canal, shut off supplies of British oil to Europe, and forced Britain to spend its scarce dollar reserves to buy oil from other sources.[44] Moreover, when Soviet premier Khrushchev threatened Britain, France, and Israel with "rocket attacks"—implying that the Soviets might consider the use of nuclear weapons—the United States did not immediately respond in kind. "In what situation would Britain find herself," the Soviets wrote, "if she were attacked by a stronger power possessing all types of modern weapons of destruction? . . . for instance rocket equipment."[45] Eisenhower did not act immediately because he did not believe that Soviet nuclear threats were credible and because he thought that the United States had already extended to its allies sufficient guarantees against nuclear attacks.[46] But Israel, Britain, and France did not see it this way. They felt threatened by the Soviets and abandoned by the United States. Yaacov Herzog, Ben-Gurion's principal political adviser, wrote that Ben-Gurion was "entirely unprepared by the vehemence of President Eisenhower's backing of the General Assembly's call for immediate and unconditional Israeli withdrawal. What the U.S. did then was to remove Israel's—as well as Britain's and France's—protective shield against possible [nuclear] retaliation, leaving them all exposed."[47]

No longer able to bear the brunt of American "economic artillery," the British and French accepted a cease-fire on November 6, the day President Eisenhower was elected to a second term, and agreed to withdraw a month later. Israel's withdrawal followed a few months after that.[48] Eisenhower had also used economic pressure on Israel to force concessions, threatening to block the sale of Israeli government bonds in the United States.[49]

While regional conflicts sharpened in the Middle East in 1956, they also became acute in Eastern Europe, particularly in Poland and Hungary. The attack on Egypt and the Suez Canal was followed by revolt and Soviet invasion in Hungary in October-November 1956.

The crisis in Eastern Europe began in February, when Soviet premier Nikita Khrushchev denounced Stalin and attacked his policies at a "secret" session of the Twentieth Communist Party Congress.[50] Khrushchev attacked Stalin to shore up his new leadership position and to open the door to domestic reform. Reform in the Soviet Union made it possible for Communist governments to consider similar reforms in Eastern Europe. Khrushchev then abolished the Cominform in April and sought to improve relations with Yugoslavia, which resulted in a joint declaration recognizing the "different roads to socialism."[51]

In Poland and Hungary the response to Soviet de-Stalinization and reform was mixed. Economic difficulties throughout the early 1950s had convinced some Communist Party leaders—Wladyslaw Gomulka in Poland and Imre Nagy in Hungary—that domestic economic and political reform was necessary. Gomulka wanted to reduce government bureaucracy and increase opportunities "for artisans and small private-service industries"; Nagy wanted to slow the pace of industrialization, provide more consumer goods, and permit some farmers to leave collective farms.[52] But reformers represented only a minority in Communist parties. Gomulka and Nagy were excluded from a central role in political power, and the Communist majority did not want to abandon Stalinist policies or surrender power to the reformers, believing that Soviet enthusiasm for reform would soon wane.[53]

In Poland in June and in Hungary in October, demonstrators began to demand reform, tipping the balance of power to reformers and propelling Gomulka and Nagy back into power in late October.[54] Strikes and riots in Poznan and other Polish cities in June and a massive demonstration at the burials of Hungarian Communists executed during anti-Tito purges in the late 1940s signaled popular discontent with Stalinist government and support for reform.[55]

Popular enthusiasm for reform grew, and public demonstrations against domestic Communist government and Soviet military occupation turned violent. The crisis became particularly acute in Hungary, where demonstrators toppled a monumental statue of Stalin and skirmished with Soviet troops and with domestic security forces still under the control of antireform Communists. The Soviets now reconsidered their support for reform.[56] But although the Soviets were alarmed by events in both Poland and Hungary, they handled the two crises in different ways.

In Poland Khrushchev and a delegation of top Soviet officials flew to Warsaw unannounced and forced a showdown with Gomulka and the Polish government. The Soviets agreed to a deal allowing Gomulka to stay in power and allowing him to pursue limited domestic reform. In return Gomulka promised that Poland would remain under Communist control, that it would continue to be an active participant in the Warsaw Pact, and that it would recognize the Soviet sphere of influence in Eastern Europe.[57]

But although the Soviets were willing to accommodate Poland, they would not do the same for Hungary. Nagy made clear his desire to pursue domestic reform, to end Communist rule, and to de-align from the Soviet sphere. When he announced on October 30, 1956, Hungary's "abrogation of the one-party system and the formation of a government based on the democratic co-operation among the coalition parties of 1945" and vowed to open talks with the Soviets "about the withdrawal of Soviet troops from Hungary" and of Hungarian forces from the Warsaw Pact, the Soviets decided that Nagy had gone too far and that his government must be brought down.[58] In the confusion created by the Suez crisis, then reaching its apogee, the Soviets were able to quickly achieve their aim. They first withdrew and regrouped, then used their troops to assault Budapest on November 4, leading to pitched battle between Soviet tanks and Hungarian irregulars.[59] Khrushchev "listed as one of several reasons for the Soviet decision [to invade Hungary] the Anglo-French intervention at Suez, which would direct the world's attention away from the Soviet Union's 'assistance' to Hungary."[60] Because the Hungarian army did not join the battle, anti-Soviet resistance was crushed by mid-November, Nagy was arrested and later executed, and conservative Communist Party rule was restored.[61]

The United States condemned the Soviet invasion of Hungary but did nothing to assist the Nagy government. Indeed, prior to the invasion the U.S. delegation to the United Nations argued that Nagy was indistinguishable from other Communists and "that the whole dispute was a falling out of thieves."[62] The United States did not intervene because it recognized Hungary as part of the Soviet sphere and worried about antagonizing the Soviets.[63] "The Russians were scared and furious," Eisenhower argued, "and nothing is more dangerous than a dictatorship in that frame of mind."[64] U.S. officials also expected that even if the Soviets had "lost a Satellite and gained a conquered province . . . the myth of [the] sweet reasonableness of communism had been destroyed," which would have important ramifications around the world.[65]

Both the United States and the Soviet Union achieved their immediate objectives in the Middle East and Eastern Europe. The United States had forced the withdrawal of British, French, and Israeli troops from the Suez Canal. The Soviets had forced independent-minded Polish and Hungarian reformers to remain within the Soviet sphere in Eastern Europe. But these immediate successes created difficult and continuing problems for both superpowers.

For many countries in the West, the U.S. behavior in the Middle East demonstrated that the United States *could* turn against any of its allies who departed from the U.S. foreign policy line, and U.S. inaction in Hungary showed that the United States would ignore and disappoint potential allies who rose to challenge the Soviet Union and depart from its sphere of influence. For many countries in the East and for many nonaligned countries like Yugoslavia, Egypt, and India, Soviet behavior similarly demonstrated that it could turn against any of its allies who departed significantly from Soviet foreign and domestic policies. For example, after the crises in Suez and Hungary abated, Nasser told U.S. Ambassador Raymond Hare that he did not intend to exchange one form of superpower domination for another. Nasser noted that the Soviets had waited nine days before delivering their nuclear ultimatum to Britain, France, and Israel, and during that period, "We had not the slightest intimation of support from any foreign state, even the Soviet Union. We relied on God and ourselves."[66]

For countries that had already expressed their discomfort with superpower spheres at the 1955 Bandung Conference, events in 1956 sharpened their objections to Cold War assignments. In a sense, the effect of the events of 1955 and 1956 was a movement for independence within both superpower spheres.

Events in 1955–1956 persuaded the leaders of some countries allied with the United States and the Soviet Union to pursue policies that would change their relation to the U.S. and Soviet spheres. For U.S. allies, the Suez crisis was a profound shock. For the British, Suez demonstrated their reliance on U.S. economic assistance and their vulnerability to pressure when they failed to conform with U.S. policy. Successive economic crises in Britain had been eased by such U.S.-sponsored measures as the lend-lease program, postwar loans, the Marshall Plan, and post-Suez loans. And with each crisis the British transferred a measure of power or regional authority to the United States as payment for their debt. As John Darwin argued,

> [Suez] precipitated a crisis within the Commonwealth, which was fiercely divided over the propriety of British action. It revealed the vulnerability of sterling to American financial pressure and the danger that independent action might jeopardize Britain's revival as a premier trading and financial power. . . . It generated acute political division at home, enforced a change of prime minister and threatened to bring down the government altogether. And it exposed the weakness of British military power and the unreliability of foreign bases in times of crisis.[67]

Formerly a great power ally of the United States, Britain was demoted to junior partner in the course of these events, particularly those associated with Suez. British Foreign Secretary Macmillan admitted that "the British action [at Suez] was the last gasp of a declining power. . . . perhaps in two hundred years the United States would know how we felt."[68]

Whereas Britain remained in the U.S. sphere in a junior role, Suez propelled France out of the U.S. sphere altogether. For the French, Suez illustrated the danger of relying on the United States as an ally. As one French official observed, "The United States will not feel any scruple in siding against its loyal allies on behalf of its potential allies [Egypt], against two essential members of the Atlantic Alliance on behalf of those for whom anti-Westernism is a political, racial and religious objective."[69] It also demonstrated French vulnerability vis-à-vis the Soviet Union, which had used nuclear weapons to threaten nonnuclear France. After Suez the French government's "previous hostility toward atomic weapons was transformed overnight into a determined and positive interest in national nuclear armament."[70] The subsequent development of a *force de frappe,* or independent nuclear force, would enable France to distance itself from one superpower and protect itself from the other.[71]

For De Gaulle, who became premier of France in 1958, Suez reinforced his long-held view that the United States would take measures inimical to French interests. Accordingly, he took two steps to promote French "independence," which he defined as its ability to "decide on what we have to do and with whom, without its being imposed by any other state or by any other collective body."[72] First, he rapidly developed French nuclear weapons, testing the first French atomic bomb on February 13, 1960.[73] The development of these weapons would enable France to rebuff Soviet nuclear threats. "Once reaching a certain nuclear capability," De Gaulle said, "one has the means to wound the possible aggressor mortally."[74]

Second, De Gaulle demanded greater French control over U.S. nuclear forces based in Europe. "[France] *obviously* cannot entrust her life or her death to any other state whatsoever, even the most friendly," De Gaulle explained to Eisenhower in 1958. "For this reason, France feels it is essential to participate . . . in any decision which might be taken by her allies to use atomic missiles or to launch them against certain places at certain times." (emphasis added)[75] But the United States was not willing to meaningfully share authority over the use of its nuclear weapons with its junior allies. De Gaulle thus began taking steps to restrict French participation in NATO, forcing the evacuation of NATO forces from France in 1966, then withdrawing from NATO altogether.[76] France's withdrawal from NATO and development of its own nuclear force effectively took France out of the U.S. sphere of influence and also altered relations with the Soviets, who became more friendly during the 1960s.

The Suez crisis also had an important impact on Israel. Like Britain, Israel had tried to repair its relations with the United States after 1956. But like France, and with French assistance, Israel also began developing its own nuclear weapons to enable it to conduct an independent foreign policy should the United States again fail to support Israel during a crisis. The *force de frappe* became the common French and Israeli response to superpower behavior during the 1956 Suez crisis.[77]

In the same way that some U.S. allies responded to the events of 1956, some Soviet allies began to depart from the Soviet sphere. China was the most important country to do so. Like the French, who saw U.S. behavior during the Suez crisis as another example of its unreliability, the Chinese viewed Khrushchev's behavior in 1956 as one more example of Soviet perfidy. The Chinese Communists had already drawn up a long list of their grievances with the Soviets—their wartime support for Chiang Kai-shek's Nationalist government, the inadequacy of postwar Soviet financial aid, and the Soviet Union's unwillingness to assist them in China's conflicts with the United States.[78] When China entered the Korean War, the Soviets did not invoke the Sino-Soviet Treaty, a mutual defense agreement, nor did the Soviets send troops to join the fighting. After Presidents Truman and Eisenhower repeatedly threatened China with nuclear weapons during the Korean War (1950–53) and the Quemoy-Matsu crises (1954–55), the Soviets did not counter these threats with nuclear warnings of their own, despite the fact that the Sino-Soviet Treaty contained an implicit Soviet pledge to provide China with nuclear weapons.[79] Like the French, the Chinese concluded that they could not rely on their allies to protect them from superpower nuclear threats. As Chinese foreign minister Chen Yi said of Soviet nuclear guarantees, "How can any one nation say that they will defend another—promises are easy to make, but they are worth nothing. Soviet protection is worth nothing to us."[80]

Although the Soviets first agreed to help the Chinese develop nuclear weapons, they balked after Chinese leader Mao Tse-tung dismissed Soviet fears of nuclear war. "No matter what kind of war breaks out—conventional or thermonuclear—we'll win," Mao bragged. "We may lose more than 300 million people. So what? War is war. The years will pass, and we'll get to work producing more babies than ever before."[81]

Khrushchev withdrew Soviet advisers from the Chinese nuclear program in 1959, which helped precipitate the rupture of Sino-Soviet relations in 1960.[82] Accumulated Chinese grievances were reinforced by events in 1956. The Chinese were upset not so much by the Soviet invasion of Hungary but by Khrushchev's attack on Stalinism, which they viewed as an attack on their own domestic policies.[83] They saw efforts to reform the Soviet Union and to permit reform elsewhere as a betrayal, much as Stalinist leaders in Eastern Europe saw Soviet-initiated reform as a betrayal that threatened their hold on power. For the Chinese, the Soviet willingness to betray their Stalinist allies in Eastern Europe, coupled with their *un*willingness to assist Chinese economic and nuclear programs, demonstrated a Soviet capacity to betray even their closest allies. In 1960 the Chinese departed from the Soviet sphere and began to develop their own nuclear weapons. The Chinese nuclear program, Mao said, was designed to "boost our courage and scare others," not just the United States but also the Soviet Union.[84] China exploded its first nuclear weapons on October 16, 1964.[85]

The departure of China from the Soviet sphere in 1960, its adoption of a nonaligned foreign policy during the 1960s, when it attacked both the United States and the Soviet Union as "imperialist" powers, and then its entry into close relations with the United States in 1972 made it possible for other Communist countries in Asia (North Korea and North Vietnam) and Europe (Albania) to distance themselves from the Soviet Union and pursue more independent foreign policies.[86]

Events in 1956 had other consequences as well. The British and French failure to discipline postcolonial Egypt demonstrated that colonial authority had been greatly weakened, that independence movements might soon be entirely successful, and that postcolonial states might be able to exercise greater independence after decolonization than they had previously expected. After 1956 decolonization accelerated, both because efforts by independence movements intensified in such colonies as British Cyprus, Kenya, and Malaysia and French Algeria and because British and French determination to retain their colonies waned after Suez.[87] As a result, in the four years after Suez twenty-six countries in Africa won their independence from British, French, and Belgian rule, along with Cyprus and Malaysia.[88]

As these countries joined the United Nations, the number of countries determined to pursue nonaligned policies grew. "By 1958 . . . the Afro-Asian states held a third of the [U.N.'s] Assembly seats. This gave them a 'collective veto' since important Assembly resolutions require a majority of two to one and can be defeated by a 'blocking third.' Soviet commentators gleefully argued that the 'American voting machine was no longer working,'" one commentator observed.[89] But what was true of waning U.S. power in the U.N. General Assembly was even more true of Soviet power.

By 1955 the United States and Soviet Union had resolved postwar problems and divided the world into two exclusive spheres. But events in 1955 and 1956 led Third World countries to contest these superpower spheres. The ability of some states to contest Cold War assignments, first Yugoslavia, India, and Egypt, then France and China, and, to some extent, countries like Israel and Poland, made it possible for other states to attempt to de-align, realign, and nonalign. After 1956 many states gradually increased their independence from both superpowers, contributing to the erosion of superpower spheres.

Cold War Dictators

By 1955 the United States and Soviet Union had settled most of their postwar disputes and agreed to recognize each other's spheres of influence, which then extended around the world. But as soon as U.S.-Soviet spheres reached their global apogee, they went into eclipse. In 1955 independent-minded states began creating a "Third World," a political space outside U.S.-Soviet spheres. And in 1956 states that had been disenchanted by events in Suez and Hungary began to distance or remove themselves from their assigned superpower spheres, slowly wearing at the base of superpower bulwarks. During the 1960s China and France, along with countries like Yugoslavia, India, and Egypt, Albania and Cuba, would breach these walls and weaken their structural integrity.

The superpowers, however, were not prepared to sit idly by and watch their spheres disintegrate. They were instead determined to protect and preserve them. Indeed, the defection of a few states prompted the superpowers to intensify their efforts to fortify their spheres by binding those states within them more tightly to superpower policies, encouraging states to defect from the other's sphere, and punishing defectors from their own.

To police crucial boundaries between spheres and maintain the political and economic integrity of their spheres, Soviet and then U.S. officials adopted dictatorships as a necessary expedient in many states, encouraging or allowing dictators to take power in many of the new republics.[90] The Soviets initiated this process in Eastern Europe during the late 1940s, when Communist parties backed by Soviet occupation armies took power in Poland, Hungary, Czechoslovakia, Bulgaria, Romania, East Germany, and Albania. In Yugoslavia Communist dictatorship was established, but by indigenous Communists.[91]

Then in the late 1940s and early 1950s, largely as a result of civil war in China and conflict in Korea, one-party dictatorships on both sides of the superpower divide emerged in East Asia. The Soviet Union supported one-party Communist rule in North Korea, mainland China, and North Vietnam. The United States backed one-party Nationalist rule in Taiwan and supported the dictatorships that emerged in South Korea and South Vietnam. It also sponsored a 1953 coup in Iran that led to the creation of a dictatorship that later established itself as a monarchy. During the 1950s the United States enlisted as its allies fascist dictatorships that had survived the war in Spain and Portugal, allowing Portugal's Salazar regime to join NATO in 1949 and providing economic and military aid to Franco's dictatorship in Spain in 1953 in return for base rights in the Azores and the Iberian Peninsula.[92] The United States also used a surrogate "contra" army in Guatemala to depose an elected leftist regime and establish a military dictatorship there in 1954.[93]

In Latin America dictatorship was common before World War II. Dictatorships in Argentina, Paraguay, Nicaragua, the Dominican Republic, and Cuba survived the war intact, though some were reconstituted in the 1950s, when collective military regimes, or juntas, replaced individual rulers, or "caudillos."[94] Venezuela oscillated between dictatorship and democracy, while Mexico was ruled by a one-party, non-Communist regime throughout this period. Although some of these dictatorships had been sponsored or installed by the United States, some, like François "Papa Doc" Duvalier in Haiti in 1957, acquired power on their own in struggles unrelated to events outside the region.

External events began to influence the region after 1959, when Communist guerrillas in Cuba overthrew the Batista dictatorship and established a Communist regime led by Fidel Castro. As the first one-party Communist regime in Latin America, Castro took Cuba out of the U.S. sphere and into the Soviet sphere, a development that led to a U.S.-sponsored "contra" invasion at the Bay of Pigs in 1961 and to a U.S.-Soviet confrontation over the placement of Soviet nuclear missiles in Cuba one year later. Events in Cuba introduced sphere-of-influence conflicts into the region and intensified U.S. support for anti-Communist dictatorships throughout Latin America. U.S.-supported military forces then mounted coups that led to new dictatorships in Honduras in 1963, Brazil and Bolivia in 1964, Peru in 1968, Panama in 1969, Chile in 1973, Argentina in 1976, and Surinam in 1980.

In the Middle East and Africa dictatorships frequently emerged on the heels of decolonization. Political parties, military elites, and charismatic leaders moved after independence to consolidate or seize power. Although dictatorships were usually initiated by indigenous groups, they were soon courted and enrolled into superpower spheres. Some, like Iraq, followed Egypt's example and played both superpowers against each other, siding first with one and then the other. During the 1950s and 1960s most African dictatorships enrolled in the U.S. sphere, with the exception of leftist regimes that ruled briefly in Ghana and the Congo and for a long time in Tanzania. The success of Communist guerrilla movements in the Portuguese colonies of Angola, Mozambique, and Guinea Bissau in 1974; coups by Communist military officers in Libya, Sudan, and Somalia in 1969; and the overthrow of the Ethiopian monarchy in 1973 by Communist military forces brought these countries into the Soviet sphere, at least for a time (Somalia later left and Ethiopia joined the Soviet sphere).

In the Middle East one-party, non-Communist regimes that took power in Iraq and Syria, like Egypt, enlisted in the Soviet sphere during the 1960s and 1970s. The new Iranian monarchy and residual monarchies in Jordan and Saudi Arabia enrolled in the U.S. sphere. The 1979 overthrow of the Shah of Iran and the eventual seizure of power by Islamic revolutionaries led to Iran's abrupt departure from the U.S. sphere and the adoption of a nonaligned foreign policy, while the 1978–79 coup by Communist forces in neighboring Afghanistan moved that country from its nonaligned position into the Soviet sphere.

Of course, dictatorships emerged elsewhere, at different times in Pakistan and Bangladesh, as well as in Burma, Thailand, Laos, and Indonesia. These were largely indigenous in origin, though the United States supported military rule in Thailand and defended anti-Communist dictatorship in Indonesia in 1965.

When they enlisted dictatorships and democracies into their spheres, the United States and the Soviet Union provided food, extended loans, purchased commodities, provided education and training for bureaucrats and military officers, and, significantly, furnished military arms to their clients and allies. The U.S. government provided more than $70 billion in military assistance to countries in Asia, Africa, and Latin America in the thirty years after World War II.[95] The Soviet Union, followed by the United Kingdom, France, and China, also transferred or sold tens of billions of dollars in arms to postcolonial states. From the mid-1950s until 1978 the Soviet Union provided $29.7 billion in military aid to other countries, most of them dictatorships.[96] The provision of superpower arms increased over time. U.S. military sales averaged about $1 billion per year in the 1950s and 1960s, $12 billion per year in the late 1970s, and $21 billion in the early 1980s.[97]

One important difference between the prewar, imperial interstate system and its postwar republican successor was that the prewar European empires reserved military arms for themselves. They engaged in an intramural arms race but did not distribute advanced weaponry to their colonies or to independence movements in colonies around the world. This changed after World War II, when the superpowers and great powers armed the world. They provided sophisticated, lethal weapons to postcolonial states and, sometimes, to opposition movements within them. The proliferation of arms stimulated local and regional arms races and put automatic weapons like the ubiquitous AK-47 into the hands of people around the world. The irony, of course, was that the provision of weapons by the superpowers increased the ability of postcolonial states to initiate and wage war unilaterally. As these states grew more powerful, they became less tractable and more independent of both superpowers. The superpowers evidently believed that the provision of arms would bind these regimes to superpower spheres. As U.S. Undersecretary of State James L. Buckley argued in 1981, "Arms transfers serve as an important adjunct to our own security by helping deter acts of aggression [and] by enhancing the self-defense capabilities of nations with which we share close security ties."[98]

But this confidence was frequently misplaced. For example, the Soviet provision of arms to Egypt and Somalia enabled them to initiate wars that the Soviets did not sanction. The provision of U.S. arms to Great Britain, France, Israel, Turkey, and Argentina helped these countries initiate wars that the U.S. did not support. "The arms suppliers themselves undermine their ability to dominate certain Third World conflicts by this very effort to secure political advantage by the transfer of increasingly sophisticated arms," Barry Blechman, Janne Nolan, and Anal Plat observed in *Foreign Policy*. "Selling arms . . . may not be like throwing a lighted match into a gasoline tank, but it is like adding more gasoline to a tank that has exploded in flaming destruction over and over in the past few years," Senator William Proxmire argued.[99]

As the journalist Walter Lippmann observed, "The sweeping terms of [Cold War] containment obliged [the United States] . . . to recruit, subsidize and support a heterogeneous army of satellites, clients, dependents and puppets."[100] The same, of course, was true of the Soviet Union. But why did both superpowers promote and support the emergence of this "hetero-geneous army" of dictatorships in their spheres?

The superpowers supported dictatorships because they were determined to defend their spheres and to prevent defection from them. As U.S. Secre-tary of the Treasury George Humphrey argued in 1955, "The United States should back strong men in Latin American governments [because] where ever a dictator was replaced, communists gained."[101] U.S. officials worried that if Communists gained, they would bring the country into the Soviet orbit, a process generally described as the "domino" effect.[102] "If we let Korea down," Truman argued, "the Soviets will keep right on going and swallow up one piece of Asia after another. . . . if we were to let Asia go, the Near East would collapse [and there would be] no telling what would hap-pen in Europe."[103] Subsequent U.S. presidents subscribed to this view, as did Soviet leaders. Khrushchev worried that Soviet concessions over Berlin would be viewed by U.S. leaders as a

> strategic breakthrough and would in no time broaden their range of demands. They would demand the abolition of the socialist system in the German Demo-cratic Republic. If they achieved this too, they would . . . undertake to wrest from Poland and Czechoslovakia the lands that were restored to them under the Potsdam agreement. . . . And if the Western powers achieved all this, they would . . . demand that the socialist system be abolished in all the countries of the socialist camp.[104]

Because the defection of a single state could trigger falling dominoes else-where, according to this shared perspective, President Kennedy admitted: "I don't know where the non-essential areas are."[105]

The superpowers also promoted dictatorships because they regarded civil-ian democratic governments as too weak, corrupt, or unreliable, making them unsuitable allies in the global contest between the superpowers. As U.S. diplomat George Kennan argued after a 1950 tour of Latin America,

> Where the concepts and traditions of popular government are too weak to ab-sorb successfully the intensity of communist attack, then we must concede that harsh governmental methods of repression may be the only answer. Those measures may have to proceed from regimes whose origins and methods would not stand the test of American concepts of democratic procedure; and such regimes and such methods may be preferable alternatives, and indeed the only alternative, to further communist successes. Extreme weakness in the po-litical and social structures of small states has always made them vulnerable to diplomatic pressures and penetration by [Communist political forces].[106]

Although U.S. officials viewed civilian democratic governments as weak in many countries, they saw the military as more capable of promoting stability or of introducing desirable social change. U.S. officials were of two minds about whether dictatorship should promote stability or change. Some, like U.N. Ambassador Jeane Kirkpatrick, argued that "traditional autocrats leave in place existing allocations of wealth, power, status and other resources . . . but they do not disturb the habitual rhythms of work and leisure . . . habitual patterns of family and personal relations," suggesting that dictatorships promoted stability.[107] But others, like President Nixon, regarded military dictatorship as "a progressive force able to carry out social change in a constructive way."[108] Although they differed as to whether dictatorships should be "conservative" or "progressive," U.S. officials agreed in any case that they were more effective and capable than civilian governments in many countries.[109]

The Soviets, too, were of two minds about the non-Communist states they supported. In the early 1950s they regarded Nasser's nationalist dictatorship as a "reactionary," or conservative, social force, but as Nasser drew closer to the Soviet sphere, they began to regard him as a progressive, even a revolutionary.

The United States and Soviet Union provided arms to dictators within their spheres for many of the same reasons. Arms sales and transfers and military grants helped establish and maintain friendly political relations, cultivate support for their policies among elites, secure overseas bases, generate substantial income, and provide employment in domestic arms industries.[110]

Some of the dictatorships that emerged in superpower spheres in the postwar period were self-made, while others were boosted into power by the United States or the Soviet Union. Some were organized as one-party regimes, while others were led by caudillos, juntas, hereditary dynasties, and even putative monarchs. But whatever their origins and political composition—characteristics we will explore in greater detail in subsequent chapters—most of the dictatorships in Southern and Eastern Europe, Latin America, and in postcolonial states around the world shared three important characteristics: they were republican, developmentalist, and ruthless.

First, most dictatorships adopted "republican" institutions and norms. That is, they adopted constitutions, though they frequently revised them to suit the exigencies of power; established representative assemblies, usually called congresses, though they often closed them; held elections to choose congressional delegates, though they typically rigged procedures to ensure prearranged outcomes; and insisted that their country was a "republic" despite these qualifications.

It is remarkable that most postwar dictatorships maintained republican institutions and practiced republican norms. Paraguay's dictator, General Alfredo Stroessner, for example, took over the Colorado Party in May 1954,

had himself elected as the only official candidate, was 'elected' in July, and remained thereafter as 'constitutional' president of Paraguay. Confirmed in the presidency by plebiscite in 1958, he [was] elected every five years with a clock-work regularity that is astonishing. . . . Making use of some minor constitutional changes, on 12 February 1978 he accepted a sixth mandate for 'order and peace' in Paraguay.[111]

Stroessner was elected to yet another term in 1983. But his situation was not unusual. Indeed, these practices were almost universally the *norm* in postwar dictatorships, with the exception, perhaps, of Portugal, Spain, and Greece, where dictatorships retained their prewar, "fascist" antipathies to constitutional "republican" government.

Of course, the fact that dictators wrote and amended constitutions, held elections, and convened congresses did not make these "republics" democratic. But the existence of these republican political infrastructures would play an important role in the collapse of dictatorships and transfer of power to civilian democrats in the 1970s and 1980s. In a sense the road to democracy was paved with republican institutions and norms. The existence of these republican institutions made the journey to democracy easier than it would have been if dictators had demolished them completely.

Perhaps contrary to expectation, dictators typically retained republican institutions and observed republican norms because it helped them maintain their political legitimacy in both international and domestic settings. For dictatorships in the U.S. sphere, the occasional election helped maintain official U.S. support and deflect critics who might otherwise hold up congressional appropriations earmarked for dictators. And the maintenance of republican institutions and norms allowed dictators to encourage some public participation in government, which secured the loyalty of some social groups and made the regime more credible. At times opposition movements were even successful in using elections called by dictators to their advantage.

A second common feature of postwar dictatorships is that almost all adopted developmentalist economic policies in an attempt to promote economic growth and "catch up" with superpowers and postimperial European states.[112] They did so because they believed that economic development would secure their hold on power. Many dictators in the U.S. sphere even expected that once they had achieved a certain level of economic development, it would be possible to return power to civilian democrats, a common assumption among "modernizationist" social scientists in the United States. Communist dictators subscribed to the idea that economic development would bring an end to the "dictatorship of the proletariat" and set the stage for the eventual emergence of egalitarian communism.

To achieve development, dictatorships in both spheres adopted mercantilist economic policies, reserving for the state an important role in economic development and using the government to direct or control important economic activities.[113] Dictatorships in both spheres took control of important economic assets, a process described as "nationalizing" or "socializing" private industry. They also protected domestic industry from international competition by erecting trade barriers, restricting currency movements, and directing investment decisions. Although state participation in and control over the economy was more pronounced in Soviet-sphere dictatorships, regimes in the U.S. sphere also played important and directive roles in the economy and adopted many of the same mercantilist policies.

The developmentalist orientation of postwar dictatorships was actively encouraged by the United States and the Soviet Union, which both provided large amounts of financial aid and technical assistance through global, regional, and domestic institutions. Between 1945 and 1988 the United States provided $94.8 billion in economic aid to the Third World, while the Soviet Union provided a total of $17.1 billion in the same period.[114] Having established economic development as one of the two pillars of the postwar world (the other was republican government), the superpowers believed that economic growth would simultaneously solve their own domestic problems and secure world peace. For practical reasons, too, both U.S. and Soviet leaders advocated economic development in other countries, hoping they would become more self-sufficient and less dependent on superpower aid over time.

Neither superpower was prepared to provide economic assistance to its allies indefinitely. Summarizing his economic principles in a 1954 memorandum, President Eisenhower described foreign aid as something "which we wish to curtail."[115] The Soviets came to this conclusion more slowly. After stripping Eastern European countries, particularly Germany, of their economic assets after World War II, the Soviets reversed these policies and began to promote economic development through the Council for Mutual Economic Assistance (COMECON). Established in 1949, the council was designed to provide their allies with "material aid in their economic development, simultaneously protecting newly established communist dictatorships and reducing their dependence on Soviet economic aid."[116]

Although they promoted development, the Soviet Union required and the United States tolerated the adoption of mercantilist economic policies by dictators in their spheres. The Soviets insisted on them because they wanted other states to conform with Soviet economic policies, which were an extreme form of mercantilism. Although the United States had itself recently abandoned mercantilist policies, replacing them with the multilateral developmentalist policies embodied by Bretton Woods, U.S. leaders tolerated mercantilist dictators in the hope that their allies would become self-sufficient, not dependent, and mercantilism seemed to promise greater self-reliance. The United States also found it could still sell important goods—surplus U.S. food, capital goods, dams and ports, and military arms—to mercantilist regimes and obtain many of the benefits of mercantilist economic development. The establishment of U.S. corporate subsidiaries inside the mercantilist screens erected by dictators and the commercial loans offered to regimes in need of cash for domestic development programs benefited both the United States and its allies.

After 1980 this would change. The United States then began insisting that dictators abandon mercantilist policies, reduce state intervention in the economy, open the economy to foreign investment and trade, and eliminate restrictions on currency movements and investment decisions, moves that would bring their economies more into line with the economic objectives outlined at Bretton Woods. U.S. officials would later use the debts incurred by military regimes to compel their compliance with new, non-mercantilist economic policies.

A third common feature of postwar dictatorships is that they appeared quite strong. The use of terms like "authoritarian" to describe dictatorships in the U.S. sphere or "totalitarian" to identify regimes in the Soviet sphere suggests that they were strong, capable, and durable political organizations. But they should be more accurately described as "ruthless," which is *not* the same as "strong."

Certainly, postwar dictatorships were able to terrorize and cow unarmed civilian populations and cripple civil society by recruiting informants and using purges, death squads, jail, exile, torture, arbitrary law, and capricious or opaque bureaucracies to stifle dissent, break trade unions, cripple political parties, suppress religious institutions, and promote public cynicism and political lethargy. But they engaged in this ruthless behavior not because they were strong but because they were weak. They were weak because most regimes shared a number of common structural flaws.

Despite the fact that the military played a leading or prominent role in most dictatorships, most military forces were actually quite weak and ineffective outside their own country. They could terrorize unarmed civilian populations, but they could not easily wage conclusive wars with their neighbors, much less defeat great power adversaries. If these regimes were effective militarily, one might have expected them to initiate wars with their neighbors or to serve as surrogates in superpower conflicts. But most of these regimes did neither. Dictatorships in Egypt, Pakistan, North Korea, Somalia, and Iraq sometimes initiated wars with their neighbors. But they found they could not wage conclusive wars, proof that even their large armies were relatively ineffective instruments of foreign policy. And when dictators in Argentina and Iraq initiated wars with great power adversaries, they were quickly and decisively crushed and humiliated.

Although the superpowers made a big show of enlisting dictatorships in military alliances around the world, they rarely invoked the treaties that bound them or insisted that these military forces participate in superpower conflicts. The Soviets asked Warsaw Pact forces to participate in its invasions of Hungary and Czechoslovakia, but it did not assign them an important military role because it regarded them as unreliable and ineffective. The Soviets did not request even token participation by its military allies in the war in Afghanistan. Among its allies, the only military forces the Soviets regarded as effective and capable were the Vietnamese and the Cubans.

The United States asked its military allies to participate in its wars in Korea, Vietnam, and the Persian Gulf, but the few detachments that did participate—from sixteen countries in Korea, for example—were not given any serious military role. As MacArthur said during the Korean War, "The entire control of my command and everything I did came from our own Chiefs of Staff. Even reports which were normally made by me to the United Nations [which was nominally in charge of the war effort] were subject to censorship by our State and Defense Departments."[117] No doubt much the same could be said of allied participation in the 1991 Persian Gulf War. Like the Soviets, U.S. officials held the military capabilities of allied dictatorships—those in South Vietnam, Taiwan, Egypt, Iran, Iraq, Greece, Spain, Portugal, and throughout Latin America—in low regard. South Korean forces were the only troops that U.S. officials esteemed.

Of the many dictatorships in the U.S. and Soviet spheres, only two proved effective in war. Cuba demonstrated that it possessed an effective military against the Batista regime, against U.S.-sponsored contras during the 1961 Bay of Pigs invasion, and then against insurgent movements that threatened Communist governments in Angola and Ethiopia. Vietnamese Communists demonstrated their military effectiveness against French colonialists, neighboring dictatorships in South Vietnam, the United States, and Communist governments in Cambodia and China. In the postwar period Vietnamese Communist military forces were exceptionally effective. Measured against the bright light of Vietnamese military success, the military effectiveness of other dictatorships falls into deep shadow.

Most dictatorships were as weak economically as they were militarily. Although they all aspired to economic development and assiduously practiced mercantilist strategies to promote growth, only a few were able to achieve *sustained* economic growth. Most enjoyed some economic growth during the 1950s and 1960s, but much of this can be attributed to the recovery of economies that had declined dramatically during the ruinous years of the Great Depression and world war. Dictatorships in Spain, Brazil, South Korea, Taiwan, Hungary, Czechoslovakia, and East Germany recorded rapid rates of growth during the 1960s that made them the envy of dictatorships everywhere and held out the promise of eventual development for all. But economic growth slowed for these countries in the 1970s and 1980s. As for those countries with less envious economic records, their developmentalist projects faltered somewhat earlier. By 1967 William Clark, director of the Overseas Development Institute, noted that "the Development Decade" had run its course, a sentiment echoed in 1970 by former World Bank President George Woods.[118] "The development business is in trouble," he told the World Conference of the Society for International Development. "Some of the high resolve with which the business was begun 20 years ago has gone. A sense of disillusionment is not confined to the industrial countries; in the less developed countries too, there is disappointment and an impatience for results."[119] Economic weakness, evident by the late 1960s, did not augur well for developmentalist dictatorships. Of these dictatorships, only South Korea and Taiwan remained strong economically into the 1980s, though they too experienced economic difficulties. As we will see, Asian economic "strength" depended on special factors that were not widely shared.

Dictatorships shared another common weakness. Because the superpowers helped install and maintain them, dictatorships were vulnerable to changing superpower policies and U.S.-Soviet relations. Changing superpower relations, periods of U.S.-Soviet détente, and the realignment of U.S.-Sino relations made dictators vulnerable. The 1972 Chinese realignment with the United States, for example, was a political thunderclap for dictatorships in North Korea and Vietnam, which was then waging a war with the United States, just as it was for dictatorships in South Korea and Taiwan, which had long identified China as its adversary and the United States as its friend.

Changed or unexpected superpower behavior that was first made evident by the events of 1956 in Suez and Hungary underscored for dictatorships the real or potential weaknesses of their international positions. What the superpowers created they could also undo. And because most dictators lacked global political institutions of their own to promote their collective interests as *dictators*—they never created an organization like the non-aligned movement, for instance—most would face the consequences of changing superpower policies alone.

Some dictatorships belonged to such collective military alliances as the Warsaw Pact, the Rio Pact, NATO, SEATO, or CENTO. But these organizations were created to defend *superpower* spheres, not to provide collective security for members who wanted to pursue their own military policies. The French discovered at Suez that its membership in NATO did not allow it to call on U.S. support for its military intervention in Suez or its war in Algeria. Argentina discovered that its Rio Pact allies would not join it in its war against the United Kingdom over the Falklands. Hungary and Czechoslovakia discovered that their Warsaw Pact allies would not protect them from Soviet invasion. And China discovered that the Soviet Union would not honor its treaty obligations and come to its assistance during the Korean War.

Postwar dictatorships were also weak in important political and social respects. As Joel Migdal pointed out in *Strong Societies and Weak States,* mercantilist regimes typically create large state agencies and enterprises to promote and direct economic development.[120] But dictators pay a price for this directed economic growth, as the existence of state bureaucracies and enterprises often provides a political and economic basis for social groups that might eventually challenge the regime and seek power on their own terms. To prevent state development agencies from assisting political challengers, dictators shuffle the heads of these agencies, appoint inexperienced cronies and loyalists to important positions, purge possible challengers or imprison them, and frequently charge them with corruption, a crime that is usually tolerated as long as its perpetrators do not present a threat to the regime.[121] These practices impair the efficiency and effectiveness of state agencies and make low-level, frontline bureaucrats and officials wary of taking any action.[122] The result is the creation of large and seemingly powerful but actually ineffective regimes. Like their armies, the bureaucracies of many dictatorships were imposing simply because of their size, but they were actually unwieldy and inefficient.[123] As Nasser once explained, "You imagine that we are simply giving orders and the country is run accordingly. You are greatly mistaken."[124]

Finally, dictatorships often succeeded in eviscerating civil society by breaking unions, destroying opposition parties, censoring the press, weakening religious institutions, squelching dissent, spreading cynicism, and promoting political lethargy. But ruthlessness had collateral effects, damaging areas of social life that dictatorships needed for economic development. The destruction of labor unions, for example, may have muffled political dissent, but it also stifled technological innovation, reduced labor productivity, and stunted the growth of domestic markets, which were essential to the success of mercantilist policies based on promoting domestic self-sufficiency. The means that dictators used to protect their political power often worked at cross-purposes with their economic objectives.

Of course, the fact that postwar dictatorships were weak in important respects does not mean that they could not survive. Indeed, during the 1950s, 1960s, and early 1970s dictatorships proliferated and even thrived. But events in the mid-1970s would expose their weaknesses, first in capitalist dictatorships in Southern Europe, Latin America, and East Asia, then in Communist dictatorships in the Soviet Union and Eastern Europe, and finally in Communist and non-Communist regimes in Africa.

four

OIL CRISIS AND DICTATORSHIP IN SOUTHERN EUROPE

Fascist dictatorships in Italy and Germany were crushed during World War II. But dictatorships in Portugal and Spain survived and in Greece revived during the postwar period. Although dictatorships on the Iberian and Ionian Peninsulas persisted into the 1970s, a shared economic crisis compounded by separate political crises in the mid-1970s would undo these dictatorships and lead, by the end of the decade, to the creation of socialist governments and republican states in Portugal, Spain, and Greece.

In the years before World War II dictators took power in all three countries, dismantling the nascent republican states that had emerged in Portugal in 1910, in Spain in 1931, and in Greece in 1924.[1]

Portugal and Salazar

In Portugal the republican state established after the abdication of Manuel II in 1910 was beset by economic problems and political turmoil after World War I.[2] During the 1920s successive republican governments wrestled unsuccessfully with growing budget deficits. The use of foreign loans to repay war debts to Great Britain and to cover normal government expenses increased government spending. In addition, the collapse of Portuguese banks and of private companies in Portugal's African colonies plunged the domestic and overseas colonies into a recession and reduced government income, leading to large and growing public deficits.[3] Between 1910 and

1927 the national debt grew from 692,000 to 7,449,000 contos, more than a tenfold increase.[4] To cover its deficits the government printed more money, leading to inflation and currency depreciation.[5] By 1926 "prices multiplied by twelve times, wages by [only] four and a half times," and the currency was worth only one thirty-third as much as it had been just sixteen years earlier.[6]

Political turmoil compounded the republic's economic difficulties. The rapid succession of weak republican governments—from 1910 to 1926 there were nine presidents, forty-four governments, twenty-five uprisings, and three temporary dictatorships—made it difficult to address the economic crisis.[7] On June 17, 1926, General Gomes de Costa established a dictatorship, and in 1928 one of his successors, General Carmona, appointed Dr. Antonio de Oliveira Salazar, a conservative economist at the University of Coimbra, to manage the government's finances.[8]

Salazar used his position to consolidate control of all government spending and the country's economic and monetary policy.[9] He cut government spending, consolidated debts, issued new bonds, and revised the tax code to produce more income. By 1928 Portugal realized its first surplus in many years.[10] During the next four years Salazar used his position and performance to maneuver past political competitors and become prime minister in 1932.[11] By rewriting the constitution and arranging for its ratification in a rigged election in 1933, Salazar effectively abolished the republic and established himself as dictator of Portugal and its colonies in Africa and Asia.[12]

Salazar was fully aware of the extent of his powers, boasting once that "when it comes time for me to give orders I expect [the nation] to obey." But he did not rule alone.[13] His dictatorship was buttressed by a variety of institutions and social groups. Salazar was supported by the army, which had been ignored and mistrusted by civilian democrats in the republic and which welcomed increased spending under Salazar. Small groups of corporate and banking interests that monopolized business in Portugal and the colonies supported Salazar's determination to curb government deficits and manage the economy. The Catholic Church also supported the dictatorship because it advocated collective religious responsibilities and opposed the republican emphasis on individual liberties and the organization of political parties that competed for their parishioners' loyalties. The government bureaucracy embraced the new regime and welcomed the abolition of meddlesome political parties and the consolidation of the bureaucracy as the country's central economic institution.[14] "We are anti-parliamentarians, anti-democrats, anti-liberals," Salazar said of this conservative, anti-republican coalition. "We are opposed to all forms of internationalism, Communism, Socialism, syndicalism and everything which may divide or minimize or break up the [national] family."[15] Later, when Portugal joined NATO, Salazar ridiculed NATO principles of "democracy, individual liberty and the rule of law" as "unfortunate" and "doctrinaire."[16]

Salazar dismantled the republican state because "parliamentary democracy has resulted in instability and disorder," but he did not restore the Portuguese monarchy.[17] Although he described himself as a monarchist and was briefly expelled from the university for advocating monarchy, he did not create a royalist state after he came to power.[18] Instead, Salazar contended, "Dictatorships are created . . . so that a new beginning can be made," and he argued that the state should be neither royalist nor republic, but "corporatist," the term he preferred.[19]

Spain and Franco

In Spain a republican state was established in 1931 when King Alfonso XIII decided "to avoid a fratricidal war" and to abdicate, noting that "we are out of fashion."[20] Coexisting with the royalist state, the dictatorship established by Miguel Primo de Rivera in 1923 failed to address mounting economic problems and the sharpening conflict between conservatives, who defended the royalist state, and republicans, who wanted to end the monarchy. As the Portuguese had done during the 1920s, the Rivera dictatorship ran budget deficits to avoid levying higher taxes on the upper classes and to meet the growing costs of improvements to Spain's archaic roads and railways. The global economic crisis of 1929–30 brought an end to economic growth.[21] The king asked Rivera to resign in 1930, but his replacement, General Berenguer, could do little to address the economic crisis. The republicans, meanwhile, pressed for a democratic government in a republican state. After republicans won the 1931 elections, Alfonso abdicated the throne.[22]

To consolidate the new republican state, successive governments retired conservative army officers, abolished aristocratic privileges, introduced land reform, and forced the Catholic Church out of the schools, antagonizing the army, landlords, and the church.[23] But the rapid succession of elections—in 1931, 1933, and 1936—and of parliamentary governments made it difficult to implement economic or political reforms. The stalemate ended when separate republican forces joined a unified popular front to win the 1936 parliamentary elections.[24]

In response to the decisive republican victory at the polls, Major General Francisco Franco and other army officers launched a military revolt from bases in Spanish Morocco and northern Spain, leading to the bloody civil war of 1936–39.[25] With assistance from other fascist countries, Franco eventually defeated republican forces. German aircraft ferried Franco's troops from Morocco to Spain and then bombed republican positions throughout the war, some fifty thousand Italian troops were sent into battle, and Hitler and Mussolini provided $570 million in arms and aid to Franco's cause. Divided between moderate, communist, and anarchist factions, the republican coalition was deprived of substantial foreign military aid after the Soviets withdrew their support in 1938.[26] Restricting the terms of its support, the Soviet Union had insisted that its arms be paid for in gold; the Soviets then abandoned the republicans altogether after Stalin moved into an alliance with Hitler. Franco's ability to call upon Hitler and Mussolini forced different conservative factions within his government to submit to his authority. Franco was named generalissimo and chief of the new anti-republican state in September 1936. "We did not win the regime we have today, hypocritically with some votes," Franco later said of the civil war. "We won it at the point of the bayonet and with the blood of our best people."[27]

In all, perhaps 1 million people died as a result of combat or starvation during the war and 250,000 more were executed after the war, many of them strangled by garrote.[28]

Like Salazar in Portugal, Franco did not rule alone but forged a coalition of militarists, fascists, conservatives, and monarchists. He was, in turn, a proponent of each group. He was a militarist during the civil war but later cut military spending.[29] He supported the Falangists, Spain's fascist party, to create a popular political base, but he abandoned it after the war, voiding the law that made the fascist salute obligatory.[30] Franco supported conservatives and Catholics, particularly after the Vatican signed a 1953 concordat that helped legitimize the regime, but his enthusiasm cooled after Pope John XXIII and the Second Vatican Council endorsed individual liberties and human rights and urged the separation of church and state.[31] He also supported the monarchy but not the king. Although Franco restored the king's flag and established the "Royal March" as the national anthem, he said the actual installation of a new king was "a goal we can sense but which is so distant that we cannot make it out yet," preferring instead to invest himself as "caudillo."[32]

In 1947 Franco proclaimed that Spain would be a royalist state and established himself as regent for the monarchy, but he did not invite the heir to the throne, the exiled Don Juan de Borbon, to return to Spain. "When Franco talked of bringing back the monarchy, he was careful not to use the verb *restaurar,* which means to restore, but *instaurar,* which means to set up or establish," noted historian David Gilmour.[33] As regent, Franco groomed Prince Juan Carlos as the possible heir to the throne but did not make this formal until 1969.[34]

Franco's dictatorship drew its ideology from diverse militarist, fascist, Catholic, and monarchist social groups and institutions. But it never departed from its anti-republican orientation. The historian D. A. Puzzo said of this eclectic ideology that "[Franco's] head was a cemetery of dead ideas."[35] For Franco and the conservative coalition, parliamentary democracy under monarchy was responsible in the nineteenth and early twentieth centuries for "the loss of immense [colonial] territory, three civil wars, and the imminent danger of national disintegration."[36] According to Franco, the defeat of the republican state during the civil war "liquidated the 19th century, which should never have existed."[37] Although Franco preserved the Cortes, or Spanish parliament, he would not permit its members to exercise parliamentary democracy.[38] David Gilmour noted that in Franco's regime the democratic "principle of 'one man, one vote' applied only to one man."[39] The anti-republican state that he established would be a royalist monarchy without a monarch, only a caudillo.

Greece and Metaxas

In Greece royalists and republicans waged a protracted contest for power during the interwar period. Indeed, "the principle and most enduring source of political division in the history of modern Greece [before and after World War II] has been over the question of whether Greece should be a Republic or a monarchy."[40] Greek kings abdicated the throne or were exiled five times in the twentieth century, in 1917, 1922, 1924, 1940, and 1968. Following each incident except the last, the monarchy was restored to power. In 1968 the Greek military dictatorship abolished the monarchy after the king bungled an attempt to overthrow the junta, and the royal family remains in exile to this day, clinging to its hopes for an eventual restoration.

For much of the interwar period royalists and republicans were evenly matched. Both sides found it difficult to obtain or consolidate power, though successive abdications and a coup by the army led to the creation of a republic on March 24, 1924.[41] As in Portugal and Spain during this period, republicans found it difficult to maintain power. "Between 1924 and 1928, there were ten Prime Ministers, three general elections and eleven military coups . . . [and] the President of the Republic was deposed once and resigned twice, only to revoke his resignation," observed the historian Constantine Tsoucalas.[42] The government was undermined by a falling demand for Greek agricultural products during the Great Depression, poor harvests, and mounting government debt, which led to national bankruptcy and the republican government's fall in 1932.[43] After much debate the monarchy named General John Metaxas to head the government. Metaxas quickly suppressed the republican opposition, declared martial law, and suspended the constitution on August 4, 1935, bringing the interwar contest between royalists and republicans to a close.[44]

Like his contemporaries in Portugal and Spain, Metaxas represented a coalition of conservative forces, though in Greece this included the Greek Orthodox, not Roman Catholic, Church. Also like his contemporaries, Metaxas was fiercely anti-republican, arguing that "the old parliamentary system had vanished forever" and that Greece was now "an anti-communist, anti-parliamentary, totalitarian state."[45] But whereas Salazar did not create a royalist state and Franco established a monarchy without a monarch, Metaxas established a military dictatorship modeled along fascist lines in a restored royalist state. Because the monarchy, not Metaxas, controlled the army and directed the country's foreign policy, Metaxas recognized that his rule was based on "monarchy, religion, country and family."[46] In Spain monarchy served Franco. In Greece Metaxas served the monarchy.

Dictatorships, World War, and Cold War

During the 1930s conservative coalitions led by Salazar, Franco, and Metaxas defeated their republican opponents and created anti-republican states, some of which were more royalist than others. Of course, dictatorships emerged in many other countries during the interwar period, most notably in Italy and Germany. But although these European dictatorships were equally antidemocratic and anti-republican, they were not equally royalist. Adolf Hitler, for example, complained that Franco's Spain was not run by proper fascists but by what he called "the clerico-monarchical muck."[47] For their part, Southern European dictators sometimes regarded the more secular fascism of Italy and Germany with distaste. Salazar, for example, argued that Mussolini's Italy was "leaning towards a pagan Caesarism, towards a new state which recognizes no limitations of legal or moral order," an order he insisted was provided in Portugal by its alliance with the Catholic Church.[48] But whatever their precise characters, anti-republican dictatorships in Portugal and Spain survived the war intact, whereas those in Italy, Germany, and Greece were extinguished.

The Iberian dictatorships survived the war for a number of reasons. Salazar survived because he successfully managed the prewar economic crisis, because he kept Portugal neutral during the war, because neutrality enabled Portugal to profit as a black-market, backdoor entrepôt between Allied and Axis blocks, and because he obtained British credit to use the Azores as an antisubmarine base during the war.[49] Franco, like Salazar, kept Spain neutral during the war, though he briefly supplied troops to Nazi Germany to fight against the Soviet Union, repaying Germany for its support during the Spanish civil war.[50] But the nonaligned policies of Franco and Salazar assisted the Allies more than they assisted the Axis powers.[51] Because Spain remained neutral, the Allies allowed it to obtain goods and food that it could not otherwise have acquired during the war.[52]

Dictators in Portugal and Spain deftly survived the war, but dictatorship in Greece did not. Metaxas also adopted a nonaligned foreign policy, one that would have favored the Allies because the king retained close ties with Great Britain. But neutrality did not serve Metaxas as it did Salazar and Franco. Assaulted first by Italian and then German forces, Greece was drawn into the fray of world war. After invading and occupying Albania in 1939, Mussolini invaded Greece in 1940. Greek forces repelled the Italian invasion but were crushed when the Germans, aided by Bulgarians, launched a second attack in 1941. The Greek dictatorship collapsed under the combined assault, the king fled, and the country was occupied and divided between German, Italian, and Bulgarian armies.[53]

At war's end the prospects for dictators, kings, and conservatives looked bleak in Portugal, Spain, and Greece. Portugal's wartime prosperity ended with the conclusion of the war, and austerity loomed ahead. Spain had not yet recovered from its destructive civil war—national income had fallen to 1914 levels, wages were one-half of their 1936 levels, and rationing cut meat and milk consumption to one-half of prewar levels.[54] In Spain the end of world war meant the continuation of *los años del hambre* (the hungry years).[55]

In postwar Greece, meanwhile, radical republicans stood on the verge of victory. The collapse of dictatorship, the flight of the king, and occupation by foreign fascists gave rise to resurgent republican forces. Republicans were strong both in the Communist-led resistance, which had tied down nine Axis divisions during the war, and among the remnants of the Greek army that had been evacuated by the British to bases in the Middle East.[56] Before the war Greek Communists had represented only 6 or 7 percent of the electorate. By war's end, however, they dominated the resistance movement and moved to establish a *laokratia*, or "People's Republic," and were determined to prevent a royalist restoration.[57]

Dictatorships in Portugal and Spain weathered the postwar crisis, and royalist rule was restored in Greece after the war as the result of several similar developments. Wartime neutrality in Portugal and Spain and armed resistance in Greece convinced U.S. and British leaders to offer dictators and monarchs a reprieve. As Churchill told Franco, "So don't let's all be too spiteful about the past."[58] The strategic locations of all three countries—Portugal's Azores in the Atlantic, Spain's proximity to the Straits of Gibraltar and the western Mediterranean, and Greece's proximity to the Bosporus, the Suez Canal, and the eastern Mediterranean—made them valuable military assets. And their anti-Communist credentials, derived from their suppression of the Left in Portugal and their victory in Spain's civil war, convinced U.S. and British officials to view them as increasingly valuable allies as the Cold War sharpened in the late 1940s and early 1950s.

In Greece the British were determined to deter republican enthusiasm. Britain first crushed the successive mutinies of exiled republican forces in 1943 and 1944, purged the Greek army of republican sympathizers, assisted the return of royalist forces to Greece after the Axis surrender, and established a conservative government that restored the monarchy in a rigged election in 1947.[59] The British-backed restoration of the monarchy triggered a two-year civil war that left fifty thousand dead, put forty thousand more in prison, and sent sixty thousand others into exile.[60]

The postwar Greek civil war, like the prewar Spanish civil war, pitted a royalist-conservative coalition against radical republicans. In Spain the con-

servatives had been supported by Italy and Germany and the republicans
by the Soviet Union. In Greece the conservatives and royalists were supported first by Great Britain, but after the British could no longer bear the
costs, the United States came to their aid, providing $300 million to the
royalist army in 1947.[61] Meanwhile, the Communist republicans were supported initially by the Soviet Union and Yugoslavia. But the Soviet Union
withdrew its support (as it had in Spain) after Stalin agreed with Churchill
to exclude Greece from its postwar sphere of influence.[62] "Might it be
thought rather cynical if it seemed we had disposed of these issues, so fate-
ful to millions of people, in such an offhand manner? Let us burn the
paper," Churchill told Stalin. "No, you keep it," Stalin replied.[63] After its
1949 split with the Soviet Union persuaded Tito to seek a rapprochement
with Great Britain and the United States, Yugoslavia withdrew its support
for the Greek Communists in exchange for British and U.S. aid.[64] Facing a
royalist army backed successively by two great powers and abandoned by
its Communist allies, the Greek Communist-republican resistance collapsed
in 1949.[65] The victorious monarchy then established a conservative government led by General Papagos, who rebuilt royalist-conservative rule without overt dictatorship.[66]

Their strategic locations and anti-Communist credentials enabled Iberian
dictators and Ionian royalists to move into an alliance with the United
States. With U.S. backing, Portugal and Greece first joined the United Na-
tions and then became members of NATO, Portugal in 1949 and Greece in
1950. European animosity toward the Franco regime prevented the United
States from admitting Spain to NATO, while opposition in Latin America,
Europe, and the Soviet Union delayed Spain's admission to the United Nations.[67] But U.S. officials concluded a separate military base agreement with
Spain in 1953, effectively welding it to the West, and in 1955 persuaded the
Soviet Union to drop its opposition to Spanish membership in the United
Nations in return for U.S. support for the admission of Eastern European
dictatorships.[68] "In the last resort, if you don't get what you want, sign
anything [the United States] puts in front of you," Franco told his negotiators during base-agreement discussions. "We need that agreement."[69]

For his part, Franco adopted a law of succession and held a referendum
approving the new law to demonstrate Spain's "democratic" character to
the world.[70] "The only formula possible for us," Admiral Luis Carrero
Blanco advised Franco, "is order, unity and hang on for dear life."[71] This
Franco managed to do.

To cement its Cold War alliances, the United States provided substantial
economic benefits to dictators in Portugal and Spain and to conservative
royalists in Greece. Between 1953 and 1961 the United States provided
Spain with $618 million in grants, $404 million in loans, and $437 million
in military aid, while Greece received more than $2 billion in U.S. military
aid and economic assistance between 1947 and 1956.[72] In addition, U.S.

and NATO troops based in these countries spent their salaries near their bases, injecting hard currencies into local economies and providing Spain, Portugal, and Greece with further economic benefits.

During the 1950s U.S. aid helped dictatorships and conservatives survive and helped their economies grow. But generous economic and military aid masked a fundamental problem in all three economies. In Portugal, Spain, and Greece, domestic industries were too weak to absorb displaced agricultural workers who were migrating to the cities. Neither were they able to create jobs for the growing urban work force, produce a full range of goods for the domestic market, or compete on equal terms with U.S. or Western European industries. Because these countries typically imported more goods than they exported, all three ran trade deficits. "None of the southern European countries (except Spain in 1951 and 1960) ran a commodity trade surplus in all the years between 1946 and 1974. . . . [They] never reached a point at which their economies generated sufficient exports to pay for their imports," noted the economist Caglar Keyder.[73]

Persistent trade deficits typically compelled countries to use up their reserves of foreign exchange and gold, forcing them to devalue their curren cies and making imported goods more expensive. For countries that relied on foreign imports, such as oil, to keep their economies afloat, devaluation raised the costs of essential imports for domestic industries. Devaluation made domestic goods cheaper and therefore easier to sell abroad, but rising prices for essential imports wiped out the putative benefits of devaluation.

During the 1950s U.S. economic aid helped Portugal, Spain, and Greece to cover their trade deficits and allowed these countries to live beyond their means, importing more goods than they exported. For a time, this contributed to economic growth. But as U.S. aid waned in the late 1950s, trade deficits reemerged as a central economic problem for Iberian and Ionian regimes, once again threatening their survival. The solution to these economic problems was the same for all three countries. By exporting workers and importing tourists, they were able to promote economic development during the 1960s and early 1970s.

Developmentalist Dictatorships

During the 1960s regimes in Portugal, Spain, and Greece discovered they could solve their central economic problem—persistent trade deficits—by exporting workers and importing tourists. Income from Southern European workers employed in Western Europe and money from Western European workers who spent their savings on holidays in Southern Europe provided regimes with the hard currency they needed to create jobs and promote domestic economic growth. Earnings from émigré workers and vacationing tourists "made it possible [for these countries] to realize . . . rapid growth without running up against the balance of payments problems that bring growth to a grinding halt in most poor economies."[74]

Beginning in the late 1950s and throughout the 1960s and early 1970s, a flood of Portuguese, Spanish, and Greek workers emigrated to Western Europe in search of employment. Nearly 100,000 workers left Portugal annually, most legally but many illegally, reaching a peak of 180,000 in 1970.[75] By the end of the 1960s nearly 1 million people, more than 10 percent of Portugal's total population, lived in Western Europe, most of them in France.[76] Workers from Spain emigrated at about the same rate, and, like the Portuguese, most Spanish émigrés made their way to France.[77] With assistance from the Spanish Institute of Emigration and from governments in Western Europe, about eighty thousand Spanish workers traveled legally each year to Western Europe, while between thirty-five thousand and one hundred thousand more made the journey illegally.[78] About one hundred thousand workers annually left Greece during this period, and by 1965 nearly 7 percent of the Greek population lived abroad, most of them in West Germany.[79]

Workers from Southern Europe emigrated to Western Europe in search of work for a number of reasons. Assisted by Marshall Plan aid and by their newfound economic cooperation in the Common Market, the economies of Western European countries grew rapidly in the 1950s. But they soon began to experience labor shortages, particularly in West Germany, where high wartime casualty rates reduced the labor force. The influx of refugees from Eastern Europe—13 million between 1945 and 1961—helped alleviate West German labor shortages in the 1950s, but continued economic growth and the end of migration from the East, which was curtailed by closure of the inter-German border and then by the construction of the Berlin Wall in 1961, forced the government to draft foreign workers. The West German government signed treaties with Spain and Greece in 1960 and with Portugal in 1964 to provide workers from these countries with unskilled jobs in West Germany.[80] Other Western European countries drafted foreign workers to provide unskilled labor in their growing economies, and by the early 1970s about 7.5 million of these foreigners had migrated into the developed European countries.[81]

Although many Southern European workers were drawn to the employment opportunities in Western European economies, for many of them emigration was not an option but a necessity. The consolidation and mechanization of domestic agriculture displaced farmers from their lands and drove many Southern Europeans abroad. In all three countries about 50 percent of the labor force worked in agriculture in 1950. But by 1970 the share of agricultural workers in the work force had fallen to 30 percent in Portugal, 20 percent in Spain, and 25 percent in Greece.[82] Agricultural consolidation and weak domestic industries that could not provide jobs for displaced agricultural workers forced many workers to seek employment in Western Europe. Migration emptied the countryside and rural villages. As the Spanish novelist Miguel Delibes wrote of one small village, "Cortiguera is a dying village, in agony. Its winding streets, invaded by weeds and nettles, without a dog's bark or a child's laugh to break the silence, enclose a pathetic gravity, the lugubrious air of the cemetery."[83]

Portuguese workers were also driven abroad by their desire to avoid conscription and escape military service in Portugal's colonial wars, which began in earnest in 1961.[84] The percent of Portuguese workers emigrating illegally climbed during the 1960s as colonial wars in Africa became more intense and military service more onerous.[85]

The export of Southern European workers to Western European economies provided substantial economic and political benefits to Portugal, Spain, and Greece. Workers typically saved some of their earnings to send back to their families. As these "remittances" came in the form of "hard," or sound, Western European currencies, they could be used to purchase imports and pay foreign debts. Remittances were deposited in domestic banks, enabling the government to pay for imports, providing the banks with money to lend, which financed industry, created jobs, and helped fuel economic growth. Moreover, the departure of these workers eased the political problems associated with high domestic unemployment.[86] Émigré workers remitted more than $1 billion a year to Portugal by 1970, a sum greater than the country earned from the sale of exports to other countries.[87] From about $100 million a year in Spain in the late 1950s, remittances rose to $1.414 billion in 1973, for a total of $8.1 billion between 1961 and 1975.[88] Greek workers, meanwhile, injected more than $6 billion into the Greek economy between 1960 and 1976.[89]

Tourism provided another important source of income for Southern European states during the 1960s. The number of tourists annually vacationing in Portugal grew from 70,000 in 1950 to 1.5 million in 1970, in Greece from 33,000 to 1.6 million in the same period, and in Spain from 456,000 in 1950 to 3 million in 1960 and 24 million in 1970.[90] Spain captured the lion's share of the tourist trade, and by 1973 the 34 million tourists annually visiting Spain even exceeded the number of people who lived there.[91] Of every six international tourists in 1973, one was visiting Spain.[92]

The growth of tourism was driven by a number of developments. The introduction of jet aircraft in the 1950s made it possible to travel great distances over short periods of time. Western European tourist agencies and airlines worked together aggressively to promote inclusive overseas vacation packages (airfare, hotels, meals, and ground transport), and longer vacations and rising wages for skilled and typically unionized Western European workers gave them the time and money to spend on trips abroad. Tourists were drawn to Southern Europe, to Spain in particular, by the availability of the "four Ss"—travel bureau shorthand for "Sun, Sand, Sea, and Sex" (Spain's Costa del Sol records 300 days of sun every year)—and by the cheap prices of goods and travel in these relatively poor economies.[93]

In Spain tourist receipts grew from $500 million in 1962 to $3.3 billion in 1971, all together contributing $10 billion to the Spanish economy between 1961 and 1970.[94] Tourists also poured smaller but still substantial sums into the Portuguese and Greek economies. Whereas tourism provided more than 35 percent of Spain's export earnings, it provided nearly 20 percent of Portugal's and 15 percent of Greece's export earnings in the 1970s.[95]

Imports of vacationing foreigners, like exports of domestic workers, injected substantial amounts of hard currency into the Iberian and Ionian economies, promoting the construction of infrastructure (airports, railroads, ports, roads, and hotels) and providing jobs in both large and small service industries.[96]

Although émigré workers and vacationing foreigners injected their savings into Southern European economies, providing the hard currency fuel for economic growth in the 1960s, domestic workers also contributed to economic development, though they did so involuntarily. In Portugal and Spain dictators banned unions, prohibited strikes, and regulated wages. During the 1950s wages rose, but did so more slowly than the cost of living, which resulted in the halving of the overall standard of living between 1936 and 1956.[97] Franco, who told his economic ministers, *"Hagan lo que les de la gana"* ("Do whatever you wish"), agreed in 1959 to an IMF economic stabilization plan that required Spain to devalue the peseta, open the economy to foreign investment and trade, cut government spending, and freeze wages.[98] These measures led to a recession, rising unemployment (34.7 percent between 1959 and 1960), and falling incomes for the domestic work force, reducing real wages by as much as 50 percent.[99]

Not surprisingly, Spanish workers who were pressed into the service of domestic economic development objected, organizing illegal strikes. The number of strikes increased from 179 in 1966 to 3,156 in 1975, and the number of working days lost as a result increased from 184,000 in 1966 to 1,800,000 days in 1975.[100] The growing number of labor conflicts during the 1960s and early 1970s, which Franco permitted as long as they were based on economic and not political grievances, increased wages in real terms, but they still lagged behind the pace of rising productivity in industry.[101]

The export of workers, import of vacationing foreigners, and the suppression of domestic workers solved the problem of perennial trade deficits and provided the means to spur rapid economic growth in the 1960s. The simultaneous emergence of emigration and tourism as pillars of economic development were products of good fortune, necessity, and design. All three countries had the good fortune to possess sunny beaches, which they could mine for the tourist trade, and they found that their relative poverty enabled them to sell scenery to tourists seeking cheap vacation venues. In Spain the devaluation of the peseta led immediately to domestic recession and rising unemployment, but it also made Spain an inexpensive tourist destination. The creation of a ministry of tourism in 1955 enabled the government to design the expansion of the tourist industry and capture a large share of the growing international tourist trade. The three countries were also fortunate that Western European economies drew on their labor supplies just when domestic workers were being crowded out of agricultural employment at home. Finally, the suppression of the domestic workforce enabled economic development. In Spain labor policies were designed to keep wages low. The income forfeited by workers was used to keep domestic firms in the industrial and service sector competitive and promote capital accumulation that could be used to promote other kinds of development.

For a time these developments, what the economist Paul Samuelson called "Market Fascism" in Spain, made rapid economic growth possible in all three countries.[102] High rates of growth enabled all three to double their gross national product (GNP) between 1958 and 1969.[103] On a per capita basis annual income grew in Portugal from about $200 in 1950 to nearly $900 in 1970; in Spain from $324 in 1958 to more than $1,000 in 1970; and in Greece from $350 in 1954 to $1,133 in 1970.[104] As elites captured much of the income in each country, increasing per capita income did not automatically translate into increased wealth for workers. Still, economic growth and rising per capita income made it possible for developmentalist dictators to remain in power.

Although many economists described the rapid economic growth and rising national income in all three countries as "nothing short of phenomenal," even a "miracle," the fact that these countries were recovering from the Great Depression, World War II, and, in the cases of Spain and Greece, destructive civil wars had much to do with their "miraculous" advances.[105] As a result of civil and world war, between 1938 and 1948 Spain's per capita GNP fell from 41.6 percent to 18.4 percent of the average per capita GNP of the United States and Western European countries. It stayed at this low level throughout the 1950s, then grew from 18.6 percent in 1960 to 28.9 percent in 1970 as a result of rapid growth during the 1960s.[106] Economic growth in Spain and in Portugal and Greece during the 1960s recovered ground lost during the Great Depression and civil and world war, but by 1970 these economies had still not recovered their pre-civil war strengths vis-à-vis the West.

While the rapid growth made possible by émigré workers and tourism helped the three countries keep pace with, though not catch up to, the growth rates of Western European economies, this form of developmentalism was vulnerable to changing economic conditions.[107] During the early 1970s the three dictatorships experienced a shared economic crisis.

Dollar Devaluation and Oil Crisis

On August 15, 1971, U.S. President Richard Nixon announced that the dollar would be devalued so that U.S. firms could become more competitive with businesses in Western Europe and Japan. "Now that [Western Europe and Japan] have become economically strong," he said, "the time has come for exchange rates to be set straight, and for the major nations to compete as equals."[108] Nixon reasoned that a cheaper dollar would enable U.S. firms to sell more goods overseas, discourage American consumers from buying more expensive foreign goods, and close the $2.3 billion U.S. trade deficit.[109]

The U.S. dollar devaluation increased the value of the currencies of Portugal, Spain, and Greece, making it harder for them to sell their goods abroad and making it more expensive for American tourists vacationing in Europe. Then in 1973–74, Soviet crop failures sent world food prices soaring. And the 1974 Yom Kippur War between Egypt, Syria, and Israel triggered an oil embargo by many oil-producing countries, leading to soaring world oil prices. The rising cost of food and fuel provoked a global inflationary spiral that would last nearly a decade.

Because all three countries exported agricultural products, rising world food prices were something of a boon for domestic farmers. But rising oil prices were a more serious problem. Because they were all heavily dependent on imported oil, rising oil prices greatly increased the cost of imports, contributing both to growing trade deficits and to rising domestic inflation. In Spain, for example, "a favorable balance of $557 million in 1973 turned into an unfavorable balance of $3.245 billion in 1974."[110] Rising oil prices triggered inflation, which "rose from 4.2 in 1972 to 15.5 percent in 1973 and a whopping 26.9 percent in 1974."[111] Because wages failed to keep pace with rising prices—in 1973, Spain's wholesale price index shot up by 48.3 percent, but wages rose by only 16.4 percent—the inflation triggered by the oil embargo lowered real wages and promoted widespread discontent.[112] In Greece the wholesale price index rose 48.3 percent in 1973, while wages increased only 16.4 percent.[113]

Although rising energy prices increased the cost of imports, they also reduced the two main sources of income for Portugal, Spain, and Greece. The oil embargo triggered a recession in Western Europe, bringing an end to the decades-long economic boom. Faced with growing unemployment, the West German government in late 1973 announced that it would stop importing workers from abroad, and France followed suit in the summer of 1974.[114] Emigration from Southern European countries dropped and émigré workers began returning home. Between three hundred thousand and four hundred thousand of them returned from Western Europe, many to the Iberian and Ionian Peninsulas, in the four years between 1973 and 1977.[115] "There are fewer Spanish, Greeks, Portuguese, Italians," observed a Spanish priest working in West Germany. "All except the Turks. The Turks hang on and the Germans can't shake them off. But the rest of our foreign legion of Mediterranean workers is slowly going home and not being replaced. Of the 5,000 Spaniards who worked in this factory in 1968, less than 900 remain."[116]

As émigré workers returned home, income from remittances declined and domestic unemployment rose.[117] In Spain only 1 percent of the domestic work force had been unemployed in the late 1960s. But unemployment rose to 3.2 percent in 1974 and then continued to rise throughout the decade, reaching 12.6 percent by 1980.[118] Rising unemployment, coupled with falling real wages, promoted worker discontent. Because recession, inflation, and rising unemployment reduced incomes throughout Europe, fewer Western Europeans took vacations in Southern Europe, thereby reducing Southern European income from the tourist trade.

Stronger currencies, mounting costs for imported oil, and falling income from émigré workers and foreign tourists led to growing trade deficits, rising inflation, and increasing unemployment. These developments fueled domestic discontent and created a shared economic crisis for the three dictatorships in 1973 and 1974.

This economic crisis was compounded in Portugal by the high cost of fighting wars against independence movements in its African colonies. "By 1974, a population of less than 9 million [1 million more lived and worked in Western Europe] was sustaining a 200,000-man army in Africa and spending over 45 percent of its annual budget on the military," wrote Kenneth Maxwell.[119] The war absorbed government resources and exposed domestic and returning émigré workers to conscription and service in an increasingly unpopular conflict.[120]

In Greece the weakness of export industries and the decline of foreign investment as a result of the 1967 military coup led to trade deficits even before the 1973 crisis hit. As the trade deficit grew from $400 million in 1970 to $1.2 billion annually from 1973 to 1978, the junta borrowed money to cover its trade shortfalls.[121] Foreign debt grew from $1.1 billion in 1969 to $1.9 billion in 1970 and to $2.3 billion in 1971.[122] Thus the dictatorship was already burdened by substantial debt on the eve of the crisis.

Although the dictatorships in Portugal, Spain, and Greece shared a common economic crisis in the early 1970s—a crisis compounded by colonial war in Portugal and foreign debt in Greece—they each experienced separate political crises that would bring an end to old Iberian and new Ionian dictatorships.

Colonial Rebellion and Domestic Revolt in Portugal

For the Portuguese dictatorship, the economic crisis of 1973 was compounded by the defeat of its military forces in its overseas colonies.[123] Portugal's military problems had begun a decade earlier in 1961, when India invaded Portuguese Goa, crushed Portuguese forces, and incorporated the city into India.[124] Radical republican independence movements also began guerrilla wars against Portuguese rule in Angola and Guinea-Bissau in 1961 and in Mozambique in 1964.[125] Nationalist and Communist guerrillas emerged in response to Portuguese forced-labor practices, falling wages for African workers, falling prices for rural farmers, and the arrest and torture of middle-class dissidents like Agostinho Neto, a physician who later organized and led the Popular Movement for the Liberation of Angola (MPLA).[126] The Portuguese responded with savagery. "We will hunt the terrorists like game," one Portuguese air force officer told reporters in 1961. "We have no alternative but extermination."[127]

Guerrilla movements sometimes massacred civilian settlers, a practice that triggered massive reprisal and mutual atrocity. In return, the Portuguese frequently targeted rebel leaders for assassination, murdering Robert Modlane, head of the Front for the Liberation of Mozambique (FRELIMO), with a letter bomb on February 3, 1969, and Dr. Amilcar Cabral, head of the African Party of the Independence of Guinea and Cape Verde (PAIGC) on January 20, 1973.[128]

Like the Spanish and Greek civil wars, in which anti-republican conservative forces battled against radical republican movements, the wars in Portugal's African colonies pitted the anti-republican Portuguese dictatorship and white settler communities in the colonies against radical republican independence movements. Different guerrilla groups also waged war with one another. By 1969 the U.S. National Security Council reported that "the outlook for the rebellion [in Portuguese Africa] is one of continued stalemate: the rebels cannot oust the Portuguese and the Portuguese can contain but not eliminate the rebels."[129]

Wars in the colonies created a series of problems for the Salazar regime and, after 1969, for the regime of Marcello Caetano. First, African wars reduced the government's income from the colonies and consumed a growing share of government spending. In 1961 military expenditures consumed 36.5 percent of government revenues, but by 1974 the cost of deploying a two hundred thousand–man army in Africa consumed 45 percent of its income.[130] Second, Portugal's colonial wars also led to its growing isolation in the United Nations and tested U.S. support for its dictatorship. During the 1950s the Salazar regime argued that its African territories were not colonies but an indivisible part of Portugal. "We know what you [the United Nations] mean by colonies, but our territories are different; they do not belong to that category," Portugal's Foreign Minister Franco Nogueira argued.[131] But the United Nations passed resolutions demanding a timetable for independence, which Portugal refused to recognize or provide.[132] Third, the long colonial wars led to the radicalization or flight of Portuguese students and workers who were subject to conscription and long military service. Many of them migrated legally and illegally to Western Europe, both to find work and avoid the draft.

By the early 1970s military stalemate convinced an important group of republican-minded army officers to bring an end to the conflict by overthrowing the dictatorship and granting independence to the colonies.[133] The prospect of defeat persuaded some officers to search for political alternatives. Some found them in the radical republican ideas of their African opponents. Many soldiers fighting in Africa studied the writings of Che Guevara and Mao Tse-tung and the work of African insurgents like Amilcar Cabral.[134] These works provided a source of radical republican ideas and showed how Portuguese officers could organize in secret.[135] Dissident officers organized an inchoate but radical republican movement they called the Movimento das Forcas Armadas, or "Armed Forces Movement" (MFA), on March 5, 1974. "I lack political coordinates," Otelo Carvalho, one MFA leader, later admitted. "If I had these, I could have been the Fidel Castro of Europe, but I had a limited culture. . . . This is the first revolution I have been involved in [in] my life."[136]

The growth of radical republicans in the Portuguese army led to the emergence of what MPLA president Agostinho Neto described as "the fourth liberation movement."[137] Members of this movement began planning a mutiny.[138] After a premature effort failed on March 16, they launched a successful coup on April 25, 1974, deposing Caetano and seizing power.[139]

After forming a junta with General António de Spínola at its head, the MFA announced it would decolonize Portuguese overseas territories, recognize the "right of the people to self-determination," promote economic development on behalf of the "laboring classes," improve "the quality of life of all Portuguese," and dissolve the junta "as soon as the constituent national assembly and the new president of the *republic* are elected by the nation." (emphasis added)[140] Coming as it did during a deep economic crisis, after years of grinding war, and under a regime that had not fully established itself as the legitimate successor to Salazar's government, the overthrow of Caetano by this small group of anticolonial republicans in the military was widely celebrated by social classes and political forces throughout Portugal.[141] But the coup also triggered a contest for political power by groups who did not participate in it, leading to a succession of provisional governments, attempted military coups (both by conservatives and by radical Communist republicans), and, in April 1976, to parliamentary elections that brought a socialist government to power in a newly established republic.[142]

During this chaotic period of rapid and sometimes revolutionary change—what some government officials called "carnival democracy"— political parties emerged from decades of clandestine activity and others were newly formed. Workers occupied factories and seized land, parties organized massive demonstrations and sometimes battled each other on the streets, and dissidents returned from exile along with settlers who journeyed to Portugal from the colonies.[143] Reformed conservatives, now minimally republican, joined with moderate republicans, including the newly created Socialist Party under Mário Soares, against radical republicans in the army and in the revived Communist Party. Radical and Communist republicans enjoyed considerable support among working people and the poor, particularly in southern Portugal and in Lisbon. But the Socialists could make a wider appeal to these and *other* social classes, who were ready to accept moderate republicans but not radical internationalists, who they associated with Communists in the colonies (the MFA) or with the Soviet Union (the Portuguese Communist Party). "What divides us is not Marx or the creation of a classless society," Soares said of the difference between moderate and radical republicans. "What divides us is Stalin, the all-powerful party, the rights of man and the problems of liberty."[144]

In the April 25, 1975, elections, the Socialists received 37.9 percent of the vote and the Communists only 12.5 percent.[145] After a series of provisional governments, the moderate republicans triumphed over the radicals, forming a socialist government in a republican state.

Cyprus and the Greek Junta

For Greece, the 1973 economic crisis was compounded by military defeat in Cyprus, which led to the collapse of the Greek dictatorship on July 23, 1974, just a few months after the fall of the Portuguese dictatorship.

The Greek military defeat in Cyprus proved to be a major turning point in Greek history. An eastern Mediterranean island with a Greek-speaking majority and a Turkish-speaking minority, Cyprus had become a British colony in 1878. Because it served as an important military base, British officials refused to surrender it after World War II.[146] In the early 1950s Greek-speaking conservative Cypriots led by Archbishop Makarios III organized a movement that demanded independence from Great Britain *and* union with Greece, what they called enosis. But British officials rejected both independence and enosis. In 1954 Minister of State for Colonial Affairs Henry Hopkinson said of Cyprus, "It has always been understood and agreed that there are certain territories in the Commonwealth which, owing to their particular circumstances, can *never* expect to be fully independent." (emphasis added)[147]

Determined to press for independence despite British intransigence, Makarios allied himself with an armed independence movement—the National Organization of Cypriot Fighters (EOKA)—under the command of Colonel George Grivas.[148] Guerrilla warfare after 1955 eventually persuaded the British to grant independence to Cyprus. During negotiations in 1958–59 the British insisted they be permitted to keep important military bases on Cyprus and that the new republic provide constitutional guarantees for its Turkish minority. Makarios reluctantly accepted guarantees that the Turkish vice president could veto many presidential decisions and that Turkish-speaking citizens be given 30 percent of the positions in the bureaucracy and 40 percent of the ranks in the army. Although Makarios had won independence for Cyprus—he became its first president in 1960—constitutional provisions protecting the Turkish minority effectively prevented realization of enosis, primarily because the Turkish minority adamantly opposed a Greek-Cypriot *anschluss*. As one observer noted, "Cyprus was the first country in the world to be denied majority rule by its own constitution."[149]

After taking power, Makarios took steps that antagonized the Turkish minority in Cyprus and the Turkish government, pro-enosis militants and their supporters in Greece, and the United States government, which assumed a role as arbiter in disputes between its two NATO allies. In 1963, for example, Makarios introduced proposals that would amend the constitution and strip the Turkish vice president of his veto powers.[150] But Makarios's effort to win greater independence and establish majority rule triggered conflict between Greek and Turkish Cypriots, each side supported by the governments in Greece and Turkey. Because the Turkish Cypriots bore the brunt of the violence, the Turkish government threatened to invade the island and intervene on their behalf.[151] The Turkish invasion was forestalled by U.S. officials, who used the U.S. Navy to block the departure of the Turkish fleet, and by the arrival of U.N. peacekeeping forces, which inserted themselves between the warring groups.[152] Turkey briefly threatened a second invasion in 1967 after pro-enosis militants led by Colonel Grivas renewed their attacks on Turkish Cypriot communities.

The outbreak of violence and threat of invasion persuaded Makarios to abandon his goal of enosis with Greece. In 1968 he conceded that a solution to conflict in Cyprus "must necessarily be sought within the limits of what is *feasible*, which does not always coincide with the limits of what is *desirable*," admitting that enosis was no longer a feasible political project. (emphasis added)[153]

The Makarios government managed to antagonize most Turkish-speaking Cypriots, a minority of Greek Cypriots, and the governments of Turkey, Greece, and the United States. Although all of these groups wanted to depose the increasingly autonomous Makarios, it was the Greek dictatorship and Greece's militant Cypriot allies who acted first, to the detriment of all.

A conservative government led by Marshal Alexander Papagos and then Constantine Karamanlis took power in Greece after the civil war, presiding over a royalist state during the 1950s and early 1960s.[154] In 1963 and 1964 successive elections brought moderate republicans to power, first as a plurality and then as a majority. Their leader, George Papandreou, promised to wage a "relentless struggle" against conservative forces and challenge the royalist state.[155] But Constantine II, who had become king on March 6, 1964, was determined to preserve the royalist state and blunt the growing republican challenge.[156] His intervention in 1965 secured Papandreou's resignation. He then installed a succession of weak minority governments between 1965 and 1967, hoping to stall the republican ascent.[157] But the elections scheduled for April 1967 promised to end the political stalemate and bring a republican majority to parliament. The king and his supporters began planning an *ektoropi* (deviation), or coup, to preempt a republican victory, but a group of military officers launched their own coup on April 21, 1967, using ready-made NATO plans designed to counter a Communist takeover.[158]

The Greek colonels were based in an organization called IDEA (Sacred League of Greek Officers) that was similar in its clandestine nature to Portugal's MFA. But unlike the radical republicans in the MFA, the Greek conspirators were anti-republican royalists, determined to root out electoral democracy.[159] As their leader George Papadopoulos argued, "Responsible democracy . . . cannot be merely the democracy which is expressed by the casting and canvassing of votes. . . . There is no possibility of [this kind of] democracy ever returning to Greece. Democracy means the exercise of responsible authority . . . for the satisfaction of the public interest."[160]

Like Franco, the Greek colonels were more interested in defending the monarchy, which provided a source of political legitimacy, than in serving the king, whom they regarded as ineffective. Although the king immediately vouched for the new dictatorship, he recognized that the colonels had acted on their own, without any loyalty to him.[161] Fearful that he would become a figurehead, the king launched his own coup on December 13, 1967, to reassert royal authority. But the coup failed miserably and the king was forced into exile.[162] A subsequent royalist coup by the navy in May 1973 also failed. Angry at the king's attempts to dislodge the junta, Papadopoulos dissolved the monarchy, denouncing it as "an outdated leftover of past ages," installed himself as president, and arranged a rigged plebiscite to ratify the new republic on July 29, 1973.[163]

To secure support for the new constitution, Papadopoulos suggested that some kind of democracy or civil liberties might eventually be restored.[164] But his military colleagues in the junta viewed this nascent republicanism with alarm. They were alarmed, too, by growing domestic opposition to the regime. In mid-November 1973 students at the polytechnic in Athens demonstrated against the junta. The demonstration was crushed by tanks and soldiers who were ordered to use their rifles to "slug the flesh" of unarmed students, killing between forty-three and eighty youths. Anti-republican forces in the military then deposed Papadopoulos on November 25 and consolidated authority in the hands of Dimitrios Ioannidis.[165] Having successfully preserved anti-republican dictatorship in Greece, Ioannidis decided to launch another anti-republican coup in Cyprus.[166]

On July 15, 1974, just eight months after the anti-republican military coup in Greece and only two months after the pro-republican military coup in Portugal, the Greek dictatorship and pro-enosis militants led by Nicos Sampson launched a coup against the Makarios government in Cyprus. They seized power after bombarding the presidential palace but failed to capture and kill Makarios, who escaped into the hills and then fled to London.[167]

Unable to capture Makarios, the new regime could not easily claim legitimacy or secure diplomatic recognition.[168] Fighting between Greek and Turkish Cypriots also erupted. Four days later, Turkish forces began landing on Cyprus as a part of a larger invasion fleet. This time the United States did not block the Turkish invasion, and Great Britain did nothing to oppose Turkey's actions, despite its obligations to maintain the "independence, territorial integrity and security [of Cyprus]."[169]

The leaders of the Cypriot coup were not prepared to defend Cyprus against a Turkish invasion. And after their Greek allies incurred heavy casualties during the initial Turkish invasion, it became clear that Greece was in no position to help.[170] As the Greek military situation on Cyprus deteriorated, Ioannidis ordered the Greek army to mobilize its forces and prepare for general war with Turkey.[171] But the army balked, knowing that it could not win a war against the superior Turkish forces without assistance from the United States. Furthermore, army leaders realized that the U.S. government had already abandoned its support for the Greek junta. Frontline troops thus demanded that the junta dissolve, that a "Council of National Salvation" be established, and that former Prime Minister Constantine Karamanlis be allowed to return from exile in Paris to head a new government in Greece.[172]

On July 23, 1973, the military juntas in Cyprus and Greece both collapsed.[173] Karamanlis arrived from Paris to head a civilian government in Greece. Makarios eventually returned to Cyprus in December. But in the interim a second, larger Turkish invasion force occupied the northern half of the island, which was subsequently annexed by Turkey, and republican government was restored only to the southern half of Cyprus.[174]

In some ways the installation of the Karamanlis government in Greece returned Greek politics to where they had been in 1963, when Karamanlis last headed a conservative government and faced opposition from a republican opposition headed by George Papandreou. In 1974 Karamanlis led a conservative government that faced opposition from republican forces led by Papandreou's son Andreas. But the balance of political forces had changed between 1963 and 1974. In the interim royalist forces had dispersed after the king fled ignominiously into exile, and conservative forces that had supported the army and its successive dictatorships were discredited by military disaster in Cyprus, by the torture and massacre of unarmed students at home, and by economic crisis and growing foreign debt. An abortive coup by last-gasp conservatives in the military on February 24, 1975, further diminished their appeal in the eyes of the populace.[175]

By contrast, republican forces in Greece emerged from dictatorship reinvigorated. Andreas Papandreou swiftly organized PASOK, a new socialist party, which grew rapidly, capturing 13.6 percent of the vote in 1974, 25.3 percent in 1977, and 48.1 percent—and a parliamentary majority—in 1981.[176]

PASOK attracted growing electoral support because it offered a youthful alternative to aging conservative rule. It promised to address the continuing economic crisis and benefited from Papandreou's long opposition to NATO. Both Andreas and his father had long opposed Greek participation in NATO. For many Greeks, events in Cyprus demonstrated that Turkey, Great Britain, and the United states were unreliable allies. Greek hostility toward the United States was particularly keen because although the United States had asked for and received Greek bases for its Mediterranean fleet, it only casually supported the Greek dictatorship and then abandoned Greece in Cyprus and allowed the island to be occupied and divided by Turkey. The Karamanlis government, citing the French example, withdrew Greece from NATO, proving to voters that Andreas Papandreou's anti-NATO and nonaligned policy had been right all along.[177]

Although the Greek dictatorship fell largely as a result of its involvement in the coup in Cyprus, it did not escape the consequences of its misadventures. In January 1975 the parliament resolved that the 1967 seizure of power was a criminal act, not a legitimate revolution, and that its leaders should be tried for staging the coup in Greece, for killing students and torturing dissidents, and for launching the coup in Cyprus.[178] Psomiades noted that "before the end of the month, criminal procedures were initiated against 104 ministers, undersecretaries, and secretaries-general who had served the dictatorship . . . [and] 50 officers and non-commissioned officers of the army and police forces, who had been accused of torturing political prisoners."[179] Many were subsequently convicted and jailed.[180]

The Death of Franco

In Spain the fall of dictatorship was triggered not by defeat in war, but by a crisis of succession. At a time when Portugal was experiencing radical republican revolution and Greece was prosecuting former dictators for their crimes, Franco's death on November 20, 1975, created problems that his anti-republican regime could not survive.[181]

Born in 1892, Franco had grown old by the late 1960s. A hunting accident and then illness persuaded him to designate political successors and to strengthen institutions so that they could sustain the dictatorship after his death. [182] An organic law adopted on January 10, 1967, provided the institutional framework for a post-Franco dictatorship.[183] In July 1969 Franco designated Prince Juan Carlos (the son of Don Juan and grandson of the last king of Spain) to succeed him as head of state, and the Cortes automatically ratified the decision.[184] When Franco became seriously ill in July 1974, Juan Carlos briefly assumed his duties until Franco recovered.[185] In 1973 Admiral Luis Carrero Blanco became the regime's president, effectively its prime minister, after serving as Franco's chief political aide for many years.[186] Franco groomed Blanco to play the same role in the Spanish government that Caetano assumed in Portugal after Salazar became incapacitated.[187]

Although Franco attempted to lay the groundwork for a smooth transition, the power that he had aggregated was not easily delegated. Nor were his delegates easily controlled. The orderly succession of power did not occur as Franco imagined.[188] On December 20, 1973, Admiral Blanco was assassinated by radical republican Basque guerrillas, who planted a bomb that blew his car "five stories into the air, over the roof of the church, and deposited it onto a high patio wall" in downtown Madrid.[189]

The death of Franco's irreplaceable confederate meant that Juan Carlos would not only serve as head of state but also play an important political role in the selection of a post-Franco government. But instead of consolidating anti-republican dictatorship or reviving the royalist state, Juan Carlos presided over the democratization of government in a republican Spain. The new king "used . . . quasi-authoritarian power . . . to implement reform initiatives, divest himself of his powers, and assume the largely ceremonial role of constitutional monarch in a parliamentary democracy," wrote historians Maxwell and Spiegel.[190]

After Franco died, Juan Carlos assumed the throne and chose reformist conservatives to head the first government of the monarchy. The new government announced on December 15, 1975, that it would "consider with special priority the widening of civil liberties, especially the right of association, and the reform of the representative institutions to broaden their bases. . . . The Government proposes to persevere in the construction of a Spanish democracy which will be secure from any totalitarian menace."[191]

When premier Carlos Arias moved too slowly toward reform, the king dismissed him and replaced him with Aldolfo Suarez, who became the Karamanlis of Spain. Led by Suarez and backed by the king, the new government persuaded the Francoist Cortes to dissolve itself in November 1976, a decision ratified by popular referendum a month later. He then legalized political parties, held an election in June 1977 to select deputies for the new congress, and charged its members with the duty of drafting a new constitution.[192] In December 1978 the constitution was approved by parliament and ratified by referendum.[193]

Spain's devolution of power, from dictatorship to democracy, was largely instigated by royalist conservatives. But why did royalist conservatives initiate democratic reform? Although the king has never fully explained why he acted more as republican than royalist, it is evident that he wanted to retain some role for the monarchy in the post-Franco state. He was no doubt keenly aware that his royal predecessors and contemporaries had not fared well. His grandfather had been forced to abdicate, and his father remained in a humiliating though luxurious exile, snubbed by Franco.[194] Carlos's marriage to Princess Sofia, the eldest daughter of King Paul and Queen Frederika of Greece and the sister of Constantine II, no doubt acquainted Carlos with the trials of royalty in exile.[195] To survive as king, Carlos had to act with more intelligence than had his royal relations.

The king and conservative elites also initiated reform to avoid both past conflicts and present turmoil. During his dictatorship Franco had kept the memory of civil war alive, celebrating wartime victories and building huge monuments to commemorate the victors and demean the vanquished.[196] But memorializing the war also reminded people of the war's immense pain and suffering. "At least 300,000 Spaniards were killed during the hostilities; 440,000 went into exile, 10,000 of them were to die in Nazi concentration camps; another 400,000 in Spain spent time in prison, concentration camps, or labor battalions," and "anything from 22,000 to 200,000 Spaniards were executed" in the years after the war under the 1939 Law of Political Responsibilities.[197] The regime's determination to savor and celebrate this searing experience also kept the victims from forgetting. The wounds of civil war thus remained open and unsutured more than thirty years later.

The king and conservative elites wanted to close these wounds, fearing that such wartime memories might help spark renewed hostilities in the unstable climate that followed Franco's death. The outspoken insistence of Franco's many supporters to remain in power, perhaps even by military coup, and the determination of radical Basque republicans in the Euzkadi Ta Azkatasuna, or "Basque Nation and Liberty" (ETA), which had first taken up arms against Franco in 1967, made the prospect of renewed civil war seem real. The ETA's destruction of the Cafe Rolando in central Madrid—killing thirteen and wounding eighty-four—and its assassination of Admiral Blanco made Spain's civil war past seem a contemporary reality for Spanish elites.[198]

The new government was very aware of events unfolding in Greece and Portugal. The collapse and prosecution of former dictators in Greece worried Spanish elites who thought Francoists might take drastic steps to avoid such a fate. And the revolution in Portugal gave rise to fear of mass revolution. Indeed, domestic labor unrest was a potential starting point for insurrection. Despite the Franco regime's ban on labor unions, *comisiones obreras*, or worker's commissions, had organized strikes to demand higher wages or improved working conditions during the 1960s. The regime tolerated them as long as they confined their demands to economic, not political, issues. Because they had become a base for radical republicans—the outlawed Communist Party was an active participant in many worker's commissions—Franco cracked down on them in 1967, arresting hundreds of activists. But strike activity continued, and the resulting lost working hours rose from 8.7 million in 1970 to 14.5 million in 1975, raising wages and presenting a demonstrable challenge to the dictatorship and to the new royalist-conservative regime.[199]

It was in this context that elites initiated reform. "It is only by taking the risk of possible change . . . that one can control the change," Suarez argued. "Otherwise, the social forces which are bringing pressures to bear on the institutions of the state will end up by triumphing as did Ho Chi Minh in Saigon. By rubbing out everything and starting again."[200]

Taken together, contemporary developments in Greece, Portugal, and Spain made radical republican alternatives seem a real possibility to the new Spanish regime. Of course, it may have been that elites had greatly exaggerated fears of renewed civil war or radical revolution. But whatever the actual prospects for war, what mattered more was that these past histories and contemporary possibilities became "virtual realities" for ruling elites. As Walter Lippmann observed in *Public Opinion* long ago, "it is very clear that under certain conditions men respond as powerfully to fictions as they do to realities, and that in many cases they help to create the very fictions to which they respond. . . . Whatever we believe to be a true picture [of the outside world], we treat as if it were the environment itself."[201] In this context, the commemoration of the Spanish civil war created a powerful contemporary political environment. It was a "fiction" because it combined real memory with imaginary possibilities. And elites responded to this fictional environment, which they had helped create, as if it were real.

The virtual realities of civil war and contemporary revolution persuaded elites that democratic reform was necessary. Elites aligned themselves with moderate republicans outside government to forestall more radical change by, or conflict between, radical *immobilista* conservatives and radical *ruptura* republicans.[202] Moderate republicans, who were represented in Spain by the Socialist Party and led by Felipe Gonzalez, agreed to participate in an alliance with the king and with moderate *aperturista* conservatives because they shared many of the same virtual realities. They too worried about civil war. They feared that radical conservatives might do in Spain what they had recently done in Chile, overthrowing Salvador Allende's democratically elected socialist government in 1973.[203] They also worried that precipitate action by radical republicans—the Communist Party or Basque guerrillas—might trigger a coup by *immobilistas*. Accordingly, they agreed to support a slow, cautious devolutionary process directed and managed by this centrist condominium. As Gonzalez explained, "At times it's most revolutionary to be moderate."[204]

The combined weight of royalist conservatives and moderate republicans enabled them to push the *immobilistas* aside and consigned the radical republicans to the periphery. The determination of the two groups to avoid past and present virtual realities enabled them to compromise on most important issues. For example, the 1977 Moncloa Pact purchased labor peace and brought an end to escalating strike activity, which threatened both economic recovery and government stability.[205] In 1978 the hours lost to strikes were less than half of the 1976 figure, and by 1980 the editors of *Euromoney* could report that "the once feared militancy of the Spanish trade unions has . . . faded."[206] Despite the deliberately slow pace of democratization, these developments bolstered its progress.[207]

After the new Spanish constitution was adopted in 1978, the alliance between royalist conservatives and moderate republicans dissolved, and they soon began competing for political power. Within a few years the Socialist Party emerged as the uncontested victor. The ascent of the Socialist Party in 1982, when it won 48.4 percent of the vote and 57.7 percent of the seats in parliament, occurred for several reasons.[208] First, the Socialist Party was led by the young and charismatic Felipe Gonzalez. Under his direction the party received money and organizational assistance from the German Social Democrats, which helped it become a serious contender in the political scene in a few short years.[209] Second, the party benefited from the collapse of Suarez's royalist-conservative party, the UCD. By initiating sweeping tax reform, legalizing divorce and the Communist Party, and granting greater autonomy to Basque and Catalan republicans, Suarez antagonized members of his own party, which had cobbled together "an electoral alliance between Suarez's *Franquista* reformers and a galaxy of fourteen minor parties."[210] In the early 1980s wide fissures opened in the alliance and the party collapsed.[211] And third, the Socialists benefited from the collapse of the Communist Party. In 1975 the Communists had strong support among workers and trade unions and possessed a determined, militant membership, numbering some two hundred thousand in 1978.[212] But Santiago Carillo, the party's aging leader, adopted policies that antagonized its members and supporters. By abandoning Soviet-style Marxism and promoting a more moderate variety of "Eurocommunism" and by restraining labor militancy during the long democratization process, he disappointed old hard-liners and young militants alike.[213] Tensions within the Communist Party led to formal splits, and by 1983 it had broken into three separate parties.[214] The collapse of parties to its right and left enabled the Socialist Party, supplied with able leaders and considerable German support, to capture and hold on to political power throughout the 1980s and into the mid-1990s.

The 1973 oil crisis created common problems for old Iberian and new Ionian dictatorships, bringing an end to economic development based on the export of domestic workers and the import of tourists. Added to this shared economic crisis were different military and political crises that occurred close to each other in time or space. The shared economic crisis made subsequent military and political crises acute rather than just problematic. All three dictatorships collapsed in rapid succession: in Portugal on April 25, 1974; in Greece on July 23, 1974; and in Spain on November 20, 1975.

All three dictatorships fell not because they were structurally connected. Indeed, there were very few institutional or political ties between the regimes. They collapsed because similar processes were at work in each state. Although the Portuguese and Greek regimes disintegrated independently, their fall contributed to events in Spain. Spanish elites democratized because they were determined to avoid the kind of developments—radical revolution in Portugal and the humiliation and prosecution of former rulers in Greece—that accompanied the collapse of dictatorships in those countries.

The governments that took power in Portugal, Greece, and Spain used existing political institutions to write new constitutions, legalize political parties, and hold referendums and elections to ratify constitutions and elect delegates to revived parliaments.[215] And socialist governments came to power in all three countries, a development that would have seemed unimaginable in 1974. By reorganizing social and political alliances, socialist governments not only consolidated and defended democratic regimes, but they also established, on a more permanent basis, republican *states*. Given the history of bitter conflict between royalist, anti-republican conservatives and republicans in all three countries throughout the twentieth century, this was perhaps the most significant achievement of provisional, interim, and then socialist governments. Anti-republican forces have been eclipsed and royalists have since retired in all three countries. Republicans—conservative in Portugal and moderate in Spain and Greece—have gained the field.

Democratization in the Iberian states had an important impact on Latin America and the Philippines, where Spain and Portugal had once held colonies. Because the Iberian states retained close economic, political, and cultural ties with their former colonies, the fall of Iberian dictatorships was felt by regimes across the Atlantic in Latin America and across the Pacific in the Philippines.

five

DEBT AND DICTATORSHIP IN LATIN AMERICA

Democratization in Latin America and the Philippines was triggered by a shared economic crisis. The crisis began when the 1971 dollar devaluation and 1973 oil crisis created economic problems for Latin American dictatorships, just as they had for Southern European regimes. Although the 1971–73 crisis contributed to the collapse of Southern European regimes, it did not topple Latin American dictatorships. They survived this first crisis because the oil embargo indirectly provided them with the money they needed to address the problems created by rising oil prices. By using borrowed money to promote "indebted development," dictators unwittingly paved the way for a second and more intense "debt crisis" by the end of the decade.[1]

In Latin America the first stage of the economic crisis began in 1971 and consisted of three related developments: the 1971 dollar devaluation, the 1973 oil embargo, and the 1972–75 grain shortages in the Soviet Union. These events created problems throughout Latin America, though their impact differed from one country to the next.

On August 15, 1971, U.S. President Richard Nixon announced that he would devalue the dollar to help U.S. firms compete more effectively against their rivals in Western Europe and Japan.[2] For most Latin American countries, the U.S. dollar devaluation raised the value of their currencies and made their exports more expensive, making it harder for them to sell their goods overseas. As it had for the Southern European dictatorships, this generally reduced their export income. And while the dollar devaluation cut into export earnings, the 1973 oil embargo and 1972–75 grain shortages increased the cost of essential imports for most Latin American countries.

The 1973 oil embargo by members of the Oil Producing and Exporting Countries (OPEC) was partly a response to the U.S. dollar devaluation and to political developments in the Middle East. Because the world's oil trade was, and is, conducted in dollars, the 1971 dollar devaluation lowered the real income of oil-producing countries, which had also seen nominal oil prices fall slowly since 1960. Determined to regain lost revenues, OPEC in 1973 imposed an oil embargo during the Yom Kippur War between Egypt and Israel, raising the price of a barrel of crude oil from $3.00 to $12.50.[3] Along with the rest of the world, Latin American countries paid more for their oil imports, spending $5 billion in 1974 compared with $1.6 billion in 1973.[4] The oil shortages resulting from the Iranian revolution in 1978–80 increased prices again, from $12 to $30 a barrel, raising the cost of imported oil in Latin America from $7 billion in 1978 to $15 billion in 1980.[5]

Rising oil prices created enormous problems for oil-poor countries like Argentina, which saw its oil bill rise from $58 million in 1972, or 3.1 percent of its total imports, to $586 million in 1974, or 15.1 percent of its imports, and Brazil, which relied on imports to supply more than 80 percent of its total oil consumption.[6] But it provided enormous benefits to oil-rich Venezuela, one of OPEC's founding members, Mexico, which was just beginning to exploit newly discovered reserves, and Ecuador, which began producing from its east Amazonian oil fields in the early 1970s.[7]

Latin American countries also paid more for food imports in the 1970s. Global grain prices increased sharply as a result of poor harvests in the Soviet Union, where grain production fell by 14 to 34 percent between 1972 and 1975, and the rising demand for food by oil-producing countries and rapidly growing East Asian countries like South Korea and Taiwan.[8] Wheat prices more than doubled, from $54 to $110 per ton between 1972 and 1974, and corn prices increased by one-third, from $46 to $79 per ton.[9] Rising grain prices increased the cost of food imports at a time when the price of fuel was also mounting. Although all Latin American countries paid more, the rising cost of food was particularly hard for food-deficit countries that exported most of their agricultural produce and relied on imports to feed their residents.[10]

During the 1960s many Latin American countries received food aid from the United States.[11] But when global food prices surged, the U.S. government scaled back its food aid programs to take advantage of rising prices, reducing its deliveries from 18 million tons to only 3 million tons between 1965 and 1974.[12] As U.S. food aid disappeared, countries that had relied on First World imports were forced to buy food on global markets at record-high prices. Poland, Argentina, Brazil, and Mexico, for example, all made major grain purchases during this period, borrowing money to finance grain imports.[13]

The 1971 dollar devaluation weakened the market for Latin American exports and reduced export income. The rising prices associated with the 1973 oil embargo and 1972–75 grain shortages increased the cost of fuel and food imports for most Latin American countries. These two developments combined to create large trade deficits, which in turn forced many countries to spend their foreign exchange reserves on necessary imports.[14] Rather than devalue their currencies to cover their trade deficits, many Latin American governments began to borrow money instead.[15]

The rising costs of food and fuel had another consequence: They contributed to inflation. During the 1960s the inflation rate for Latin America was 12 percent.[16] But as the price of oil tripled between 1973–74 and then doubled again between 1978–80 and as the price of food doubled from 1973–80, inflation reached an annual rate of 75 percent and averaged 128 percent a year between 1976 and 1980.[17] The economic crisis of 1971–75 finally brought an end to decades-long developmentalist policies in Latin America and introduced "indebted development" as the common strategy for economic growth.

During the 1950s and 1960s many Latin American governments encouraged private or public industry to produce domestic goods to serve as replacements for expensive imports, a process known as import substitution.[18] They also adopted essentially mercantilist policies, erecting high tariff barriers to protect these industries from foreign competition and using foreign-exchange controls to discourage domestic industries from purchasing essential capital goods from abroad.[19] For a time, import substitution and government mercantilism promoted modest economic growth in Latin America, 5.3 percent on average in the 1950s and 5.4 percent in the 1960s.[20] But as the 1971–75 economic crisis threatened these modest economic gains, governments abandoned their import-substitution strategy and embarked on a policy of borrowing money to promote development.

Oil Crisis and Debt

As export income declined and the cost of imported oil and food rose, trade deficits mounted, creating a major economic crisis for dictatorships throughout Latin America. Dictators averted the 1971–75 crisis by borrowing heavily. But although borrowed money helped them solve the immediate problems associated with the crisis and helped promote economic development in the 1970s, reliance on indebted development would make them more vulnerable to the second crisis that emerged at the end of the decade.[21]

Before the 1971–75 crisis governments in Latin America had borrowed only modest amounts of money, about $20 billion between 1950 and 1970, most of it from the IMF and the World Bank. Latin American governments found it difficult to borrow heavily because loan capital was relatively scarce. But the creation of the Eurodollar market made a growing supply of funds available to Latin America and other Third World borrowers during the 1970s.

The Eurodollar market emerged during the 1950s and 1960s, when governments and private investors from around the world took the U.S. dollars and other hard currencies they had earned in trade and deposited them in subsidiaries of U.S. banks in Europe.[22] Governments and private corporations found these accounts to be safe places for their dollars; further, they were not subject to the same regulations that applied to currencies deposited in domestic banks.[23] The money available in this Eurodollar banking pool grew to $10 billion by 1960 and to $110 billion by 1970.[24] During the 1970s money from another source began to deepen and expand this reservoir of funds. The 1973 oil embargo raised oil prices for consumers around the world and increased oil revenues for oil-producing countries. "Between 1973 and 1974, the current account surplus of OPEC countries rose from $7 billion to $68 billion," noted economist Barbara Stallings. "The newly wealthy OPEC countries wanted to keep their expanded export revenues in a highly liquid form, so a large percent was deposited with the Euro-banks."[25] With the influx of dollars from oil-producing countries, the pool of money in the Eurodollar market grew from $110 billion in 1970 to $1,525 billion by 1980.[26]

As the pool of money in Eurodollar accounts grew, bank officials began pumping out loans to borrowers in Eastern Europe, Africa, East Asia, and Latin America. Of the $810 billion loaned to developing countries between 1970 and 1983—an amount split equally between loans made by private banks and government lending agencies like the World Bank—Latin America's share was nearly half of these loans, or $350 billion.[27]

Private banks made loans from Eurodollar supplies to afford the interest they owed to their depositors. In addition, private banks seeking to invest growing Eurodollar deposits found it more profitable to lend money to Third World borrowers than to domestic borrowers (more "risky" Third World borrowers paid higher interest rates than "safer" First World borrowers). First World industry also encouraged private and government lending agencies such as the World Bank and export-import banks to make loans so that Third World countries would be able to purchase their goods. The U.S. government's Export-Import Bank, for example, loaned money to Latin American governments so they could purchase U.S. airplanes. As Boeing President Malcolm Stranger explained, "The Ex-Im Bank . . . was created to help promote exports . . . to help foreign firms and their nations to buy big-ticket goods that would be of social and economic benefit. Airplanes certainly meet this description. . . . Airplane exports are also very good business for this country's own economy, by the way."[28]

Because loans to Latin American countries promised substantial profits for private banks and provided these countries with the means to purchase First World goods, loans were made widely available to Latin America and other Third World countries. The oil embargo, in a roundabout way, provided a temporary solution for the problem it created.

Governments in countries throughout Latin America took advantage of newly available resources and borrowed heavily. In 1974 alone Brazil doubled its net external debt from $6.2 billion to $11.9 billion, and its debt tripled to $32 billion by 1977 and tripled again to $95 billion by 1983.[29] In the same period debt in Mexico climbed to $85 billion, in Argentina to $40 billion, in Venezuela to $33 billion, in the Philippines to $20 billion, in Chile to $18 billion, in Peru to $11.6 billion, and in Colombia to $10 billion.[30]

Perhaps because they were eager to lend, international banks did not seem overly concerned about how their money was spent. "Indeed," economic historian Victor Blumer-Thomas noted, "the banks were unaware of the purposes for which most of their loans were used: nearly 60 percent of all U.S. bank lending in the 1970s was devoted to 'general purpose,' 'purpose unknown,' or 'refinancing.'"[31]

The Latin American governments used these loans in a variety of ways. First, they borrowed money to pay for costly imports and to cover mounting trade deficits.[32] Second, governments borrowed money to promote economic growth, using funds to expand energy production, agriculture and fisheries, industry and mining, and transportation and communications.[33] By developing infrastructure and expanding the production of agricultural and industrial goods, governments reduced unemployment and increased government income from project revenues and worker taxes.[34] Third, much of the money was used to repay previous loans. Economists Sue Branford and Bernardo Kucinski estimated that 60 percent of the $272.9 billion borrowed by Latin American countries between 1976 and 1981 ($170.5 billion in all) "was immediately paid back to the banks as debt repayments or interest. Another $22 billion remained with [First World] banks as reserves against potential losses, which were a kind of additional guarantee for the debt itself," leaving only a fraction of the total debt for productive investment.[35] Fourth, governments spent borrowed money on the military. They did so in part because U.S. military aid to Latin American countries declined from $210 million in 1977 to just $54 million in 1979, reflecting growing U.S. concern about the poor human rights records of most Latin American dictatorships.[36] Governments borrowed money both to replace lost U.S. aid and to increase military spending in real terms. Military spending by Latin American countries doubled during the 1970s as dictators moved to strengthen the armies that served them.[37] Finally, although governments borrowed most of the money from private banks and public lending agencies, private debt was also on the rise, increasing from $15 billion in 1972 to $58 billion in 1981 and accounting for about 20 percent of the total.[38] Domestic firms and even some foreign multinationals operating in these countries borrowed heavily to finance the expansion of their businesses.[39]

Borrowed money helped fuel economic growth throughout Latin America during the 1970s, as did rising commodity prices for many Latin American exports. Between 1970 and 1982 the terms of trade for Latin American goods was extremely favorable, more so than at any time in the preceding or succeeding decades.[40] Between 1975 and 1984 real gross domestic product (GDP) in Latin America increased 31 percent, from $257 billion to $336 billion.[41] The Mexican economy grew 57 percent and the Brazilian economy 37 percent between 1975 and 1981, growth rates described as miraculous by economists.[42]

Borrowed money spurred economic growth and secured some popular support for dictatorships during the 1970s. But it also contributed to inflation, which began to erode popular support by the end of the decade. Two factors contributed to inflation during the 1970s. First, fuel and food prices increased as a result of the oil embargo and grain shortages. And second, the rising supply of money and credit made available by heavy government borrowing and massive public spending made it possible for some groups to demand and receive higher prices and wages.[43]

Inflation is a discriminatory economic process. Some businesses and workers are better able to demand and receive higher prices or wages than other groups. Generally speaking, firms that produce necessary and essential goods or firms that exercise monopoly power in the market can demand and receive higher prices than businesses that produce less essential goods or that operate in competitive markets. Likewise, workers who possess essential or scarce skills or who belong to strong unions can demand higher wages than unskilled workers in nonunionized trades. Because some groups can raise prices or wages while others cannot, inflation effectively discriminates against the latter groups, increasing their costs and reducing their purchasing power.

In Latin America ogopolistic firms and state-run enterprises were able to keep up with inflation because of their access to money or credit to pay for more expensive imports and because of their central position in the domestic market—a position created by the import substitution policies of previous decades—which enabled them to demand and receive higher prices for the goods they produced. As prices climbed, unionized workers in private and state-run industries, government workers in expanding bureaucracies, and, importantly, soldiers in growing armies were able to demand and receive higher wages from private firms and the state, which could pass on these additional costs to consumers in the form of still higher prices or taxes. Of course, dictatorships often dismantled unions or tried to curb their power in the private and public sector. But they could not easily refuse wage demands by government bureaucrats and military personnel who provided them with essential political support. Although the demands of these groups were generally satisfied, the demands of others were neglected. Despite rapid economic growth in most Latin American countries, real wages fell and the gap between rich and poor widened during the 1970s, largely as a result of the discriminatory effects of inflation.[44]

Inflation eroded support for dictatorships among those groups it adversely affected, particularly the poor, unskilled, and nonunionized workers in agriculture and industry. Of course, these groups did not provide the dictatorships with much political support. But inflation also eroded support among the more important middle- and upper-class constituencies, even among those groups who were not adversely affected by inflation. As the economist Anthony Compagna noted about the psychology of inflation, "If someone's income increased by $1,000 (which he or she regards as due to merit, conveniently forgetting that inflation boosts other people's income as well) and rising prices take away $500 of the $1,000, the person is still better off but feels cheated anyway [because] $1,000 at the old prices would have meant a [more] significant increase in living standards."[45]

Inflation simultaneously *differentiated* social groups, making some poorer, and *united* them in a common antipathy to its real or imagined consequences. Borrowed money enabled dictatorships to promote economic growth, which helped them avert the 1971–75 crisis. But inflation distributed the benefits of indebted development unequally and eroded support for dictators among all sectors of society as the decade progressed.

As the debts of Latin American and other Third World countries mounted, First World lenders began to worry about increasing risk. They began hedging their bets, insisting in the late 1970s that borrowers agree to convert their fixed-interest loans to loans with floating interest rates, which would be adjusted every six months, bringing interest rates into line with current market rates.[46] Because lenders made future loans contingent on converting loans from fixed to adjustable rates, borrowers generally agreed to convert their loans. By 1983 nearly 70 percent of all loans made to Latin America were subject to floating interest rates, which meant they would rise or fall depending on the interest rates set in First World countries.[47] This provision made Latin American debtors extremely vulnerable to changing interest rate policies in the United States. After 1979 new U.S. economic policies raised interest rates, increasing the cost of borrowed money and triggering the second major economic crisis of the decade. Although Latin American dictatorships survived the first crisis, they would not survive the second.

Debt Crisis and Structural Adjustment

In 1979 inflation in the United States rose to 14 percent annually, a product of the oil price increases associated with revolution in Iran. As rising inflation and lengthening gas lines undermined President Jimmy Carter's popularity, Carter appointed Paul Volcker to head the Federal Reserve and lead the government's battle against inflation.[48] On October 6, 1979, Volcker announced that the Federal Reserve would fight inflation by raising interest rates, thereby restricting the supply of money and credit.[49] After "fluctuating between 6.8 percent and 9.1 percent in the late 1970s," U.S. interest rates climbed to "12.7 percent by 1979, 15.3 percent by 1980, and 18.9 percent by 1981," rising briefly to 20.2 percent in the fall of 1981.[50] Climbing U.S. interest rates and the rising London Interbank Offered Rate (LIBOR), which set interest rates for Eurodollar loans, created two problems. First, they greatly increased the payments on Latin American loans, most of which were now pegged to floating Federal Reserve or LIBOR rates.[51] Latin American interest payments rose from nearly $6.9 billion in 1977 to over $39 billion in 1982, a more than fivefold increase.[52]

A second problem was that high U.S. interest rates acted like a magnet, attracting money from investors around the world. Because U.S. Treasury bonds, bills, and notes were offered at higher interest rates than government bonds elsewhere and because investors regarded them as extremely safe investments in uncertain economic times, purchases of U.S. Treasuries and corporate securities skyrocketed. The massive influx of money from around the world drained money from distant countries, a process known as capital flight.

In 1978 Latin American investors had spent about $7 billion to purchase safe U.S. securities, a process Filipino investors described as "dollar salting." Many Latin American and Filipino investors would deposit or "salt away" their capital in U.S. banks or financial institutions, then use these deposits as collateral to borrow money from First World lenders to run their businesses. Dollar salting was an attractive option for these investors, as their governments would often offer to repay money borrowed from foreign sources if the business should fail; meanwhile, their foreign investments were safe from the risk of bankruptcy or expropriation. But in 1980 Latin Americans invested $25 billion abroad, a threefold increase from 1978.[53] "From 1973 to 1987," Manuel Pastor wrote, "capital flight from Latin America added up to $151 billion, or about 43 percent of the total external debt during those years."[54]

Capital flight reduced the amount of money available for domestic investment.[55] This resulted in higher levels of unemployment, deprived governments of the foreign currency they needed to pay for imports and repay foreign debts, and eroded the tax base as investors withdrew taxable savings from domestic banks and placed them in tax-free deposits in U.S. banks. As Volcker observed, "In many [Latin American and Third World countries], their excessive debt burdens can be traced in large part to capital flight by their own citizens discouraged from investing at home."[56] He might have added that U.S. interest rate policies under his direction accelerated capital flight and attracted it to the United States, where it was used to finance growing defense spending and mounting federal budget deficits.[57]

As debt-related costs increased after 1979, Latin American countries saw their export incomes fall. In contrast to the 1970s, when the price of metals, raw materials, food, and—for some countries—fuel rose, prices for these goods declined dramatically during the early 1980s. Export earnings were crucial to Latin American countries because the "hard currencies" (dollars, deutsche marks, yen) they earned by selling their goods to First World countries were used to repay their loans and purchase essential imports. First World lenders insisted on repayment in dollars or other hard currencies, not in Mexican pesos or Argentine astrals, because they worried that indebted governments would simply print more money—which they did in any event—and repay loans in worthless, depreciated currencies.

In the late 1970s higher prices for many commodities led to strong export earnings throughout most of Latin America. But between 1980 and 1982 world commodity prices fell by more than one-third to their lowest level in thirty years, a disastrous blow to countries relying on commodity exports to repay their debts.[58] A World Bank index of raw material prices, which started at 168.2 in 1980, fell to 100 by 1990 and 86.1 in 1992, the lowest prices in real terms since 1948.[59] As the economist Darrell Delmaide noted, "The beef that Argentina [exported] fell from $2.25 a kilogram . . . in 1980 to $1.60 by the end of 1981. Sugar from Brazil and the Caribbean fell from 79 cents a kilo to 27 cents by 1982. And copper, a big ticket item for the likes of Chile . . . fell from $2.61 a kilo to $1.66."[60]

Falling prices were particularly devastating for countries that relied on one crop or on raw materials for the bulk of their export earnings.[61] Although between 1960 and 1980 most Latin American countries had reduced their dependence on primary commodities for export earnings—Argentina from 96 to 77 percent, Brazil from 97 to 61 percent, Chile from 96 to 80 percent, Colombia from 98 to 80 percent, Mexico from 88 to 61 percent, Peru from 99 to 84 percent, and Venezuela from 100 to 98 percent—they still relied heavily on primary goods for more than two-thirds of their export income.[62] When commodity prices fell, the loss of income was considerable.

A variety of related developments triggered the fall of commodity prices. First, they fell because high U.S. interest rates spurred a recession in the United States and around the world, thus greatly reducing the demand for Latin American goods by the United States, the principle market for Latin American exports. U.S. demand for Latin American goods also fell because the United States and other First World countries had begun to develop new technologies and to substitute new domestically produced goods for Third World imports. Increasing U.S. sugar beet production and the development of high fructose corn sweeteners reduced the demand for imported cane sugar from Brazil and the Philippines, while weight-conscious consumers who switched from sugared soft drinks to artificially sweetened beverages reduced the demand for sugar in any form. Likewise, the development of fiber-optic glass cable reduced the need for copper cable from Chile. Technological innovation enabled the United States to implement import substitution policies of its own, replacing Latin American imports with high-technology domestic goods.[63]

Second, commodity prices fell because the supply of many Latin American products had recently grown. During the 1970s Latin American countries had used borrowed money to expand the production of agricultural and industrial goods. For example, world coffee production had increased from 3.8 million tons in 1970 to 4.9 million tons in 1979, while world sugar production had increased from 585 million tons to 754 million tons in the same period.[64]

Taken together, the mounting costs associated with high interest rates and falling income from exports created an economic hurricane that built to gale-force strength by 1982. Lesser winds, though of the same type, first stormed and overwhelmed low-lying economies in Peru and Jamaica (1979), Nicaragua (1980), Bolivia (1981), and Guyana (1982).[65] The center of the storm then shifted to Eastern Europe, where on March 27, 1981, Polish government officials in London told representatives of five hundred Western banks that Poland could not repay the $27 billion it had borrowed.[66] In July the Romanian government followed suit, suspending payments on its more modest $7 billion debt.[67]

The financial problems created by these defaults seemed relatively insignificant in August 1982, when Mexico's finance minister Jesus Silva-Herzog announced that Mexico could no longer make payments on its $90 billion foreign debt. During the following year more than forty other countries around the world, most of them in Latin America, ran out of money and announced they could no longer repay the interest or principle on the $810 billion they owed.[68] "Never in history have so many nations owed so much money with so little promise of repayment," *Time* observed.[69] This economic hurricane, which threatened to destroy North American lenders and South American borrowers alike, was deflected from North America by the Federal Reserve and the World Bank. But it hit Latin American economies with full force.

First World lenders were able to escape catastrophe because they created what Princeton economist Robert Gilpin called a "creditor's cartel," which allowed lenders led by the Federal Reserve and the World Bank to practice a "divide and conquer strategy" and insist that debtor states take steps to ensure full repayment.[70] "Interest payments on the debt would not be decreased across the board nor would commodity prices received by debtors be increased," Gilpin observed. "The burden of solving the problem would remain squarely on the debtors."[71]

While Federal Reserve and World Bank officials managed the debt crisis in dozens of countries, private First World lenders moved to protect themselves from the consequences of the crisis by reducing credit to debtors. Although they did not entirely cut off new loans, private lending to Latin American countries fell by one-third between 1982 and 1984, and public agencies assumed the burden of lending to debtor states during this time. Private lending fell despite U.S. Treasury Secretary James Baker's 1985 plan to encourage renewed private lending during the crisis.[72] After lending $38 billion in 1981, public and private lenders supplied only half as much, $16.8 billion, in 1982 and only $5.3 billion in 1983.[73]

Although First World lenders averted catastrophe—no major First World bank failed during the crisis—Latin American countries did not. By 1982–83 rising costs and declining incomes had exhausted the foreign currencies held by Latin American governments, preventing purchases of imported food or fuel. Because foreign loans were scarce and domestic capital supplies had flown abroad, agriculture and industry were directly threatened. To avert massive layoffs and economic collapse, Latin American governments needed to obtain sufficient foreign exchange and working capital from First World lenders, especially from the World Bank and other multilateral lending agencies. First World lenders agreed to provide credit, foreign exchange, and standby loans only if Latin American governments adopted stringent economic programs designed to ensure debt repayment.

These pay-it-back, "structural adjustment" programs imposed by creditors and adopted by Latin American governments during the early 1980s had three important features. First, creditors demanded that governments assume responsibility for repaying private debts that they did not themselves incur. Private firms had borrowed $58 billion from foreign lenders, about 20 percent of the outstanding debt. In Venezuela and Argentina nearly 60 percent of the total debt had been acquired by private businesses, domestic and foreign.[74] But governments and taxpayers were told to repay this debt, as if it were their own. "In country after country," wrote Harvard economist Jeffrey Sachs, "governments took over the private debt on favorable terms for the public sector firms, or subsidized the private debt service payments, in order to bail out the private firms. This 'socialization' of the private debt resulted in a significant increase in the fiscal burden of the nation's foreign debt."[75]

Second, in order to repay all loans, public and private, as a condition for receiving short-term capital, Latin American governments needed to create trade surpluses and government budget surpluses. Trade surpluses would allow them to acquire foreign currency, which could then be used to repay debts and purchase essential imports. Accordingly, most Latin American countries expanded the production of their hard currency-earning exports and devalued their own currencies. Officials in Argentina, Bolivia, Brazil, Chile, the Dominican Republic, Ecuador, Mexico, Paraguay, Peru, the Philippines, Uruguay, and Venezuela hoped that currency devaluations would simultaneously make their exports cheaper abroad and make imports more expensive. Devaluations would stimulate exports, reduce the domestic demand for imports, and create trade surpluses.[76]

Expanded production and currency devaluations helped Latin American countries export more goods, and the "trade balance, which had been negative until 1982, became positive, with a surplus of $30 billion recorded in 1983 and nearly $40 billion in 1984."[77] From 1980 to 1985 Latin American countries increased the volume of goods they exported by 23 percent.[78] But falling prices, caused in part by increasing supplies, meant that the value of these exports remained the same, despite their increased volume. In fact, the value of the region's exports was the same in 1985 as it was in 1981, and after oil prices fell in 1986, the value of exports dropped nearly 20 percent.[79]

With export incomes holding steady, the only way Latin American governments managed to create trade surpluses was by severely reducing imports. Whereas they imported $95.8 billion in goods in 1981, they imported only $54.4 billion in 1983, staying at this level throughout the mid-1980s.[80] By slashing imports Latin American governments created between $30 and $40 billion in trade surpluses, which they used to repay First World loans. As Mexican finance minister Silva-Herzog observed, "The much heralded improvement in Latin America's current accounts therefore is attributable mostly to import reduction, rather than to export increase."[81]

Finally, while they took steps to create trade surpluses, Latin American officials also moved to generate government budget surpluses that could be used to repay their debts. One way to reduce government spending and earn hard currency was to sell off state assets, such as the government-owned phone company, airline, cement factory, and coffee company. In debt crisis negotiations First World lenders insisted that Latin American governments privatize state-run businesses and change their laws to allow foreigners to purchase these assets. But because most countries had devalued their currencies *prior* to privatization, state assets were more cheaply available to foreign buyers. As a result, state assets were frequently transferred to foreign rather than domestic owners.

State assets could only be sold once, and thus their sale generated fixed returns. But to tackle their debts governments required steady sources of income. Generally they did this by increasing taxes and cutting public spending. During the 1970s Latin American governments used borrowed money to keep rising oil and food prices artificially low so that transportation, cooking fuel, and basic foods would remain affordable for poor and working people. Dictators reasoned that subsidies would purchase support or, at least, public indifference to their rule. But in the 1980s they were forced to eliminate these subsidies, which accounted for a considerable percentage of government spending.[82]

The result was sharply rising prices for basic necessities, which helped fuel inflation. Governments also cut salaries and laid off government workers while simultaneously raising taxes. Generally speaking, they reduced taxes on corporations and the rich and increased excise and sales taxes, which fell most heavily on the poor. One 1986 study of ninety-four structural adjustment programs found that most contained wage restraints, most cut subsidies and transfer payment programs, such as social security and unemployment assistance, and nearly half raised taxes.[83]

Indebted Dictators

During the 1970s and 1980s U.S. economic policy underwent a series of changes that worked to the disadvantage of Latin American dictatorships. Although U.S. officials encouraged dictators to borrow heavily in the 1970s, the U.S. government contributed to the crisis by devaluing the dollar, which reduced export earnings for many Latin American countries. The elimination of U.S. food aid programs under Nixon and the reduction of military aid under Presidents Ford and Carter contributed to the pressure on governments to borrow. By insisting that Latin American governments convert low, fixed-interest loans to floating rates, U.S. and IMF officials made dictatorships extremely vulnerable to shifting interest-rate policies. When Volcker changed U.S. interest-rate policy to battle domestic inflation, Latin American governments saw their costs increase and their incomes fall. After the debt crisis broke, the U.S.-led creditor's cartel insisted that Latin American governments assume all private debts and adopt painful structural adjustment programs.

In economic terms the debt crisis and structural adjustment programs led to contraction, declining living standards, and rising inflation. Latin American economies shrank by about 10 percent in the early 1980s.[84] Because their populations continued to grow, real wages and consumption fell. In just three years, between 1980 and 1983, real consumption per capita fell 8 percent in Brazil and Mexico, 14 percent in Peru, 17 percent in Argentina and Chile, and 39 percent in Nicaragua.[85] As the economy contracted, unemployment rose. Between 1981 and 1986 the number of people living below the poverty line in Latin America increased from 150 to 170 million.[86]

Moreover, inflation rose throughout most of Latin America, reaching double-, triple-, and even quadruple-digit annual rates.[87] Inflation rates spiraled upward because governments pumped money into the economy to prevent a complete economic collapse during the implementation of austerity programs.[88] In Argentina, for example, the money supply and consumer prices increased in lockstep during the 1980s: A 362.0 percent increase in the 1983 money supply matched the 343.8 percent increase in consumer prices; the 546.7 percent increase in the 1984 money supply translated into a 626.7 percent increase in prices; and the 697.9 percent increase in 1985 was matched by a 672.2 percent increase in prices.[89]

Jeffrey Sachs argued that as a result of these developments, "the debtor countries may have fallen into the deepest economic crisis in their histories. . . . Many countries' living standards have fallen to levels of the 1950s and 1960s. A decade of development has been wiped out throughout the debtor world."[90]

This second economic crisis created serious political problems for Latin American dictators. The humiliating negotiations and punitive economic programs adopted in response to the debt crisis made "strong" regimes look "weak" in their confrontations with the United States and multilateral lending agencies. Structural adjustment programs created the economic basis for political protest throughout the region. Sociologist John Walton recorded fifty major protests, what he called "IMF riots," in thirteen countries between 1976 and 1986.[91] He found that when governments cut subsidies for food and basic necessities, increased fares for public transportation, or eliminated government jobs, riots frequently resulted. In September 1985, for example, "hundreds of Panamanian workers invaded the legislature chanting, 'I won't pay the debt! Let the ones who stole it pay!'"[92]

Although IMF riots were disorganized and spontaneous forms of protest and usually had meager immediate effects, they brought poor and working people into the streets to protest the economic policies of dictators. In some cases even middle- and upper-class groups joined these protests.[93] It was not long before economic demands were joined by political demands, as in Brazil during early 1984, when demonstrators in massive street marches demanded *"Diretas Ja!"* ("Direct Elections Now!").[94] When economic crisis combined with political crisis, dictators throughout Latin America began to lose their hold on power.

SIX

DEMOCRATIZATION IN LATIN AMERICA

During the 1970s the majority of states and the bulk of the territory and population of Latin America were controlled by dictatorships of different types. Individual dictators and their families headed dictatorships in Nicaragua and Haiti, collective military juntas, sometimes assisted by surrogate political parties, held or took power in Argentina, Brazil, and Chile, while "revolutionary" political parties wielded singular authority in Mexico and Cuba. Countries led by civilian democratic governments were rare. Colombia and Venezuela were the only large democratic countries in the region. They were joined by Costa Rica and the small island democracies in the eastern Caribbean.

But although dictatorships controlled most of Latin America, they held power in *republican* states. Unlike the anti-republican Iberian and Ionian dictatorships, Latin American dictators adhered to republican political conventions. They regularly held elections and promised to restore democracy at the earliest opportunity. Of course, they also tried to rig or annul elections and defer any real devolution of their political power, making the transition to democracy a permanent stage. In Brazil, for example, the decade-long transition to democracy, or *abertura* (opening), initiated by the military junta became a nearly permanent state of affairs. These practices promoted cynicism at home and derision abroad as scholars and governments mocked the tragicomic features of "banana republics" and "facade" democracies.[1]

But dictatorships practiced these republican charades for important reasons. They could not easily jettison the republican ideology of nineteenth-century Latin American revolutionaries who had carved independent states out of Iberian empires. To do so would undermine their claims, real or imagined, to be seen as the legitimate heirs of Latin American liberators: Simon Bolivar, Jose de San Martin, Bernardo O'Higgins. They were also pressed by the United States to defend their republican credentials in the interstate system, primarily to blunt Soviet criticism of Western democracies and their allies. Dictatorships also recognized that elections and parliaments enabled select social groups to participate in the decisionmaking process, which was essential for dictators who wanted to run the government and manage the economy effectively. For these reasons most Latin American dictatorships cast themselves as republicans, maintaining republican institutions and practicing republican norms, albeit reluctantly. As one Brazilian army officer explained in 1977, "I'm a hard liner, but I'm not a fascist Nazi."2

Even Augusto Pinochet, leader of the military regime that deposed and murdered Chile's President Salvador Allende in a brutal 1973 coup, used the language of democracy. In 1975 Pinochet argued that "the world today beholds a generalized crisis of the traditional forms of democracy" and promised that the junta would "resolutely advance toward the creation of a new democracy by means of a new political and institutional regime."3 In 1983 Pinochet reiterated these republican themes, insisting that his goal was "the establishment of an authentic and effective democracy ... [that would] preserve our most sacred republican traditions, avoid the distortions which an unbridling of partisanship would bring, and give to democracy an authentic representative dimension."4

Although Pinochet and his collaborators were more inclined toward the anti-republican fascism and royalism of the Iberian and Ionian dictators, they paraded as democrats in a defense of republic. Latin American political traditions, foreign policy concerns, and domestic political pragmatism compelled them to play the roles of democrats on the republican stage. Of course, some dictators embraced republican traditions with enthusiasm. Military juntas in Bolivia, Peru, and Ecuador described themselves as "revolutionary" republicans, as did those leading regimes in Mexico, Cuba, and, for a time, Nicaragua.5

The "republican" dictatorships in Latin America survived the 1971–75 economic crisis by borrowing money and pursuing indebted development. But they would not survive the second economic crisis, which had been triggered by their reliance on foreign debt. Between 1978 and 1994 most of these dictators transferred power to civilian democrats. An account of democratization can be told in three parts. During the first period, between 1978 and 1982, dictatorships collapsed in the Dominican Republic, Nicaragua, Ecuador, Honduras, Peru, and Bolivia. Democratization in these countries was a welcome development, but did not yet signal a general trend. At first democratization in these countries was dismissed simply as another swing of the political pendulum and as evidence of continuing turmoil in weak and unstable states. As one political scientist wrote, "Typically a Latin American country changes its regime once every 7.2 years. There have been 140 political regimes between 1940 and 1980. Half did not last 48 months."[6]

Democratization assumed wider significance in its second phase, after powerful dictatorships fell in Argentina, Uruguay, Brazil, the Philippines, and Chile between 1982 and 1989. The democratization of large and populous states indicated that the process was not simply an idiosyncratic, cyclical process but a generic and secular development. Finally, between 1989 and 1994, democratization occurred in Panama, Paraguay, Nicaragua (again), El Salvador, and Haiti.

Four caveats must be made before beginning an account of these developments. First, although democratization was widespread, it was not ubiquitous. Significantly, it did not extend to Mexico or Cuba. I will explain why these regimes did not democratize during this period after examining why others did. Second, democratization was typically initiated by dictators, not by revolutionary mass movements. Dictators democratized when they "became convinced that their institutional, party, class or other collective interests could be better protected by relinquishing power voluntarily rather than risking forced eviction."[7] Only in Nicaragua and El Salvador did radical republicans overthrow or seriously challenge entrenched dictatorships. But although these revolutions were rare, they became important "virtual realities" for other dictators, much as civil wars with radical republicans had become worrisome for dictatorships in Spain and Greece.

Third, democratization did not necessarily result in democracy, at least not right away. In Nicaragua, for instance, revolution and the overthrow of the Somoza regime in 1979 certainly widened participation in politics and government. But the Sandinista government that took power was not wholly democratic and excluded some social groups who took up arms against it. Although relatively fair elections in 1984 gave large majorities to the Sandinistas, it was not until 1990 that most social groups participated in an election that brought anti-Sandinista groups to power. In a sense Nicaragua democratized twice.

Democratization elsewhere occurred in a similar fashion. Successive referendums and elections democratized the political process and distanced civilian governments from their military predecessors. But the continuing participation of former dictators like Pinochet in the political process and the restoration of conservative political elites as in Nicaragua suggest that even democratizing states may not yet have arrived at fully democratic destinations. In most cases democratization was limited, resulting in the transfer of political power to groups that had been excluded from power. But power was often transferred to elites and sometimes even to previous rulers, not to the poor or their representatives.

Finally, democratization was a contingent process. The fact that dictatorships have disappeared in most Latin American states during the last fifteen years does not mean that democratization has become a permanent feature of the political landscape. Military leaders have returned to the barracks, not retired from politics.

Democratization in the Small Republics

The Dominican Republic

For some Latin American dictatorships the second economic crisis of the 1970s followed too quickly on the heels of the first. In the Dominican Republic world sugar prices rose in 1975–76, temporarily buoying the economy, but then quickly declined, reducing exports and government revenues.[8] A second oil price increase in 1979 was not accompanied by rising sugar prices, so rising trade deficits consumed the foreign exchange that had been briefly accumulated, leading to currency devaluations.[9] Heavy government spending and widespread corruption, meanwhile, created government budget deficits and brought the country to the brink of bankruptcy by 1982.[10] The economic crisis in the Dominican Republic was not associated so much with foreign debt, as it was elsewhere, but by falling commodity prices and government budget deficits.

Juaquin Balaguer was elected president of the Dominican Republic in 1966 after U.S. troops intervened to prevent the return of Juan Bosch to power. Bosch had won the 1962 presidential election but had been deposed by a coup in 1963 and reinstated by a popular uprising in 1965. After 1966 Balaguer became a civilian dictator who was regularly returned to office "in plebiscites in which he was the only candidate."[11] As the economy soured in 1978, the opposition led by Antonio Guzman mounted a serious challenge to Balaguer. When it became apparent that Guzman was winning in the May 16, 1978, election, military officers who supported Balaguer seized ballot boxes and jailed opposition leaders. But widespread popular protest and U.S. diplomatic objections prevented Balaguer from stealing the election, forcing him to relinquish power to Guzman on August 16, 1978.[12]

Once in power, however, Guzman tried to enrich his family and created patronage jobs in government to establish an independent political base. Widespread corruption and a bloated bureaucracy forced the government into insolvency. After he failed to win reelection in May 1982, Guzman committed suicide, and Jorge Blanco took office in August. But Blanco was unable to resolve the country's economic problems, and in May 1986 Balaguer, the former dictator, was reelected to office.[13] The return of the rehabilitated Balaguer demonstrated the political limits of democratization in the Dominican Republic. Political power was exercised more democratically after Balaguer's return than it had been before 1978, but he still kept his old rival, the radical Juan Bosch, and the poor groups he represented at some distance from power.[14]

Nicaragua

In Nicaragua the economic crisis of the early 1970s was compounded in 1972 by a devastating earthquake that resulted in economic losses of $845 million.[15] The quake leveled Managua and forced the government to borrow heavily to finance the reconstruction of the capital, but the Somoza dictatorship somehow "misappropriated" the funds earmarked for this purpose.[16] Foreign debt mounted, doubling between 1972 and 1974, and by 1978 it made up 51 percent of the country's GDP.[17] By December 1978 the dictatorship could no longer service its debt and turned to the United States and the IMF for loans to stave off economic collapse. Pressured by U.S. officials, the IMF approved a $65 million loan only nine weeks before the regime fell.[18]

The Somozas had established a hereditary dictatorship, headed successively by Anastasio Somoza Garcia (1937–56), his son Luis Somoza Debayle (1956–67), and Anastasio's younger brother Anastasio "Tachito" Somoza Debayle (1967–79).[19] Anastasio "Tachito" Somoza's 1974 decision to rewrite the constitution to allow him to run for reelection triggered opposition from radical and conservative republican groups.[20] The Sandinista National Liberation Front (FSLN), a small Communist group founded in Cuba in 1961, took wealthy hostages at a 1974 Christmas party, enabling it to obtain a large ransom, win the release of political prisoners, and spotlight its opposition to the dictatorship.[21] The FSLN subsequently launched an insurrection in the countryside in 1977 and in 1978 seized the National Assembly, holding its members hostage while making ransom and political demands.[22] These bold guerrilla actions and the dictatorship's savage military response helped the FSLN grow from fewer than 150 armed fighters in 1974 to 3,000 in 1978 and 5,000 in July 1979, posing a serious military threat to the regime.[23]

Somoza's 1974 decision to seek reelection also led *La Prensa* publisher Pedro Joaquin Chamorro to form a political party representing conservative elites who were opposed to the dictatorship.[24] As the country's economic crisis deepened, elites defected to Chamorro's Democratic Union of Liberation (UDEL), praising the FSLN's opposition to Somoza.[25] The January 1978 assassination of Chamorro, like the subsequent assassination of Benigno Aquino in the Philippines, galvanized and united conservative and radical opponents of the regime. After Chamorro's death leadership of the conservative opposition passed to his wife, Violeta, much as it would from Benigno to Corazon Aquino in the Philippines.[26] The UDEL and FSLN formed a de facto coalition, calling urban strikes and waging rural guerrilla war, which then led to a wider civil war between Somoza's national guard and opposition groups that resulted in the deaths of more than fifty thousand people between 1977 and 1979.[27]

As the economy deteriorated and political opposition mounted, U.S. officials reassessed their support for Somoza. Although the Carter administration defended Somoza and helped Nicaragua secure IMF loans in April and May 1979, it also cut off U.S. aid in February 1979 and in July "invited" Somoza to retire in Miami.[28] Somoza resigned on July 17 and went into exile in the United States, and the national guard surrendered to the FSLN two days later, on July 19, 1979.[29]

During Carter's administration U.S. officials did not intervene on the dictatorship's behalf. But after the FSLN victory the new Reagan administration supported a surrogate contra army in a war against the newly established government. Based in Honduras and Costa Rica, the contra armies were composed of national guard remnants and led by conservative republicans like Alfonso Robelo and Violeta Chamorro, who left the coalition government in 1979 after the FSLN came to dominate the junta.[30] FSLN leader Daniel Ortega won the presidency and FSLN representatives won a majority of assembly seats in the 1984 elections, which were boycotted by conservative opponents. The civil war between radical and conservative republicans continued for a decade, while economic sanctions imposed by the Reagan administration battered the economy.[31] The Sandinista government ratified a new constitution in 1987 and held elections in 1990 that brought Chamorro and moderate-conservative republicans to power, ending the long civil war.[32] In a sense Nicaragua democratized twice, in 1979 and again in 1990. In the intervening decade political participation was successively widened by revolution and elections. But the eventual transfer of power to conservative elites meant that democratization was also significantly limited, its extension confined to fairly narrow social and economic circles.

Honduras

In Honduras the military under Melgar Castro began discussing a return to civilian government in 1976. But opposition within the military led to Castro's removal and a delay in elections for a constituent assembly until April 1980. U.S. officials pressured the military to restore civilian government because they wanted to use Honduras as a bulwark against the spread of communism from Nicaragua, a project that would earn U.S. congressional support only if Honduras's military junta stepped down.[33] The new constituent assembly then set presidential elections for November 1981.[34] Suazo Cordoza and his Liberal Party won the elections and Cordoza was inaugurated in January 1982.[35]

Honduras was heavily indebted and experienced a serious economic crisis during the early 1980s. Although the bulk of U.S. economic and military aid—ranging from $80 million to $110 million per year from 1982 to 1984 and increasing to $229 million in 1985—was used to support the anti-

Sandinista contra army based in Honduras, it was also used to prevent the economic crisis from become acute during the first few years of civilian rule.[36] U.S. determination to protect the civilian government in Honduras also prevented the military, which had reserved an important role for itself under the new government, from aborting civilian rule during this period. But as U.S. congressional support for the contra war waned, U.S. aid for Honduras declined. Jose Azcona Hoya, who became president in 1985, was forced to declare a moratorium on the country's debt in 1989.[37]

Civilian rule in Honduras was limited by the central role played by the military after the 1980–81 elections, by its financial dependence on U.S. aid, and by U.S. insistence that it remain a frontline U.S. ally in the irregular war against Nicaragua.[38]

Ecuador

Like the Dominican Republic, Ecuador also found riches during the crisis of the early 1970s. The first oil embargo boosted the price of Ecuadoran oil, providing the government with unprecedented income.[39] The dictatorship used these revenues as collateral for foreign loans in an effort to industrialize the economy, what the government called "aggressive indebtedness."[40] But spending on industrialization soon outstripped oil revenues, while inflation eroded living standards, fueling widespread political discontent and leading to a general strike on November 13, 1975.[41] Oil prices rose again in 1979–80 but then began a decade-long decline that lowered the real price of oil to pre-embargo levels.

Deteriorating economic conditions and a more vocal political opposition, signaled by the 1975 general strike, persuaded the military junta to transfer its power through a series of referendums and elections. It took some time to write a new constitution, which was approved in a referendum on January 15, 1978.[42] Two rounds of presidential elections followed, on January 16, 1978, and on April 22, 1979.[43] Despite efforts by factions within the military to obstruct, delay, or void the results, Jaime Roldos was elected and installed as president on August 10, 1979.[44]

Peru

The "Revolutionary Government of the Armed Forces," as the Peruvian dictatorship called itself, faced severe trade deficits as a result of the 1971–75 crisis. By 1976 the government was forced to seek international loans to cover its balance of payments deficits. U.S. and other lenders agreed to loan money to the chronically weak Peruvian economy only on the condition that the government devalue its currency, impose austerity measures, and "accept financial supervision by a commission that would be appointed by the banks."[45] One year later, as the government approached the brink of insolvency, the IMF imposed additional conditions, which contributed to escalating protests, strikes, demonstrations, and military uprisings that the government could not easily contain.[46]

Democratization in Peru began soon after it began in Ecuador in 1975–1976. In July 1977 Peruvian President Morales Bermudez announced that the military would transfer power in two stages, first by electing representatives to a constitutional convention on July 18, 1978, and then, after the representatives had rewritten the constitution, by electing a president in May 1980.[47] Having announced that it would transfer power, the military then used force to prevent its early relinquishment, employing "openly repressive measures to contend with growing labor militancy."[48] The 1980 presidential election was won by Fernando Belaunde, who had been ousted as president and exiled by the military during the 1968 coup.[49] The return and rehabilitation of the former president demonstrated that democratization resulted in the status quo ante, not the emergence of a new, more participatory form of government.[50] In Peru democratization did not extend political power to the urban or rural poor, who were then organized by radical republicans and groups like Sendero Luminoso to oppose moderate and conservative republican governments led by Belaunde, Alan Garcia, and then Alberto Fujimori.[51] Whereas conservative republicans had led armies against the radical republican government in Nicaragua, in Peru the radical republicans led the insurrection against conservative republicans. In both cases, however, the civil wars that emerged after the initial phases of democratization pitted conservative and radical republicans against each other. Because the Peruvian government was unable to cope either with the ongoing civil war or the economic problems associated with its debt crisis, Alberto Fujimori eventually disbanded the assembly, imposed martial law, and assumed dictatorial powers. Because democratization was limited in important ways from the outset—excluding important social groups and political parties from power—it resulted in dictatorship, albeit in a reconstituted social and political form.

Bolivia

One of the poorest countries in Latin America, Bolivia achieved some economic growth during the 1970s because rising oil prices increased revenues from the sale of its oil and gas reserves. But Bolivia exhausted its oil and natural gas supplies by the end of the decade, so rising oil prices in 1979–80 provided few economic benefits. The price of tin continued to fall, which cut into revenues provided by Bolivian tin exports, and Bolivian agriculture was devastated by drought and floods in 1983.[52] The collapse of Bolivian export industries made it impossible for the government to repay its foreign debts or to balance its budget, and the government was bankrupt by 1982.[53]

Dictators in Ecuador had called for elections in 1976. Dictators in Peru did so in 1977. And the Bolivian dictatorship issued the call in 1978.[54] Like its contemporaries, the Bolivian regime, led by General Hugo Banzer, hoped to manipulate the election process in a way that would produce a civilian government acceptable to the military. This proved to be a difficult and time-consuming process. Three presidential elections were held during the next four years. Because the military's candidates failed to win the first election on November 24, 1978, rival military officers seized power, annulled the election, and called for a second election in July 1979.[55] Inconclusive results in this election forced the political parties to appoint an interim president pending new elections in 1980. The interim president served only a few months before he, too, was deposed by a coup, whose leaders agreed to install Lydia Gueiler as the second interim president.[56] The June 1980 election was won by Hernan Siles, but he was prevented from assuming office by yet another coup on July 17.[57] Because this regime had little social and no political support, other military officers forced it from power and began to "negotiate the military out of power."[58] Negotiations resulted in an agreement by rival political parties and the military to reconvene the congress that had been elected in 1980 and to elect Siles as president.[59] In October 1982 Siles was reinstalled as Bolivia's president. In 1985 deteriorating economic conditions and pressure from former President Banzer forced Siles to leave office a year early. Although Banzer then won a narrow plurality of the vote, the congress blocked his return to power and elected former President Paz Estenssoro.[60] In Bolivia, as in the Dominican Republic and Peru, democratization resulted in the reelection of a former ruler.

During the late 1970s and early 1980s democratization in these small republics seemed the product of idiosyncratic developments, not the harbinger of change. Of course, U.S. officials and dictators throughout Latin America worried that insurrection in Nicaragua might itself signal radical change. But the Nicaraguan revolution remained an anomaly, and Nicaragua's radical republican character was slowly curbed.

Because the transfer of power from dictators to democrats was tumultuous and the outcome uncertain in the Dominican Republic, Nicaragua, Honduras, Ecuador, Peru, and Bolivia, it is not surprising that scholars were then reluctant to announce that a "trend" had emerged. Most scholars were skeptical of suggestions that democratization might be in the offing elsewhere on the continent.[61] As Malloy and Gamarra wrote in 1982,

Like other Latin American countries, Bolivia has been attempting to move from repressive authoritarian modes of government to more open modes of ... representative democracy.... [But this development] has not been in any real sense democratization.... Since 1978, national political life has been rather chaotic and the country has lurched through three abortive elections and a variety of de facto regimes based on coups and countercoups.... At this writing, it is far from certain that civilian democratic government will be able to establish itself firmly. In short, representative democracy remains more an aspiration than a reality in Bolivia.[62]

This well-founded skepticism about events in Bolivia, and for that matter about events in the rest of Latin America, would diminish only after Latin America's large and powerful regimes democratized. When they did, in Argentina, Brazil, and Chile, the idiosyncratic transitions in the Dominican Republic, Nicaragua, Honduras, Bolivia, Ecuador, and Peru would then be seen as initiating an important general trend.

Democratization in the Large Republics

Argentina

The debt crisis, which grew to gale-force strength by 1982, undermined the economic legitimacy of dictators throughout Latin America. But economic crisis alone did not lead to the collapse of dictatorships. In Argentina, for example, economic crisis was compounded by military defeat. And the collapse of a "strong" dictatorship there helped to trigger democratization elsewhere.

In Argentina the dictatorship that came to power in 1974 borrowed heavily. Foreign debt tripled from $6.4 billion in 1978 to $19.4 billion by 1980, doubled again to $43 billion by 1982, and reached $48.4 billion in 1984, prompting one World Bank official to describe Argentina's economy as a "financial Hiroshima."[63]

Under economic duress, General Roberto Viola opened negotiations with opposition trade union leaders and politicians in 1981 to enlist their support for a program that would address the economic crisis and return government to civilian authority.[64] But hardliners in the military opposed Viola's opening to civilian democrats and replaced him with General Leopoldo Galtieri in December 1981.[65]

Galtieri opposed any devolution of power, promising that the military would retain its authority until 1990.[66] But he did vow to address Argentina's economic and political crisis. "The time for words and promises has ended," he proclaimed. "The time has come for action."[67] For Galtieri, "action" meant invading the Falkland Islands (referred to as the Malvinas by Argentines) and wresting them from Great Britain, which had possessed the disputed islands for more than 150 years.[68] As Galtieri later explained, he planned to invade the islands, both because it would be an extremely popular move and because it would deflect domestic attention from the economic crisis, and then hold presidential elections, which he would then be "sure to win."[69]

As soon as he took power, Galtieri began preparing the invasion. The regime's plan to use invasion as a solution to its domestic economic and political problems was based on two important assumptions.[70] First, Galtieri expected that the United States would either support the invasion or remain neutral in a conflict between two of its allies. The United States would not interfere, Galtieri believed, because the Monroe Doctrine and the 1947 Rio Treaty obligated the U.S. government to "defend" its Latin American allies against "outside power," presumably even Great Britain. He also thought U.S. support might be forthcoming because Argentina had recently provided military assistance and financial aid to the U.S.-supported contras in Nicaragua and because the United States had long supported dictators in Latin America and Argentina.[71] Even after President Reagan told Galtieri on the eve of invasion, "I do not want to fail to emphasize pointedly that the relationship between our two countries will suffer seriously [if war breaks out]," Galtieri continued to believe that the United States would not interfere.[72]

Second, Galtieri did not think that the United Kingdom would defend the sparsely populated Falklands. He thought that Margaret Thatcher's government would respond to an Argentine invasion in the same way that Portugal had responded to India's 1961 invasion of Goa, when Portugal had surrendered its distant outpost.[73]

Based on these expectations and assumptions, Argentine troops crossed three hundred miles of the southern Atlantic Ocean and landed at Port Stanley on April 2, 1982, claiming the Falklands for Argentina. But although demonstrators in Buenos Aires celebrated the "return" of the Malvinas, the regime had completely misjudged the U.S. and British response. The Reagan administration promptly condemned the attack, called for a withdrawal of Argentine troops, and took the issue to the U.N. Security Council, which adopted U.S.-sponsored resolutions against Argentina.[74] U.S. officials and the European Economic Community imposed economic sanctions, sent U.S. Secretary of State Alexander Haig on a diplomatic mission to negotiate a peaceful end to the conflict, and, after negotiations failed, moved to support their British ally against their Argentine ally. As full-blown war approached, the United States provided decisive military assistance to the British, supplying aviation fuel, air-to-air missiles, and satellite intelligence to British forces.[75]

Although author Jorge Luis Borges wrote that the struggle over the remote islands was "like two bald men fighting over a comb," the British were not prepared to forfeit the Falklands like the Portuguese had surrendered Goa.[76] "The time for weasel words has ended," Conservative Bernard Braine told Parliament. "I expect action from the government; and I hope we shall get it. . . . The very thought that . . . 1,800 people of British bone and blood, could be left in the hands of such criminals is enough to make any normal Englishman's blood—and the blood of Scotsmen and Welshmen—boil too."[77]

The Thatcher government quickly assembled a naval armada and sent it south to recapture the islands. Defended by nuclear submarines powerful enough to destroy the Argentine fleet wholesale (one British sub sank the Argentine cruiser *Belgrano* as a warning), backed by nuclear weapons lethal enough to destroy the whole country, and armed with sophisticated weapons that the Argentine forces did not possess, the British navy landed its troops in the Falklands on May 21, 1982.

The battle was brief. The British fleet prevented Argentina from resupplying or rescuing its ten thousand troops that were occupying the islands. The British air force, supplied with effective U.S. missiles, decimated the Argentine air force, destroying forty aircraft in one three-day period. British marines then outmaneuvered and crushed ill-equipped Argentine forces on the ground, forcing General Mario Manendez to surrender the Argentine garrison on June 14, 1982.[78]

In Buenos Aires demonstrators took to the streets again, this time demanding an end to dictatorship.[79] Galtieri was forced to resign, and his replacement, General Reynaldo Bignone, promised that elections would be held on October 30, 1983. Raul Alfonsin won 52 percent of the vote in the election, and he was inaugurated in December 1983.[80]

Events in Argentina demonstrated the weakness of even "strong" Latin American dictatorships. The debt crisis, IMF-mandated austerity programs, and the imposition of economic sanctions against Argentina during the war demonstrated the regime's weakness vis-à-vis such foreign economic powers as the United States, the IMF and World Bank, and the European Economic Community. The crushing defeat of its armed forces exposed Argentina's putative military power as a chimera. Although the military could wage a lethal war against civilian dissidents, its vast army, assembled at considerable expense during the 1970s, was humbled by a foreign military power.[81] U.S. support for Great Britain, which was regarded by Argentines as a great "betrayal," showed that the dictatorship was vulnerable to changing U.S. foreign policies.[82] The regime complained that "the Argentine people will never understand or forget that at one of the most crucial moments in their history . . . the United States preferred to take the side of an extra-hemisphere power."[83] But they should not have been so surprised. This was the same geopolitical lesson taught earlier to the Greek dictatorship when it sponsored a coup in Cyprus without first obtaining U.S. approval. Forced to choose between an allied democracy and an allied dictatorship, the United States delivered defeat to the dictatorship.[84] Finally, the rapid and humiliating defeat exposed the regime to domestic ridicule and public censure, which helped drive the dictatorship from power.

After Alfonsin took office, pressure mounted to prosecute military officers for their conduct during Argentina's "Dirty War," just as officers had been in Greece. Since 1974 the Argentine military had waged this war against civilian dissidents, kidnapping, jailing, torturing, and murdering its opponents, often pushing drugged prisoners out of airplanes over the Atlantic Ocean.[85] As General Iberico St. Jean explained, "First we'll kill the subversives, then their collaborators, then . . . their sympathizers, then . . . those who remain indifferent, and finally we'll kill the timid."[86]

In October 1984 the Alfonsin government tried and then convicted a number of senior military officers for their conduct during the Dirty War and the Falklands War, sentencing some to life in prison.[87] This was followed in 1987 by the prosecution of lower-ranking officers.[88] But a military revolt in April 1987 and a December 1988 decision to exempt junior officers from prosecution slowed government efforts to put criminals of the Dirty War behind bars. Then in October 1989 the newly elected President Carlos Menem pardoned Galtieri and dozens of other officers for their crimes.[89] Although government efforts to prosecute war criminals wound down in Argentina, the attempt to hold military leaders accountable had important consequences elsewhere. It demonstrated to other dictators that they too might be prosecuted for violating human rights—most had conducted "dirty" wars of their own—and that they might be tried for political or economic crimes. As a result, dictators often initiated a devolution of power in order to negotiate their immunity from prosecution in advance.

The collapse of dictatorship in Argentina was significant because dictators elsewhere realized they shared many of the same problems. They too were vulnerable to debt crisis, to changed U.S. foreign policy, to domestic pressure for democratization, and to liability for human-rights violations. An awareness of these weaknesses persuaded many dictators to consider devolving power in order to protect some measure of their political power, economic wealth, and personal security.

Events in Argentina accelerated democratization in neighboring Uruguay and Brazil, where dictators had already promised to return power to civilian governments.

Uruguay

Although Uruguay's economy had grown rapidly during the 1970s, its debt quadrupled between 1972 and 1983.[90] Rising oil prices in 1979, falling exports, and a declining number of Argentine tourists after 1980 slowed growth and precipitated an economic crisis.[91] Economic decline was compounded by the dictatorship's failure to win a 1980 plebiscite to ratify its continued rule.[92] Although the military was divided on this issue, General Gregorio Alvarez in 1981 promised to democratize.[93] The collapse of dictatorship in neighboring Argentina and massive public demonstrations and strikes between May and November 1983 persuaded the regime to negotiate the transfer of power in earnest.[94] The agreement reached in the Naval

Club Talks provided for elections but also protected military officers from prosecution after they surrendered power.[95] Although political parties were allowed to participate in the elections, the leaders of two parties—Wilson Ferreira Aldunate and Libar Seregni—were excluded, and Wilson remained in jail.[96] When elections were held in November 1984, Julio Sanguinetti, a moderate who was acceptable to the military, was elected president and assumed office on March 1, 1985. "A remarkable aspect of the 1984 elections was the extent to which they represented continuity with the [precoup] period," historian Henry Finch observed. "Not only was the electoral system unchanged, but the party hierarchies were also little altered by the passage of time and residual military interference."[97]

Brazil

The Brazilian dictatorship under General Ernesto Geisel first promised to pursue *abertura* in 1974. He did so to blunt enthusiasm for democratization that was then underway in Portugal. Political scientist Paul Buchanan noted that "it was no coincidence that *abertura* was initiated when a wave of re-democratization was washing over Southern Europe. By reorganizing legal and administrative structures and the general parameters of arenas of social conflict, the regime was able to adopt new patterns of behavior in response to social pressures and change."[98]

General Joao Figueiredo reiterated this promise in 1980, saying, "As I have already promised to make this country a democracy, I now affirm to all Brazilians that we, the 1964 revolutionaries, shall not deviate from our course of pursuing the normalization of the political process."[99] But although the Brazilian junta regularly promised to move the country toward democracy, it did so at a glacial pace. The government restored some civil and political liberties but used authoritarian controls and torture to contain dissent and limit political opposition to its continued rule.[100] As a result, the decade-long *abertura* threatened to become a permanent state, not a transition to democracy. In the early 1980s, however, a number of developments pushed the frozen *abertura* toward its democratic conclusion.

During the 1970s the dictatorship had borrowed heavily to promote economic growth, and foreign debt increased from $6.6 billion in 1971 to $100 billion by 1984.[101] As a result of the mounting debt crisis, per capita income began to fall, inflation climbed, and the IMF in 1983 demanded that the dictatorship impose an austerity program that would further erode incomes, which had already fallen between 10 and 15 percent between 1980 and 1984.[102] Public support for the government's political party, the Partido Social Democrática (PDS), continued to decline. In 1966 it had captured 50.5 percent of the votes for the federal assembly (the military permitted elections for the assembly but appointed senators, and it did not permit direct presidential elections, which the junta controlled) but won only 48.4 percent in 1970, 40.9 percent in 1974, 40.0 percent in 1978, and only 36.7 percent in 1982.[103] Widespread opposition to the government's austerity program and massive demonstrations between January and April 1984 for direct presidential elections forced the government to finally make good on its promises for real democratization.[104] At this point the military could not agree on a successor to Figueiredo, while the opposition united behind a ticket composed of Tancredo Neves, a moderate civilian opponent of dictatorship, and his running mate, Jose Sarney, a conservative who had led the military's political party.[105] On January 15, 1985, the electoral college elected Neves, but he died one day before his inauguration after emergency surgery. Sarney assumed the presidency in his place on March 15, 1985.[106] Brazil's transition to democracy had resulted in the inauguration of a conservative politician who had been part of the regime's civilian political apparatus.[107] The military thus had little reason to object to the process it had reluctantly initiated.

The Philippines

Events then shifted to the Philippines, a country that more closely resembles Latin American states in social, political, and economic terms than its Asian neighbors. Like most Latin American countries, the Philippines was colonized and converted to Catholicism by Spain, then brought into the U.S. sphere of influence as a colony after the 1898 Spanish-American War. After securing its independence first from Japanese invasion and occupation during World War II and then from the United States in 1946, the Philippines retained closed ties with the United States. Given this history, the Philippines can be described as a Latin American country in East Asia.

Also like Latin American countries, the Philippines borrowed heavily after President Ferdinand Marcos declared martial law and assumed dictatorial powers in 1972. The country's foreign debt grew to $26 billion by 1985, an amount equal to its annual GNP.[108] Although debt had contributed to economic growth and enriched the country's corrupt elite during the 1970s, wages for the majority of the population continued to fall, and unskilled workers in 1980 received only half of what they had earned in the 1970s.[109] By the end of the 1970s Benedict Anderson observed that "5 percent of the country's income earners received, probably, about 50 percent of the total income. At the time, over 70 percent of state revenues came from regressive sales and excise taxes. . . . Combined with a characteristically tropical-Catholic birth rate of over 3 percent . . . the result was a massive pauperization of the underprivileged."[110]

Debt-related economic crisis after 1981 led to a sharp decline in per capita GNP. But the sharpest drop occurred after 1983, initiating the most severe economic crisis in post-war Philippine history.[111] Economic problems were compounded by the August 21, 1983, assassination of Benigno Aquino, the leader of the conservative republican opposition to the Marcos regime. His murder by government soldiers shook confidence in the regime, leading to massive capital flight.[112] In October 1983 the government was forced to suspend payments on its debt and begin austerity program negotiations with the IMF and World Bank.[113] During the next two years the economy registered negative growth, shrinking by nearly 9 percent.[114] Economic developments, particularly the "pauperization of the underprivileged," created domestic military problems for the regime, which contributed to foreign policy problems with the United States.

During the 1970s rural insurgents began waging a guerrilla war against the Marcos regime. The New People's Army (NPA), which led the uprising, was formed in 1968 when a group of leftist university students joined the remnants of a Huk guerrilla unit.[115] Like Greek Communist irregulars who had fought Axis occupation during World War II, the Hukbo ng Bayang Laban Sa Hapon (People's Army to Fight Japan), or "Huks," had been formed by peasants and Communist intellectuals during World War II to fight the Japanese occupation.[116] After the war U.S. officials arrested many Huk leaders and reinstalled Filipino political elites, many of whom had collaborated with the Japanese.[117] Government crackdowns on rural protest and massive election fraud after the war led to open insurrection by 1949, much as it had in Greece in the same period. And like the Communists in Greece, the Huks were crushed by an effective counterinsurgency campaign, which was led by Secretary of Defense Raymond Magsaysay and assisted by the CIA and the U.S. military (the entire Huk leadership was captured in Manila in 1950).[118]

Isolated Huk units survived and were revitalized in the 1970s by new student activists and pauperized peasants in the countryside.[119] By 1981 the NPA had five thousand to seven thousand irregulars under arms and had moved from "early" to "advanced" guerrilla operations.[120] And by 1985 the NPA had grown to thirty thousand full-time and part-time troops who were deployed in fifty-nine guerrilla units operating in fifty-nine of the country's seventy-three provinces.[121]

To contain renewed rural insurrection, the Marcos regime expanded the military from 57,000 troops in 1972 to 113,000 in 1976 and 158,300 by 1985, assisted by another 124,000 irregulars.[122] Military spending "as a percentage of total government expenditures doubled from 9 percent in 1972 to 18 percent in 1977."[123] Government forces conducted regular and dirty wars against rural insurgents, arresting 70,000 and murdering 602 dissidents between 1972 and 1985. A total of 2,225 were "salvaged," or executed, by soldiers in the field, and 300 women or young girls were raped by military personnel during this same period.[124] Despite government military efforts, however, the NPA grew in strength. In 1981 Defense Minister Juan Ponce Enrile admitted that "the real danger to Philippine society is the

Communist Party of the Philippines and its military arm, the New People's Army."[125] A 1984 U.S. Senate mission reported that NPA units "now challenge the Armed Forces of the Philippines [AFP] across the length and breadth of the Philippine archipelago. Although the AFP still has greater numerical strength . . . it is already spread thinly trying to divide its attention and forces throughout the countryside on numerous islands."[126]

As rural insurrection grew more widespread, U.S. officials began to worry about another "Nicaragua" and changed their attitude toward Marcos. In 1981, after Marcos had been reelected in a fraudulent election, Vice President George Bush had offered this toast: "We stand with you sir. . . . We love your adherence to democratic principles and to democratic processes."[127] But by 1985 the Reagan administration pressed Marcos to hold a "snap" election, and, when he could not win it legally, the United States took measures to prevent him from stealing it. The regime's shaky relations with the United States, a product of its inability to contain rural insurrection, contributed to other domestic political problems.

After Marcos declared martial law in 1972, he used successive plebiscites through select "citizens' assemblies" to rewrite the constitution, ratify continued martial law, and demonstrate his domestic popularity for the benefit of foreign governments and international lending agencies.[128] Like dictators in Latin America, Marcos promised in 1978 to "normalize" the political process and "shift from authoritarianism to liberalism," and in January 1981 he formally ended martial law.[129] But normalization in the Philippines, like *abertura* in Brazil, did not guarantee any real devolution of power. That would come only after important political and social groups withdrew their support for the regime and defected to the non-Communist opposition following the Aquino assassination.[130]

The murder of Aquino, like the assassination of Chamorro in Nicaragua, galvanized the opposition. It pushed the Catholic Church and its leader, Cardinal Jaime Sin, into the opposition camp and united moderate and conservative forces behind Aquino's widow, Corazon.[131] Like Violeta Chamorro, Corazon Aquino inherited her husband's political role. But unlike Chamorro, she did not ally herself with radical insurgents because she could rely on support from the Catholic Church and, increasingly, from the U.S. government.

In November 1984 the U.S. National Security Council (NSC) developed a new policy toward the Marcos government. It argued that the 1983 Aquino assassination had "destroyed most of the political credibility the 19-year old Marcos government enjoyed and exacerbated a shaky financial situation," that the threat posed by the NPA "will doubtless continue to grow in the absence of progress toward credible democratic institutions," and that "President Marcos at this stage is part of the problem." To address these problems, the NSC urged a "revitalization of democratic institutions, dismantling 'crony' monopoly capitalism . . . and restoring professional, apolitical leadership to the Philippine military to deal with the growing communist insurgency."[132]

With these instructions in hand, U.S. officials then took a series of steps to implement their new policy. In May 1985 CIA director William Casey told Marcos to hold early elections, a message reiterated by Reagan emissary Senator Paul Laxalt, who told Marcos in October to hold elections and to stop "screwing up" the counterinsurgency effort.[133] Two weeks later, thinking that he could win or steal the "snap" election, Marcos announced he would hold an early presidential election in early 1986, largely to deflect U.S. pressure.[134] But the opposition united rapidly behind Aquino's candidacy, and U.S. officials sent observers, funded an independent election-monitoring organization to prevent Marcos from tampering with the results, and lobbied the military to stay out of the contest.[135]

Aquino emerged the winner in the February 7, 1986 vote, but the official government tally gave the election to Marcos, leading to a political impasse.[136] The stalemate was broken on February 22 when Defense Minister Enrile and General Fidel Ramos led a small mutiny against the dictatorship. Civilian demonstrators then rushed to protect the rebels from assault by troops loyal to Marcos, and the army balked. President Reagan then asked Marcos to step down and invited him into exile in Hawaii. Marcos fled on February 25, and Aquino assumed the presidency.[137]

After the dictatorship collapsed, Aquino revised the constitution, elected a new assembly, and negotiated a cease-fire with the NPA.[138] Attempted military coups in 1987 and 1988 shook the Aquino government and prevented it from making further accommodations with the NPA. Aquino then lost the presidency to Fidel Ramos in the 1992 elections.[139] In the Philippines, as in much of Latin America, democratization led first to the emergence of a moderate-conservative republican government, then to a government led by a former official of the dictatorship.

The fall of the Marcos regime was significant because it demonstrated that the U.S. government was capable of abandoning its long-standing support for dictators, even its close allies. It was important, too, because although the Philippines was in many respects a Latin American country, it was also located in Asia. Dictatorships in neighboring Asian countries closely watched events in the Philippines. Regimes in South Korea and Taiwan, like the Philippines, were dependent on U.S. support and were vulnerable to changing U.S. foreign policies. Developments in the Philippines persuaded them to review domestic policies in light of a changed U.S. foreign policy environment.

Chile

After a brief pause between 1986 and 1988 democratization in Latin America resumed in Chile. Like other Latin American dictators, Chile's General

Pinochet promised in the mid-1970s to democratize the regime—eventually. But the Chilean *abertura,* outlined in a July 9, 1977, speech at Chacarillas, would take at least a decade, Pinochet said, and at the end of this decade he would try to extend his presidency into the late 1990s.[140] In the meantime, Pinochet, like Marcos and many others, revised the constitution and held elections to ratify his continued rule. Like them, he manipulated the electoral process to secure overwhelming approval—75 percent voted for Pinochet in a 1977 referendum and 67 percent approved a revised constitution in a 1980 referendum—despite the fact that opinion polls showed that only 25 percent of Chileans actually supported the dictatorship.[141]

During the 1970s the regime could move toward democratization at a glacial pace, if at all, because it was buoyed by economic development. The government and private industry borrowed heavily to finance growth, and Chile's foreign debt grew from $3.67 billion in 1973 to $17.2 billion in 1982 and to $21.0 billion in 1985.[142] Chile's economic program, drafted by economists trained at the University of Chicago, opened the country to foreign investment and trade and sold off state assets. These policies increased the elite's share of the country's wealth. The top 20 percent increased its share of total income from 43.2 percent in 1969 to 58.2 percent in 1978 and to 64.2 percent in 1988, while the bottom 20 percent saw its income cut by half between 1969 and 1978.[143] And their support for the regime helped keep Pinochet in power. In many ways these policies anticipated the policies adopted by other Latin American countries in response to their debt crises. In a sense, Chile adopted "structural adjustment" policies before the debt crisis occurred, rather than after. The Chicago-trained economists anticipated subsequent developments, but they could not prevent them. When the debt crisis struck Latin American in the early 1980s, Chile was hard hit, and in 1982 "Chile suffered the worst fall in GNP of any Latin American nation."[144] The economy contracted and business failed, forcing the government to nationalize many banks. Industrial production fell to 75 percent of its 1970 level, the currency was devalued, per capita income fell, and unemployment rose to 28.5 percent by 1983.[145]

Economic crisis led to popular protest. A call by the copper miner's union for a day of national protest on May 11, 1983, was met with widespread enthusiasm, leading to strikes, street marches, hunger strikes, pot-banging protests, and rock-throwing street battles. For the next three years poor, working-, and middle-class protesters continued to denounce the regime's economic policy and demand a return to democracy.[146] Political parties regrouped, and a coalition of grassroots groups in 1986 organized the Asamblea de Civilidad (Civic Assembly).[147] The government's use of troops against demonstrators, the 1984 reimposition of a state of siege, military sweeps of shantytowns, the detention of twenty-five thousand activists, the continued use of torture, and the burning alive of two young Chileans in 1986 blunted but did not deter mounting social pressure for political change.

For the Pinochet regime, the problems associated with economic crisis and domestic political protest were aggravated by shifting U.S. policies. After 1985 U.S. officials began distancing themselves from dictatorships throughout Latin America and pressed the Pinochet regime to change. Assistant Secretary of State Elliot Abrams made this policy change plain in 1985, saying that "the Reagan administration . . . is 100 percent in favor of electoral democracy, and wants nothing to do with the overthrow of democratic governments by the military."[148] The U.S. government objected to Pinochet's new state of siege, signaling its disapproval by abstaining on voting on multilateral development bank loans to Chile, voting four times between 1986 and 1988 for U.N. resolutions criticizing the government's human rights record, and suspending some export preferences and investment incentives for Chile.[149]

As in the Philippines, the dictatorship in Chile was persuaded by these events to call an election to quiet domestic opposition and deflect U.S. criticism. Pinochet, like Marcos, called a "snap" election, hoping that a brief campaign would not allow the opposition time to unite against him. But unlike Marcos, Pinochet did not risk running against an opposition candidate when he called, on August 30, 1988, for an October 5 election.[150] Instead, he organized a plebiscite and stood alone for president. The electorate, which had been limited by restrictive registration laws that prevented the poor from voting, could only vote for or against Pinochet.[151] But like Marcos, Pinochet miscalculated. When the election was held, 55 percent of the electorate voted against him.[152]

During the next year, in preparation for the December 14, 1989, election that would select a new president and transfer military authority to civilian government, political parties organized feverishly, while the regime tried to fortify its base of power. The government stacked the senate, rigged electoral procedures, which prohibited Marxist parties from participating, packed the judiciary, and passed laws that reserved an important role for the military, with Pinochet as its head, while also protecting the military from prosecution for human rights violations.[153]

When Patricio Aylwin Azocar, the head of the Christian Democratic party, won the election, the transfer of power to civilian government on March 11, 1990, was restricted in important ways.[154] The new head of state, for example, could not dismiss Pinochet, the head of the army.[155] When the government opened limited prosecutions against military leaders for murdering civilians, the military made public displays of force in December 1990 and May 1993 to curb civilian authority.[156] In Chile democratization returned Christian Democrats to power, the party that ruled for many years prior to Allende's election in 1971. The political status quo ante was restored with one important difference. Under Christian Democratic government in the 1960s the military had played a peripheral political role. But under Christian Democratic rule in the 1990s the military insisted on a central role.

Between 1982 and 1989 strong, or at least prominent, dictatorships fell in the large and populous Latin American states. The fall or withdrawal of dictators in Argentina, Uruguay, Brazil, the Philippines, and Chile demonstrated that democratization was not an idiosyncratic phenomenon but a universal achievement. Although debt crisis and democratization swept away most of the dictators in Latin America, a few still remained. During the next few years most of them would also depart.

Residual Dictatorships

During the next five years, from 1989 to 1993, dictatorships fell in Panama (1989) and Paraguay (1989–93), power devolved in Honduras (1989–90), Nicaragua (1990), and El Salvador (1991), and democratization was reintroduced in Haiti (1994). Except in Paraguay, where the dictator was driven out of power by indigenous forces, in other states the United States played an important, even central, role in democratization during this period. U.S. forces invaded Panama, landed troops without opposition in Haiti, and used its military-civilian allies to press for political change in Honduras, Nicaragua, and El Salvador, brokering an easy peace between radical and conservative republicans in Central America.

Panama

Democratization in Panama was the end product of foreign and domestic economic and political developments. Led by Omar Torrijos from 1968 until his death in 1981 and then by Manuel Noriega, the military regime borrowed heavily to promote growth, like dictatorships throughout Latin America. Panama's foreign debt reached about $5 billion by 1985.[157] Panama's debt crisis was compounded by the second devaluation of the U.S. dollar. In September 1985 U.S. officials secretly agreed with their principal economic partners in the Group of Five (the United States, the United Kingdom, West Germany, France, and Japan) to devalue the dollar against "the main non-dollar currencies."[158] The Plaza Accords, as the agreement was called, effectively reduced the value of the dollar by one-half over the next three years, while doubling the value of the Japanese yen and the West German mark.[159] Since Panama uses the U.S. dollar as its own national currency—both because dollars are used to pay Panama Canal transit fees and because U.S. troops protecting the canal spend the dollars they earn in the country—the dollar devaluation had adverse economic consequences for Panama. As the value of the dollar fell after 1985, Panamanians found it more difficult to import goods from non-dollar countries.[160] The resulting trade deficits exacerbated its already serious debt crisis. This dual economic crisis, which was specific to Panama, was then compounded by U.S. economic sanctions, which were imposed in 1988 as part of the U.S. effort to depose General Noriega.[161] These developments combined to cripple the economy, leading to a 17 percent decline in GNP and 25 percent unemployment by 1989.[162]

The events of September 1985 also proved to be important for the Noriega regime. In that month the Panamanian defense forces murdered opposition leader Hugo Spadafora after he returned from abroad.[163] Like the murders of Chamorro and Aquino, the Spadafora assassination undermined domestic and foreign support for the regime. When Panama's President Nicolas Barletta, who was installed by Noriega in a fraudulent 1984 election, began to investigate the Spadafora murder, Noriega forced him to resign and replaced him with Eric Devalle.[164] Devalle later tried to fire Noriega in 1988 but failed and fled into exile. These developments greatly reduced the regime's credibility and contributed to the emergence of the domestic opposition. Reports in 1986 that Noriega had been a paid CIA agent and a drug trafficker embarrassed the Reagan administration and persuaded it to press for Noriega's ouster and, eventually, to impose economic sanctions.

In May 1989 Noriega annulled the presidential election results, preventing opposition candidate Guillermo Endara from assuming power, and ordered thugs to beat Endara in public.[165] As the economic and political situation deteriorated, Noriega cast himself as a nationalist opposed to foreign intervention by the United States. But when his troops attacked U.S. military personnel, killing one, President George Bush ordered U.S. troops to invade Panama, despite U.S. assurances that its forces would "never be directed against the territorial integrity or political independence of Panama," a commitment made to reassure Omar Torrijos during the completion of the 1979 Panama Canal Treaty.[166] Noriega was captured and deported to the United States, where he faced trial on drug-trafficking charges. Like Somoza and Marcos, Noriega was "invited" into exile in the United States, though he was also asked to spend his exile in jail. (He is now serving a forty-year sentence for drug trafficking.)

After the December 20, 1989, invasion, U.S. officials installed Endara as president and used U.S. troops to rebuff subsequent coup attempts by unreconstructed military forces. Although Endara survived the military coups, his popularity plummeted from 70 percent approval ratings in 1990 to only 9 percent in 1992, both because his government was installed by a foreign power and because he was unable to solve the country's economic and political problems.[167]

Paraguay

Paraguay's democratization, if it can be called that, was extremely limited. In 1989 General Alfredo Stroessner had ruled for more than thirty-four years, having been regularly reelected as president in elections controlled by his Colorado party. But economic crisis eroded his support among economic elites, and his effort to have his son succeed him antagonized his military associates, who wanted their share of power and resented the fact that Stroessner's son Gustavo—whom they called "La Coronela"—was a homosexual.[168] On February 3, 1989, General Andres Rodriguez, a close associate whose daughter had married Stroessner's other son, Hugo, but who was also Stroessner's chief rival, organized a bloody coup and forced Stroessner into exile.[169]

Rodriguez then called elections for May 1, presenting himself as the candidate for the Colorado party. In Paraguay "snap" elections worked to the regime's advantage. The opposition, silenced for thirty-four years, could not quickly organize, while the deeply entrenched Colorado party rallied behind its new candidate after obtaining from Rodriguez a pledge that he would not seek a second term.[170]

El Salvador

Democratization in El Salvador, as in Nicaragua, was largely a product of civil war, which began in 1980 and ended only in 1992. The 1960s and 1970s witnessed economic growth and a rise in GDP per capita from $185 to $289, but the concentration of wealth was such that in 1977 the wealthiest 6 percent earned as much as the poorest 63 percent of the population. The same 6 percent also controlled most of the country's arable land, leaving 41 percent of rural families without land in 1975.[171] Rapid population growth in a land-scarce rural economy contributed to massive migration into neighboring Honduras during the 1960s. But the 1969 "Soccer War" between Honduras and El Salvador, a conflict fueled by problems associated with El Salvadoran immigration, curbed migration and intensified conflict between land-poor rural groups and oligarchy in El Salvador during the 1970s.[172] In 1971 several radical republican groups began organizing insurrections in the countryside, while the moderate opposition challenged the military government after it defrauded the 1972 election and exiled the Christian Democratic candidate, Jose Napoleon Duarte.[173]

Several political developments between 1979 and 1980 sharpened social conflict and led to civil war. In 1979 a military coup installed a junta that represented military factions, conservative politicians, and representatives from the moderate opposition. The urban radical and rural insurgent opposition was excluded from the junta, however.[174] Uniting after being politically divided during the 1970s, radicals and insurgents launched demonstrations and strikes to oppose the regime. The March 1980 assassination of Archbishop Oscar Romero, like the assassinations of Chamorro, Aquino, and Spadafora, galvanized the radical opposition. The radicals then combined to form Farabundo Marti para la Liberacion National (FMLN) in the autumn of 1980, leading to civil war between the military-conservative-moderate regime and the urban radical and rural insurgent opposition.[175]

Emboldened by Sandinista success in neighboring Nicaragua, the FMLN launched a "final offensive" in January 1981, sending its seven thousand combatants into battle against the government's thirty thousand–strong army.[176] But the FMLN offensive failed, and opposing sides settled into a twelve-year civil war that the FMLN could not win and the U.S.-backed government could not lose.

To retain U.S. support, the coalition junta held elections for a constituent assembly in 1982 and then held successive presidential elections in 1984 and 1989. The 1984 election was won by Duarte, who had been prevented from assuming the presidency a decade earlier. Duarte's narrow victory over Roberto D'Aubuisson, a conservative associated with death squads and the government's dirty war, allowed the government to claim that El Salvador had democratized. This enabled the Reagan administration to secure continued congressional support for massive aid to the Duarte government and its war against the radical opposition.[177]

The U.S. government provided about $6 billion in financial and military aid to El Salvador during the civil war, helping to keep the economy afloat and the government in power during the 1980s, much as it did in Honduras.[178] The regime also benefited from another source of revenue. The war drove many poor people out of rural El Salvador, and nearly six hundred thousand of them migrated to the United States.[179] Economic and political refugees working in the United States sent more than $1 billion annually back to El Salvador, providing an important infusion of cash into the war-torn economy.[180] Ironically, people driven out of the country by war helped keep the war going. But although U.S. aid and emigrant remittances kept the economy afloat and prevented the government from collapsing, economic conditions still deteriorated and per capita income fell 15 percent between 1980 and 1989.[181]

In 1989 the two sides grew both stronger and weaker. Alfredo Cristiani, a member of D'Aubuisson's conservative party, won the 1988 presidential elections, consolidating conservative power and marginalizing Duarte's moderate Christian Democrats. The next year, in November 1989, the FMLN launched an offensive that nearly captured the country's capital.[182] But although conservatives and radicals were growing stronger, they were also growing weaker. With war in Nicaragua winding down, U.S. enthusiasm for continuing war in Nicaragua and El Salvador abated, and the Cristiani government faced the prospect of declining U.S. aid. The government also realized that tightened U.S. immigration policies might force the return of many emigrants and a subsequent reduction in the flow of remittances. Meanwhile, the FMLN realized that its 1989 offensive was its best effort and that popular support for the war was waning. Although both sides were in relatively strong positions at the time, in 1990 they began negotiating an end to the civil war, aware that their respective positions would only weaken with time.

The U.N.-sponsored negotiations proceeded slowly during 1990 and 1991, but eventually produced an agreement that was signed on January 16, 1992. The agreement allowed the Cristiani government to remain in power but opened future elections to participation by radical groups and promised land reform and the distribution of 650,000 acres to the landless poor. Further, it required FMLN forces to lay down their arms and the government to cut the army in half and retire many officers, providing a general amnesty for military personnel but allowing a few to be prosecuted for human rights violations.[183]

Civil war and democratization in El Salvador resulted in a conservative civilian government, much as it had in Nicaragua. But in El Salvador radical republicans never controlled the government, as they had for a decade in Nicaragua.

Haiti

Democratization in Haiti was also a protracted and turbulent process that began in 1986 and reached a conclusion only in 1995–96. Between 1957 and 1986 Haiti was ruled by a hereditary dictatorship. Like the Somoza dictatorship in Nicaragua, Haiti was ruled by a political dynasty. François "Papa Doc" Duvalier took power in 1957 and designated his son Jean-Claude "Baby Doc" Duvalier as his successor shortly before he died in April 1971.[184] U.S. navy patrols prevented exiled political and military leaders from returning to challenge the succession, and Jean-Claude soon consolidated his position. During the 1970s high sugar prices promoted modest economic growth, but oil price increases in 1979–80, falling sugar prices, and a devastating hurricane wiped out these economic gains.[185]

As in El Salvador, migration and U.S. aid helped the Duvalier regime survive the economic crisis of the early 1980s. U.S. aid grew from $25.0 million in 1980 to $34.6 million in 1981, $55.0 million in 1985, and $101.0 million in 1987, making Haiti the largest recipient of U.S. economic aid to Latin America outside of Central America.[186] While U.S. aid and IMF loans pumped money into the country and into Duvalier's personal coffers (a $20 million IMF loan found its way into Duvalier's presidential accounts), emigrant remittances injected money into the economy. During the 1980s two hundred thousand poor Haitians migrated to the Dominican Republic to cut sugarcane, and five hundred thousand made their way to the United States, many by boat, with fifteen hundred landing on Florida's beaches every month in 1980–81.[187] Those Haitians driven by poverty to migrate returned as much as $100 million a year during the 1980s to their poor relatives in Haiti, a sum equal to U.S. aid in 1987.[188]

Massive migration helped buoy the economy and for a time reduced political pressure on the Duvalier regime. But worsening economic conditions, a plague of swine fever that required the destruction of the country's black pigs—for many Haitians, their only capital investment—and a new U.S. policy of returning Haitian boat people led to riots and demonstrations in November 1985.[189] Opposition to the Duvalier regime was led by the Catholic Church, while restive military officers plotted coups. Politically isolated by February 1986, Duvalier accepted a U.S. offer of exile, and he flew to France on February 7.[190]

Political power was quickly assumed by a military-dominated junta led by General Henri Namphy, who promised elections on November 29, 1987.[191] But violence by conservative elites and the military forced him to cancel the election.[192] When it was held on January 18, 1988, the major opposition candidates refused to participate, and army candidate Leslie Manigat was elected. Four months later, however, Manigat was overthrown in an army coup.[193]

Disappointed with this result, U.S. officials suspended economic aid and pressured the military to hold new elections. The December 1990 elections were won by Jean-Bertrand Aristide, a Catholic priest and radical republican who mobilized poor voters and vowed to "cleanse" Haiti of wealthy elites, corrupt government officials, *tonton macoutes* (brutal thugs), and the military personnel who protected them.[194] His September 1991 speech defending the practice of *Pere Lebrun,* or mob lynching via flaming tires, triggered a conservative reaction, and the military led a coup that forced him into exile a few weeks later.[195]

Although U.S. officials thought Aristide too radical, they were even less satisfied with the new dictatorship led by Raul Cedras. The United States responded to its growing disappointment in the Cedras regime by imposing successively stronger economic sanctions and embargoes, which drove Haitians in large numbers to U.S. shores, and eventually established a naval blockade around the island. On the verge of economic collapse, Haiti saw a decline in its per capita income from $390 to $240 between 1991 and 1994 and a 34 percent fall in its real GDP, while 75 percent of the nation's workforce was unemployed or underemployed.[196] Under these conditions the military was forced to negotiate, agreeing to restore Aristide in October 1993. Noncombat troops were assigned by the United Nations to ensure a peaceful transition, arriving in Haiti by ship on October 11, 1993, but were turned away by violent conservative mobs.[197] Continued U.S. pressure, high-level negotiations, and preparation for a massive U.S. invasion one year later finally forced the military to retire. In September 1994 Cedras flew into exile in Panama, U.S. troops landed without opposition, and Aristide was reinstalled as president on October 15, 1994.[198] As part of the deal, however, Aristide was forced to agree not to serve his full four-year term, but to step down after elections in December 1995, which were won by Rene Preval, a member of Aristide's Lavalas Platform coalition.[199] In Haiti successive economic crises, domestic opposition, and U.S. diplomatic intervention and near invasion forced successive dictators from power, resulting in a radical and then moderate republican government by the mid-1990s.

Patterns of Democratization in Latin America

In Latin America fifteen countries democratized in the fifteen years between 1978 and 1993. Economic and political crises combined to force dictators from power. Economic problems related to the debt crisis undermined dictatorships in most countries, though some countries were affected earlier than others, and a few, like El Salvador and Haiti, managed to defer the crisis for some years because U.S. aid and emigrant remittances kept their economies from collapsing. In some countries debt-related crisis was compounded by economic sanctions or embargoes imposed by others, as was the case in Argentina during the Falklands War, Nicaragua during the contra war, Panama in its conflict with the United States, and Haiti after the 1987 and 1991 military coups. Crisis was also complicated by natural disasters: earthquake in Nicaragua, flood and drought in Bolivia, swine fever in Haiti.

Economic crisis joined with different kinds of political crisis. The assassination of prominent dissident leaders—Chamorro in Nicaragua, Aquino in the Philippines, Spadafora in Panama, and Romero in El Salvador—galvanized opponents who then challenged the regime. Demonstrations organized by opposition political parties, trade unions, grassroots groups, and sometimes the Catholic Church helped force dictators to relinquish power in Argentina, Brazil, the Philippines, Chile, and Haiti.

Military defeat played an important role in the collapse of dictatorship in Argentina, with consequences that reverberated across the continent, while insurrection and civil war propelled the process of democratization in Nicaragua, El Salvador, and the Philippines. But although Central American civil wars were prominent—absorbing the attention of neighboring states and the United States—they were also rare. Democratization was, by and large, peacefully accomplished.

Changing U.S. foreign policy played an important political role. Time and again U.S. officials abandoned dictators in their hour of crisis. Successive U.S. administrations—Carter, Reagan, Bush, and Clinton—withdrew long-standing U.S. support for allied dictatorships in the Dominican Republic, Nicaragua, Argentina, the Philippines, Chile, Panama, and Haiti, "inviting" dictators into exile and, for Noriega, also into jail. When diplomatic pressure did not produce sufficient change, U.S. officials supported a surrogate contra army to wage war in Nicaragua, used its own military to invade Panama, and landed troops in Haiti to force political change. The "betrayal" of dictators long allied with the United States signaled an important change in U.S. foreign policy, persuading other dictators to relinquish power before they were forced from office.

Economic and political crises resulted in the collapse of Latin American dictatorships. In most cases conservative or moderate civilian governments then assumed power. Indeed, former dictators like Joaquin Balaguer in the Dominican Republic or former presidents like Fernando Belaunde in Peru and Paz Estenssoro in Bolivia resumed their duties as heads of state after military interregnums. In other countries the political parties that had led government prior to dictatorship returned to power. The Christian Democrats returned to power in Chile, the military's political party returned to power in Brazil after the death of Tancredo Neves, and the Peronist party returned to power in Argentina. Throughout much of Latin America democratization resulted in the status quo ante, in which governments were led by the same people, the same parties, or, in the case of the Philippines, members of the same social elite that had held office prior to the dictatorships. Only in Nicaragua and Haiti did radical republicans take power, and they only held power for a time before returning it to conservative or moderate governments. Democratization was thus limited by the inability or unwillingness of Latin American countries to move beyond their pasts.

The moderate-conservative outcome of democratization is striking given the fact that dictators were discredited by economic crisis and corruption, frequently implicated in political assassinations and dirty wars, betrayed by their allies, coerced by international lending agencies to accept painful austerity measures, and humiliated by military or electoral defeat. Under these circumstances it would be easy to assume that radical republicans would triumph when dictators fell, as they did in Portugal, Greece, and Spain. In Latin American, by contrast, radical republicans were generally excluded from power.

Radical republicans in Latin American did not effectively compete for political power during the democratization of the 1980s because they had been twice defeated during the postwar period. They were defeated first during the onset of the Cold War in the late 1940s and again during the dirty wars waged by dictators during the 1960s and 1970s. After World War II there was "a sudden and dramatic advance of democracy throughout Latin America," and most of the region's dictatorships were swept away.[200] But as the U.S.-Soviet conflict sharpened, U.S. diplomats began criticizing the participation of radical republicans—Communists, Socialists, and left-liberals alike—in government, arguing that their participation undermined democracy.[201] Conservative republicans and the military were mindful both of shifting U.S. policy and of their need for U.S. economic assistance. Because the United States was providing only $400 million to Latin America (Belgium and Luxembourg alone received more U.S. aid than the whole of Latin America), Latin American governments relied on private U.S. investment to assist their postwar economic growth. But U.S. investment would not be forthcoming until "the left, especially the Communist left . . . [was] marginalized, and the working class brought firmly under control."[202]

In this context conservative elites cracked down on organized labor, purged radicals from unions, expelled radicals from government, outlawed Communist parties, and restricted the franchise.[203] The conservative counterattack succeeded because the urban working and middle classes that supported and sometimes defended democratization were still relatively small, because radical forces were frequently divided (relations between Communist and Socialist parties were bitter in many countries), because conservatives enjoyed the support of powerful domestic institutions, particularly the Catholic Church and the military, and because conservatives could now rely on U.S. diplomatic approval and economic assistance if they succeeded in gaining power.[204] By the end of 1954 "there were no fewer than eleven dictatorships in Latin America (Guatemala, El Salvador, Nicaragua, Panama, Cuba, the Dominican Republic, Venezuela, Colombia, Peru and Paraguay) . . . thirteen if Ecuador and Argentina are included . . . [and] only four democracies remained: Uruguay, Costa Rica, Chile and Brazil."[205]

Of course, radical republicans did not always concede without a fight. Civil war briefly erupted in Costa Rica in 1948 and also in Colombia after the April 9, 1948, assassination of Jorge Eliecer Gaitan, leading to a protracted conflict between 1946 and 1958, a period known as *La Violencia* (The Violence).[206] In Guatemala the radical republican governments of Juan Jose Avevalo (1945–51) and Jacobo Arbenz (1951–54) were brought to an end by a U.S.-supported surrogate army, the first "contra" army of the postwar period, which invaded Guatemala from Honduras in June 1954.[207] Coups, civil wars, and invasion brought an end to the brief period of postwar democratization, and "the left, and democracy itself, suffered a historic defeat in Latin America."[208]

The collective defeat of radical republican forces after World War II was followed by a second defeat during the one-sided dirty wars initiated by dictators in the 1960s and 1970s. In these "uncivil" wars dictators deployed regular armies, introduced irregular death squads, and incited vigilantes to murder, "disappear," "salvage," and terrorize not only armed, radical republican insurgents, but also unarmed dissident and moderate leaders of trade unions, student groups, and political parties. The regular and irregular forces marshaled by dictators effectively eliminated an entire generation of radical republicans in many countries, reducing the strength and confidence of these forces on the eve of democratization. In the absence of a radical republican presence, democratization was a less risky process for dictators to initiate.

During the 1960s, 1970s, and 1980s radical republicans organized rural guerrilla movements in Cuba, Venezuela, Guatemala, Colombia, Peru, Bolivia, Nicaragua, Mexico, El Salvador, and the Philippines, and urban guerrilla movements in Argentina, Uruguay, Chile, and Brazil.[209] But they had little success because they were politically divided, because they received little outside support, and because they tied their fortunes to an inappropriate model of revolution.[210]

Most radical movements adopted Cuba as their model and subscribed to Ernesto "Che" Guevara's assertion in 1959 that "the example of our revolution for Latin America and the lessons it implies have destroyed all the cafe theories; we have shown that a small group of resolute men supported by the people and not afraid to die can take on a disciplined regular army and defeat it. This is the basic lesson."[211] But Guevara's own attempt to apply this lesson in Zaire and then in Bolivia failed. His band of guerrillas was ambushed, and he was captured on October 8, 1967, and killed the next day. Guevara told his executioners: "Shoot, cowards! You are going to kill a man!"[212] But even after his death, even after other small groups of resolute men tried and failed to take on disciplined regular armies and undisciplined death squads, many radical republicans persisted in their efforts to emulate Che.[213] The Cuban model was inappropriate elsewhere, however, because it was the product of unusual circumstances: widespread popular support, an extraordinarily weak dictatorship, U.S. inattention, and, later, Soviet assistance. Its success changed all of these conditions, and subsequent movements found narrow social support, ruthless and implacable dictators, a determined United States, and an indifferent Soviet Union. As a result, they were defeated, and successive failures pushed radicals into the political margins by the 1980s. When democratization finally occurred, they generally played only a minor role.

Mexican and Cuban Exceptionalism

Although most Latin American countries experienced successive economic crises in the 1970s and 1980s and most of them democratized, Mexico and Cuba did not. Why were dictatorships in these countries exceptions to the general rule?

Mexico

The economic crisis that struck Mexico in 1982 was as strong as any in Latin America. Like other states, Mexico borrowed heavily in the 1970s. Its foreign debt quintupled from $4.2 billion in 1970 to $17 billion in 1975, doubled to $30 billion in 1977, climbed further to $48 billion in 1980, then doubled again to $80 billion in 1982, topping out at about $100 billion in 1987.[214] Mexico's 1982 debt crisis signaled the arrival of the economic hurricane for countries across the continent. Yet debt crisis in Mexico did not precipitate substantial political change.

Economic crisis did not topple the Partido Revolucionario Institucional (PRI), the party that has monopolized power since 1928, because it could draw on a deep reservoir of popular support. This support was based on its legacy as a radical republican party that subscribed to an anti-imperialist tradition and provided real benefits to rural and urban workers.[215]

After the 1910 revolution against the Porfirio Diaz dictatorship, a long and bloody civil war ensued. Nearly 1 million died and another million emigrated between 1910 and 1934.[216] In 1917 warring factions agreed to a radical constitution that provided for land reform, worker's rights, the separation of the Catholic Church from the state and education, and ownership of the country's mineral wealth for the people.[217] But civil war continued during the 1920s, and a succession of generals claimed the presidency. In 1929 General Plutarco Elias Calles established a new official political party to consolidate radical republican power and institutionalize the revolution.[218] But it was not until Lazaro Cardenas assumed the presidency in 1934 that the government's political party took its contemporary shape.[219] Cardenas began by purging conservatives from power in the army and the party, elbowing the Catholic Church aside, and unceremoniously exiling Calles, his chief rival, to the United States in 1936.[220] He then took two important steps to build support for the party among rural and urban workers.

First, he accelerated the redistribution of land, providing more land, nearly 50 million acres, to more people, about 764,000 poor peasants, than all of his predecessors.[221] By delivering on the republican constitution's promises, Cardenas secured the support of rural workers. Although his successors did not practice land reform with such enthusiasm, they all redistributed some land, continually reminding the rural poor of the regime's commitment to its radical origins.[222] Second, on March 18, 1938, Cardenas nationalized the U.S. and British oil companies that controlled the oil industry in Mexico.[223] This decision won the enduring support of Mexican oil workers and rallied the country behind the government's anti-imperialist, republican nationalism, much as Nasser's decision to nationalize the Suez Canal had secured his popularity in Egypt.[224] Unlike Nasser, however, Cardenas escaped economic sanction and possible invasion. The Roosevelt administration was determined to secure Mexico's political support and its oil supplies on the eve of world war and thwarted private U.S. and official British efforts to punish Mexico.[225]

The decision to nationalize oil had other long-term benefits. Oil provided the government with substantial new revenues, which were used to expand government "para-statal" businesses, provide patronage jobs, create bedrock political support for the party, and deliver substantial social services for the poor and working classes that the government could not otherwise afford.[226] The discovery of vast new oil reserves in the mid-1970s—proven oil and gas reserves increased from 6,338 million barrels in 1976 to more than 72 billion barrels in 1981, and earnings from oil exports grew from $3.9 to $14.5 billion between 1979 and 1981—capitalized on the oil embargo crises of the 1970s.[227] Of course, falling oil prices after 1980 and plunging oil prices after

1985 contributed to Mexico's debt crisis because the country's heavy borrowing was premised on the expectation that oil prices would remain high.[228] But it was still better to have oil at any price than no oil at all—the predicament of most Latin American countries. Mexico's vast oil reserves both caused and cushioned the impact of the debt crisis.

Over the years popular support for the PRI eroded. The government's massacre of student demonstrators in Mexico City in 1968, the 1985 earthquake in the capital, and massive corruption and political assassinations in the 1980s and 1990s have diminished the party's reservoir of popular support.[229] Whereas the PRI captured more than 70 percent of the vote in the 1940s, it managed to win only 30 percent in the mid-1980s, retaining its hold on power because the opposition was divided and because it was able to manipulate election results when necessary.[230]

The Mexican government has also benefited from its particular relationship with the United States.[231] Although the United States has many times invaded Mexico and taken much of the territory it has claimed, it has also provided crucial political and economic support for the Mexican regime since the 1930s. Roosevelt retained good relations with Mexico despite the nationalization of U.S. oil companies, and U.S. immigration policies during and after the World War II allowed many Mexicans to work and settle in the United States. Mexican emigration has relieved unemployment among Mexico's growing rural poor and provided the government with substantial income from émigré remittances.[232]

U.S. officials have taken other steps to ease Mexico's economic problems. In 1982 high-level U.S. officials personally managed Mexico's debt crisis, extending terms that they did not subsequently offer to other countries. U.S. officials also promoted U.S. investment in Mexican free trade zones, the *maquiladoras* along the border, and negotiated a free trade agreement with Mexico and Canada that provided real economic benefits to the Mexican economy.[233] When Mexico's trade deficit soared in 1994 and the value of the peso plunged, the Clinton administration provided nearly $50 billion in loans to ease the crisis. To some extent Mexico's economic problems were eased by its incorporation into the U.S. economy, much as the economic problems of Spain, Portugal, and Greece were eased by their entry into the European Community. As a result of its long-standing domestic political and economic policies and timely U.S. support, the Mexican government survived the debt crisis intact.

Cuba

Like Mexico, Cuba's one-party regime survived the debt crisis intact. The Cuban Communist Party, led by Fidel Castro, has monopolized power since it overthrew the Fulgencio Batista dictatorship in January 1959.[234] Party-based dictatorship in Cuba, as in Mexico, is relatively rare in Latin America, where dictatorships are typically organized by caudillos or military juntas. But the rarity of such dictatorships may account in part for their survival.

High sugar prices in the mid-1970s helped Cuba deflect problems associated with the oil embargo. But declining sugar prices, which resulted in export earnings falling from a high of $719.9 million in 1977 to only $179 million in 1978, forced Castro's government to borrow heavily.[235] Cuba's foreign debt rose from $1.3 billion in 1975 to $4.5 billion in 1980 and to $7.3 billion in 1989.[236] During the 1980s sugar prices continued to fall, and the harvest declined from 8.0 million tons in the early 1980s to only 4.2 million tons in 1993 because Cuba lacked the hard currency necessary to purchase fertilizer or farm machinery.[237] As a result of rising debt and declining export income, per capita GDP fell from $1,686 in 1985 to $1,278 in 1991.[238]

The Cuban regime survived its debt-related crisis because it still possessed considerable popular support, which it could draw on in difficult times. The continuing legitimacy of Castro's regime is based on the legacy of its radical republican foreign policies and its domestic economic policies. By routing the corrupt and disorganized Batista dictatorship in 1958 and 1959, Castro and Guevara and their "small band of resolute" guerrillas won the support of most Cubans, though many soon became disenchanted and fled. About two hundred thousand people left Cuba for the United States between 1960 and 1962.[239] With U.S. support, some émigrés organized a contra army that prepared to invade Cuba and overthrow the new regime.[240] But their April 17, 1961, invasion at the Bay of Pigs was quickly defeated, and 1,180 contra soldiers were captured.[241] The regime's military victory helped consolidate Castro's political power. The Cuban missile crisis in October 1962 brought the United States and the Soviet Union to the brink of nuclear war, but they soon reached an agreement that averted potential disaster. The Soviets agreed to withdraw their nuclear missiles in return for the withdrawal of U.S. missiles from Turkey, and U.S. officials indicated that they would not threaten Cuba with invasion.[242] These developments protected Cuba from U.S. invasion and secured a special relationship with the Soviet Union, which subsequently provided financial and military aid and purchased Cuban sugar above world market prices. Soviet aid enabled the regime to survive the withdrawal of U.S. investment and the U.S.-imposed embargo. In return for Soviet economic aid the Cuban government provided troops to radical republican movements in the 1960s and to Communist governments in Africa during the 1970s, becoming what U.S. Senator Daniel Moynihan called the "Gurkhas of the Russian Empire" (a reference to the role played by Indian troops in Great Britain's imperial armies before 1948).[243]

Unlike dictatorships in Greece, Portugal, or Argentina, Cuban forces enjoyed considerable battlefield success in foreign wars. Cuba's fifty thousand troops fought in Angola with distinction and in 1988 helped Angolan forces defeat the South African army, which contributed to democratization in South Africa and Angola.[244] Cuban forces also fought effectively on behalf of the Communist government in Ethiopia, though the regime there was later overrun by Eritrean guerrillas.[245] About twenty-three hundred Cubans died in the foreign wars, but their participation demonstrated the regime's military effectiveness, which contributed to its domestic legitimacy. Because the Soviet Union and foreign governments compensated the Cuban regime for its military assistance, foreign wars also provided real economic benefits. The Cuban government, for example, received $250 million for its military and civilian operations in Angola in 1981.[246]

The Castro regime also used domestic economic policies to win the support of rural and urban workers in Cuba, spending heavily on education and health care and providing services that were superior to those provided by dictators elsewhere in Latin America.[247] In 1980, for example, Cuba had the lowest infant mortality and longest life expectancy of any Latin American country.[248] With deteriorating economic conditions in the 1980s eroding much of the regime's popular support, Castro adopted an economic strategy that mimicked the policies of Southern European dictatorships in the 1960s: exporting workers and importing tourists. Beginning in 1980 during the Mariel boat lift, the Castro regime allowed Cubans to emigrate to the United States. Successive waves of émigré boat people gave the regime an outlet for domestic dissent, while creating the basis for a new source of income—emigrant remittances—a situation similar to developments in El Salvador and Mexico in the same period.[249] Cuban émigrés contributed $120 million to the Cuban economy in 1993, an injection of hard currency that helped keep the tattered economy from falling apart.[250] Ironically, it was dissidents driven from Cuba that helped keep Castro in power. At the same time, with foreign investment from Spain, the regime began redeveloping its tourist industry. The number of tourists visiting Cuba increased from 130,000 in 1980 to 326,000 by 1990.[251] The government earned $200 million from tourism in 1989, a fivefold increase over 1980.[252] Given Cuba's beautiful beaches and cheap accommodations, the switch from a sugar-dominated to a tourist-based economy has been relatively successful, as it was for Spain, Portugal, and Greece.

Because the one-party regime in Cuba can draw on its tradition of radical republican foreign and domestic policies, it still enjoys considerable, though declining, political support. This tradition and the charismatic leadership provided by figures both living (Castro) and dead (Guevara) enabled the Cuban regime to survive its debt crisis intact.

seven

GROWTH AND DEMOCRATIZATION IN EAST ASIA

Because the Philippines is a Latin American country located in East Asia, the fall of Marcos in 1986 was felt both in Latin America and East Asia. Events in the Philippines contributed to Latin American democratization, a process that was already well underway. In East Asia it helped initiate a process that had not yet begun.

The withdrawal of U.S. support for Marcos, a close U.S. ally, and the emergence of a mass-based opposition movement demanding "People Power" were extremely worrisome developments for dictatorships in neighboring South Korea, Taiwan, and China. They too were wrestling with changed superpower policies, growing domestic political opposition, and serious economic crisis. But the political and economic crisis in East Asia was different from the crisis in the Philippines and Latin America. Instead of debt crisis, East Asian dictators confronted problems associated with rapid economic growth. During the late 1980s dictators in South Korea and Taiwan would democratize in an effort to solve these problems. In China, however, the dictatorship would abort incipient democratization, reforming the economy while preserving Communist political rule, an outcome described by one observer as "Market-Leninism."[1]

In some respects East Asian regimes resembled dictatorships in Latin America. They shared a common poverty in the early postwar period and used control of the state to protect domestic industry and promote economic growth. The military regime in South Korea resembled the regimes in much of Latin America, whereas the one-party regimes in Taiwan and China resembled the one-party dictatorship of Mexico's PRI. All three "revolutionary," "nationalist," and "republican" parties emerged during civil wars in the 1920s and managed to become durable and relatively popular political institutions in their respective states. Like their Latin American counterparts, dictatorships in South Korea during the 1970s and China during the 1980s also borrowed heavily to finance economic growth. By 1986, for example, Korea had borrowed $54.4 billion (up from $2.2 billion in 1970 and $27.1 billion in 1980), China $26.6 billion, and Taiwan $12.7 billion, debts on par with regimes in Argentina, the Philippines, and Peru.[2] But where Latin American dictators tried and eventually failed to overcome their debt-related crises, regimes in South Korea and Taiwan succeeded, raising themselves from a common poverty to an exceptional prosperity.

In 1950 South Korea and Taiwan were poor countries, like many others in Latin America, Africa, and Asia. But their economies grew much more rapidly than did those of their poor counterparts. In South Korea double-digit annual growth rates increased per capita income from $87 in 1962 to $6,498 in 1991, while per capita income in Taiwan rose from $153 in 1952 to $7,600 in 1989.[3] This kind of rapid growth—in 1983 18 million people in Taiwan exported as many goods as 130 million Brazilians and four times as many goods as 75 million Mexicans—was unmatched by any country in Latin America during this period and was exceeded only by Japan. It was described by economists as an "economic miracle."[4]

What accounts for the economic success of East Asian "dragons," or "tigers," as South Korea and Taiwan are sometimes called, particularly in light of the comparatively poor economic record of dictatorships in Latin America or, for that matter, Southern Europe? And why did East Asian economic growth, the envy of countries around the world, create a crisis for dictators in the late 1980s, a crisis that led to democratization in South Korea and Taiwan?

The exceptional economic growth achieved by South Korea and Taiwan in the postwar period was fostered by Japanese colonial policies before World War II, by U.S. and Japanese policies after the war, and by domestic policies adopted by their governments after 1950.

Before 1945 Taiwan and South Korea were both colonies of Japan. Formosa, as Taiwan was called by Japan, was colonized after the first Sino-Japanese war in 1894–95. Korea was occupied and then annexed by Japan in 1910. Initially, Japanese administrators exploited their new colonies ruthlessly, much as their European counterparts were exploiting their own in Africa. Japanese colonial policies were designed to keep both colonies at the "fundamental level required to maintain [them] as a source of cheap raw materials, especially rice, for Japan."[5] But during the 1920s Japanese administrators departed from an extractive economic and punitive political approach and developed infrastructure, educational institutions (in 1926 they founded Keojo Imperial University in Seoul), and industry in both colonies, realizing that colonial industries could produce goods for East Asian markets.[6] During the 1930s Japan's rulers sought to create an integrated and self-sufficient economic sphere to weather the effects of the Great Depression.[7] "Japan is among the very few imperial powers to have located heavy industry in its colonies: steel, chemicals, hydroelectric facilities in Korea and Manchuria," the historian Bruce Cumings observed, "[while] Taiwan 'had an industrial superstructure to provide a strong foundation for future industrialization.'. . . By 1945, Korea had an industrial infrastructure that . . . was among the best developed in the Third World."[8]

As a result of "colonial enclave" industrialization and integrated economic development, the GDP in all three countries grew substantially between 1911 and 1938: Japan by 3.36 percent, Korea by 3.57 percent, and Taiwan by 3.80 percent.[9] As Carter Eckert noted, "Korean capitalism thus came to enjoy its first real flowering under Japanese rule and with official Japanese blessing."[10] But economic growth was not necessarily counted as a "blessing" by colonized people in Korea and Taiwan, who "remember this period with intense loathing" because they were forced to worship the Japanese emperor, adopt alien Shinto beliefs, speak Japanese, and take Japanese names.[11]

After World War II the Allies dismantled the Japanese empire, returning Formosa, now Taiwan, to China, and dividing Korea between Soviet and U.S. occupation armies pending the outcome of elections for an indigenous government in an independent Korea.[12] But the retreat of Japanese empire did not mean an end to Japanese participation in the Korean and Taiwanese economies. Close economic relations between Japan and its former colonies survived the war and the end of empire. During the postwar period Japanese firms provided loans and invested heavily in both countries.[13] South Korean and Taiwanese businesses were ideal subcontractors for Japanese firms because U.S. trade privileges allowed them to export goods to U.S. markets unobstructed.[14]

While Japan played the dominant role in Korea and Formosa during the prewar period, the United States played the dominant role in the postwar period. Initially, U.S. officials regarded South Korea and Taiwan as outside the U.S. sphere of influence. In January 1950 U.S. Secretary of State Dean Acheson placed Korea, Taiwan, and Indochina outside the "defensive perimeter" of the United States, arguing that "it must be clear that no person can guarantee these areas against military attack."[15] But after South Korea was invaded by Communist forces from North Korea on June 25, 1950, U.S. policy changed. Led by General Douglas MacArthur, U.S. and U.N. military forces intervened on behalf of South Korea, drove North Korean armies back across the thirty-eighth parallel, and approached the Chinese border. This triggered Chinese intervention, created a military stalemate that resulted in the repartition of Korea at the thirty-eighth parallel, and brought South Korea into the expanding U.S. sphere of influence. U.S. troops have remained in South Korea ever since.[16]

Events in Korea also affected U.S. relations with Taiwan. During the final phase of the Chinese civil war (1947–49), Chiang Kai-shek's defeated Nationalist army retreated to Taiwan. As Communist armies prepared to invade the island, U.S. officials prepared to abandon Chiang. In January 1950 U.S. President Harry Truman announced, "The United States has no predatory design on Formosa or any other Chinese territory. . . . Nor does it have any intention of utilizing its armed forced to interfere in the present situation . . . [and] will not pursue a course which will lead to involvement in the civil conflict in China."[17] U.S. officials prepared to forsake the Nationalists because they believed that U.S. intervention was no longer useful and because U.S. officials and both Chinese combatants regarded Taiwan as an inseparable part of China.[18] But the outbreak of war in Korea changed U.S. policy toward Chiang and brought Taiwan into the U.S. sphere of influence. When war erupted in Korea, President Truman immediately ordered the U.S. Seventh Fleet into the Taiwan Strait "to prevent any attack on Formosa [by Communist China]."[19] The Korean War thus divided both Korea and China and brought South Korea and Taiwan into the U.S. sphere of influence.[20]

Because U.S. officials now regarded both South Korea and Taiwan as frontline, anti-Communist states, they provided substantial economic and military aid to governments in both countries.[21] To shore up Chiang's one-party dictatorship in Taiwan and the military regimes that ruled South Korea after 1962, the U.S. government provided $5.6 billion in economic and military aid to Taiwan and $13 billion to South Korea between 1945 and 1978.[22] U.S. aid to Korea was greater than U.S. aid to *all* of Africa ($6.89 billion), India ($9.6 billion), and nearly as much as to all of Latin America ($14.8 billion) in the same period.[23] About half of the aid provided by the United States was in the form of military aid.[24] These figures do not include the benefits to the South Korean economy that accrued from the stationing of U.S. troops in the country for decades. Troops based in South Korea, like tourists, spent some of their salaries there, pumping hard currency into the economy and providing jobs in military service industries. No troops were based in Taiwan, but during the war in Vietnam the island did benefit from the influx of servicemen who were sent there for rest and recreation, what might be called military tourism.[25]

Wars in Korea and in Vietnam provided other economic benefits to South Korea and Taiwan. By purchasing food and other goods for the war effort and providing contract and subcontracting work for businesses during these wars, the United States provided jobs and income for both countries.

As Chan and Clark noted, "Taiwan [and South Korea] eagerly seized the business opportunities provided by the massive U.S. spending related to the Vietnam War."[26] For Korea, as much as 20 percent of its foreign exchange earnings in the late 1960s could be attributed to the Vietnam War.[27] The expertise gained by Korean firms from construction work under the direction of U.S. engineers also contributed to the emergence of a strong construction industry. By the 1970s South Korean construction firms began to win overseas contracts in the Middle East, such as Hyundai's $931 million contract to build a harbor complex in Saudi Arabia in 1976, and by 1980 approximately 132,000 South Korean construction workers were based in the Middle East.[28] Remittances from overseas construction workers poured hard currency into the economy and helped offset the rising cost of oil from the Middle East during the 1970s.[29]

The United States also provided other economic benefits to South Korea and Taiwan during this period, such as large quantities of surplus grain and other agricultural commodities though the PL 480 food-aid program. Lower food prices kept wages low in Korea and Taiwan, which in turn helped keep businesses competitive throughout much of the postwar period.[30]

The United States also allowed governments in South Korea and Taiwan to set very favorable exchange rates. Like Japan, South Korea and Taiwan benefited from rates that made their goods cheap in the U.S. market and made U.S. goods too expensive for most domestic consumers to buy. This encouraged export industries and protected domestic firms from foreign competition. Low exchange rates in the 1950s, which remained virtually unchanged until President Nixon abandoned the Bretton Woods system of fixed exchange rates and devalued the dollar in 1971, provided real advantages to their growing economies. Like golfers whose handicap remains the same even though their game has improved, low and fixed exchange rates increased the competitiveness of firms in South Korea and Taiwan as the postwar period progressed. As frontline states, South Korea and Taiwan also earned preferential trading privileges from the United States, helping their businesses compete in the important U.S. market.[31] The fact that Taiwan could still count on a weakened but still influential China lobby in the U.S. Congress no doubt helped secure and defend its U.S. economic benefits during the 1950s and 1960s.[32]

Taken together, U.S. aid to South Korea and Taiwan had an important impact on postwar economic development in both countries. According to one estimate, "in the absence of . . . U.S. aid, Taiwan's annual GNP growth rate would have been cut by half, its per capita income would have been reduced by three-quarters, and it would have taken the island 30 more years to reach its 1964 living standards."[33] For South Korea, which received even more U.S. aid than Taiwan, these estimates might have been even more dramatic.

Prewar Japanese colonialism and postwar investment and U.S. aid and trade policies after the war spurred economic growth in South Korea and

Taiwan. But domestic policies also played an important role in their post-war success. In both countries regimes adopted land reform and export-oriented industrialization to promote rapid economic growth.

During the 1950s governments in both South Korea and Taiwan introduced land reform. The governments took land from large landlords and sold it at low prices to peasants who had been leasing the land. The number of peasant owners rose and the number of tenant farmers fell.[34] As land ownership encouraged farmers to work harder and more efficiently, agricultural production grew rapidly. In Taiwan agricultural production increased 5 percent a year in the 1960s.[35] By extending landownership to rural farmers, the government won their gratitude and helped establish a conservative base of support for the regime in the countryside. For the Nationalists in Taiwan, this was a constituency that had been lost on the mainland to the Communists, who had promised land reform to China's tenant farmers.[36]

Although governments in both countries used land reform to increase peasant ownership and production, they did not neglect the landlords whose land they had seized. Regimes compensated landlords by giving them government bonds and stocks in manufacturing and transportation industries.[37] The difference between early land reform in Taiwan and China was that the Kuomintang compensated landlords, whereas the Communists did not.[38] By buying out the landlords in Taiwan, the regime converted them from a rural class that earned income from rent to an urban class that earned income from interest and dividends. Financial dependence and economic growth cemented their political allegiance to the regime.[39]

Peasants and landlords were not the only beneficiaries of land reform. The government in Taiwan purchased a large amount of rice from owner-cultivators at less than world market prices, then exported rice at higher, world market prices, using the surplus to finance industrial development. From 1954 to 1960 this practice resulted in an annual profit of $10.5 million for Chiang's government.[40] And because it paid landlords less than market prices for their land and paid below-market interest rates for the bonds it issued as compensation, the government created an even greater surplus to finance industrial growth or military spending.[41]

Land reform had another important consequence. Changing rural relations and increased food production created a labor surplus in rural areas, which resulted in migration to the cities. In South Korea the urban population increased from 38 percent to 61 percent of the total population between 1960 and 1982.[42] The massive influx of workers into the cities created the core of a large, low-paid work force in the growing industrial sectors of both countries.[43]

In South Korea and Taiwan, Japanese investment, U.S. aid, and income received from the mandatory purchase and forced savings programs in rural areas provided an important source of capital for industrial development. In Taiwan the bullion reserves taken from China by the Nationalist regime during the civil war and the capital provided by Chinese émigré communities around the world provided additional sources of investment.[44] Overseas Chinese communities provided between 18 and 28 percent of Taiwan's cumulative foreign investment during the postwar period.[45]

With the capital provided by foreign and domestic sources, regimes in South Korea and Taiwan developed policies to assist industrial firms produce goods for domestic and foreign markets. Both countries introduced restrictive labor laws, and Taiwan also introduced martial law between 1949 and 1987 to control the expanding urban labor force and to keep wages low. Dictatorships in both countries used their control of banks, credit, and interest rates to organize capital and create firms that could compete effectively in domestic and foreign markets, though each country encouraged the expansion of different kinds of firms.[46] The South Korean government created huge private monopoly firms, called *chaebol,* that dominated the country's economic landscape. As the scholars Bello and Rosenfeld noted, "In 1988, the combined revenues of the top four *chaebol*—Samsung, Hyundai, Lucky-Goldstar and Daewoo—topped $80 billion, or an astonishing 60 percent of Korea's total GNP of $135 billion."[47] By contrast, the regime in Taiwan created some large firms, called *caifa,* but it also encouraged the proliferation of small firms in a more competitive economic environment.[48] "More than 90 percent of Taiwan's 90,000 industrial enterprises are companies with fewer than 30 employees," wrote Bello and Rosenfeld.[49] Throughout the postwar period the formal structure of the big monopoly firms in South Korea and the small, competitive firms in Taiwan has been less important in determining success than the fact that both receive considerable guidance and investment from state agencies.

Like their counterparts in Latin America, governments in South Korea and Taiwan adopted import substitution policies during the 1950s. But unlike regimes in Latin America, East Asian regimes soon abandoned these policies, Taiwan in the late 1950s and South Korea between 1960 and 1964.[50] Using their financial, administrative, and political resources, East Asian regimes pushed firms, large and small, into production for export markets, particularly in Japan and the United States. They used high tariff barriers to protect domestic industries and to prevent domestic consumers from purchasing goods from abroad, which could produce trade deficits. Imports of many goods were banned outright. Until the mid-1980s, smoking a foreign cigarette in South Korea could result in a jail sentence.[51]

By 1970 export policies began to pay large dividends. Taiwan achieved its first trade surplus in 1970, just when U.S. aid was winding down, and went on to record a surplus every year thereafter. Although growing slowly in the 1970s and more rapidly in the 1980s, Taiwan's surplus stood at $15.6 billion in 1986. By 1990 Taiwan had built up foreign exchange reserves worth more than $80 billion, up from only $2 billion in 1980, second in the world only to Japan's reserves of $98 billion in 1988.[52]

South Korea and Taiwan benefited from these foreign and domestic economic developments. But they also benefited, indirectly, from one important and shared political-military development: partition. The partitions of Korea and China in the early 1950s meant that governments in South Korea and Taiwan could pursue economic development for their relatively small populations. This was particularly important for Taiwan. Although economic growth in Taiwan raised per capita GNP from $153 in 1952 to $7,500 in 1989, even double-digit economic growth would not have raised incomes as far and as fast if the 18 million people in Taiwan had been yoked politically to the one billion people in China, either under Nationalist or Communist rule.[53] People in Taiwan now recognize the economic advantages of smallness, which is why enthusiasm for reunification with the mainland has cooled. "When people [in Taiwan] think about unification, they think: 'What's in it for us? [Do] you want to equalize incomes with the mainland?'" explained Chang Liang, president of Shearson Global Financial Services in Taipei.[54] Or as one Taipei judge argued,

> Let me illustrate to you why Taiwan should not unify with China. The average annual income of the people on mainland China is only about $250, but that of the Taiwan people is about $5,000 . . . What is Taiwan's annual income going to be when it is unified by China? Maybe less than $500. If you think it is a good thing to reduce our annual income from $5,000 down to $500 you must have some serious mental problems.[55]

Partition simultaneously gave the United States a reason to provide substantial aid to frontline dictatorships, which helped spur economic growth, and enabled relatively small populations in South Korea and Taiwan to secure the benefits of post-partition economic growth.

Growth and Crisis

Japanese colonialism before 1945, U.S. aid after 1945, and domestic economic policies that created and seized economic opportunities enabled South Korean and Taiwanese economies to grow rapidly throughout most of the postwar period. Although successive oil crises in the 1970s briefly slowed growth, they did not create serious structural crises for either country. Sustained economic growth consolidated the political support provided by rural farmers and industrial elites and reinforced the support of landlords who had become shareholders, providing considerable political legitimacy for dictatorships. But changing political conditions in the 1970s and new economic developments in the early 1980s made it increasingly difficult for both countries to maintain high rates of growth. Changing U.S. policies pressured them from above, low-wage countries created economic competition from below, and domestic working classes demanded change from within. As these pressures mounted, dictatorships in South Korea and Taiwan began to democratize.

U.S. support for dictatorships in South Korea and Taiwan was crucial to both countries. The U.S. government protected them from invasion and assisted their economic recoveries, providing economic aid and markets for their goods. But changed U.S. political policies in the 1970s and economic policies in the mid-1980s presented a series of problems for dictatorships in South Korea and Taiwan.

In 1971 Nixon signaled an important change in U.S. policy toward both countries by recognizing and then traveling to China to establish a new relationship with the Communist government. After admitting China to the United Nations, the United States no longer provided Taiwan and South Korea with the extraordinary political attention and economic assistance they had previously received as frontline anti-Communist states. U.S. economic and military aid fell off dramatically, though more for Taiwan than for South Korea, which still confronted Communist North Korea (though no longer China) across the thirty-eighth parallel.[56] The Nixon administration kept U.S. troops in South Korea, but withdrew a division to signal its changing policy in the region.[57] During the 1970s the United States gradually cut back its military presence and support for Taiwan, and in 1979 the Carter administration ended official recognition of Taiwan, abrogated a 1954 mutual defense treaty, and recognized the Communist dictatorship as China's sole legal government.[58] It did not, however, cut its *economic* relations with Taiwan.[59] And the Carter administration discussed but did not proceed with plans to slash the number of U.S. troops based in South Korea, largely because the Park Chung Hee dictatorship threatened to develop its own nuclear weapons if the United States withdrew its forces.[60]

Although U.S. foreign policy changed dramatically in the 1970s, its economic relations with South Korea and Taiwan remained unchanged until the mid-1980s. But growing U.S. trade deficits prompted new economic policies toward both countries. In 1971 the United States recorded its first postwar trade deficit. To improve the U.S. trade position, Nixon devalued the dollar and abandoned the system of fixed exchange rates established by the Bretton Woods agreement. But despite this substantial devaluation, U.S. trade deficits continued to rise, reaching $25.3 billion in 1980 and climbing to $122 billion in 1985.[61] Although the bulk of the U.S. trade deficit was produced by trade with Japan and with oil-producing countries, U.S. trade deficits with Taiwan and South Korea were still significant. The U.S. trade deficit with Taiwan increased from $2.3 billion in 1979 to $16 billion in 1985.[62] In 1980 the United States posted a $266 million surplus in its trade with South Korea but recorded a $4.2 billion deficit by 1985.[63]

To reduce growing trade deficits, particularly with its Asian partners, U.S. officials took three steps that dramatically changed its economic relations with South Korea and Taiwan. First, at the 1985 Plaza Accords U.S.

officials persuaded its Group of Five partners to devalue the dollar, resulting in the dollar's fall to one-half its 1985 value against the yen and the deutsche mark by 1987 and to one-third its 1985 value by the early 1990s.[64] As it turned out, the U.S. dollar devaluation had important, though different, consequences for South Korea and Taiwan.

In Taiwan the government had tied the value of the New Taiwan Dollar to the value of the Japanese yen. As a result of the Plaza Accords, the value of Taiwan's currency, like that of the yen, increased as the value of the U.S. dollar declined. The value of the Taiwan dollar rose almost 40 percent against the U.S. dollar between 1985 and 1988, slowing Taiwan's exports to the United States slowed and reducing its trade surplus from $16 billion to $10 billion in the same period.[65] Moreover, because most of Taiwan's foreign exchange reserves consisted of U.S. dollars and securities, the value of its enormous holdings declined in real terms.[66]

South Korea adopted a different currency strategy. Unlike Taiwan, the South Korean regime had pegged its currency, the won, to the dollar, not the yen. On the eve of the U.S. dollar devaluation the South Korean government in mid-1985 devalued the won and continued to devalue it against the dollar during the next few years. So while Taiwan's exports to the United States declined during this period, South Korean exports surged, not only to the United States (where the price of Korean goods remained about the same), but also to Japan and Western Europe (where the price of its goods fell).[67] As a result, South Korea's trade surplus with the United States increased despite the Plaza Accords, from $4.2 billion in 1985 to $8.7 billion in 1988.[68] It is important to note, however, that although both Taiwan and South Korea posted trade surpluses with the United States, they recorded trade deficits with Japan, a residue of their neocolonial relations with Japan.[69] South Korea's substantial currency devaluations did not prevent its trade deficit with Japan from increasing from $3.0 billion in 1985 to $3.8 billion in 1988.[70] And although Taiwan recorded a trade surplus of $10.4 billion with the United States in 1988, it suffered a $6 billion deficit in its trade with Japan.[71]

But although the South Korean currency strategy was more effective than the strategy adopted by the regime in Taiwan, it did not blunt the second part of the U.S. plan, which was to force both countries to lower their tariffs, particularly on U.S. agricultural goods, and to restrict the export of some goods to U.S. markets. The former eroded rural support for the two regimes, and the latter created problems for export-oriented industries.

During the 1980s, but particularly after 1985, U.S. officials demanded that South Korea and Taiwan (and other countries around the world) reduce their tariffs and open their markets to U.S. goods. This was part of an overall strategy to use various kinds of free trade agreements—Section 301 of U.S. trade law, the Uruguay Round of negotiations in the General Agreement on Tariffs and Trade, and regional trade agreements with Canada and then with Canada and Mexico—to promote U.S. exports and reduce trade deficits.[72] U.S. officials were particularly keen on opening markets in South Korea and Taiwan to U.S. grain, rice, tobacco, beef, and fruit. Reluctantly, officials in South Korea and Taiwan yielded to U.S. demands. They did so in part because they feared that the United States would retaliate against their manufactured exports if they did not and in part because the high cost of domestic produce contributed to demands for higher wages by urban workers (cheaper U.S. imports could help them contain wage demands). But by opening their domestic markets to U.S. produce, the regimes destroyed the livelihoods of many domestic farmers who had long supported dictatorships in both countries.[73] On May 20, 1988, farmers in Taiwan rioted, protesting foreign competition, in Taipei's worst riots since the 1940s, and protests by rural farmers mounted in South Korea.[74]

Not only did the United States demand open markets for its goods, but it also called for restrictions on South Korean and Taiwanese exports to the United States, negotiating voluntary export restrictions and using legislation under Section 301 to retaliate against unfair traders who "dumped" goods in the United States.[75] U.S. officials invoked Section 301 trade sanctions twice against South Korea after 1985 and used the threat of sanctions to negotiate concessions on other occasions.[76] These developments brought an end to cordial U.S. economic relations with South Korea and Taiwan and demonstrated U.S. determination to change postwar economic rules. Changed U.S. foreign and economic policies placed real pressure on dictatorships in South Korea and Taiwan, pressure that threatened to slow their economic growth and perhaps even to reverse it.

Under mounting pressure from the United States and Japan during the mid-1980s, South Korea and Taiwan began to experience a second problem: competition from low-wage countries in Asia. Economic success in South Korea and Taiwan had not gone unnoticed. Other Asian countries developed export industries of their own. These industries became increasingly competitive, largely because labor costs in Thailand, Indonesia, Bangladesh, and, importantly, China were even lower than in South Korea and Taiwan. In 1988 workers earned $610 a month on average in South Korea and $643 a month in Taiwan.[77] But this was considerably higher than the $209 a month paid to workers in Indonesia, $132 in Thailand, and $129 in Malaysia.[78] By 1989 the gap between wages in South Korea and Taiwan and wages in other Asian countries had grown even wider. The average textile operator earned $3.56 an hour in Taiwan and $2.87 in South Korea, while operators earned $0.68 in India, $0.65 in Thailand, $0.40 in China, $0.26 in Sri Lanka, and $0.23 in Indonesia.[79] For South Korea and Taiwan economic growth had a price: higher wages and reduced competitiveness.

As a result, industries in South Korea and Taiwan began losing business to Asian competitors. In the important textile industry, for example, South

Korea's share of the U.S. market remained at 17.3 percent between 1979 and 1982, whereas China's rose from 1.1 percent to 7.8 percent.[80] Faced with increasing competition from their neighbors, businesses in South Korea and Taiwan sought investment opportunities outside their countries for the first time.[81] South Korean businesses invested more money abroad in one year, 1988, than they had during the previous twenty years, while in Taiwan a poll indicated that only a third of the owners of 1,000 manufacturing companies were willing to continue investing in Taiwan, and a tenth were planning to invest elsewhere.[82] The resulting falling market shares and increased capital flight put real economic pressure on both South Korea and Taiwan and forced them to consider measures to address this rising competition.[83]

If regimes in South Korea and Taiwan had been able to keep their domestic wages low, competition from low-wage Asian neighbors would not have presented serious problems. But wages were rising because domestic social groups were demanding economic change and, increasingly, political reform.

Dictatorships in South Korea and Taiwan had long suppressed labor organizations and opposition political parties to keep wages low and maintain their monopoly on power.[84] Regimes in both countries had killed opposition demonstrators—in Taiwan in 1947 and in South Korea in 1980—to discourage demands for economic and political change. In 1947 the Nationalist regime massacred between eight thousand and ten thousand opponents in Taiwan and then imposed martial law.[85] The 1947 massacre, like events during the civil wars in Spain, Greece, and Latin America, effectively deterred the emergence of opposition groups for many years. The massacre of civilians by the regime in South Korea in 1980 was also designed to curb opposition to the regime. But although it suppressed dissent, it did so for only a short time.

On October 26, 1979, South Korea's President Park Chung Hee was assassinated at a dinner party by Kim Jae Kya, head of the Korean Central Intelligence Agency, in a dispute over how to handle recent protest rallies in the cities.[86] Six weeks later Chun Doo-Hwan launched a coup to steal a march on his competitors for the leadership and to prevent the opposition from democratizing government.[87] In May 1980 Chun declared martial law and imprisoned opposition leaders.[88] When students organized a rally against martial law in Kwangju on May 18, police savagely attacked demonstrators, which prompted wider riots and forced the military to withdraw from the city.[89] Paratroops returned in force on May 27, killing hundreds and perhaps thousands of civilians before retaking the city.[90]

After the traumatic events in Kwangju and the subsequent crackdown on dissent the number of unions dropped from 6,011 before May 1980 to 2,618 by the end of the year, the number of union members declined from 1,120,000 to 950,000 during the same period, and the number of labor disputes fell by more than half.[91]

But the Kwangju massacre only suppressed dissent for a few years. By the mid-1980s opposition groups had forged what some sociologists have called a *minjung* (people, or the masses), "a broad alliance of 'alienated classes,' people alienated from power and the distribution of the fruits of economic growth."[92] In the Korean context the term connotes "a strong [populist] nationalist desire for economic and political independence."[93] At the center of this *minjung* were student-intellectuals and workers, but the flanks of this core alliance were occupied by white-collar workers and rural farmers opposed to changed agricultural policy.[94]

Social groups in South Korea recovered quickly from the Kwangju massacre and created an effective political alliance because they shared common economic problems and an antipathy for what they regarded as corrupt political institutions. For many groups in South Korea and also in Taiwan, rapid economic growth had not greatly increased their economic well-being. To promote low-wage, export-oriented growth, the regimes had kept real wages behind productivity increases, and manufacturing wages remained low, particularly for women, compared with wages in the United States and Japan.[95] Workers were asked to work long hours—the work week in South Korea actually increased from 50.5 to 54.3 hours between 1975 and 1983—and under dangerous conditions, with Korea leading the world in its rate of industrial accidents and of occupation-related illnesses.[96] Because South Korea did not spend much on housing to accommodate the influx of workers into the cities, housing was scarce and extremely expensive.[97] One study reported, "In 1985, the poorest 30 percentage of the population had an average of two square meters per person and three families per house. It is common for one family to live in one or two small rooms and often, three generations live together—in some cases in one room."[98] In Seoul, home to one-quarter of the country's population, 2 million people, or one-fifth of the city's residents, were squatters.[99] Because the regime had long used high tariff barriers to protect domestic farmers and industry, workers and consumers paid high prices for food and other goods.

Common economic grievances led to renewed labor militancy by the mid-1980s. New unions were organized, membership rolls in nongovernmental unions grew, and the number of labor disputes multiplied. The share of organized labor in the labor force increased, rising from 14.4 percent in 1986, 17.3 percent in 1987, 22 percent in 1988, and 23.7 percent in 1989.[100] In South Korea the number of labor disputes rose from 98 in 1983 to 265 in 1985, then exploded from 276 in 1986 to 3,749 in 1987, a more than thirteenfold increase.[101] One economist noted that "32 percent of all manufacturing firms with 300 or more employees struck in 1987 and that 1.225 million workers were involved in strikes between June and October 1987."[102] The organization of white-collar unions during this period broadened the social base of the *minjung*.[103] In Taiwan labor disputes followed a similar pattern, rising from 700 in 1980 to 1,622 in 1985 and then to more than 2,900 in 1987 and 1988.[104]

The *minjung* in South Korea and its counterpart in Taiwan shared a common hostility to existing political institutions. South Korea's 1980 constitution, which "provided for an indirect electoral college system that effectively gave Chun the power to name his successor," was widely regarded as corrupt.[105] After the ruling party won only 35.3 percent of the vote in the February 1985 legislative elections, its manipulation of electoral rules to retain control of the National Assembly discredited the dictatorship. President Chun's decision on April 13, 1987, to suspend debate on direct presidential elections and then in June to nominate former general Roh Tae Woo as the ruling party's candidate in the next presidential election, "all but guaranteeing that [Roh] would gain the presidency," created a pervasive political hostility to the regime.[106]

In Taiwan the political institutions transferred to the island in 1947 came to be regarded widely as old and obsolete. When Chiang Kai-shek moved his government to Taiwan in 1947, he maintained that it still represented all of China. Legislators elected to the national assembly from mainland districts in 1947 and 1948 were thus given permanent seats pending all-China elections at some later date.[107] When legislators died, they were replaced by first, second, and even third runners-up from the 1947–48 election, and no new parliamentary elections were held until 1969, when the government began holding "supplementary" elections to replace dead legislators.[108] Because the average age of legislators in 1988 was eighty years and because fourteen legislators on average died annually in office between 1980 and 1986, legislators were widely referred to as the *zou rou*, or "walking dead."[109]

By the mid-1980s the government's ossified and geriatric political institutions had become objects of public ridicule, and opposition groups demanded their reform. Hostility to the regime's political institutions crystallized on September 28, 1986, when 112 *dangwai* (outside the ruling party) leaders announced the formation of the opposition Democratic Progressive party, a move that was then still illegal under martial law provisions.[110] But they were allowed to participate in Taiwan's first two-party elections in December 1986.[111] By demanding economic change and political reform, the *minjung* in both South Korea and Taiwan was able to put real domestic pressure on both regimes.

After 1985 a number of factors combined to create a serious crisis for dictatorships in both South Korea and Taiwan. The economic stability of both regimes was affected by the U.S. determination to reduce its trade deficits with Asian states and by increasing competition from low-wage neighbors and the "slow" growth rates that resulted—in South Korea the economy grew "only" 4 percent, about half the 1983 rate, and the same was true in Taiwan. Meanwhile, the emergence of a socially diverse movement demanding economic change and political reform and the hapless demise in 1986 of the Marcos dictatorship at the hands of Corazon Aquino's "People Power" movement, which made Asian *minjung* movements bold, persuaded leaders in South Korea and Taiwan 1987–88 to initiate political reform, an Asian *abertura* that would result in real but limited democratization.[112]

Democratization in South Korea and Taiwan

On June 29, 1987, Roh Tae Woo, whom Chun had selected to be the ruling party's presidential candidate, announced that he would amend the constitution to permit direct presidential elections, change election laws to promote fair, multiparty competition, pardon jailed opposition leaders—particularly the radical dissident Kim Dae Jung—so they could participate in future elections, restore civil rights and abolish press censorship, and undertake serious social reforms.[113] This dramatic departure, made without consulting Chun, transformed Roh from military leader—he had participated in Chun's 1979 coup and helped direct the Kwangju massacre—to civilian presidential candidate.[114] "Park Chung Hee built Korea's high-growth economy," he said. "It is left to me to bring Koreans democracy. That, I hope, will be my monument."[115]

In the short run Roh evidently believed that open elections could restore the government's declining political legitimacy and bring an end to street protests and labor unrest. In the long run he hoped that the creation of a multiparty system dominated by the ruling party would marginalize the radical opposition and reinvigorate the economy.[116] "The old political, economic and social systems and orders started to crumble, and we thus had to grapple with the formidable task of building new systems and orders to replace them," he later recalled.[117] Cho Soon, Roh's minister of economic planning, worried that unless something dramatic was done, what Roh had called "sweeping, epoch-making, bold-measures," the Korean "economy will collapse like some of the Latin American countries."[118] U.S. officials also encouraged Roh to move in this direction, arguing against continued military rule.[119]

In the December 1987 elections Roh was elected president with 37 percent of the vote after Kim Young Sam (27 percent) and Kim Dae Jung (28 percent) split the opposition vote.[120] As a democratically elected president, Roh was able to contain street protest and host the 1988 Olympics. Then in 1989–90 Roh cracked down on labor disputes, arresting militants, deploying fourteen thousand troops to break a strike at Hyundai's giant shipyards in 1989, and banning one important trade union because it was "leading a vicious conflict with an ideology of class struggle for the liberation of labor."[121] In the case of South Korea, political reform helped curb economic revolt.

Roh then made a deal with Kim Young Sam's moderate opposition party to exclude Kim Dae Jung's radical opposition party from power. On January 22, 1990, Roh announced that the ruling party would merge with Sam's party and with Kim Jong Pil's conservative party (Kim Jong Pil had been a prime minister during Park Chung Hee's dictatorship) to form a center-right coalition.[122] To cement this "Grand Conservative Coalition," as it was called, Roh agreed to support Sam's candidacy for president in 1992, and Sam was duly elected.[123] As Roh later explained, "The role of my presidency is to serve as a kind of large furnace in which all extremes of controversy are melted. In the end we can make stronger steel out of the mixture."[124] The democratization initiated by Roh and the moderate-conservative merger he engineered forged political institutions that were both stronger and more democratic than their predecessors, though they also rehabilitated the ruling party and excluded the radical opposition.

In 1986 Chiang Ching-kuo initiated a protracted process of democratization in Taiwan that is still underway. The eldest son of Chiang Kai-shek, Chiang Ching-kuo inherited the dictatorship when his father died in 1975.[125] By 1986 Chiang Ching-kuo was seventy-seven years old, and he began casting around for ways to transfer power to a successor after his death, one who could democratize Taiwan but also maintain the Nationalist Party's grip on power. In 1984 he designated Lee Teng-hui as his successor.[126] At the March 1986 meeting of the Central Committee of the KMT (National People's Party) Chiang argued that the regime should move toward a constitutional democracy. In April he appointed a task force to suggest possible reforms, such as permitting participation by other political parties, lifting martial law, and reforming the parliament.[127] After the opposition *dangwai* leaders formed a new political party in September, Chiang told his colleagues in October that "the time is changing and so is the environment. To fit in with these changes, the KMT must adopt new concepts and new forms according with the basic spirit of the democratic and constitutional system. Only by doing so can the KMT be in line with current trends and forever be together with the public."[128]

Chiang permitted the opposition to participate in the December 1986 elections, though restrictive electoral rules allowed them only token success, and he finally lifted the decades-long martial law on July 15, 1987.[129] When he died in January 1988, power passed to his designated successor, Lee Teng-hui.[130] Lee continued to democratize, but slowly. The representation of non-KMT political parties increased, but the *zou rou* remained in office for several more years. It was only in 1990 that the Supreme Court ruled that senior legislators would be retired by the end of 1991.[131] And in December

1992 Taiwan held its first general elections for representatives to the legislature, though direct elections for president were not permitted until December 1996, a decade after Chiang Ching-kuo began to democratize Taiwan.[132] In the 1992 elections the opposition won 30 percent of the seats, and the ruling Nationalist Party retained its parliamentary majority.[133]

Although other dictatorships had tried to manage the democratization process so they could retain their hold on power, the Nationalist regime in Taiwan was more successful than most. Unlike South Korea, where Roh transformed the military regime into an electoral party, the Nationalist Party in Taiwan has democratized *without* having to share power with some of the opposition. In South Korea Roh was able to consolidate continued conservative rule, but he was not able to prevent his or Chun's indictments in 1995 for political crimes related to the coup and to the Kwangju massacre and for economic crimes related to bribery and corruption. Roh was jailed, accused of accepting $370 million in bribes while president.[134] In Taiwan, by contrast, the Nationalist government has so far escaped any accounting for events under the two Chiang dictatorships.

Why have the Nationalists been able to democratize slowly, without surrendering or sharing power, and without being subjected to the kind of legal scrutiny given many other fallen dictatorships in countries around the world? Perhaps the answer is that Taiwan's Nationalist Party resembles revolutionary dictatorship in Mexico. Like the PRI in Mexico, the KMT dates back to the revolutionary period, to 1912 in China, when it helped overthrow the Qing dynasty. With Soviet assistance, it was reorganized along Leninist party lines in the 1920s.[135] Like the PRI in Mexico, the KMT in Taiwan possessed a revolutionary heritage, providing land reform and promoting real economic growth. This created a reservoir of support among émigré Chinese in Taiwan, though less among indigenous Taiwanese who were long excluded from political power. The fact that, with U.S. assistance, the regime successfully defended the island from Chinese invasion no doubt won the loyalty of many—émigré or indigenous—who were hostile to the Communists. Taiwan's ability to withstand the retraction of U.S. diplomatic and military aid after Nixon's opening to China demonstrated to many that the regime could maintain Taiwan's independence under difficult diplomatic circumstances. For these reasons the Nationalist regime was able to retain power even as it democratized.

For both Taiwan and South Korea rapid economic growth contributed to a crisis that resulted in democratization. But although rapid growth helped cause the crisis, it also helped solve it. As they democratized in the late 1980s and early 1990s, both countries saw their economies revive and rapid growth resume. This gave new legitimacy to the political arrangements then being created. In South Korea renewed growth helped consolidate the new Grand Conservative Coalition, which contained "reformed" elements of former dictatorships (Kim Jong Pil represented the Park Chung

Hee dictatorship and Roh Tae Woo the Chun Doo-Hwan regime). In Taiwan continued growth enabled the ruling party to retain power, though it now faces nominal political competition from other parties.

East Asian Exceptionalism

Like South Korea and Taiwan, China appeared to be on the verge of democratization in the late 1980s. In the spring of 1989 students and workers in Beijing occupied Tiananmen Square and demanded political reform, much as demonstrators in Seoul had been demanding reform for some years. But the government's forcible removal of protesters camped in the square, its massacre of civilians in Beijing on June 3, and the subsequent arrest of dissidents around the country aborted incipient democratization. Events in China did not lead to the collapse of communism, as it would in Eastern Europe and the Soviet Union. Even though they too faced serious economic problems, dictatorships in China, North Korea, and Vietnam did not succumb, like their Communist counterparts in Europe, or democratize, like their neighbors in South Korea and Taiwan.

China

Economic and political problems in China first assumed crisis proportions in the mid-1970s. In 1976 economic growth slowed, partly as a result of the disastrous Tangshan earthquake. China's trade deficit with capitalist countries was growing rapidly—from $1.2 billion in 1977 to $4.5 billion in 1979—and economic stagnation threatened.[136] Workers and peasants staged strikes, and demonstrators marched in Tiananmen Square.[137] The deaths of Premier Zhou Enlai in January 1976 and then of Mao Tse-tung on September 9, 1976, created a succession crisis for the Communist leadership, which was struggling to recover from the decade-long vicissitudes of the Great Proletarian Cultural Revolution (1966–76).[138] After a two-year political struggle for control of the party, Deng Xiaoping ousted Hua Kuofeng and assumed power in December 1978.[139]

Once in power Deng initiated a series of important economic reforms to restructure the economy and promote growth, what was called *tiaozheng* (readjustment) and *jingii tizhi gaige* (reform of the economic structure).[140] He also introduced modest political reform, or *fangsong,* to encourage wider participation in decisionmaking so that people could "supervise political power at the basic level, as well as in all enterprises and undertakings."[141] Deng promoted limited political reform because he believed that "without reforming the political structure, it will be impossible to safeguard the fruits of economic reform or to guarantee its continued advance."[142]

Because Deng and the ruling party initiated economic and political reforms without first developing a comprehensive plan and because the reforms were introduced piecemeal after 1978, the regime was compelled, in its words, to "cross the river by groping for stepping stones."[143] The stepping-stone approach to economic reform that emerged after 1978 had several key features.

The centerpiece of the regime's economic restructuring was agricultural reform. The government turned land over to farmers, effectively privatizing land ("the land remains collectively owned, but it is now allocated for 15 years or more to individual families"), increased the prices paid to farmers for produce delivered to the state by about 25 percent, and allowed farmers to sell food produced in excess of their quotas on the open market for even higher prices.[144] The government also helped farmers by building irrigation works, extending power lines, and making more fertilizer and new seeds available, while allowing farmers to cultivate higher-value commercial and industrial crops.[145] By privatizing land and increasing farm income the government hoped to increase productivity and boost crop yields. "If agricultural development is not accelerated," the regime worried in 1978, "industrial and other construction projects cannot be achieved."[146]

Agrarian reform was an enormous economic and political success. Rural farm income more than doubled between 1978 and 1984, and food grain production increased 50 percent, from 305 million tons in 1978 to 407 million tons in 1984.[147] As food production expanded and per capita consumption increased, diets improved.[148] The dramatic improvement of rural income and diet won widespread rural support for the regime's reforms. This helped the regime recapture much of the rural support it had lost during the disastrous agrarian reforms of the late 1950s, which had led to poor harvests and massive starvation: Between 14 and 26 million people died of hunger between 1959 and 1961 alone.[149] The agrarian reforms introduced after 1979 simultaneously boosted food production and secured new political support for the regime in the countryside.

Although agriculture was the cornerstone of post-1978 reforms, the Deng regime also wanted to introduce new technology to spur economic growth in industry. To do this the government borrowed heavily from foreign creditors and encouraged foreign investment in China.[150] China's foreign debt increased from less than $5 billion in 1980 to $40 billion in 1988.[151] By 1988 foreign investors had committed $28.06 billion to projects in China.[152] The Chinese dictatorship borrowed heavily in the 1980s to promote exports. And to make its exports more competitive, the regime also devalued its currency, the yuan, slowly during the early 1980s, then sharply in 1986 after the Plaza Accords began depreciating the dollar. The yuan declined from 1.5 to the dollar in the late 1970s to 3.7 in 1986, 4.7 in 1989, 5.22 in 1990, and 5.3 in 1991.[153]

The regime's strategy of using borrowed money, foreign investment, and currency devaluations to promote export-oriented industrial growth proved very successful. Chinese exports to the United States increased from $9.7 billion in 1978 to $52.5 billion in 1989, and its overall foreign trade grew from $20.5 billion in 1978 to $111.7 billion in 1989.[154]

In addition to its foreign economic policies, the regime also adopted new domestic budgetary policies to promote growth. In 1979 it increased government spending and began running budget deficits, which grew from zero in 1978 to 50 billion yuan annually by 1990.[155] To keep its deficits from growing too large the regime cut military spending in half. Defense spending fell from 20.0 percent of the budget in 1979 to 12.0 percent in 1985 and to 8.2 percent in 1987.[156] In 1985 the army was cut by 1 million men, or 25 percent, and the regime planned to cut between three hundred thousand and five hundred thousand more in 1989. In the wake of Tiananmen Square, however, the regime reversed course and increased military spending.[157] Deficit spending and budget cuts thus made it possible for the regime to increase spending on products designed to promote economic growth.

At the outset Deng hoped that these steps would result in rapid growth and higher incomes.[158] "If by the end of the century we can achieve a GNP per capita of $1,000, we will have become well off," he said.[159] Economic growth between 1978 and 1984, when China's economy grew as fast as any in the world, promised to make Deng's aspirations a reality.[160] But after 1985 economic and then political problems emerged, threatening to derail economic growth and destroy the regime.[161]

Although agrarian reform led to increased food production, grain production leveled off in 1984 even as the population continued to grow by 15 million a year, this despite China's stringent policies holding each family to a one-child limit.[162] Food production increased again in 1992, but food prices rose anyway.[163] Rising agricultural prices were good for farmers, increasing their incomes and shrinking the gap between rural and urban incomes, which closed from 1 to 4.6 in 1978 to 1 to 3.1 in 1987.[164] But rising food prices were not good for the government because its own food purchases became more expensive, which contributed to growing budget deficits, and because rising prices contributed to inflation.[165]

Inflation in China gathered speed in the mid-1980s, reaching double-digit annual rates in 1985 and rising to 28 percent annually by 1989.[166] In addition to rising agricultural prices, the influx of money and credit into the economy from foreign loans, foreign investment, and heavy government spending greatly increased the money supply and fueled price increases.[167] Inflation, then, was largely a by-product of the regime's rapid-growth reform policies.[168]

In China the discriminatory effects of inflation were hardest on urban residents, particularly on those who received fixed government salaries. In 1987 the real incomes of one-fifth of urban households had declined, and by 1988 inflation had reduced incomes for more than half of these households.[169] As one Shanghai worker complained, "I wish we could go back to Mao's day. At that time, we had no inflation and we were guaranteed a certain living standard. Now I can hardly afford to feed my family."[170]

To check rising inflation the government implemented austerity measures in 1986, curbing bank loans, raising interest rates, rationing food for urban residents, raising taxes, and cutting spending to reduce government budget deficits.[171] In August 1986 a state-run enterprise was forced into bankruptcy, the first in China since 1949.[172] But although austerity programs contained inflation, they did not eliminate it, resulting instead in stagflation, which resulted in additional problems, particularly for the country's urban residents.[173] "The austerity programme . . . did not yield the desired results: [It] led to stagflation rather than stabilization," wrote Marie-Claire Bergere. "Thus, besides being deprived of the security and guarantees they had enjoyed . . . the urban blue- and white-collar workers now also saw the benefits they had received from the [initial] economic reform (higher salaries and more bonuses) threatened. Discontent and unrest spread."[174]

The problems associated with reform—inflation and then austerity programs—were keenly felt by urban residents. "As early as mid-1985, public opinion polls began registering a slight downturn in popular enthusiasm for reform," Richard Baum noted. "By early 1986 . . . only 29 percent of urban residents surveyed felt the reforms provided equal opportunity for all."[175]

When students assembled in Tiananmen Square on April 16, 1989, to mourn the death of Hu Yaobang and again on May 16 to welcome Soviet leader Mikhail Gorbachev, they were able to rally urban blue- and white-collar workers to their calls for greater democracy.[176] A student-worker alliance was forged when the All-China Federation of Trade Unions announced its support for the student movement on May 19.[177] This Chinese version of the South Korean *minjung* was possible in 1989, unlike in earlier years, because students, workers, and white-collar professionals all experienced economic problems as *urban* residents, problems they blamed on the reforms implemented by the Communist Party.[178]

Initially, the regime negotiated with demonstrators camped out in Tiananmen Square and tried to persuade them to depart. But determined hunger strikes, mounting protest, and the movement's "near universal support in major urban areas, including support by workers, citizens and many party members, constituted a direct threat to party rule."[179] The regime declared martial law on May 30 and sent troops into Beijing.[180] But with massive nonviolent protests blocking their progress toward Tiananmen Square, the troops balked at using force and withdrew on May 22–23.[181] Faced with humiliation and political defeat, hard-liners around Deng purged their opponents from the party, regrouped the regime's military forces, and assaulted central Beijing on June 3–4, clearing the square. The government had reasserted its authority, killing between 1,000 and 2,600 people in the process.[182] Tiananmen became the regime's Kwangju. "This was a test," Deng said a few days later, "and we [the regime] passed."[183]

The dictatorship "passed" its most serious political test for a variety of reasons.[184] First, the urban *minjung* in China was weaker and smaller than its counterparts in South Korea and Taiwan. Although China's urban population, which constituted the social base of this alliance, was large in absolute terms—297 million in 1990—it was small in relative terms, comprising only 26 percent of the total population.[185] Despite recent growth and considerable illegal migration from the countryside during the 1980s—there may have been as many as 80 million illegal or transient sojourners living in China's cities—the urban population was smaller than it might have been because the regime used extensive migration controls in the 1950s and 1960s to prevent urban growth and sent tens of millions of city dwellers to live in rural areas during the 1960s.[186] As a result, the *minjung*'s social base was smaller than comparable movements in South Korea and Taiwan, where rapid growth had already emptied rural populations into the cities. As Singapore's Prime Minister Lee Kuan Yeuw observed, "students in China had been watching on Chinese TV . . . the almost nightly demonstrations of 'people power' in the Philippines and South Korea and forgot that China was a very different country."[187] China was "different" in part because its urban population was not as large.

Second, the regime was able to retain widespread support among the rural population during the 1989 crisis. The regime's agrarian reform had provided real benefits to rural farmers, who had seen rural poverty decline and their incomes increase relative to those of urban residents, who they regarded as more privileged. Although rural farmers also experienced problems with rapid growth, the number of people living at or below subsistence levels declined from 28 percent of the population in 1980 to only 10 percent in 1989.[188] Economic growth during the decade preceding the events of Tiananmen Square helped secure the loyalty of the rural population.

The fact that the regime had established itself as a revolutionary party in the 1920s and again during the Cultural Revolution of the 1960s and 1970s and had "defeated" foreign imperial powers—Japan during World War II and the United States during the Korean War—and its domestic rival (the Nationalists) during the Chinese civil war contributed to its reservoir of political support, as did the fact that the regime had 48 million party members in place to remind the populous of this heritage.[189] In these respects the Communist regime resembled dictatorships in Mexico, Cuba, and Taiwan. During the crisis the regime could eventually rely on the People's Liberation Army, which had "deep rural roots."[190] In the contest between the urban, student-worker opposition, and the regime's rural, peasant-military supporters, the latter weighed more heavily in the balance. After the revolt the regime moved to shore up its support in the military, which had briefly balked during the crisis, by doubling the military budget between 1989 and 1994.[191]

Third, while the regime's assault on its domestic opposition provoked international censure, it was able to count on continued foreign political and economic support. Unlike many other dictatorships in Southern Europe, Latin America, and East Asia, the great powers did not abandon China during its crisis. Indeed, foreign investment increased dramatically. Foreign firms made contracts to invest $77 billion between 1979 and 1991 but made contracts worth $251 billion during the next three years.[192] Because it received 17 percent of the *world's* total foreign direct investment, equal to one-third of all foreign investment going to developing countries, the regime was rewarded, not punished, for its crackdown on dissent.[193]

Japan continued to provide aid, loans, grants, and investments after Tiananmen Square, the United States continued trading with and investing in China, and in October 1990 the European Community lifted its nonmilitary sanctions on China, in part to reward China for its support of U.N. resolutions against Iraq.[194] Taiwan increased its investment in China to $20 billion by 1993 and permitted residents to visit China as tourists, which provided the Communist regime with an important source of hard-currency earnings.[195]

Finally, by adopting what some observers have called "Market-Leninism" or what Deng called "communism as basis, capitalism as means," a pragmatic approach that combines the defense of dictatorship with economic reform, the regime was able to create and maintain rapid economic growth.[196] As in Taiwan, rapid growth was a problem, but it was also a solution to political problems encountered by both regimes in the late 1980s.

North Korea

As in China, one-party Communist regimes in North Korea and Vietnam also survived economic and political crises during the late 1980s and early 1990s. Although banners in North Korea proclaimed, "We have nothing to envy in the world," Kim Il Sung's regime confronted several serious economic and political problems.[197] According to Barry Gills, in 1990 "the North Korean economy suffered perhaps its worst year since the Korean War. GNP declined nearly 4 percent and per capita GNP by 5.25 percent. External trade declined by 4 percent, the trade deficit stood at some $600 million and external debt grew to $7.86 billion," up from $3 billion in 1982.[198]

In addition to these economic problems, which were largely related to growing debt and frequent defaults—the North Korean regime had been forced to default on its debts in 1976 and again in 1987—the regime also faced political problems as former allies embraced old foes.[199] In June 1990 Soviet leader Mikhail Gorbachev visited South Korea, a "betrayal" comparable to Mao Tse-tung's 1972 meeting with Richard Nixon.[200] Changing superpower relations undermined the diplomatic support that had long been provided to the North Korean regime, much as it did for the dictatorship in Taiwan. Declining Soviet and Chinese support for North Korea was significant because they had provided crucial military support and substantial economic aid to the regime during the 1950s and 1960s. Military intervention during the Korean War and $2.8 billion in foreign aid from China and the Soviet Union between 1945 and 1978 rescued the regime from defeat and laid the basis for considerable economic growth after the war.[201] The changing foreign policy environment in the 1980s weakened the regime at a time when the aging dictator Kim Il Sung was nearing the end of his life. After ruling North Korea since the late 1950s, Kim died on July 8, 1994.[202] But the Communist regime survived these economic and political problems and Kim's death, as power passed to his son, Kim Jong Il.

North Korea's self-imposed isolation has prevented scholars and journalists from studying its economic and political developments closely. It is clear, however, that the regime's continued survival was due to several historical and contemporary developments. Although economic problems became acute in the late 1980s, the regime managed to promote economic growth. National income increased 1.8 times between 1977 and 1984, raising per capita income to $900 by the mid-1980s, a figure that compared poorly with the incomes of South Korea and Taiwan but favorably with those of China ($300) and Vietnam ($150).[203] Income was equitably distributed, and half of the work force remained in agriculture.[204]

To ease the crisis the government opened the economy to limited foreign investment and trade in the 1990s.[205] Like Cuba, North Korea began promoting tourism for the first time to earn the foreign currency it needed to repay its debt, encouraged North Korean émigrés living in Japan to send home more of their earnings, and sent workers and soldiers abroad. North Korean military instructors were sent to more than a dozen countries, while construction workers were sent to Iran to erect apartment buildings in exchange for 1 million tons of oil.[206] The admission of North and South Korea to the United Nations in 1991 also made it easier for the regime to secure economic aid from international lending agencies.[207]

Although the death of a dictator can create a crisis for a regime based on singular leadership, as it did, for example, in Franco's Spain, Kim's death in 1994 did not precipitate any appreciable political crisis. The transfer of Kim's power to his son may have provided a solution to potential crisis, much as it did in Nicaragua under successive Somozas or in Taiwan under successive Chiangs. Perhaps hereditary dictatorship is effective politics in a setting in which dictatorship takes a patrimonial and corporatist family form and in which primogeniture is a widely shared cultural value.[208] Young Whan Kihl argued that this practice is "reminiscent of the feudalistic hereditary system of bygone eras . . . [an] archaic system of father-son leadership," while Bruce Cumings argued that it is a modern adoption of twentieth-century corporatism, not feudalism.[209] But in either case it is an effective political practice not only in North Korea, but also in India, Pakistan, and Bangladesh, where daughters have frequently assumed their fathers' political powers.

Moreover, North Korea, like "revolutionary" regimes elsewhere, garnered a certain legitimacy from having "defeated" foreign powers, Japan during World War II and the United States during the Korean War. It also "defeated" its domestic rival during the Korean civil war, though in this context "victory" meant averting annihilation and reestablishing the status quo ante. Partition, which created ongoing conflicts with South Korea and its superpower ally, may also have helped legitimize North Korea's continued rule, much as partition helped the government in Taiwan to portray itself as a defender of independence from its sibling state. Certainly the regime relies heavily on this theme, using terms like *chajusong* (self-reliance), *minjok tongnip* (national or ethnic independence), and *charip kyongje* (independent economy) to reinforce its claims as a radical republican state.[210]

It may also be that because South Korea now recognizes that unification would be a real economic burden, requiring it to spend billions on its neighbor, South Korea has allowed more extensive investment in and trade with the North. This may help the Kim Jong Il regime survive. For South and North Korea, partition increasingly seems to be an *economic* good rather than a *political* evil.[211] One scholar has argued "that both countries now fear reunification, the North because it would imply the victory of capitalism and the South because of the cost [from $200 to $500 billion over five to ten years]; the South's policy is now to avoid a collapse in the North which would make immediate reunification a possibility."[212]

Vietnam

Like North Korea, the Communist regime in Vietnam also faced a serious economic and political crisis in the mid-1980s. Although the Communists had forced U.S. troops to withdraw, defeated the regime in the south, and reunited the country in 1975, the country was exhausted after thirty-five years of war. To recover from the war the regime borrowed heavily from the Soviet Union, about $14.4 billion by 1990.[213] But the country needed much more than this to repair and rebuild its war-torn economy. A decade after the war ended Vietnam's per capita GNP was only $200, its population of 71 million was growing rapidly, food production was falling, and by 1988 "the government was forced to appeal to the international community for help because of near famine conditions in the north."[214]

At the Sixth Party Congress in 1986 the regime admitted that "numerous difficulties still beset the life of our people. . . . The countryside is running short of common consumer goods and medicines; housing, sanitary conditions and cultural life in many areas still leave much to be desired."[215] One critic within the party argued that "Vietnam hasn't advanced to socialism. Vietnam is the poorest and most backward country in the world at present."[216] General Vo Nguyen Giap told a rally, "My generation washed away the shame of losing our country's independence, and now it's your turn to wash away the shame of a poor and backward country."[217]

Vietnam's political problems were as serious as its economic problems. The country faced continuing hostility from Communist China. China had skirmished with Vietnam in a 1979 border war and opposed Vietnam's 1978 invasion and occupation of Cambodia, which had deposed the brutal Khmer Rouge regime, an ally of China. These wars meant that the regime continued to spend heavily on the military, making it difficult to devote its scarce resources to economic reconstruction. Vietnam also faced continuing hostility from the United States, which had imposed economic sanctions and withheld diplomatic recognition pending resolution of their dispute over the 2,273 U.S. soldiers listed as missing in action during the war.[218]

To address these problems the regime initiated a series of economic reforms and diplomatic initiatives at the December 1986 party congress. The party appointed Nguyen Van Linh, a reformer who had earlier been kicked off the Politburo, as general secretary. Like Gorbachev in the Soviet Union, Linh promoted *doi moi* and *cong khai,* or "renovation" and "reform," a Vietnamese form of perestroika and glasnost.[219] In the Vietnamese context this meant promoting agrarian reform—allowing farmers to leave collectives and farm on their own—opening the door to foreign investment and trade, and reducing restrictions on private economic activity in Ho Chi Minh City (Saigon), allowing it to become an engine of the country's economic growth.[220]

During the next few years economic reforms produced important results. After facing near famine in 1988, farmers increased food production dramatically, and in 1990 the government exported 1.3 million tons of rice, the country's first rice exports since the 1930s, becoming the third largest rice-exporting country in the world.[221] Attracted by Vietnam's large supply of skilled but cheap labor, foreign businesses, principally from Taiwan, Hong Kong, and France, invested $2.1 billion between 1988 and 1991.[222] Ho Chi Minh City also began growing rapidly, recording a growth rate of 15 percent in the early 1990s, which increased the incomes of urban residents dramatically.[223]

Vietnam also took new diplomatic initiatives after 1986. The regime began negotiating an end to its occupation of Cambodia and in 1989 announced that it would withdraw its fifty thousand troops.[224] This enabled it to reduce its heavy military spending and begin to repair its diplomatic relations with neighboring states. Vietnam also began working with U.S. officials to resolve disputes over U.S. servicemen missing since the war. These efforts were rewarded in February 1994, when President Bill Clinton lifted U.S. economic sanctions, and on July 11, 1995, the United States restored diplomatic relations with Vietnam.[225]

Economic reform and diplomatic initiatives helped the regime weather its difficult economic crisis. But other political resources and developments also contributed to its survival. Like the traditions of Communist parties in Cuba, North Korea, and China and of nationalist parties in Mexico and Taiwan, Vietnam's radical republican tradition dated back to the 1920s, and the regime could boast of its charismatic leaders, living (Vo Nguyen Giap) and dead (Ho Chi Minh). By defeating foreign opponents during long wars— Japan, France, the United States, China, Kampuchea/Cambodia—and domestic rivals, the regime had established its credentials as a nationalist party defending Vietnamese independence, a position that helped it secure considerable loyalty. Like Cuban troops fighting in Africa, the Vietnamese troops fighting in Cambodia were seen by some sectors of the domestic population as fighting for a worthy cause, in this case for an end to the Khmer Rouge dictatorship that had murdered millions of its own citizens.[226]

Of course, many opponents of the regime fled the country after the Communists reunited the country by force in 1975. But the flight of Vietnamese boat people during the 1970s and 1980s probably helped strengthen the regime, much as successive flights of Cuban boat people indirectly assisted the Cuban dictatorship. Because many urban workers and intellectuals fled the country, the base of domestic opposition to the regime—the *minjung* that emerged during this period in South Korea, Taiwan, and China—was reduced. The fact that the Vietnamese regime took steps to improve economic conditions for its urban residents probably reduced or mitigated opposition from this important quarter. Moreover, after fleeing their homeland, Vietnamese émigrés living in the United States sent remittances to their families in Vietnam and then returned as tourists in the 1980s and early 1990s. Income from émigré remittances and from tourism provided a valuable source of hard currency for the regime, much as it did for governments in Cuba and elsewhere.[227] In this regard the regime in Vietnam most closely resembled Castro's Cuba. For many of the same reasons both governments survived domestic crises and the fall of communism in other countries.

eight

CRISIS AND REFORM IN THE SOVIET UNION

The Soviet Union was beset by a series of problems during the 1970s and 1980s. Agricultural, industrial, and military crises led first to economic stagnation, or *zastoi*, and then to decline.[1] "Between 1980 and 1985, the rate of economic growth [in the Soviet Union] appears to have fallen to zero," one economist observed.[2] The standard of living in the Soviet Union fell from fifty-sixth place in the world in 1976 to seventieth in 1982.[3] Soviet leader Mikhail Gorbachev admitted, "By the beginning of the 1980s, the [Soviet Union] found itself in a state of severe crisis which embraced all spheres of life."[4]

The Soviet crisis confronted its leaders with their most serious challenge since World War II. Prime Minister Nikolai Ryzhkov compared the situation to the crisis "following the October Revolution in 1917, when national income was cut by 50 percent and industrial production by 80 percent" and to the crisis during World War II "when the occupation of a large segment of Soviet territory resulted in a 34 percent decrease in national income and a 23 percent decrease in industrial production."[5]

The Soviet crisis was shared by Communist regimes in Eastern Europe because their Soviet-installed dictatorships suffered from many of the same ills plaguing the Soviet Union and because their collective political, economic, and military institutions were linked to those of the Soviet Union. The Communist Information Bureau, which was created in 1947, provided the political link between the Communist Party in the Soviet Union and Communist parties in Eastern European regimes. The Council for Mutual Economic Assistance (CMEA or COMECON), which was established in 1949 as a Soviet response to the U.S. Marshall Plan, organized economic relations among Communist states.[6] And the Warsaw Pact, which was created in 1955 to counter the formation of NATO, integrated the armies of member countries under a single military command.[7]

These institutions, which were created and dominated by the Soviet Union, extended and consolidated Soviet authority and Communist government in Eastern Europe. During the postwar period these institutions helped the Soviet Union create a pro-Soviet bloc in the United Nations and extract economic resources from East Germany but also from other Eastern European countries.[8] Poland, for example, "was forced to hand over all [industrial] plants that had even the least connection with Hitler's war machine."[9] When domestic opposition movements emerged to challenge Communist authority, these collective institutions were used to rationalize Soviet military intervention in East Germany (1953), Hungary (1956), and Czechoslovakia (1968).

But although collective institutions initially provided important political, economic, and military benefits to the Soviet Union, they became increasingly burdensome. By the 1970s the Eastern European countries, not the Soviet Union, received most of the economic benefits from these institutional affiliations.

The 1973 oil crisis was the turning point for economic relations between the Soviet Union and Eastern Europe. Because the Soviets had agreed in 1971 to supply Soviet oil to Eastern European countries at fixed prices for five years, Eastern European countries obtained cheap oil from the Soviet Union as world oil prices climbed.[10] The Soviets, in effect, were forced to subsidize their Eastern European partners.[11]

Not only did the Soviets provide oil subsidies, they extended loans and economic and military subsidies to their allies in Eastern Europe and around the world. The Soviets, for example, paid four times the world price for Cuban sugar to assist Castro's regime during the 1960s and 1970s, a subsidy that grew larger as world sugar prices fell in the late 1970s. Between 1979 and 1987 the Soviet Union provided nearly $29 billion in economic and military aid to Vietnam and Cambodia, $11 billion to Cuba, $9 billion to Afghanistan, $8 billion to Angola, and $3 billion to Nicaragua.[12] One U.S. study found that the "costs of Soviet empire rose from $18 billion in 1971 to $24 billion in 1976 and about $41 billion in 1980, an annual growth rate of nearly 9 percent for the decade."[13]

By 1980 the cost of maintaining Soviet power exceeded the benefits it received from its allies. As former President Richard Nixon observed, "Every one of the Soviet Union's 'colonies' is a drag and has to be subsidized."[14] Evidence of the changing relations between the Soviet Union and its Eastern European allies could be seen in a comparison of per capita income figures. In 1984 Soviet citizens earned a per capita income of $7,120, whereas income in East Germany was $9,800 and in Czechoslovakia was $8,250.[15]

Because dictatorships in the Soviet Union and Eastern Europe were linked by shared institutions, crisis for one became crisis for all. Soviet efforts to address domestic problems in the late 1980s, which resulted in a reduction of Soviet military spending in Eastern Europe, transferred Soviet problems to Eastern Europe and triggered a fatal crisis for Communist regimes in 1989. The collapse of Eastern European Communist regimes, in turn, contributed to a coup and collapse of Communist rule in the Soviet Union in 1991. Reciprocating crises resulted in democratization for both regions. But in the Soviet Union, Yugoslavia, and Czechoslovakia democratization also led to the dissolution of central authority, the division of states, and the creation of multiple republics in their stead.

The crisis, which Gorbachev said "embraced all spheres of life" and would engulf one-party dictatorships in the Soviet Union and Eastern Europe, first emerged during the 1970s, when Soviet grain harvests withered. Crop failures in 1972, 1974–75, 1977, and 1979–82 created a series of problems for the regime.[16]

The collapse of Soviet agriculture can be traced to agricultural policies dating back to the 1930s. During the 1920s and 1930s the Soviet dictatorship under Joseph Stalin forced farmers to join large-scale, state-owned collective farms. The government seized land without compensating owners, used collectives to requisition food supplies without paying producers, and used the agricultural resources it obtained to finance rapid urban industrialization.[17] Collectivization was an extremely disruptive process. The regime killed or deported farmers who resisted the seizure of land or goods, and farmers slaughtered their livestock rather than surrender them to the state. "Thus the cattle herd which totalled 70.5 million head in 1928 before collectivization was cut to 38.4 million after collectivization. The pig herd and the stock of horses were actually cut by more than half . . . [and] the stock of sheep and goats was reduced to a third of what it had been."[18] As a result, agricultural output plummeted, the Soviet Union became the world's foremost grain importer, and many regions experienced widespread famine.[19]

After World War II the Khrushchev regime invested heavily in agriculture and increased the wages of workers on collective farms to increase yields and expand grain harvests. The grain harvest doubled from 81 to 171 million metric tons between 1950 and 1966 (a crop still smaller than Russia's harvest in 1913), and peasant incomes doubled between 1956 and 1966.[20] But after 1966 harvests did not regularly exceed these levels, and peasant incomes remained low, only about half of incomes earned by urban workers.[21] Because low rural incomes provided workers with few incentives, crop yields remained poor. Between 1966 and 1970, for example, Soviet wheat yields were only one-half of U.S. yields, corn only one-third, and potatoes only one-fifth of yields in the United States, particularly disturbing given the fact that the Soviet and American populations were roughly the same size.[22]

As Soviet harvests stagnated, the growing population increased its demand for food. Harvest failures in the 1970s and 1980s and the resulting food shortages thus created a series of problems for the regime. First, the government had to import grain to cover its food deficits. Whereas the regime had exported 5.1 million metric tons of grain in 1971, it imported 10.5 in 1972, 19.0 in 1973, 22.5 in 1979, 33.0 in 1980, and 40.0 in 1981, an eightfold increase.[23] The cost of Soviet food imports quadrupled between 1974 and 1981, rising from $5.1 billion to $20.9 billion.[24] Massive grain imports contributed to growing trade deficits and drained the government's foreign currency reserves but did not greatly alleviate chronic food shortages.[25]

Second, the regime was forced to spend more to keep urban food prices low. Like dictatorships in Latin America, the Soviet regime was determined to keep urban food prices low, both because it had long provided this benefit and because it wanted to prevent the social unrest and inflation associated with price increases. Food subsidies were thus increased. In 1980, for example, the government spent 35 billion rubles ($50 billion) and by 1986 nearly twice as much, 57 billion rubles ($97 billion), or 13 percent of its budget.[26] Increased government spending on food subsidies during the 1970s and 1980s contributed further to government budget deficits, which quadrupled from 13.9 billion rubles in 1985 to 58.8 billion rubles in 1990.[27]

Third, food shortages encouraged domestic producers and consumers to behave in ways that undermined the government's system of food rationing. During the 1970s and 1980s farmers began withholding more of their produce from the government, largely because the regime did not greatly increase farm prices or farm incomes despite widespread shortages and rising world prices. Farmers began selling a growing share of their crops through unofficial or "black" markets that sold goods for higher prices.[28] This decreased the supply of low-priced food available in government stores. As a result, consumers either had to wait in long lines to purchase food that was low-cost but in short supply in the government stores or buy food that was expensive but readily available on the black market. Actually, they did both. When low-priced food was available in state-run stores, they bought more than they needed, hoarding it, and this created scarcity even when food supplies were plentiful. One survey found that 57 percent of consumers were "stocking up" on products for future use.[29] When the food they needed was not available in government stores, they purchased high-priced food on the black market. Although the incomes of rural farmers rose and urban residents had access to more goods, this two-track system created resentment and contributed to inflation. It caused resentment because urban residents spent long hours or much of their incomes to purchase food. It led to inflation because consumers bid up prices in the unofficial markets, particularly in the big cities, where food prices were typically three to five times higher than in rural areas.[30] The emergence of a two-track food system undermined government authority, fueled inflation, and contributed to growing resentment among urban consumers.

The agricultural crisis that first emerged in the early 1970s was compounded by a growing military crisis. During the 1970s the regime increased already high levels of military spending and in 1979 began waging war in Afghanistan. But massive defense spending and military intervention created domestic economic and foreign policy problems for the regime.

During the Cold War the Soviet Union spent heavily to defend its sphere of influence and maintain its status as a military and political superpower. How much it spent is the subject of intense debate. According to Ruth Sivard, the Soviets spent $4.6 trillion on the military between 1960 and 1987, or between 12 and 15 percent of its annual GNP, a figure commonly used by analysts in the late 1980s.[31] But more recently, some analysts have argued that the Soviets spent much more, as much as 20 to 28 percent of GNP.[32] By comparison, the United States spent between 6 and 8 percent of its GNP on the military during the Cold War.

Whatever the actual amount, the Soviets spent heavily on the military and spending grew during the late 1970s, at a time when U.S. officials reduced military spending as a percentage of GNP after the end of the Vietnam war.[33] The growing intensity of war in Afghanistan and renewed U.S. military spending under the Reagan administration further increased Soviet spending in the early 1980s.

Cold War military spending enabled the Soviet regime to maintain a large occupation army in Eastern Europe, assist Communist governments fighting wars in Latin America (Nicaragua against contras and Cuba in Angola and Ethiopia), in Africa (Angola, Mozambique, and Ethiopia), and Asia (Vietnam), and to aid non-Communist governments in the Middle East (Syria and Iraq) and North Africa (Libya and Algeria).[34] The sale of Soviet arms—assault rifles, tanks, helicopters, and jet aircraft—enabled the regime to obtain a substantial and growing income from allied and client states. Annual Soviet arms sales to non-Communist countries grew from $2.72 billion in 1975 to $10 billion in 1982 and amounted to $52.1 billion between 1974 and 1982.[35] During this period the Soviet Union overtook the United States, which sold $37 billion in arms, as the world's largest arms dealer.[36] Because they demanded hard currency as payment for most of their arms, the Soviets obtained valuable currency reserves that they used to purchase food and industrial imports.[37]

But although arms sales helped defray the regime's military costs, heavy defense spending did not provide domestic economic benefits or secure military advantages abroad. Domestically, heavy military spending absorbed scarce supplies of capital, skilled labor, and natural resources, diverting these resources from other sectors of the economy. As a result, military spending retarded economic growth and contributed to stagnation and decline.[38] Gorbachev later said that increased military spending during the Afghan war and the renewed arms race with the United States "exhausted our economy."[39]

It also became apparent during the 1980s that massive military spending had not enabled the Soviets to produce weapons that could compete with U.S. and Western European arms on battlefields in the Middle East or secure victory against mujahedin rebels in Afghanistan. In 1982, for example, during an air battle over Lebanon, Israeli pilots flying U.S. and French jets shot down eighty Soviet-produced planes flown by Syrian pilots but lost none of their own.[40] Likewise, in competitions with Western tanks Soviet T-62 battle tanks did not perform nearly as well.[41] In Afghanistan mujahedin insurgents armed with U.S. Stinger ground-to-air missiles fired 340 of them in combat, downing 269 Soviet aircraft. Introduced in late 1986, the Stinger missiles helped the Afghan rebellion and ultimately made Soviet military victory impossible.[42] In 1987 Mathias Rust, a West German youth, piloted his Cessna through Soviet air defenses and landed his plane on Red Square, the center of Soviet power.[43]

The poor performance of Soviet arms was dramatically underscored during the 1991 Persian Gulf War, when the U.S.-led coalition crushed Iraqi forces supplied with Soviet arms, destroying four thousand Soviet-made tanks in the process. The failure of Soviet weaponry in the Gulf War led some Soviet military planners to conclude that the Soviet military model was "obsolete."[44] As Soviet Marshal Dmitry Yazov admitted, "What happened in Kuwait necessitates a review of our attitude toward the [Soviet Union's] entire defense system."[45] Soviet arms had greater success in southern Africa, where Cuban and Angolan forces using Soviet arms were able to compete effectively with South Africa's armies. But in this contest South Africa was prevented by embargo from obtaining more advanced U.S. and Western European arms.

While the force of Soviet arms prevented countries in Eastern Europe and, for a time, Afghanistan from exiting the Soviet sphere of influence, they did not prevent others from disengaging. Yugoslavia and China departed in the 1940s and 1950s, and Egypt severed its military ties with the Soviets in the early 1970s. These developments eroded Soviet influence around the world.

War in Afghanistan

The problems associated with heavy military spending were, of course, exacerbated by the Soviet Union's war in Afghanistan. Until 1973 Afghanistan was ruled by Mohammed Zahir Shah's constitutional monarchy.[46] Although the monarchy received about $2.5 billion in economic and military aid from the Soviet Union between 1956 and 1978 and $533 million in economic aid from the United States in the same period, both superpowers regarded Afghanistan as a "buffer state," a nonaligned state between competing Soviet and U.S. spheres.[47] But a 1973 coup by Shah's cousin, Mohammed Daoud Khan, who abolished the monarchy, suppressed Islamic dissent and arrested domestic Communists, led to a 1978 coup by the People's Democratic Party of Afghanistan followed the coup of 1973. Led by Hafizullah Amin, the Communists took power and then attacked their Islamic opponents and members of a dissident faction within the Communist Party.[48] These events effectively moved Afghanistan into the Soviet sphere and provoked domestic opponents into armed rebellion.[49] Although the Soviets welcomed Afghanistan's entry into their sphere of influence, they did not approve of Amin's attack on Communists within his own party, many of whom had close ties with the Soviet Union, and they worried that Amin's attacks on the non-Communist opposition would provoke an Islamic rebellion like the one that had just overthrown the shah in neighboring Iran.[50] So the Soviets took two steps. First, on December 24, 1979, Soviet agents assassinated Amin to consolidate a Communist government under the pro-Soviet Babrak Karmal.[51] Second, on the same day, they sent troops into the country to destroy the domestic, non-Communist opposition.[52] Soviet leader Leonid Brezhnev defended the execution of Amin and invasion of Afghanistan, claiming that "to have acted otherwise would have meant leaving Afghanistan a prey to imperialism . . . to watch passively the origination on our southern border of a . . . serious danger to the security of the Soviet state."[53] The East German ambassador in Kabul told the American chargé d'affaires in 1979 that "if the Soviet Union allowed a pro-Soviet communist government in a border state to collapse, it would have an unsettling effect on other border states within the Soviet orbit."[54]

Soviet military forces in Afghanistan grew rapidly in strength, from 350 in 1978 to 7,000 on the eve of the 1979 coup and to 105,000 troops by 1981. Soviet forces peaked at about 115,000 in 1984.[55] The Soviet war effort cost about $5 billion a year, an expense that "averaged 50 times more than [annual expenditures] . . . during the previous 25 years."[56] But the large Soviet military deployment failed to crush the anti-Communist opposition. Counterinsurgency specialists estimated that Soviet military strength was "far short of the minimum (about 500,000) . . . necessary to mount a serious military challenge to the resistance."[57] As a result, the war dragged on until February 1989. During a decade of war 15,000 Soviet troops were killed and 37,000 wounded, while it is estimated that perhaps 1 million Afghans died, and between one-fifth and one-quarter of the Afghan population became refugees.[58] In economic terms the Soviets nearly exhausted their reserves of gold and diamonds to finance the war, spending at least 60 billion rubles, close to $100 billion.[59]

In addition to the human and economic costs of war, the Soviets paid a political price for invasion. President Carter condemned it as the "greatest threat to peace since the Second World War" and took steps to increase U.S. military spending, an initiative that was soon expanded by the Reagan administration. The U.S. decision to aid the mujahedin with money and weapons, amounting to $1 billion a year between 1986 and 1989, helped the rebels enormously. Along with money from other sources, the mujahedin rebels were able to resist and then stalemate the Soviet armies.[60] The war also cost the Soviets Third World political support. The U.N. General Assembly annually voted in overwhelming numbers—104 to 18 in 1980—against Soviet intervention, demanding "the immediate, unconditional and total withdrawal of foreign troops" from Afghanistan.[61] In the Soviet Union the war became increasingly unpopular, leading to widespread disaffection with the government's foreign policy. *Pravda*, the Communist Party newspaper, "reported that most of the 'thousands' of letters it had received asked the simple question, 'When is it going to end?'"[62]

The Soviet army's inability to defeat the Afghan resistance, which became apparent during the early 1980s, created a number of serious problems for the regime. Compared with the military defeats of dictatorships in Portugal, Greece, and Argentina, the defeat of the Soviet Union in Afghanistan was more damaging given the substantial Soviet investment in the conflict.

Economic Crisis in the Soviet Union

A series of economic problems added to the onset of agricultural problems in the 1970s and military problems in the early 1980s, contributing to mounting foreign debt, growing domestic budget deficits, and rising inflation.

During the early 1970s the regime began importing goods from non-Communist countries to increase the supply of food and consumer goods and to modernize industry.[63] Although heavy imports resulted in a $4 to $5 billion trade deficit in 1975, the government was able to reduce and contain trade deficits by increasing its exports of arms, oil, and gold.[64] Rising oil and gold prices during the 1970s increased export earnings from these commodities.[65] Even so, the regime began borrowing from the West to cover its trade deficits.[66] Soviet foreign debt grew from $6.3 billion in 1975 to $11 billion by 1980.[67] After 1980 oil and gold prices began to fall. Between 1980 and 1985 oil prices fell slowly, from $35 to $27 a barrel. But after 1985 they fell rapidly. Increased oil production in Saudi Arabia lowered the price of oil from $27 to $14 a barrel in 1986, while the U.S. dollar devaluation following the 1985 Plaza Accords reduced the value of the dollars earned by oil-exporting countries like the Soviet Union.[68] As a result, Soviet trade deficits increased, this despite efforts to increase the sale of arms, oil, and gold (its sales of gold increased from 55 tons in 1983 to 338 tons in 1986 and 270 tons in 1987). Soviet debt grew to $25.5 billion by 1984, $37.4 billion by 1986, and $50.6 billion by 1989.[69] As its own debts mounted, the Soviet Union tried to collect money it was owed by other socialist countries, some $34.8 billion in 1985, but evidently with little success.[70]

Although the Soviet Union's foreign debt was not as large as that of some Latin American countries, it nonetheless depleted Soviet gold stocks and currency reserves, which gradually weakened the value of the ruble, and the influx of money and credit from abroad contributed to inflation.[71]

As the government began importing goods in the 1970s, it increased government spending to stimulate the economy, to provide credit to industry, particularly construction, to keep consumer prices low, and, after 1979, to pay for the war in Afghanistan.[72] Because the government was reluctant to raise taxes or consumer prices, the government began running budget deficits in 1978.[73] Budget deficits averaged 18.0 billion rubles a year between 1980 and 1985, then grew rapidly to 47.9 billion rubles in 1986 and to 91.8 billion in 1989, averaging 67.0 billion rubles a year between 1986 and 1989.[74] Meanwhile, the national debt grew from 142 billion rubles in 1985 to 389 billion rubles by 1989.[75]

The budget deficits produced by heavy government spending during the 1980s, particularly after 1985, contributed to rising inflation. Inflation rose because government borrowing and deficit spending injected money and credit into the economy and because Soviet consumers spent their savings to purchase scarce goods.

Although the regime had borrowed money to import food, industrial machinery, and consumer products, these goods and housing nonetheless remained in short supply.[76] During the 1980s stores were only open on average for 115 days of the year. One study reported that of one thousand types of consumer goods, only twenty were regularly available in the state-run stores, and only ten percent of all goods were not subject to some form of rationing.[77] Because goods were often unavailable, consumers were forced to save their money. And when goods were available, they were often of poor quality. One Soviet official observed that "more than 2,000 times a year color television sets catch fire in Moscow alone. Together with them the houses burn."[78] When goods *were* available the government's subsidized prices allowed consumers to buy them cheaply. Consumers were in effect forced to save money, as they could choose only between inexpensive goods or no goods at all. As a result, Soviet consumers increasingly had money to spend but few places to spend it. On average Soviet workers saved 5.8 percent of their incomes in 1985 but 11.1 percent, or twice as much, in 1989.[79] The savings deposits of Soviet workers grew from 46.6 billion rubles in 1970 to 156.5 billion in 1980, 220.8 billion in 1985, and 457.0 billion in 1988.[80]

With "money to burn," consumers began to look for ways to spend it.[81] Increasingly, people began selling or reselling goods on black and informal markets, knowing that they could obtain prices two to three times higher than official state prices.[82] As a result, the prices of many goods rose sharply, and consumer savings, which were created by the government's supply and price policies, contributed to growing inflation *despite* the fact that supplies and prices of most goods were "controlled" by the government. Between 1981 and 1985 inflation rose annually at about 5.7 percent, but it grew to 7.3 percent in 1987, 10.5 percent in 1989, 53.6 percent in 1990, and exploded to 650–700 percent in 1991.[83] Inflation in the Soviet Union, as in other countries, undermined the standard of living for people whose incomes could not keep pace with higher prices. It also caused considerable resentment among people whose incomes *did* increase.

Political Crisis in the Soviet Union

The agricultural, military, and economic crises that accumulated in the 1970s and early 1980s combined in the early 1980s with a political crisis caused when aging Soviet leaders died in rapid succession. The political crisis began when Leonid Brezhnev, who had become general secretary of the Communist Party in 1964, died suddenly on November 10, 1982, after reviewing the annual parade celebrating the anniversary of the Bolshevik Revolution.[84] A political battle over his successor ensued. Brezhnev's chosen successor, Konstantin Chernenko, was passed over, and Yuri Andropov was selected as the new Soviet leader. But Andropov, already sixty-eight years old when he assumed the party leadership, suffered from poor health, and he died after a long illness on February 9, 1984, only fifteen months after taking power.[85]

A second political battle then erupted within the party. Andropov's chosen successor, Mikhail Gorbachev, who represented the young, reform-minded wing of the party, was passed over, and Brezhnev's old protégé, Chernenko, was chosen instead. But Chernenko, at seventy-two, the oldest general secretary ever to have assumed office, was also in poor health, and he died a year later, on March 10, 1985.[86] Mikhail Gorbachev, then fifty-four, assumed power the next day.[87]

But the political battles that preceded Gorbachev's installation did not end when he took power. In many respects the reforms he initiated to address accumulating crises intensified the battle for power among his political rivals. Although Gorbachev remained in power for six years, he eventually surrendered power not to one, but to many successors.

In the Soviet Union the crisis of succession, which began with Brezhnev's death in November 1982 and ended with Gorbachev's resignation in December 1991, was a decade-long political contest. Before Gorbachev took power the battle was waged within the Communist Party itself. But after he became general secretary the contest shifted, and the battle for power was waged increasingly in public, in the parliament, at the polls, and in the streets, particularly in the streets of the Soviet Union's constituent republics.

Gorbachev and Reform

After taking power in 1985 Gorbachev initiated a series of reforms designed to address the regime's accumulating crises. Some of these reforms were first discussed by Gorbachev's mentor, Yuri Andropov, who observed in 1982 that "there were many unresolved problems in the economy," admitting that there are "no fixed prescriptions for their resolution."[88] Like the Chinese Communist leadership in 1978, Soviet leaders were searching for "stepping stones across a stream." Gorbachev developed a series of reforms that he hoped would help the regime ford deep economic waters.

To overcome the Soviet Union's economic stagnation and to prevent it from falling behind the West, Gorbachev wanted to "accelerate" the economy, what he called *uskorenie,* and to promote growth.[89] This could only be done if the economy was "restructured," a process known now as perestroika. Because important sectors of the party, the government bureaucracy, the population at large, and the military opposed substantive reform, Gorbachev soon realized that he needed to mobilize political support for this "titanic job."[90] He did this by promoting political "openness," or glasnost, and limited democratization. "We shall not succeed with the tasks of perestroika if we do not firmly pursue democratization."[91] As he explained in 1987, "Restructuring will only spin its wheels unless the main actor—the people—is included in it in a thoroughgoing way."[92] For Gorbachev, democratization was "a guarantee against the repetition of past errors and consequently a guarantee that the restructuring process is irreversible."[93] The Soviet Union had no choice, he said. It "was either democracy or social inertia and conservatism."[94]

Of course, to revive the moribund economy the regime needed to increase the productivity of agriculture and of industry. The regime allowed farmers to lease land from the state, paid farmers more for the food contracted by the state, and allowed farmers to sell surplus food through unofficial markets at higher prices.[95] By giving farmers greater control and providing them with higher incomes, the regime hoped that agricultural reforms would spur food production. At the same time the regime tried to increase production in industry by introducing new technologies and machinery imported from abroad, cracking down on alcohol use and absenteeism, and giving managers and workers more control of industrial decisions.[96]

But these reforms had several unintended effects. First, agricultural reforms did not give farmers as much control of the land as did Chinese reforms, largely because the state's leasing arrangements did not eliminate collective agricultural arrangements. Nor did they greatly increase farm incomes, largely because farmers were still required to deliver the bulk of their crops to the state. Because productivity increases were further negated by distribution losses—40 percent of the country's fruit and vegetable crops and 25 percent of its grain rotted before they reached government shops or private markets—agricultural reforms produced few real gains.[97]

Second, although farm incomes did not greatly increase, reforms did increase the price of food for urban residents. So while urban industrial workers were asked to work harder, learn new skills, and increase production, their incomes were eroded by the rising cost of food, housing, and consumer goods. The government attempted to address rising costs by raising wages and increasing food subsidies to pay farmers more but also to keep urban food prices low. But wage increases did not improve worker productivity. Because many goods were still unavailable, workers banked their savings or bid up the price of goods that were available. The resulting inflation eroded the value of their savings and reduced the gains from higher wages. As a result, the reforms did not greatly increase the real incomes of industrial workers. Without higher real wages, workers had little incentive to work harder. And without the threat of unemployment to spur great effort, worker productivity did not greatly increase. Consumer goods thus continued to be of poor quality and in short supply.

The regime faced two difficult choices. It could raise farm incomes to increase food supplies, but higher farm incomes would raise urban food prices, erode urban incomes, and antagonize industrial workers. Alternatively, it could raise the real incomes of urban workers to increase industrial production, but the regime would have to suppress agricultural income and return to Stalinist agricultural policies to keep food prices low. This was not a desirable option, as declining agricultural incomes would further reduce food supplies, forcing the government to import more food and ration its distribution. So instead of choosing one option over the other, the regime tried to do a little of both, modestly increasing both farm incomes and the wages of urban workers. But this resulted in growing budget deficits and rising inflation without greatly increasing either food supplies or industrial production.

The regime considered ending its food subsidies, which would have raised farm income and increased urban food prices substantially, but feared that such a step would shatter its support in the cities. Evidently Gorbachev was not prepared to antagonize urban workers, as the Chinese regime had done with its agricultural reforms. China had been prepared to crush urban opposition by force, however, and Gorbachev was unwilling to provoke the urban opposition and then be forced to contain it.[98]

Although Gorbachev's reforms did not revitalize agriculture or industry, the regime was able to significantly reduce the burden of military spending and shift the resources devoted to it to the domestic civilian economy, a development that Gorbachev regarded as crucial to the success of perestroika.[99] In 1985 Gorbachev called for "restricting military potential within the bounds of reasonable sufficiency," and argued that the country should rely more on the collective security provided by the United Nations and other treaty arrangements and less on the force of Soviet arms.[100] During the next few years Gorbachev took three important steps to reduce and redirect military spending. First, he withdrew Soviet troops from distant theaters and negotiated an end to regional conflicts; second, he reduced military spending and the size of the Soviet forces as these conflicts eased; and third, he negotiated arms control agreements with the United States.

Gorbachev's first priority was to withdraw Soviet forces from Afghanistan.[101] The Soviet Politburo secretly decided on November 13, 1986, to withdraw Soviet troops by the end of 1988 because Soviet intervention failed to establish a durable Communist government capable of ruling on its own and because it was unable to defeat the mujahedin, who were assisted by the United States and its allies.[102] As the war dragged on, Gorbachev admitted, "counterrevolutionaries and imperialism have turned Afghanistan into a bleeding wound."[103]

Gorbachev took several steps to wind down the war and secure a diplomatic settlement. In May 1986 he replaced the Afghan leader Babrak Karmal with Mohammed Najibullah, whom he regarded as more amenable to Soviet pressure, recalled eight thousand troops to signal Soviet determination to withdraw completely, and began negotiating in earnest with the United States and the United Nations for an end to the war.[104] Because the United States did not take Soviet initiatives seriously, negotiations dragged on until February 8, 1988, when Gorbachev announced that he would withdraw all Soviet forces ten months after a U.N.-sponsored agreement was reached. Negotiations were then rapidly concluded, and on April 14, 1988, the Soviet Union, United States, Afghanistan, and Pakistan signed an agreement providing for a full Soviet withdrawal by February 15, 1989.[105]

Although Soviet troops departed, the war continued.[106] Najibullah's regime fought on, and the mujahedin, now without superpower support and divided into warring factions, could not defeat the regime until March 1992. And when they finally dislodged Najibullah, they could not consolidate power in a unified state. Today mujahedin groups continue to battle for control of Kabul and the rest of the country.[107]

While negotiating an end to Soviet intervention in Afghanistan, Gorbachev also began winding down Soviet commitments to military interventions elsewhere. In December 1988 the Soviet Union helped secure the withdrawal of Cuban troops, which were armed and financed by the Soviets, from Angola, and in February 1989 helped persuade Vietnam to withdraw from Cambodia.[108] This latter development helped ease Soviet relations with China, allowing it to reduce its military presence along the Soviet border with China.

In 1969 Soviet and Chinese troops had clashed along the frontier, and the Soviets thereafter had stationed five hundred thousand troops, or fifty-four divisions, along the Sino-Soviet border.[109] Gorbachev began negotiating with China in 1987 to reduce conflict in this region. In 1989 the Soviets agreed to cede to China a small island that had been the site of clashes in 1969, to open the border to trade, and to reduce its forces along the border by 40 percent, withdrawing two hundred thousand troops, while the Chinese also agreed to reduce their forces.[110] These developments eased tensions considerably, and in May 1989 Gorbachev traveled to Beijing for the first Sino-Soviet summit in thirty years, an event that coincided with the occupation of Tiananmen Square by opponents of the regime.[111]

As the Soviets withdrew their troops in large numbers from Afghanistan and the Chinese border, Gorbachev could then begin to reduce defense spending. Although military spending had been frozen in 1987, Gorbachev began to reduce spending in 1989.[112] The first cuts were modest, about 8.3 percent in 1989, but became more dramatic, reaching 14 percent in 1991.[113] Modest spending cuts were accompanied by massive troop reductions that cut the army by half a million to 4.5 million in 1989, a reduction that essentially demobilized troops returning from Afghanistan and the Chinese frontier.[114]

Along with spending cuts and troop reductions, the regime began converting defense industries for civilian use. Many defense industries already produced some consumer goods—for example, all the radios and televisions produced in the Soviet Union were manufactured by defense industries—but they began producing more consumer goods and fewer arms after 1989.[115]

While reducing military spending by withdrawing Soviet troops, Gorbachev also initiated arms control negotiations with the United States. Gorbachev wanted to wind down the nuclear arms race, which he regarded as costly and dangerous. In 1987 he told the Twenty-Seventh Congress that "nuclear weapons cannot be a means of achieving political, economic, ideological or any other goals," arguing that "disarmament [would promote] development."[116]

At a series of annual superpower summits—Geneva in 1985, Reykjavik in 1986, Washington, D.C. in 1987, Moscow in 1988, and Malta in 1989—Gorbachev pressed Presidents Ronald Reagan and George Bush to undertake serious arms control negotiations that would substantially reduce or eliminate intermediate-range, strategic long-range, and space-based nuclear weapons.[117] In Reykjavik, for example, Gorbachev proposed that the United States and the Soviet Union reduce by at least 50 percent their strategic arms, consisting of land-based missiles, sea-launched missiles, and heavy bombers, leading to their total elimination by the end of the century.[118] This kind of dramatic departure from the sluggish and incremental arms control negotiations of previous decades was regarded with astonishment and skepticism by U.S. officials. But as the retraction and reduction of Soviet military power became evident, the Reagan administration began negotiating in earnest. In 1987 the superpowers signed the INF treaty, which provided for the withdrawal and destruction of intermediate-range nuclear missiles based in Europe.[119] Although the number of nuclear missiles actually affected by this treaty was not significant, representing about 5 percent of the nuclear arsenal, it marked the first time the superpowers had agreed to reduce and eliminate a portion of their nuclear forces.[120] Although they did not address issues relating to space-based weapons or "Star Wars" defenses against nuclear weapons, they eventually concluded an agreement cutting strategic nuclear weapons, which came out of the revived Strategic Arms Reduction Talks (START II). This agreement, signed by Russian President Boris Yeltsin on January 3, 1993, stipulated that two-thirds of the nuclear arsenal of both sides would be destroyed by the year 2003.[121]

The two superpowers also began negotiating a reduction of conventional military forces in Europe. Gorbachev's unilateral decision on December 7, 1988, to withdraw fifty thousand Soviet troops and five thousand tanks from Eastern Europe in advance of these negotiations and to reduce substantially Soviet military forces across Europe signaled his commitment to major troop reductions and an end to the arms race.[122]

Like Soviet troop withdrawals from Afghanistan and the Chinese frontier, troop withdrawals from Eastern Europe were part of an overall reduction in Soviet military spending. But although Soviet troop reductions in Afghanistan and along the Chinese border had few repercussions—Communist regimes in Afghanistan and China stayed in power, at least for a time—they had enormous consequences for regimes in Eastern Europe. For these regimes, Soviet troop withdrawals represented a momentous change in Soviet foreign policy.

Throughout the Cold War Soviet leaders insisted that they had a right to intervene in Eastern Europe, by force if necessary, to maintain their sphere of influence. Their "right" to do so was recognized by the United States, which conceded a Soviet sphere at summits before and after the war, and this right was reiterated by successive invasions in 1953, 1956, and 1968. During the last intervention Soviet leaders argued that "the defense of socialism is the highest international duty," and that any threat to socialism in its sphere was "not only a problem of the people of the country in question, but a general problem and concern of all socialist countries."[123]

This assertion, known as the Brezhnev Doctrine, was the cornerstone of Soviet policy in Eastern Europe and also in Afghanistan. It was subsequently used to warn Polish Communists in March 1981 that they must take steps against the trade union Solidarity and "reverse the course of events and channel them in the right direction."[124] Implicit in the Soviet warning was the threat to use its own military forces to "reverse the course of events" if the Polish government failed to act. The Polish government's decision in December 1981 to declare martial law, ban Solidarity, and arrest its leaders was taken to preempt Soviet intervention.[125]

Soviet policy toward Eastern Europe changed after Gorbachev took power. In April 1985 Gorbachev argued that "every nation is entitled to choose its own way of development, to dispose of its fate, its territory, and its human and national resources."[126] Two years later Central Committee Secretary Yegor Ligachev told Hungarians, "every country looks for solutions independently, not as in the past. It is not true that Moscow's conductor's baton, or Moscow's hand is in everything. . . . every nation has a right to its own way."[127] At a speech in Yugoslavia, which had won the right to go its own way many years before, Gorbachev argued against "any interference in the internal affairs of other states under any pretext whatsoever," noting further that "all nations had a right to 'their own roads of social development.'"[128]

These statements reduced the Brezhnev Doctrine to rubble. At a press conference on October 25, 1989, reporters asked Soviet Foreign Minister Gennady Gerasimov whether the Soviet Union still adhered to the Brezhnev Doctrine. "No," he said. Instead, Gerasimov declared, new Soviet policy toward Eastern Europe would henceforth be called the "Sinatra Doctrine," because the American singer Frank Sinatra "had a song, 'I did it my way.' So every country decides in its own way which [economic and political] road to take."[129]

Even then, dictators in Eastern Europe and many U.S. officials did not believe that Soviet foreign policy had changed or that the Brezhnev Doctrine had been abandoned. After Gorbachev told East German dictator Erich Honecker in October 1989 that "everything in the world is changing. None of us can go on acting as we used to," Honecker did not believe him.[130] So the Soviets sent Alexander Yakovlev to Berlin to "reinforce the warning. 'They just couldn't believe that we'd let things take their course. I had to keep telling them that we wouldn't interfere,'" Yakovlev recalled.[131]

Like Honecker, many U.S. officials did not believe that Soviet policy had changed. As late as November 1989 Jeane Kirkpatrick, the U.S. representative to the United Nations during the Reagan administration, argued that "the Soviet Union is not going to withdraw from Europe."[132] But changed Soviet policy should not have taken Soviet allies and U.S. officials by surprise. It had been in the making for some time. The new Soviet foreign policy fatally undermined the Eastern European governments at a time when they had already been weakened by a shared economic and social crisis in the 1970s and 1980s.

nine

DEMOCRATIZATION IN EASTERN EUROPE AND THE SOVIET UNION

Communist Party dictatorships in Eastern Europe shared an economic crisis, a social crisis, and—as a result of changed Soviet foreign and military policy—a political crisis. When these crises combined in the fall of 1989, regimes in Eastern Europe simultaneously collapsed, bringing an abrupt end to forty years of Communist rule.[1]

The economic crisis for Eastern European dictatorships began in 1970, becoming acute first in Poland. In 1969–70 the Polish economy "entered into a new period of stagnation marked by the decline in the rates of growth of national income, wages and productivity of labor."[2] Poland's leader Wladyslaw Gomulka wanted to increase government investment in industry to spur economic growth. But the government could only increase spending if it cut some other costs. In November 1970 Gomulka reduced government subsidies for food, a move that sharply raised food prices just before Christmas.[3] Food riots and strikes broke out in Gdansk and other cities. The regime called out its troops, and forty-five workers were killed and nearly twelve hundred injured in the street battles that followed.[4] Gomulka was forced to resign soon after, and Edward Gierek was chosen to replace him as party secretary.[5]

Poland had one of the largest economies in Eastern Europe, and Gomulka had been one of the more popular dictators. He had acquired considerable popularity because he had introduced limited reform, prevented the collectivization of Polish agriculture, and deflected Soviet military intervention in 1956.[6] Because the economies of other Eastern European regimes were also stagnating and because their leaders were generally *less* popular than Gomulka, "the significance of the Polish riots and the toppling of Gomulka was not lost on the other regimes. They must not only raise living standards but make it obvious that they were doing so."[7]

Determined to revive moribund economies and stave off the discontent evidenced by the Polish strikes, Gierek and other Eastern European states borrowed heavily. Like Latin American dictators, Eastern European dictators planned to use borrowed money to modernize industry and expand exports, largely abandoning the import substitution policies of the postwar period.[8] Increased export earnings would allow them to repay debts and import technologies that would increase productivity and promote further growth.[9] Of course, the same reliance on foreign debt provoked the same debt crisis, first in Poland and *then* in Mexico and Argentina.[10]

During the 1970s foreign debt increased rapidly in all the Eastern European countries, with the exception of Albania. Poland's debt increased from $764.0 million in 1971 to $24.0 billion in 1980; Bulgaria's from $723.0 million to $3.0 billion; Czechoslovakia's from $160.0 million to $3.3 billion; East Germany's from $1.2 billion to $9.7 billion; Hungary's from $848.0 million to $7.1 billion; and Romania's from $1.2 billion to $8.6 billion.[11] The debt of Eastern Europe grew from $4.9 billion in 1970 to $56.0 billion in 1980, with Poland accounting for almost half of the total.[12] In most countries indebtedness continued growing in the 1980s. Poland's debt rose to $35.2 billion by 1988; East Germany's to $20.4 billion; Bulgaria's to $6.0 billion; Czechoslovakia's to $5.0 billion; Hungary's to $15.9 billion; and Yugoslavia's to $14.3 billion. Romania's debt fell to $1.1 billion, the result of a massive and extremely painful austerity program.[13]

Dictators in Eastern Europe borrowed heavily from Western European creditors, who were eager to loan money from the growing Eurodollar pool, but they also received important economic assistance from the Soviet Union in the 1970s.[14] Soviet assistance to Warsaw Pact dictatorships took the form of Soviet energy and military subsidies. Although world oil prices climbed after the 1973 OPEC oil embargo, the Soviet Union continued to deliver oil below its world market price. Although the Soviets raised its oil price after 1974, doubling it between 1974 and 1976 and quadrupling the price between 1976 and 1983, the price paid by Eastern European countries still remained well below the world price.[15] One economist estimated that the price benefits provided by the Soviet Union to its partners amounted to between $20 and $30 billion during the 1970s.[16]

The Soviets also provided military subsidies. The Soviet Union assumed most of the costs of maintaining Warsaw Pact armies in Eastern Europe. In 1979 it spent 13 to 15 percent of its GNP on Warsaw Pact defense, while most member countries devoted only 2 percent of their GNP on their militaries. East Germany spent more than most—6 percent—but this amounted to only half of the Soviet contribution.[17] By assuming most Warsaw Pact costs, the Soviet Union provided low-cost military security for Eastern European dictatorships, which enabled these countries to spend their money elsewhere.

In addition to its energy and military subsidies, the Soviet Union also provided modest amounts of credit, loans, and hard currency to ease economic problems in Eastern Europe. For example, the Soviets provided $350 million to the Polish government in 1971 and another $4 to $5 billion in 1980–81 to ease successive crises.[18]

Foreign debt and Soviet subsidies helped spur economic growth, for a time. Poland, like Brazil in the early 1970s, grew at a rapid pace, recording 6.6 percent annual growth between 1971 and 1975 (one economist maintained that the economy grew by as much as 10–12 percent beginning in 1972).[19] Other Eastern European countries also grew at respectable rates, ranging from 3.4 percent in Hungary and Czechoslovakia to 4.5 percent in Bulgaria and 6.2 percent in Romania.[20] But economic growth stalled and then stagnated after 1975.[21]

Several factors contributed to stagnation in the late 1970s. First, Eastern European countries began to pay more for Soviet oil. Although it was still cheaper than oil on the world market, Soviet price increases hurt the Eastern European economies, with Poland being especially hard hit.[22] Second, because governments used borrowed money to invest in industry and mismanaged much of the money they borrowed, they neglected investment in agriculture and failed to raise rural incomes.[23] As a result, agricultural production stagnated and countries had to import food in increasing quantities, particularly after 1975. Eastern Europe imported 9.5 percent of the grain it consumed in 1965, but this figure rose to 14.2 percent by 1980, a nearly 50 percent increase in grain imports.[24] Moreover, Soviet grain shortages and rising world food prices translated into higher prices for imports. The rising costs of imported fuel and food made it difficult for Eastern European regimes to increase investment and to continue to expand their economies.

As the Polish economy slowed, the government, now under Gierek, again tried to raise food prices. The 60 percent increase in food prices in July 1976, like the increase in 1970, was designed to reduce government food subsidies, which amounted to 20 percent of the national income in 1977, in order to purchase imported food, fuel, and technology.[25] But the government's effort to cut subsidies and raise food prices prompted renewed strikes and demonstrations. "Once again blood was shed and once again the price rise was rescinded, after the workers' ringleaders had been imprisoned."[26] These events led in September 1976 to the formation of an alliance between workers and intellectuals.[27] This Polish *minjung* would grow during the next few years, emerging under the banner of "Solidarity" in 1980.

Solidarity: The Polish *Minjung*

The alliance between Polish workers and intellectuals was first forged in 1976. Although the regime had rescinded proposed price increases in response to massive protests on June 25, it had then cracked down on dissent, attacking demonstrators, arresting and jailing strike leaders, and firing dissident workers.[28] In September, fourteen Polish intellectuals organized a Committee for the Defense of Workers (Komitet Obrony Robotnikow), or KOR.[29] "At this stage *solidarity* is more important than demands," Jacek Kuron, a KOR leader explained. (emphasis added)[30] "Solidarity is now an absolute necessity and self-defense by the community as a whole is indispensable. . . . Every infringement that passes without comment becomes an antecedent to another transgression. We become accomplices to every violation that we let pass in silence," KOR later argued.[31] By providing financial, medical, and legal aid to "all who have been subjected to victimization," KOR hoped to create and defend a space for dissent, which could then be used "to create social movements that would oblige the authorities to carry out the reforms."[32]

At the outset, workers and intellectuals pressed only for modest reform—workers for higher wages, intellectuals for an end to the regime's suppression of workers. Intellectuals and students made common cause with striking workers because they shared common economic problems. The price increases proposed by the regime in 1976 would have increased the cost of food 40 percent for workers and intellectuals alike.[33] Declining standards of living, which became widely recognized in 1975–76, and housing shortages affected both workers and intellectuals.[34] After the police murdered a KOR student activist, Stanislaw Jyjas, on May 7, 1977, and arrested many KOR activists a week later, it was the workers who came to their defense, forcing the regime to release the activists.[35] Reciprocal interventions in the defense of others strengthened the ties between working-class and intellectual communities during the next few years.[36] The relation between them was cemented in 1980, when striking workers at the Lenin shipyards in Gdansk invited KOR intellectuals to participate in the deliberations of the strike committee and its negotiations with the regime. As strike leader Lech Walesa explained, "The whole affair [at the shipyard] is based on the fact that KOR taught us this job. Now the pupils [workers] have surpassed the teachers [intellectuals]."[37] At Gdansk the worker-intellectual alliance moved beyond demands for higher pay. Their twenty-one-point program demanded that the government lift controls on independent media and recognize their rights to form an independent trade union and to strike without reprisal.[38] Solidarity, a federation of autonomous trade unions representing the worker-intellectual alliance, was registered and recognized in September 1980.[39]

Within a year 7 million people, or nearly a fifth of the Polish population, had joined Solidarity, and by October 1981 the union adopted a program calling for the creation of a "self-governing *republic*." (emphasis added)[40]

The consolidation of the worker-intellectual alliance in Solidarity, a Polish *minjung*, created a political crisis for the regime just as the country's economic condition took a sharp turn for the worse. Sharply rising interest rates in 1979, which remained high for several years, forced the regime to pay more to service its $24 billion debt. By 1980 debt service payments represented 96 percent of the income Poland earned from its exports.[41] At the same time, the growing wave of strikes, led after 1980 by Solidarity, forced the government to pay higher wages, which undermined its ability to produce low-cost goods for export markets. As a result of mounting foreign and domestic costs, the regime was forced to default on its debt on March 27, 1981. The onset of debt crisis and the growing strength of Solidarity weakened the Communist Party, which was increasingly "unable to organize the society, to get the country out of the disaster, even to defend the state."[42]

These developments alarmed Soviet leaders, and Brezhnev demanded that the regime ban free trade unions and resolve the crisis, threatening Soviet military intervention if it did not.[43] It was in this context that General Wojciech Jaruzelski declared martial law. Arguing that "a national catastrophe is no longer days but only hours away," Jaruzelski announced on December 13, 1981, the formation of a Military Council of National Salvation, proclaimed martial law on its behalf, and moved quickly to ban Solidarity and arrest and imprison thousands of its activists around the country.[44] The regime's December 1981 crackdown was Jaruzelski's Kwangju, a dramatic attempt to crush the democratic opposition by force.

After taking power in 1981, Jaruzelski's regime was able to raise prices and cut wages, reducing the standard of living to its 1970 level.[45] This helped the regime reduce domestic spending. The regime also allowed seven hundred thousand people to emigrate between 1981 and 1988, an exodus that helped the dictatorship, like regimes in Spain, Cuba, and Vietnam, reduce unemployment and export dissent, while creating an important source of foreign exchange from emigrant remittances.[46] The regime also persuaded foreign creditors to reschedule Polish debt and secured Soviet aid worth $4–5 billion, a payment made in return for the regime's defense of Communist rule.[47] As a result, the Polish military regime survived the 1981 crisis caused by foreign debt, domestic protest, and the threat of Soviet invasion. But its crackdown on domestic opponents and its capitulation to foreign powers—both to Western European economic powers and to Soviet military power—shredded the remaining political legitimacy of Communist Party rule in Poland. As in South Korea in 1980, the Polish military crackdown in 1981 contained but did not destroy the domestic opposition.

Similarly, the regime's economic measures deferred but did not solve the economic crisis. Foreign debt continued to grow, reaching $36.6 billion by 1986, a figure representing 47.6 percent of Poland's 1986 gross national product.[48] In 1988 Poland owed Western banks $3.23 billion in debt-service payments alone.[49] Prices rose sixfold between 1980 and 1987, fueling inflation that eroded urban incomes for workers and intellectuals alike.[50] The regime reduced its imports to create trade surpluses so that it could obtain hard currency to repay foreign debt, but spare parts for industrial and agricultural machinery then grew scarce, and production suffered as a result. Because the government reduced spending on housing construction, housing also became scarce and more costly for urban residents.[51] Government austerity programs, which eroded living standards, and another food and energy price hike eventually triggered a further wave of strikes in April 1988.[52]

With workers now demanding not just higher real wages but also the legalization of Solidarity, political and economic crises again combined. This time, however, the regime faced these political and economic crises alone. Gone were Communist leaders like Gomulka, who had enjoyed some domestic popularity in the 1950s and 1960s. Gone was the Communist Party, which had proved inept and had been elbowed aside by the military during the crisis of 1980–81. Gone, too, was the Soviet Union, which under Gorbachev no longer threatened or even promised to use its army to defend Communist regimes in Eastern Europe. Jaruzelski evidently realized earlier than other neighboring dictators, like Honecker, that Soviet military policy had changed.[53] As the regime became increasingly isolated, Jaruzelski's government in August proposed a series of Round Table discussions, which opened on February 6, 1989. As a result of agreements reached the following April, the regime agreed to legalize Solidarity and schedule elections for June 4, 1989.[54] In return, Solidarity and other parties to the agreement promised to elect Jaruzelski as president following the election and allot 299 seats in the Sejm, or assembly, to the Communist Party and its allies. Campaigning under the slogan "We must win," Solidarity won 92 of 100 seats in the Senate and 160 of the 161 open seats in the Sejm.[55] The Communist Party, which campaigned on the platform "With us it's safer"—according to one observer, a slogan that sounded more like an advertisement for contraceptives than for parliamentary candidates—captured no senate seats and won only five seats in the Sejm, though they claimed and filled another 294 seats allotted to them by the Round Table discussions.[56]

After the intense negotiations that followed the election, a party representing rural farmers, who had long supported the Communists, joined Solidarity and helped to form a government headed by Tadeusz Mazowiecki, an early member of KOR, on August 24, 1989.[57]

By permitting democratization but also retaining important powers as president and reserving power in parliament for the unpopular Communist Party, Jaruzelski, like Pinochet and Roh, allowed the democratic opposition to assume power while limiting its ability to exercise power in a "self-governing republic." Although Solidarity took power, the Round Table discussions prevented the political extinction of the Communist Party. The Communists used the breathing space provided by the agreements to recover and eventually return to power in the mid-1990s. Although Solidarity allowed Jaruzelski and the Communists to retain some power, its ascent was still an enormous achievement, perhaps as important elsewhere as it was in Poland itself. It demonstrated that an opposition movement could compete for power in a Communist dictatorship and, unlike a comparable movement in China, it could also win. Its success paved the way for other, weaker movements in Eastern Europe, which then poured into the political space created by Solidarity.

Democratization in Poland was a significant development. It marked the first time that a Communist regime had surrendered its monopoly on power to a domestic opposition movement. Moreover, Poland departed from the Soviet sphere of influence without prompting Soviet military intervention. The significance of these developments was not lost on other Communist regimes, which faced many of the same problems. Like Poland, Communist regimes had borrowed heavily in the 1970s, defaulted on foreign loans in the early 1980s, and then imposed austerity programs. They too understood that austerity programs impoverished workers and intellectuals in urban areas, creating conditions for the emergence of a *minjung* alliance like Solidarity, which might compete for political power. And they knew that their continuing rule had long rested on the force of Soviet arms. But during the 1988–89 Polish crisis Jaruzelski had not requested and Gorbachev had not offered Soviet military power to defend the regime. Most Eastern European regimes now understood that Soviet foreign policy had changed and that they could no longer count on Soviet intervention in a political crisis.

The Hungarian Retreat

In Hungary events kept a close pace with developments in Poland. Like Poland, Hungary had borrowed heavily, and although its debt was lower than Poland's in absolute terms, it was higher in per capita terms.[58] Led by Janos Kadar, the regime reduced government subsidies and raised prices and taxes as part of its austerity program.[59] Although the Hungarian government was more successful than were successive Polish governments at raising prices, these developments simultaneously undermined the socialist character of the economy—the government allowed some property ownership, for example—and encouraged the growth of the anti-Communist opposition, which saw such economic reforms as higher prices and taxes undermine the standard of living.[60] Because reform failed to revive the economy while fueling opposition to Communist rule, a faction within the Communist Party organized a palace coup in May 1988, forcing Kadar into the ceremonial post of president and installing Karoly Grosz in his place.[61] Grosz tried to open the political process so that the party could retain some power, much as Jaruzelski was then doing in Poland. Opposition parties were legalized and demonstrations permitted in January 1989.[62] The opposition took the opportunity to press for further change, and in February the Communist Party "declared its support in principle for the transition to 'a multi-party system.'"[63] In May it opened the border between Hungary and Austria, which enabled migrants from East Germany to pour across the frontier.[64] In September, just after Solidarity had assumed power in Poland, the government announced it would hold multi-party elections in June 1990.[65] In October 1989 the Communist Party abandoned its Marxist-Leninist ideology and announced that it had become a "socialist" party, while the government dropped the name "People's Republic" and declared itself a "Republic."[66]

When elections were held in June 1990, newly formed opposition parties captured a majority of the votes, though the Socialist Party made a respectable showing, winning 11 percent of the vote, half as much as the Hungarian Democratic Forum and Association of Free Democrats, which captured 24 and 21 percent of votes cast.[67] By retreating from power before opposition groups gathered to force it from power, the Communist Party and its successors in Hungary were able to retain a measure of political influence in the absence of any firm guarantees or power-sharing commitments by the opposition.

But the rapid, strategic retreat of Hungarian Communists created problems for other dictatorships, particularly for Honecker's regime in East Germany. By opening the border between Hungary and Austria on May 2, 1989, the Hungarian regime exacerbated East Germany's long-standing emigration crisis.[68] The massive exodus of East German emigrants, combined with the East Germany's growing debt crisis, brought down the regime in the autumn, a development that would lead both to democratization and to German reunification the following year.

The Wall Falls

After Germany was divided by the superpowers in 1949, 3.4 million East Germans, one-sixth of its population, fled to West Germany before August

13, 1961, when Erich Honecker sealed the inter-German border and began building the Berlin Wall, or the Antifaschistischer Schutzwall (Anti-Fascist Bulwark), as it was called in East Germany.[69] The East German dictatorship built the wall because the emigration of professionals and skilled workers threatened to cripple the economy and discredit the regime. Closing the border slowed but did not end the flight of East Germans. Between 1962 and 1988 another 616,066 East Germans left the country, most of them emigrating to West Germany, where they received citizenship and economic assistance.[70] The East German regime gave official exit permits to about half of these emigrants, but most of the rest fled through neighboring countries or escaped across the border, and 29,670 were "ransomed" by the West German government, which paid about DM 100,000 for each East German dissident or political prisoner.[71] Still, many more wanted to leave. By the mid-1980s five hundred thousand East Germans had applied for official permission to leave the country.[72]

Emigration was both a problem and a solution for the East German regime. It weakened the economy and undercut its legitimacy, but it also vented dissent, secured West German ransoms, and provided hard currency from emigrant remittances, just as it did for regimes elsewhere. As long as the regime could manage emigration, it could minimize the costs and maximize the benefits associated with it. But the Hungarian border opening upset this balance. Thousands of East Germans rushed into the breech, and during the next six months 343,854 people left East Germany, half as many as departed during the previous twenty-six years.[73] By November 1989 fifty thousand people a week were pouring out of the country.[74]

The migratory flood, which now included young male workers, disrupted industry and brought the economy to a standstill. This triggered an acute economic crisis because the regime depended on a functioning economy to repay its $20.4 billion foreign debt.[75] By October 31 East German officials admitted that economic deterioration threatened the very solvency of the country and warned that only drastic reform and outside help could avoid a 25 to 30 percent drop in the standard of living.[76]

In September 1989 students in Leipzig began demonstrating against the regime. They chanted, "We want to leave!" and carried banners demanding "an open country with a free people."[77] Police attacks on peaceful demonstrators fueled protests, and demonstrations in Leipzig grew larger and spread across the country.[78] In October, when Gorbachev visited East Germany to attend celebrations marking the country's fortieth anniversary, demonstrators chanting "Gorbi, Gorbi" took to the streets in Berlin and Leipzig, much as students had done in China during the Soviet premier's visit in April.[79] Faced with mounting protests, Honecker ordered police to shoot demonstrators and restore order on October 9, 1989. But authorities in Leipzig refused to shoot, and Honecker's call for a Tiananmen Square-like massacre went unheeded.[80] On October 17 members of the regime introduced a resolution in the Politburo demanding "the removal of Erich Honecker and the election of Egon Krenz as general secretary."[81]

In an effort to dam the migratory flood, Krenz promised to introduce a bill that would give residents passports and exit visas.[82] But demonstrators demanded more. Faced with still-mounting domestic protest, continued migration, and Gorbachev's public reiteration that the Soviet Union would not intervene on the regime's behalf, the East German cabinet resigned on November 7, 1989.[83] Two days later Gunter Schabowski, secretary of the Socialist Unity Party, which had assumed power as an interim government under Krenz, announced that "applications for private trips abroad may be submitted without further conditions. . . . Permission will be granted immediately."[84] When people learned that border guards had allowed people to cross checkpoints at the Berlin Wall unhindered, East Germans flooded across, gathered at the wall and, with West Germans joining them, began to tear it down.[85]

The demolition of the wall was like a defeat in war for the residual Communist government in East Germany. As the wall fell, Communist Party rule collapsed utterly. Krenz was forced to resign on December 3, and the Communist Party dissolved itself as a political entity.[86]

Although dissidents had begun to organize opposition movements and political parties during the fall of 1989, neither they nor elected officials in the country's parliament were capable of addressing the economic crisis or coping with the political issues related to the collapse of Communist government in East Germany.[87] The economic crisis could only be addressed with help from West Germany, which was willing to extend aid provided it could fulfill its ambition, embodied in its constitution, to unite the two Germanys in a single state.[88] But because Germany had been divided by the superpowers during the Cold War, German unification could only be achieved with the permission of the great powers: the United States, the Soviet Union, the United Kingdom, and France. In practice this meant securing Soviet consent because West German's NATO allies had already agreed to support reunification efforts.

In this context democratization in East Germany became synonymous with the unification of the two German states. In March 1990 East German voters elected representatives to the Volkskammer, or parliament. After the Alliance for Germany party, which was supported by Helmut Kohl's conservative Christian Democrats in West Germany, won the overwhelming majority of seats, the Volkskammer began negotiating with its West German counterparts in the Bundestag for an inter-German treaty that would reunite the countries and provide for all-German elections in a single state.[89]

Although representatives in the Volkskammer and the Bundestag agreed on most issues, some differences surfaced. They wrangled over abortion rights (East Germans wanted a liberal law, West Germans a restrictive law), the restoration of property seized by the East German state, and access to the files of the East German secret police.[90] But aside from these issues, the two parliaments quickly agreed on the central issues related to the economy and democracy. During its final session the Volkskammer passed 164 laws in 181 days, a flurry of activity that some observers called a "tempocracy," a government ruled by deadlines.[91]

At the same time, the West German government led by Kohl's Christian Democrats began negotiating for Soviet permission to reunite the two Germanys. After Gorbachev announced on February 10, 1990, that "between the Soviet Union [and East and West Germany] there are no differences of opinion about reunification and the people's right to strive for it," negotiations proceeded swiftly.[92] The Soviets agreed to recognize a single, unified German state and allow it to retain its membership in NATO and in the European Community. For its part, West Germany agreed not to station non-German NATO troops in Eastern Germany or to acquire atomic, biological, or chemical weapons. It also agreed to limit the size of the all-German army to 370,000 and to reimburse the Soviet Union for the cost of withdrawing Soviet troops and relocating them to the Soviet Union.[93]

Economic union of the two Germany was first on the agenda. On July 1, 1990, the West German deutsche mark was introduced in East Germany to provide economic stability and to provide a kind of down payment for the West German acquisition of the East.[94] The West German government gave East German residents hard currency in exchange for rapidly depreciating East German marks, a step that helped purchase voter loyalty in all-German elections later that year. "Eating decently, [visiting] a disco or a whorehouse, that's all possible now," remarked one East German resident.[95]

Political union came next, with the dissolution of the East German state following on October 2, 1990. "East German embassies closed their doors ... ministries stood deserted ... [and] the People's Army turned its command over to the former arch enemy."[96] On December 2, 1990, the all-German elections were held, resulting in a landslide for Kohl's Christian Democrats, the party that had engineered unification.[97]

Czechoslovakia

Coming on the heels of democratization in Poland and Hungary and demonstrating conclusively that the Soviet Union would no longer intervene to save Communist regimes in Eastern Europe, the fall of the wall in Berlin and of the Communist dictatorship in East Germany had important consequences for the remaining dictatorships in Eastern Europe. The rapid emergence of a dissident-worker's alliance in Czechoslovakia, which was cemented during peaceful street protests against the regime in November 1989, forced the Milos Jakes government to open negotiations with the opposition and then quickly to resign. The "Velvet Revolution," as it was called, resulted in December in the formation of a government with a non-Communist majority headed by Vaclav Havel, a dissident poet who began 1989 in jail and ended the year as president.[98]

Bulgaria

After leading the Communist Party in Bulgaria for thirty-five years, Todor Zhivkov was forced to retire on November 10, just three days after the fall of the Berlin Wall.[99] Like Hungarian Communists, the Bulgarian Communists retreated before opposition forces could gather to throw them out. They quickly dissolved the Communist Party, reconstituted themselves as a "Socialist Party," and promised to hold multiparty elections in June 1990. Their headlong retreat was more successful than that of their Communist-turned-Socialist counterparts in Hungary. In Bulgaria they were able to win half of the votes and a parliamentary majority in the June elections and retain much of their previous power.[100] In this context, democratization was a successful survival strategy for a political elite determined to retain some hold on power.[101]

Romania

In Romania, by contrast, Nicolae Ceausescu refused to concede power in the face of growing domestic opposition and international isolation. Ceausescu ordered troops and security forces to fire on demonstrators in Timisoara and in Bucharest in December 1990. But mounting protest and the defection of army units to the opposition led to a brief and bloody civil war, which ended in the capture and summary execution of Ceausescu and his wife.[102] The National Salvation Front that came to power contained some dissidents but also many former members of the Communist Party.[103] Although the fall of dictatorship resulted in a transfer of power, democratization was limited and constrained.

Democratizations Compared

During the fall of 1989 Communist regimes in Poland, Hungary, East Germany, Czechoslovakia, Bulgaria, and Romania abruptly and simultaneously collapsed. Their collective response to economic and political crisis contrasts sharply with the responses of Latin American dictators, who were forced from power slowly.

In Latin America dictators fell sequentially, not simultaneously, during a fifteen-year period. In Eastern Europe, by contrast, they collapsed all at once, during a brief six-month period. The abrupt simultaneity of democratization in Eastern Europe was due to the fact that Eastern European regimes were linked in ways that Latin American dictatorships were not. Eastern European leaders were connected by a shared history: They had all been installed by the Soviets in the late 1940s. In Latin America dictators came to power on their own initiative, sometimes with U.S. assistance. Eastern Europeans were joined by economic institutions such as COMECON, by a shared ideology and political institution, the Communist Party, and by a shared military institution, the Warsaw Pact. In Latin America, shared economic institutions, such as regional free trade agreements, are only now being created; dictators had rather different ideologies, ranging from leftist regimes in Bolivia to neofascist regimes in Chile; and their armies hardly every marched together, though many officers attended the same military schools in the United States. The common bonds shared by regimes in Eastern Europe meant that a crisis in one country was, in effect, a crisis in all. By contrast, because Latin American countries were not joined by common economic, political, or military institutions, dictatorships there experienced shared economic crises separately.

The experience of Eastern European regimes also contrasts with that of dictatorships in East Asia, where Communist dictators in China, Vietnam, and North Korea survived economic crises and political challenges. Why were Communist regimes in East Asia or, for that matter, in Cuba, able to survive crisis, whereas their counterparts in Eastern Europe were not?

Eastern European regimes did not survive, in the first instance, because their crisis was more acute than the crisis in East Asia (though not Cuba). In Poland the regime had heavy foreign debts and faced a large interclass opposition movement that mounted determined and ongoing protest against Communist rule. The emergence of Solidarity presented a serious political challenge not only to the regime in Poland, but also to regimes in other countries, where developments had created the economic and political basis for the emergence of similar movements. Regimes in Eastern Europe recognized that Solidarity could easily be emulated, and many Communists simply retreated before Solidarity-imitators took shape in their own countries. In East Asia, only in China did a Communist regime confront a domestic *minjung*, though in 1989 it was not as strong as Solidarity had already become in 1980.

Eastern European regimes were also more vulnerable to changed Soviet policy than their counterparts in East Asia. In Eastern Europe Communist dictators were supported, in large part, by Soviet armies. In East Asia, by contrast, Communist parties could count on their own armies, which had also seen combat in the postwar period. In this respect the Cuban dictatorship resembled East Asian Communist regimes, insofar as Castro relied on a battle-tested domestic army to defend the country. As a consequence, when the Soviets rescinded the Brezhnev Doctrine and withdrew its military guarantees from Eastern European regimes, Communist parties found themselves without loyal and experienced armies to call on for their defense.

In Poland the Communist Party was able to call on Jaruzelski and the Polish army for a time. But the army did the party few favors—elbowing party members aside in government—and was never more than a stopgap solution. Jaruzelski rather reluctantly inserted the army between the disintegrating Communist Party and Solidarity to *prevent* Soviet military intervention. After Gorbachev took power and the threat of intervention had disappeared, the army lost its raison d'être, and the party lost its unflinching loyalty. Elsewhere it became clear after events in East Germany that domestic armies would probably balk at slaughtering their fellow citizens in the streets. Where they did defend the regime—as in Romania—they did so only briefly, before defecting en masse to the opposition. In China, by contrast, the army had briefly balked and then followed the party's orders.

The collective crisis caused by economic disaster, symbolized by debt, by domestic political protest, symbolized by Solidarity, and by Soviet withdrawal, symbolized by the fall of the Berlin Wall, was immediate and acute. But Communist regimes fell not only as a result of these proximate causes and "virtual realities," but as a result of long-term failures. Unlike Communist regimes in East Asia or Cuba, dictatorships had no reserves of political support to draw on when multiple crises struck. They had not won power on the battlefield, against foreign invaders or domestic opponents, or in electoral contests against other parties. They had been installed by the Soviets and owed their survival to a foreign power. Moreover, during previous crises—in East Germany in 1953 and 1961, Poland and Hungary in 1956, Czechoslovakia in 1968, and Poland in 1981—Communist regimes had capitulated to Soviet demands. East Asian and Cuban Communists as "nationalists" could rally political support and had fought in defense of their nation and homeland against foreign powers, but regimes in Eastern Europe could only point to their service in the "defense" of *another* country, the Soviet Union.

Communist regimes in East Asia and Cuba also cultivated domestic political support by introducing economic reforms that provided real benefits to crucial sectors of the population, particularly to the peasantry. By contrast, the price-hike reforms and austerity programs introduced by regimes in Eastern Europe led to falling living standards for urban and rural people alike. Government policies in Eastern Europe undermined the political support of their key constituencies. When crisis struck, regimes in Eastern Europe were abandoned by their soldiers but also by their workers. Without the support provided by at least some domestic political constituencies, Communist regimes could not long survive.[104]

Still, although Communist regimes in Eastern Europe did not survive intact, Communist *parties* were not wholly extinguished. The leaders of some parties, those who managed to wrest power from old-guard leaders on the eve of collapse, dissolved Communist parties, reconstituted them as "Socialist" parties, and competed, with varying degrees of success, in democratic, multiparty elections. In Poland and Hungary the problems associated with the introduction of free-market reforms eventually led to the return of ex-Communists to power, though not for some years. In Bulgaria they returned quickly to power, with the Socialists capturing the 1990 elections. In Romania, however, they never really relinquished power.

The situation in Yugoslavia and Czechoslovakia was complicated by the fact that democratization was accompanied by the division of these countries into separate states—eight in Yugoslavia and two in Czechoslovakia. But the pattern in these countries was much the same. By the mid-1990s ex-Communist, now "nationalist" leaders had taken power in many of the successor states, in Croatia, Bosnia, Serbia, Macedonia, and Slovakia, whereas the anti-Communist opposition retained power only in Slovenia and the Czech Republic.

Transition in Yugoslavia and Czechoslovakia

Yugoslavia: A Violent Parting

The Communist regime in Yugoslavia did not participate in the economic, political, and military institutions shared by other regimes in Eastern Europe. Unlike in Communist regimes in neighboring states, Josip Broz Tito had come to power on his own, having led an effective partisan war against Nazi invasion during World War II.[105] He then broke with Stalin in 1948, de-aligned Yugoslavia from the Soviet sphere of influence in Eastern Europe, and organized the nonaligned movement around the world. Yugoslavia received U.S. economic and military aid and was courted by the European Community, which invited Yugoslavia to participate in the European Free Trade Association.[106] Although Tito declined, he nonetheless adopted economic policies that distinguished Yugoslavia from other Communist countries in Eastern Europe. Like Southern European dictators in the 1960s, Yugoslavia exported workers to non-Communist countries in Western Europe, principally West Germany. By 1975 more than a million Yugoslavs abroad were supplying the country with their remittances, boosting the balance of payments.[107] Yugoslavia also imported tourists from Western and Eastern European countries. The 6.4 million tourists that visited Yugoslavia in 1980 injected $1.1 billion into the economy.[108] Tito also permitted extensive privatization, allowing individuals to own small-scale farms and businesses.

Tito's economic policies enjoyed considerable success in the 1960s, but Yugoslavia began to experience problems in the 1970s, much like its Southern and Eastern European neighbors. The 1973 oil crisis raised the price of imported oil and caused a recession in Western Europe, forcing many immigrants to return to Yugoslavia and reducing emigrant remittances.[109] As a result, Yugoslavia, like its Eastern European neighbors, borrowed heavily in the 1970s, and its foreign debt rose from less than $3.5 billion in 1973 to more than $20.5 billion in 1981.[110] The debt crisis that sharpened after 1979, when U.S. interest rates rose, was compounded by the return of migrant workers—five hundred thousand had returned home by the mid-1980s.[111] After the government was forced to impose austerity measures, the standard of living fell nearly 40 percent between 1982 and 1989.[112]

Yugoslavia's economic problems were compounded by Tito's death in 1980, which created a political crisis for his successors. Since the country's creation in 1946, when Tito's partisan coalition had abolished the monarchy and welded together a federal republic consisting of Serbia, Croatia, Macedonia, Slovenia, Montenegro, and Bosnia-Hercegovina, Tito had devised and revised constitutional arrangements between the Communist Party and the country's constituent republics.[113] He introduced new constitutions in 1946, 1953, 1963, 1974, which were amended twice before he died, in 1967 and 1968, and twice after he died, in 1981 and 1988.[114] The 1974 constitution was an unwieldy document—the world's lengthiest constitution, with 406 articles—that was "designed to prevent any individual from acquiring as much power as Tito himself had and to prevent any of Yugoslavia's peoples from dominating the federation."[115] Successive constitutions did little to prepare the country to deal with political and economic issues after Tito's death and set the stage for a struggle for power within the Communist Party. By the end of the decade the contest between Tito's successors within the party became a struggle between his successors in constituent republics.

During the 1980s factions within the League of Yugoslav Communists began to attach themselves to regional republican institutions, which had been provided for in the constitution. Using these institutions as a political base, they began to rally to their separate causes those who had been hurt by debt crisis and the central government's austerity program.[116] In the late 1980s the leaders of factions in Yugoslavia abandoned Communist Party labels and affiliations and created "nationalist" parties in their place.[117]

The regionalization and nationalization of factions within the Communist Party began in Serbia. In April 1987 Slobodan Milosevic began using nationalist themes—"Nobody will ever beat you [Serbs] again"—to bid for power within the Serbian League of Communists, one of the constituent groups of the League of Yugoslav Communists.[118] By September he had driven his opponents from the party. Using the Serbian Communist Party as a political base, Milosevic then rallied Serbian workers against the government's austerity program and demanded a greater share of power for Serbia relative to the other republics. These developments antagonized other factions within the Communist Party, which had also used the existing institutions in other republics to establish independent political bases to organize against central government austerity measures, which were widely unpopular, and for greater autonomy in the federation.[119] In the republics outside of Serbia Communists were often joined by other non-Communist groups that wanted greater political and economic autonomy.

In January 1990 Milosevic called an extraordinary congress of the League of Communists in Yugoslavia to bid for control of the unified Communist Party.[120] But Communist delegations from Slovenia and then Croatia walked out, the united Communist Party dissolved, and constituent factions returned to their respective republics.[121] After they left, Slovene and Croatian delegates shed their Communist identities and began campaigning for multiparty elections in their respective republics. In Slovenia the ex-Communist party lost the April parliamentary elections but retained control of the presidency.[122] Elections in Macedonia produced similar results.[123] In Croatia a non-Communist party won, though its leader, Franjo Tudjman, was a former Communist general who broke earlier with Tito and had been jailed by the regime.[124] In Bosnia-Hercegovina Communists joined a coalition government.[125] In Serbia and in Montenegro former Communists won decisively.[126]

The 1990 elections demonstrated the growing political autonomy of constituent republics. Growing political autonomy made economic cooperation more difficult as the debt crisis deepened. Then in the fall of 1990 leaders of the Yugoslav army joined the post-Tito power struggle, forging an alliance with Milosevic and Serbia.[127] Although the army was itself an important faction within the Communist Party, it had stayed out of the internal political battles that had raged during the late 1980s. It remained a popular institution, largely because it had fought effectively during World War II, deterred Soviet invasion after the war, and served with distinction in U.N. peacekeeping operations during the postwar period. But its leaders were alarmed at the growing autonomy of the republics, which threatened its role as an institution of the central government.

The army thus allied itself with Milosevic's faction because he remained a Communist (most of the other Communist Party factions had already abandoned their Communist identities), because they thought an alliance with the most powerful republic would help Communists reassert central authority, and because many of the officers were themselves Serbian. However, the army-Milosevic alliance and the 1990 army maneuvers that rehearsed military intervention in Slovenia and Croatia did not consolidate central authority but eroded it.[128] Antagonized by the army-Serb alliance and its attempt to reassert central authority under Communist government, the government in Slovenia held a plebiscite on independence, and "as soon as the result was official on December 26, 1990, the Slovene parliament declared its intent to secede from Yugoslavia in six months time if there was no progress towards a negotiated settlement of the country's future."[129]

Because federal constitutional provisions provided for a rotation of power, which allowed the Serbs to control "four of the eight seats in the federal Presidency, including that of President during the crucial year 15 May 1990 to 15 May 1991," Serb officials blocked proposals for greater autonomy and insisted on important powers in the negotiations that followed.[130] They evidently believed that their alliance with the army gave them the political weight they needed to win concessions from the other republics. But Slovenia and Croatia refused to concede, and they both withdrew from the federation on June 26, 1991. The army intervened to prevent their departure, but strong resistance from Slovene and Croat militias forced army columns to withdraw. The militias were able to rebuff the initial advance because the army's longtime policy to arm and train regional militias as reserves in the country's defense prepared them to resist invasion, in this case by the Yugoslav army itself.[131]

In Yugoslavia democratization led to partition and civil war. The country was partitioned because factions within the Communist Party were unable or unwilling to find solutions to the debt-related economic problems and the political problems left unresolved by Tito's death. Political factions retreated to their republics, where they argued that greater autonomy and, later, independence would solve their political and economic problems. The independence of constituent republics need not have led to civil war, but it did in Slovenia, Croatia, and later in Bosnia, for two reasons. First, the breakaway republics did not extend political guarantees to residual minority populations, such as the Serbs in Croatia and the Serbs and Croats in Bosnia.[132] Minorities refused to participate in multiparty elections and independence plebiscites, refused to recognize the new governments as legitimate, and took up arms against them. Second, Milosevic's Serbian government and the Yugoslav army assisted Serb militias in Croatia and Bosnia, preventing the governments of breakaway republics from consolidating power. These developments led to brutal and protracted civil wars in both republics.[133]

These civil wars have become defined increasingly in ethnic terms. But they began as a conflicts among Communist party factions within a unified Yugoslav state. The strategies used by different factions led to democratization and division. The attempt by one faction—the army-Milosevic alliance—to prevent division and reassert its own authority in a unified state failed, but the attempt ignited war between and within successor states. The governments of the new states then used ethnic appeals to rally political support. They appealed to ethnic identities rather than to class identities because ethnic appeals made it possible to create multiclass constituencies that were stronger than political constituencies based on singular class identities alone. As a result, wars between and within successor states were defined increasingly along ethnic and religious lines. Although they are now ethnic conflicts, they did not emerge as a result of antagonisms between different ethnic groups. The governments in successor states came to power in multiparty elections, but former Communist Party leaders now control the government or participate in ruling coalitions, and some, like Milosevic in Serbia and Montenegro and Tudjman in Croatia, have assumed nearly dictatorial powers.

Czechoslovakia: A Velvet Divorce

As in Yugoslavia, conflict over the distribution of political power and the direction of economic policy in Czechoslovakia resulted in partition. But in Czechoslovakia division did not lead to violent conflict.

After peaceful protest forced the Communist government in Czechoslovakia to yield power in 1989, a large number of political parties organized to compete for power. In the country's last nationwide election in 1992 forty-two different political parties fielded candidates for office. In 1990 the non-Communist Civic Democratic Party (CDP) came to power, and its prime minister, the free-market economist Vaclav Klaus, took rapid steps to dismantle socialist economic policies and introduce a capitalist economy, "capitalism without adjectives."[134] Because this led to rising unemployment, particularly in Slovakia, where the Communist regime had based much of the country's heavy industry, many people there supported the go-slow economist policies of the Movement for a Democratic Slovakia, led by former Communist Vladimir Meciar.[135] Like Communists in Yugoslavia, Meciar began organizing a political base through institutions in Slovakia, largely because he could not compete effectively for power with Klaus at the national level. And like the Yugoslav Communists, Meciar began advocating greater autonomy for Slovakia, even independence, though he used the threat of secession mostly to increase his bargaining power with the central government, trying to win economic protection from the government's free-market policies. In the June 1992 elections Klaus's CDP won one-third of the votes, enough to outdistance all other parties, including Meciar's, but not enough to form a government on its own. In an effort to form a government, Klaus began negotiating with Meciar, who had placed a distant second in the voting. Although a majority of voters throughout the country supported a *unified* country, Klaus and Meciar agreed to divide the country into two parts without putting partition to an electoral test or referendum.[136] Partition was an attractive option for both leaders, for Klaus because he could then pursue his capitalist economic policies without obstruction from the Slovak minority, and for Meciar because he could assume power on his own terms. The two parties thus agreed to a "velvet divorce," and Czechoslovakia was divided into two separate states.

Yugoslavia and Czechoslovakia were not the only countries where democratization resulted in division. Democratization would also be accompanied by division in the Soviet Union.

Democratization and Division in the Soviet Union

The succession crisis that began in the Soviet Union when Leonid Brezhnev died did not end in 1985 when Gorbachev assumed power. During the late 1980s political factions within the Communist Party continued to struggle for power. In the Soviet Union Communist Party factions, like their counterparts in Yugoslavia after Tito's death, launched their struggle for power from the country's constituent republics. Communist Party factions based in the Baltic republics, Ukraine, and Russia organized there to challenge Gorbachev and central authority. Their success in using the republics as a base to oppose Gorbachev and his reforms encouraged others to do the same. By using political institutions in the republics and by allying themselves with the emerging Soviet *minjung*, they were able to wrest power from Gorbachev in 1992 and then to democratize and divide the Soviet Union. A crisis of *succession* had become for the Soviet Union a crisis of *secession*.

After he took power in 1985, Gorbachev introduced a series of economic, political and military reforms to address the country's multiple crises. Unlike Deng in China, Gorbachev never fully consolidated power before introducing reforms, in part because he introduced political reforms designed to share power, or at least open the political process to others, something Deng never attempted. As a result, political groups opposing Gorbachev's reforms and groups proposing different kinds of reforms emerged within the Communist Party. Because they were relatively weak at first, they could not confront Gorbachev directly and contest control of the central government. For example, when Boris Yeltsin spoke critically of Gorbachev and his reforms in October 1987, he was removed from his post and exiled to the margins of central political power.[137] So rather than struggle for power at the center, Yeltsin and others moved their struggles to the republics, using the party structures and parliaments in the republics as their base of operations. The most important of these were in the Baltics—Lithuania, Latvia, and Estonia—and in Ukraine and Russia.

Communist Party factions emerged first in the Baltics. In 1988 "a group of Estonian economists, all Communist party members, came up with a plan for republican financial autonomy," and on November 16, 1989, the Estonian party "voted a declaration of sovereignty, giving Estonian laws precedence over Soviet ones."[138] On June 25, 1989, Lithuanian Communist Party leader Algirdas Brazauskas argued that "a Lithuania without Sovereignty is a Lithuania without a future," and he recommended that the Lithuanian Communist Party break from the Soviet Communist Party.[139] The Communist Parties of the Baltics then joined with non-Communist parties emerging in the republics—Sajudis in Lithuania and the Popular Front in Estonia and in Latvia—to criticize the 1939 Hitler-Stalin Pact, which was used to justify the Soviet annexation of the Baltic states during World War II. Especially given the dubious legality of the pact's terms, they demanded to exercise their right to leave the Soviet Union, a "right" given by provisions in the Soviet constitution.[140] On August 23, 1989, the anniversary of the Hitler-Stalin Pact, 2 million Balts formed a "continuous 370-mile human chain from Vilnius through Riga to Tallinn to demand independence."[141]

By breaking with the Soviet Union and allying themselves with the democratic, non-Communist opposition, Communist parties in the Baltics were able to build political support and retain power in a postcommunist state. Although the Communist Party in Lithuania initially lost elections to Sajudis, Brazauskas was soon returned to power as president in the 1992 elections. In Estonia and Latvia reformed Communists never relinquished power.

Because they were small in numbers, Communists and their new allies in the Baltics were vulnerable to any reassertion of central Soviet authority. But they had some advantages. Gorbachev was forced to admit that the Soviet Union had improperly annexed the Baltics. As Alexander Yakovlev, one of Gorbachev's chief advisers, conceded, "I had to admit to [Baltic representatives in 1988] that we had an empire, that there really was a center which dictated to the republics. I had to agree with them."[142] The Baltic republics used history and the Soviet constitution to their advantage, arguing that the Soviet annexation was illegal, and if it was legal, that they still had a right as republics to secede from the Soviet Union under its constitutional provisions. In either case, they did not have to act alone. They were soon joined by other, larger republics, which made common cause with the Baltics against the center.

Although Communists in Ukraine could not make the same historical claims against the Soviet Union, they had important contemporary grievances. Popular discontent was exacerbated by the partial meltdown of the Chernobyl nuclear reactor near Kiev in 1986, during which about sixty-three kilograms of highly radioactive material was burned and released into the atmosphere, more than ninety times the amount released at Hiroshima.[143] Communist Party leader Leonid Kravchuk took advantage of the regime's mishandling of the disaster to argue for greater Ukrainian autonomy. A September 1989 survey found that only 20.6 percent of the people in Ukraine supported independence, but 90.3 percent of the same people voted in favor of Ukraine's August 24, 1991, declaration of independence.[144] Given Ukraine's size and dense population—Ukraine was the second largest union republic, boasting 51.7 million inhabitants—the fact that its Communists broke with the center greatly strengthened similar groups in other republics.[145]

The ability of Communist Party factions to struggle for power from their bases in the republics was enormously strengthened by the emergence of party factions in the Russian republic. The Russian struggle against the center would prove decisive.

Initially, it was conservative Communists in the Gorbachev government who demanded and received approval in June 1990 to establish a Russian Communist Party and Russian legislature like those that had long existed in other republics.[146] As John Dunlop argued, "It should be underlined that these conservative communist attitudes to Russian autarchy were . . . primarily tactics to get themselves an independent power base from which to attack Gorbachev."[147]

But although conservative factions created the new institutions in the Russian republic, it was Boris Yeltsin and his allies who used them effectively. "To compensate for the weakness of [Yeltsin's faction] in the central institutions of power," Gail Lapidus argued in 1991, "Yeltsin has effectively employed a 'horizontal' strategy that seeks ties among the republics to curtail the center's political and economic dominance."[148] Yeltsin was able to seek these ties in his role as chairman of the new Russian Congress. Capturing 84 percent of the vote in his district, Yeltsin maneuvered past Gorbachev's allies and conservative Communist factions to become chairman on May 29, 1990, and then passed a declaration of Russian sovereignty in June 1990.[149] In June 1991 Yeltsin won Russia's first presidential election with 57.3 percent of the vote and was inaugurated in July.[150] The creation of republican institutions in Russia created a power base for Yeltsin, while the emergence of Yeltsin's powerful anti-Gorbachev faction made it easier for factions based in other republics to make headway against the center.

But although factions within the Communist party found a political base of support in the republican institutions, they also needed to find a social base of support to elect them to office in republican parliaments. In the

Baltics this source of support was relatively easy to find, as the population had long opposed Soviet annexation and resisted central Soviet authority. But elsewhere Communist leaders like Kravchuk and Yeltsin had to find allies among those who had long supported Soviet power. They found their support base among the Soviet *minjung*, the urban workers and intellectuals who had been adversely affected by Gorbachev's reforms.

Although Gorbachev introduced reforms to solve multiple crises, the reforms undermined the position of urban workers and intellectuals, much as they did in China and in Poland during the same period. The demilitarization of the economy increased unemployment among skilled and educated workers in defense industries.[151] Rising prices for food and housing, both in short supply, contributed to inflation and undermined the standard of living for urban residents.[152] Perhaps the most serious problem was inflation, which was caused in part by shortages but also by Soviet consumers who used their savings to bid up the prices of available goods. To reduce inflationary pressure, the Gorbachev government decided to confiscate fifty-ruble and one hundred-ruble notes and to limit cash withdrawals from the state savings bank in an effort to soak up "excess" savings that were being used to bid up prices.[153] But this greatly antagonized the populace without substantially reducing inflation. For reforms to work the government needed to eliminate subsidies and force consumers to pay market prices for the goods they purchased. As Gorbachev argued in 1990, "Without price reform, we cannot and shall not create satisfactory economic relations in the economy."[154] But the regime's repeated efforts to raise prices were met with staunch resistance, just as they were in Poland, because people understood that "price reform" would greatly reduce their standard of living.

Yeltsin and other anti-Gorbachev factions based in the republics understood that opposition to reform was widespread and growing. So Yeltsin allied himself first with the workers and intellectuals opposed to reform in Moscow, his initial base of support, and then with the coal miners who had been conducting strikes across the country since July 1989. Most of the 2.5 million Soviet miners joined the strikes because the rising prices of food and housing had eroded their real wages.[155] The government's insistence that miners pay for soap was a "symbolic last straw."[156] The strikes in 1989 and 1990 formed the basis for a Soviet movement similar to Solidarity, which demanded the right to strike and to form independent trade unions. They were supported politically by Boris Yeltsin, who defended the miners in their battles with the Gorbachev regime.[157] The miners were soon joined by other workers in heavy and service-sector industries, who conducted strikes and demanded higher wages.[158] As a result, wages increased "8 percent in 1988, 9 percent in 1989, and by 10 percent in 1990—whereas the national product increased by 4.4 percent in 1988 and by 2.5 percent in 1989, and in 1990 even decreased by 5 percent."[159]

Yeltsin and other Communist party factions capitalized on the growing hostility to the central government and to economic reform. They simultaneously campaigned *for* and *against* "reform." They were *for* political "reform," advocating Gorbachev's ouster and the dismantling of central authority, because this would enable power to be transferred to the republics. In multiparty elections in the republics the political reform they proposed was synonymous with democratization, but it also signified division. But they fought *against* economic "reform" to retain the support of their primary political constituency, the Soviet *minjung,* whose standard of living had been undermined by Gorbachev's austerity programs and price hikes.

By supporting wage hikes and opposing price increases, the *minjung* and the Communist Party factions made it impossible for the central government to implement serious economic reforms, and by 1991 Gorbachev had suspended efforts to eliminate state subsidies and increase prices.[160] Gorbachev, like Gomulka and Gierek, was unable to introduce the price increases that were essential for economic reform to succeed. The economic crisis deepened as a result. Soviet trade deficits soared, the value of the ruble fell, foreign debt increased, inflation rose, and industrial output plummeted.[161] By 1991 "aggregate output had dropped by 17 percent, a magnitude of decline not seen since the devastating Nazi invasion [in 1941]."[162] The World Bank observed that "the traditional centrally planned system had collapsed, but a functioning market system had not yet replaced it."[163]

It was in this context that a conservative faction of the Communist Party launched a coup on August 19–21, 1991, while Gorbachev was vacationing in the Crimea. The conservatives who led the coup—Vice President Gennadii Yanaev, Prime Minister Valentin Pavlov, Defense Minister Dmitrii Yazov, and KGB Chairman Vladimir Kryuchkov—were the heirs of the Brezhnev-Chernenko legacy within the party.[164] Unlike Yeltsin and Kravchuk, they had remained as a faction *within* the central government while Gorbachev pursued economic and political reform. But they finally split from Gorbachev and launched a coup to depose him because they thought he had been too accommodating to other factions, because they wanted to crush their opponents in the republics, and because they wanted to reassert central, old-school Communist authority.

But the coup quickly failed. Their attempt to emulate Roh in 1980, Jaruzelski in 1981, and Deng in 1989 failed for a variety of reasons. First, they were relatively weak. Their long association with Gorbachev and with reform had eroded their political and economic support. Second, they also proved singularly inept at organizing the coup. The opposition, meanwhile, which consisted of former Communist Party leaders based in the republics, was now relatively strong. Yeltsin could now successfully appeal for political support from the populace, at least in the political center of Moscow, and his defense of the Russian White House proved a turning point. Third, the army, an important faction in its own right, refused to join the conservatives in their attempt to overthrow Gorbachev. Indeed, many army leaders already supported factions based in the republics. But army leaders were also interested in preserving a semblance of order and realized that their intervention in a bloody conflict might lead to civil war, as it had in Yugoslavia and, on a smaller scale, in Armenia and Azerbaijan.

Without army support, the coup by conservative Communists collapsed. Gorbachev, who had been fatally weakened by his alliance with the conservatives, was gradually exiled to the margins of political power during the fall of 1991. Meanwhile, Yeltsin abolished the Communist Party, declared the independence of the constituent republics, and finally dissolved the Soviet Union on December 30, 1991.[165]

Post-Soviet Russia

By the end of 1991 multiple crises in the Soviet Union had led both to democratization and to division. In most cases the Communist Party factions that had emerged in the late 1980s became governments in successor states. Most of these factions had shed their "Communist" identities and had established political parties to be able to compete successfully in multiparty elections held before the Soviet Union dissolved. But some retained their Communist affiliations and established new governments without ever relinquishing power or subjecting themselves to electoral tests. Although some of these reconstructed and unrepentant Communists assumed power in the new republics, they no longer enjoyed a complete monopoly on political power as they had before 1985. The emergence of non-Communist parties and of new factions of old Communist Party remnants forced most governments to contend for power in a multiparty environment. Only in Lithuania did a non-Communist movement come to power, and its tenure was brief. By 1993 the Sajudis government was replaced by one headed by the former head of the Lithuanian Communist Party. Democratization thus resulted in multiparty political competition in most republics, but power was typically monopolized by former Communist Party factions.

The new republics faced the same economic problems that had contributed to the demise of the Soviet Union. In Russia, for example, Yeltsin tried to introduce reforms that he had previously opposed, raising prices and reducing government subsidies. In January 1992 average prices for all commodities had increased by 3.5 times and the prices of basic goods by 7 times their January 1991 level.[166] But because price "reforms" were not accompanied by wage increases, the standard of living fell. By March 1992 it was estimated that a majority of the Russian population lived below the poverty line.[167] Yeltsin found himself facing the dilemmas that had plagued

Gorbachev only a few years earlier. Antagonizing his political supporters with his initial reform, Yeltsin was unable to mollify them by slowing reform's pace, nor was he able to introduce structural economic change.

Moreover, when Russia became independent, Yeltsin inherited a parliament filled with conservative Communists who had been in place before the Soviet Union dissolved. The conservatives formed a faction that challenged Yeltsin's government, blocking his efforts to introduce political and economic change. By 1993 the two groups had reached a political impasse. Yeltsin decided to dissolve parliament and order new elections to break the stalemate.[168] When the leaders of the parliament refused to comply and barricaded themselves in the White House, much as Yeltsin had done in August 1991, Yeltsin ordered the military to shell and storm the parliament and jailed his opponents on October 3, 1993.[169]

In the December elections that followed, voters elected representatives from other neocommunist parties to replace many of the imprisoned Communist delegates. Yeltsin's party won only 9 percent of the vote, and the new parliament soon ordered the release of the dozen or so imprisoned Communists.[170] During the next few years Yeltsin's Communist opposition revived, and by 1996 Communist Party leader Gennadii Zyuganov challenged Yeltsin for the presidency.[171]

Not only did Yeltsin face growing opposition from Communist Party factions for control of the Russian government, much as Gorbachev had faced factions during the 1980s and early 1990s, he faced opposition from factions that had emerged in Russia's constituent republics, most dramatically in Chechnya. There, former Communist Dzhokhar Dudayev led a movement demanding independence from Russia, much as the Baltic republics, Ukraine, and Russia had done under Gorbachev. In November 1994 Yeltsin ordered the Russian army to crush the Chechen opposition, but the rebels mounted fierce resistance. After heavy bombardment leveled the capital of Grozny and killed some twenty-five thousand civilians, the Russian army finally took the city, but brutal guerrilla war continued.[172]

In short, Yeltsin faced many of the same problems that Gorbachev had faced. Yeltsin's solutions were much the same as those of his predecessor: raising prices to reform the economy, battling conservative Communist Party factions for control of the central government, and fighting Communist Party factions based in the republics that challenged central authority. Yeltsin's efforts to address economic problems and consolidate political power have met with little success, for the same reasons that Gorbachev's efforts resulted in his defeat. The problem is that the measures designed to resolve the country's multiple economic crises antagonize the *minjung*, the social constituency that holds the balance of political power. Communist opposition leaders understand this dilemma, and like Yeltsin earlier, now they argue for and against reform. They are for political reform, for ousting

Yeltsin and his supporters, but against economic reform because it hurts the *minjung*. There is little evidence, however, to suggest that they are better prepared to address these continuing problems than were Gorbachev and Yeltsin. Because it would be as hard to return to a Communist past as it seems to be to advance to a capitalist future, Communist factions that assume power in the post-Soviet republics will face the same economic problems and encounter the same political opposition as their predecessors.

ten

DEBT AND DIVESTMENT IN SOUTH AFRICA

It could be said that contemporary democratization began and ended in southern Africa. Rebellion in Portugal's African colonies, particularly in Angola and Mozambique, led to the 1974 military revolt and democratization in Portugal. Anticolonial revolution in southern Africa not only contributed to democratization and around the world, it also contributed eventually to democratization in South Africa. The collapse of Portuguese colonialism in Angola and Mozambique in 1974 marked the onset of crisis for the white regime in South Africa.

After 1974 the South African regime was beset by economic, military, and social crisis. But it did not easily succumb. The South African regime deflected growing foreign and domestic demands for democratization for twenty more years, at a time when governments elsewhere collapsed. The regime was able to resist change because of its initially strong economy and its widespread and determined political support from an interclass, multiethnic, white minority. The economic wealth of this white minority provided the government with considerable economic resources. The democratic political institutions controlled by the white minority also gave the government considerable strength and legitimacy, which enabled it to rule over non-white ethnicities and the multiethnic black majority. For many years the regime also benefited from the tacit political support of the United States. Domestic and foreign political support enabled the regime to suppress domestic opponents and wage war with neighboring countries, allowing it to delay democratization for two decades after 1974. But deepening economic crisis, military defeat, changed superpower policies, and, most importantly, the emergence of a determined domestic opposition eventually forced the regime to democratize and share the institutions long reserved for whites. Prime Minister Frederik W. de Klerk's announcement on February 2, 1990, that the African National Congress (ANC) would be legalized and ANC leader Nelson Mandela released from prison marked the beginning of democratization. Mandela's inauguration as president four years later represented its culmination. Democratization, which began in southern Africa in 1974, reached a conclusion in South Africa two decades later.

Economic Crisis

The economic crisis that first emerged in South Africa during the early 1970s brought an end to decades of rapid economic growth.[1] During the half century between 1919 and 1969 "South Africa's real national income grew an average of more than 5.5 percent per year, making it one of the fastest-developing countries in the world."[2] Of course, rapid economic growth was not widely shared. The white minority, some 17 percent of the population, took 71.9 percent of the national income in 1970, which provided whites with a per capita income of more than $10,000 a year and wages twenty times those of black workers.[3]

Sustained economic growth and the benefits it provided to whites were made possible by the exploitation of the country's natural resources and human populations. South Africa's rich natural resources, particularly its gold and diamonds, were produced cheaply because the regime used its political monopoly, which was institutionalized after 1948 in a set of laws known collectively as apartheid, to control the black labor force and supply it at low cost to industry and agriculture. Because the regime's political power kept labor costs low and profits high, between 1963 and 1972 the rate of return on invested capital was the highest in the world.[4] High profit rates encouraged massive foreign investment, which in turn reduced trade deficits that persisted from 1946–71.[5]

But South Africa's ability to attract foreign investment, which fueled economic growth in the postwar period, depended on apartheid. And apartheid was both an attraction and anathema to foreign investors. On the one hand, apartheid made foreign investment extremely profitable. U.S. manufacturers, for example, earned a 31.7 percent return on their investments in 1980.[6] But apartheid also put investment at risk because it greatly antagonized the black majority, leading to conflict and violent reaction by the regime. When conflict erupted, as it did after the 1960 Sharpeville massacre, foreign investors temporarily withdrew and economic growth briefly slowed.[7] In the aftermath of the massacre the *Economist* warned, "South Africa cannot hope to attract foreign capital on realistic terms until it has adopted a policy of racial co-existence that is acceptable to the outside world."[8]

On balance apartheid proved more of an attraction to foreign investment than an obstacle during the 1950s and 1960s. But in the 1970s and 1980s social conflict and the economic risks associated with apartheid increased investor aversion. As a result, foreign investment slowed during the 1970s. And after 1985 foreign investment was withdrawn, a divestment that crippled the economy and fractured its political foundation. To a large extent, then, foreign investment in South Africa was both an economic asset and a liability. It could promote economic growth, as it did in the 1950s and 1960s, or it could undermine the economy, as it did in the 1980s.

In the early 1970s several economic problems emerged in South Africa. In 1973 Arab oil-exporting countries imposed an oil embargo on South Africa, forcing it to pay premium prices for oil it had to obtain from third-party suppliers.[9] The oil embargo cost the South African regime between $1 and $2 billion more than other oil-importing countries, making the embargo one of "the costliest international action[s] against South Africa."[10]

While rising oil prices increased the costs of production in industry and agriculture, growing strike activity by black workers also increased business costs. Strikes by black workers, particularly gold miners, increased dramatically after 1973.[11] Because the price of gold rose rapidly after 1971 when the United States abandoned the Bretton Woods agreement and abandoned a fixed dollar price for gold, the mining industry could afford to pay higher wages.[12] But higher wages for gold miners encouraged other workers to press for higher wages, which increased production costs in other industries that could not as easily pass along their higher costs in the form of higher prices. As a result of growing strike activity, black workers were able to increase their share of national income from 20 percent in 1970 to 28.9 percent in 1980 and reduce the earnings ratio between white and black workers from 20:1 to 6:1.[13]

As the cost of imported oil and black labor rose, so too did the risks associated with apartheid. The government's slaughter of unarmed protesters during the 1976 Soweto uprising persuaded investors that the risks were rising and triggered another round of divestment, much like the one following the 1960 Sharpeville massacre.[14] But the regime was able to weather the economic problems associated with these developments in the 1970s because gold prices rose, making it possible to pay for imported oil and to pay higher wages in some industries, and because the government used borrowed money to replace capital lost as a result of foreign divestment and domestic capital flight.

Because South Africa is the largest single producer of gold in the world—gold accounted for 45 percent of its export earnings in 1984—its economic fortunes depend heavily on the price of gold.[15] As the price rose from $31 an ounce in 1971 to $820 an ounce in 1980, the economy reaped a wind-fall.[16] Rising gold prices "boosted mining profits and government tax revenues, allowing the first significant real increase in black mining wages since the early 1900s, and eased South Africa's balance of payments constraint," thereby sheltering South Africa from the economic consequences of rising oil prices during this period.[17]

While gold exports helped cover trade deficits, the South African government, like dictatorships around the world, borrowed heavily in the 1970s to replace declining foreign investment.[18] Foreign debt grew from $3.0 billion in 1970 to $18.0 billion in 1981 and then to $23.7 billion by 1985.[19] Rising gold prices and foreign loans essentially carried the South African economy through the 1970s.

But in the 1980s interest rates rose and gold prices fell. As we have seen, rising interest rates increased debt payments and made it difficult for countries like South Africa to borrow money. And like the prices of other commodities, the price of gold fell in the 1980s, from $820 an ounce in 1980 to under $300 an ounce in 1985, reducing export earnings, contributing to trade deficits, and weakening the currency.[20] The value of the rand fell from $1.35 in 1980 to $0.39 by the end of 1985.[21] The currency devaluation should have increased other South African exports, but embargoes made it harder, not easier, to export goods. As a result, the currency devaluation did not restore the trade balance, as it might have under different circumstances.

Falling gold prices also reduced government tax revenues. As the sociologist Martin Murray noted, "A standard rule of thumb used . . . in Johannesburg was that for every $10 the gold price fell, the [government] lost $200 million in tax revenues."[22] By this measure, the government in 1985 lost $10 billion in annual revenues.[23]

In 1984–85 renewed strikes and political protest raised production costs and increased risk, which accelerated foreign divestment and domestic capital flight: "International capital flows turned from an inflow of $3.5 billion to an outflow of $3.7 billion between 1981 and 1985."[24] These developments triggered a crisis of debt and divestment in the summer and fall of 1985. On July 20 the regime declared a state of emergency to contain strikes and riots throughout the country.[25] France and other Western European countries then imposed economic sanctions on South Africa, which drove down the value of the rand, accelerated capital flight, and intensified demands for repayment by South Africa's foreign creditors.[26] As the risks of doing business in South Africa rose, foreign investors and creditors withdrew their capital, draining the economy of financial resources.[27] On August 27 the government suspended trading in its currency and stock markets and on September 1 announced that it was suspending payments on half of its $24 billion foreign debt.[28]

South Africa's refusal to repay its debt and its unwillingness to alter the political structure of apartheid led to voluntary divestment by corporations and foreign investors, for whom the risks now outweighed rewards. Explaining his company's decision to sell its operations in South Africa, Exxon President Lawrence Rawl noted, "The deterioration of the South African economic and business climate caused by the continuing internal and external conflicts has affected our business and its potential for growth."[29] It also led to the imposition of economic sanctions by governments now opposed to apartheid. In 1986 the United States joined other Western European countries in imposing a variety of economic sanctions on South Africa.[30] Pushed by risk and prodded by sanctions, foreign investors withdrew about $12 billion from South Africa between 1984 and 1991, which included about $1 billion of disinvestment by U.S. firms.[31] After renegotiating with foreign creditors, the South African government managed to send $8 billion to foreign creditors in the same period.[32] Although South Africa's Prime Minister P. W. Botha insisted, "I am not a jellyfish, we're not a nation of jellyfish," the twin crises of debt and divestment crippled the country's economic spine.[33] By 1989 the Trust Bank of South Africa estimated that real average incomes were 15 percent lower than they would have been without sanctions and divestment.[34]

During the 1980s economic problems—rising interest rates and falling commodity prices, particularly for gold—added to the political problems resulting from increasing black opposition to apartheid. Taken together, these developments reduced profits and increased risk. By 1985 foreign investors, lenders, and governments became convinced that the economic and political risks associated with an apartheid-based economy outweighed the rewards. As a result, the South African regime faced an ongoing crisis of debt and divestment, which crippled the economy and reduced incomes not only for blacks but, importantly, also for whites. After 1985 the economic crisis could only be solved politically, either by silencing the black opposition or by abolishing apartheid. Unable to achieve the former, the South African government eventually abandoned apartheid in its search for a political solution to its economic problems.

Military "Defeat"

South Africa's economic crisis was compounded in the mid-1970s by a series of ongoing military problems along its borders. The collapse of Portuguese dictatorship in 1974 brought anticolonial independence movements in Portugal's African colonies to the brink of power. In Angola and Mozambique Communist guerrilla groups dominated the independence movements, but non-Communist movements contested their claim to power. When the Portuguese government granted independence to Angola on November 11, 1975, it did not designate a successor, and fighting broke out between the Movimento Popular de Libertacao de Angola (MPLA) and the non-Communist Uniao Nacional para a Independencia Total de Angola (Unita) and its ally, the Frente Nacional de Libertacao de Angola (FNLA).[35] To prevent the MPLA from establishing a Communist state along the South African border and to assist its non-Communist rivals, South African forces invaded Angola and advanced to within two hundred miles of the Angolan capital, Luanda.[36] But the arrival of three thousand Cuban troops and the dispatch of Soviet arms to the MPLA halted the South African advance on November 20, 1975, and the South African army withdrew.[37] Although the MPLA was widely recognized as Angola's legitimate government, civil war continued. During the next decade South Africa and the United States supported Unita in a "contra" war against the MPLA government and its Cuban-Soviet allies. The South African army launched cross-border raids into Angola, both to provide military support for Unita and to attack Communist guerrillas fighting for independence in neighboring Namibia.

South Africa had a long history of involvement in Namibia, having taken control of the former Germany colony under a 1920 League of Nation's mandate.[38] After World War II South Africa tried to annex Namibia, but the United Nations refused to recognize the takeover. In 1966 the United Nations revoked South Africa's mandate, and in 1971 the International Court of Justice ruled that South Africa's occupation of Namibia was illegal.[39] The United Nations then recognized the Southwest Africa People's Organization (SWAPO) as Namibia's legitimate government. But South Africa's refusal to surrender power led to war with SWAPO guerrillas, which had established bases in southern Angola.[40]

In Mozambique, where the Communist Frente de Libertacao de Mocambique (Frelimo) had come to power after independence in 1975, South Africa supported the Resistencia Naccional Mocambicana (Renamo), an anti-Communist guerrilla movement created by white Rhodesians and Portuguese intelligence officers, in a contra war against the Frelimo government.[41] In Rhodesia, where a white-minority government resisted the transfer of British colonial rule to the indigenous black majority, the South African government provided aid and assistance until 1980, when Rhodesia became Zimbabwe, an independent country with a black-majority government.[42]

South Africa reacted to the emergence of hostile Communist states and guerrilla movements by waging wars along its frontiers. In Namibia the South African government waged war on its own, in Angola alongside contra allies who were also supported by the United States, and in Mozambique through contra surrogates. The decision to wage wars against the antiapartheid "frontline" states, what the South African regime in 1977 described as a "total war" against its collective enemies, greatly increased the government's military spending.[43] Military spending grew from R 44 million in 1960 to R 1.654 billion in 1977–78, a 1,000 percent increase, then to R 2.668 billion by 1982–83 and R 8.090 billion by 1988–89.[44]

During the 1970s and 1980s South Africa's military policies produced some success. The army destroyed the ANC's guerrilla forces inside South Africa, its raids and reprisals crippled ANC forces based in frontline states, and its support for Renamo's brutal contra war in Mozambique—which killed one hundred thousand civilians, displaced nearly 2 million people, and caused widespread starvation—forced the Communist government to accommodate South African demands. In 1984 the Frelimo government was forced to sign the Nkomati Accord on Non-Aggression and Good Neighborliness, effectively ending its support for the ANC and forcing it to withdraw from the frontline states as an active opponent of apartheid.[45] Likewise, South Africa's support for Unita contras in Angola kept the MPLA government from consolidating its authority, while its continued occupation of Namibia kept SWAPO from assuming power for many years.

Although South Africa's military campaigns extended and defended its frontiers against domestic and foreign opponents for more than a decade, the cost of waging protracted wars rose sharply. Then in 1987–88 a South African expeditionary force in Angola bogged down in a war that it could not win, a "defeat" that created a crisis for the regime's military policies in Angola and Namibia.

In the summer of 1987 the MPLA's army in Angola, assisted by thirty-five thousand Cuban troops and bolstered by Soviet arms, launched an offensive in southern Angola against Unita's contra army. As they advanced, nine thousand South African troops invaded Angola to protect their contra ally, blunting the Communist offensive in November and forcing the Angolan-Cuban army to retreat to the city of Cuito Cuanavale.[46] South African and Unita forces then laid siege to the city, which produced a military stalemate that lasted until August 1988.[47] By forcing the South African army into a protracted, costly, and inconclusive battle, Cuban troops and Soviet air power persuaded the South African government to reassess its regional military policy. As Paul Moorcraft noted, the South African army "had not been defeated, but it could no longer afford the costs of trying to win."[48] In August 1988 the South African regime decided to cut its losses and withdraw its troops from Angola, and in December the combatants reached a comprehensive settlement. The Cubans and the ANC agreed to withdraw from Angola, a development that led in 1991 to an agreement ending the civil war in Angola, while the South Africans agreed to reduce their forces in Namibia and permit elections for a constituent assembly in November 1989, a development that brought SWAPO to power in a multi-party, independent Namibia on March 21, 1990.[49]

The battle of Cuito Cuanavale was a turning point that brought an end to South Africa's unilateral military intervention in the region. The battle exposed the regime's vulnerability to protracted conflict and forced the regime to reassess its foreign policy and, indirectly, its domestic policies, which had long relied on the government's force of arms. Black opposition to white rule in South Africa, which arose in the 1970s at the same time that anti-apartheid governments came to power in neighboring states, resulted in a drawn-out domestic conflict. Like the wars along its frontiers, the ongoing civil war in South Africa increased the cost of maintaining apartheid and triggered a deepening social and political crisis for the regime in the 1980s.

The Black *Minjung*

In 1948 South Africa's white electorate, which was composed of Boer and English ethnic groups, brought the National Party to power, a position it would retain for forty-three more years. During the 1950s the National Party strengthened old laws and introduced new ones that assigned land, economic resources, and political power to the white minority, while locking the black majority and "colored" minority into poverty and powerlessness, depriving both of property and citizenship in their own country.

The 1910 constitution, which reserved political power for whites, and the 1913 and 1936 Land Acts, which reserved most of the country's land for whites (93 percent in 1913, reduced to 87 percent in 1936), provided the cornerstones for the postwar system.[50] Upon this foundation the National Party regime constructed a huge edifice of laws collectively known as apartheid, or "separate development."[51]

Apartheid policies were designed to furnish black labor for white mines, farms, factories, and household by controlling black settlement and migration patterns. Blacks were assigned places to live, generally outside of towns or in small reservations called "Bantustans," or homelands, and their movement within the country and between their residence and work was strictly controlled by a series of "pass laws."[52] Between 1962 and 1980 an estimated 3,522,900 South Africans——blacks and colored minorities—were subjected to some form of forced resettlement, and between 1965 and 1975 nearly 6 million people were prosecuted for pass law violations.[53] As in China, where the Communist government directed massive resettlement campaigns to keep peasants out of the cities, the South African regime controlled resettlement and migration patterns to keep blacks out of white urban areas and provide labor where it was needed.[54] The regime feared that without these controls, black workers would abandon rural farms and mines and migrate to cities, as they had during World War II, when the black urban population grew from 25 percent before the war to nearly 40 percent by war's end.[55] The regime's resettlement and migration policies were designed to provide black labor to white employers and to divide blacks geographically, thus minimizing their ability to act collectively or organize politically.

Not only were many blacks assigned to reservations as their permanent residence, but during the 1970s the government also made these homelands "independent," which meant that the regime "officially deprived nearly eight million Africans of the South African nationality."[56] As one official explained, "If our policy is taken to its logical conclusion . . . there will be not one black man with South African citizenship. . . . Every black man in South Africa will eventually be accommodated in some independent new state . . . and there will no longer be a moral obligation on this Parliament to accommodate these people politically."[57]

To enforce apartheid's myriad laws—some of which, for example, segregated education, banned interracial marriage, and made it a crime for blacks to touch, and thereby desecrate, the South African flag—the regime banned opposition political parties and made it a crime to protest or "campaign for the repeal or modification of *any* law" or to promote the "communist doctrine" of racial equality. (emphasis added)[58]

During the 1950s the regime arrested and jailed opposition leaders, co-opted opponents by assigning them nominal powers in black townships outside of cities and in Bantustan reservations, and massacred demonstrators who opposed apartheid. On March 21, 1961, on the eve of an ANC campaign against pass laws, police opened fire on nonviolent and unarmed students in Sharpeville, killing sixty-seven, "most of whom were shot in the back as they tried to flee."[59]

After Sharpeville the regime banned the ANC (founded in 1912) and the Pan-Africanist Congress (founded in 1959) and arrested its leaders or forced them into exile, crushing first-generation opposition to apartheid and silencing protest for more than a decade.[60] Then in the early 1970s opposition to apartheid reappeared. At first it consisted of two separate movements, one composed of young students and intellectuals and another of black trade unions. But in the mid-1980s the student intellectual current finally joined the trade union movement, which had amalgamated different unions into a powerful federation in 1985, creating a South African *minjung* that posed a serious political threat to the regime.

In 1971 students and intellectuals selected Steve Biko to lead the new Black Consciousness Movement. This group of moderate dissident intellectuals vowed to fight apartheid using only legal means and included only blacks in their organization, eschewing interracial politics, which were illegal in any event.[61] Their first success came in 1976, when they helped organize demonstrations by students who objected to a law requiring black students to use Afrikaans as the language of instruction in school.[62] After police shot and killed student demonstrators on June 16, 1976, riots erupted in cities across the country.[63] Police killed 150 people during the first week of protest and more than 500 more during the next 16 months, most of them young adults.[64] Police violence, the arrest of leaders, and the murder of Steve Biko in 1977 eventually stifled the protests.[65] As in South Korea and Poland, however, the regime's crackdown did not entirely eliminate the opposition, which reemerged in the South African black townships in 1984.

While the Black Consciousness Movement was organizing students, a series of spontaneous strikes involving more than sixty-one thousand workers near Durban in early 1973 led to the creation of independent black trade unions, a development similar to events in Poland during the same period.[66] Although strikes were illegal, private employers separately agreed to wage increases, and government officials eventually allowed unions to form as long as they organized as discrete unions and eschewed any political demands.[67] As a result, black workers in many industries were able to increase their wages, improve working conditions, and form unions during the 1970s. Private industry and government officials were initially amenable to these demands because wages had been extremely low and because foreign loans and profits from rising gold prices made wage increases possible. By 1980, however, the different trade unions began organizing a trade union federation that became, like Solidarity, a collective vehicle intent on challenging the government with its economic and political demands.[68]

These two opposition currents converged in 1984–86. In February 1984 students near Pretoria began boycotting classes, and when police shot demonstrators, riots again erupted in black townships around the country.[69] During this second round of protests boycotting students were joined by other members of the community who objected to the higher prices that resulted from South Africa's deepening debt crisis. In August and September 1984 the government attempted to ease its own debt-related budget deficits by increasing rents, food prices, train and bus fares, and sales taxes.[70] This greatly antagonized urban residents, students, and workers—young and old alike—just at it had in China and Eastern Europe. Because high taxes and prices were levied by local governments in the townships, urban protest—"a widespread refusal to pay for our oppression"—was directed both at black municipal authorities and at the white regime.[71] As a result, 240 black officials, including 27 mayors, were forced to resign between September 1984 and June 1985.[72] This shared economic crisis helped link students and workers in common opposition to apartheid.

While students boycotted their schools in 1984–85, workers in separate trade unions were constructing their trade union federation. After a series of summit meetings in 1981, 1982, and 1983, thirty-four independent trade unions representing more than five hundred thousand workers finally cobbled together the Congress of South African Trade Unions (Cosatu) in November 1985.[73] Union membership grew quickly and strike activity increased. Twenty-five percent of the black workforce had joined unions by the end of 1984.[74] One month after Cosatu was formed, "South Africa experienced its most strike-bound January in a decade."[75] More importantly, the new federation abandoned its industrial-issues-only approach, demanding that the ANC be legalized, that Mandela be released from jail, and that rent, tax, and price increases be rescinded.[76] Its call for a general strike on May 1, 1986, which joined students and workers in common opposition to apartheid, marked the consolidation of a *minjung* in South Africa.[77]

On July 20, 1985, the regime responded to student riots and worker strikes by declaring a state of emergency, rounding up twenty-five thousand dissidents in the first sweep.[78] Like Jaruzelski's 1981 declaration of martial law, Prime Minister Botha's state of emergency was designed to crush the opposition. Unlike Jaruzelski, however, Botha also tried to splinter the opposition, establishing a tacit political alliance with black municipal authorities and with homeland leaders like KwaZulu chief Gatsa Buthelezi. The regime licensed or encouraged municipal authorities and homeland leaders to form vigilante groups and ethnic militias, both to defend the municipal leaders' nominal political authority and modest economic privileges and to break up the second-generation opposition, which had gravitated to first-generation ANC leadership.[79] Buthelezi agreed to a de facto alliance with the regime because he hoped to create a political base in the KwaZulu homeland, much as Communist leaders in Yugoslavia and the Soviet Union tried to create new political bases in the republics. He later demanded independence in a separate KwaZulu state as a way to exact concessions from the ANC after Mandela was released from prison, much as Meciar had done in Czechoslovakia.[80]

The violence associated with state repression, vigilante reprisal, and urban rioting took a heavy toll. From 1987 to 1990 nearly twenty thousand homes were destroyed, one hundred thousand people were forced to flee, and six thousand people died in the violence.[81] But the government and its black allies failed to crush the *minjung*. Social unrest and domestic opposition to apartheid became endemic. This domestic social crisis in turn contributed to the regime's economic and foreign problems, as the government's state of emergency and war on its domestic opposition triggered both a loss of confidence by foreign investors and banks and the imposition of sanctions by foreign governments who objected to the regime's savage assault on the black majority.

Majority Rule

The emergence of ongoing economic, military, and social crises in 1984–86 created serious problems for Botha's white-only regime. This collective crisis did not immediately force the regime to surrender power, both because the government retained the political support of the white minority, a relatively large group compared to the groups that supported other unpopular regimes around the world, and because its leaders were determined to retain power no matter what the economic or social cost. "I am not prepared to lead white South Africans and other minority groups on a road to abdication and suicide," Prime Minister Botha vowed. "Destroy white South Africa and our country will drift into factions, strife, chaos and poverty."[82]

But as the 1980s wore on, South Africa's multiple crises led to "factions, strife, chaos and poverty" despite—or rather because of—Botha's 1986 state of emergency and continued white rule. The political impasse was broken in 1989 by a succession crisis within the government and the ruling National Party. After suffering a stroke in January 1989, President Botha resigned as head of the National Party but retained his powers as prime minister, creating a constitutional crisis within the government.[83] As the prime minister was chosen by the ruling party, a bitter battle for the leadership of the National Party ensued, a contest won by Frederik de Klerk in February.[84] A period of uneasy accommodation between the two leaders—Botha as head of the government, de Klerk as head of the ruling party—followed. It was resolved on August 14, 1989, when Botha was forced to resign in a palace coup orchestrated by de Klerk and other cabinet ministers who wanted a new leadership to handle the country's ongoing crises.[85]

During the autumn, as Communist dictatorships collapsed in Eastern Europe and elections for government in an independent Namibia approached, de Klerk began serious negotiations with jailed ANC leaders, releasing four leaders on October 15 as evidence of his good faith.[86] Then on February 2, 1990, at a time when "the Communist threat has lost its sting," de Klerk went before the white Parliament and announced that he was legalizing the ANC and that he would soon release Mandela, who had been imprisoned for twenty-seven years. "The well-being of all in this country is linked inextricably to the ability of the leaders to come to terms with one another on a new dispensation," de Klerk argued. "The aim is a totally new and just constitutional dispensation in which every inhabitant will enjoy equal rights, treatment and opportunity in every sphere of endeavor—constitutional, social and economic."[87] De Klerk said he seized the initiative because "the old South Africa is burdened by inheritances from many sources of the past, which are really blocks around our neck."[88]

After his February 2 speech de Klerk released Mandela and legalized the ANC, the Communist Party, and other antiapartheid groups. In March the regime gave independence to Namibia, reduced compulsory military service, ended cross-border raids into neighboring states, and suspended aid to contra armies in Angola and Mozambique. In May it opened formal negotiations with the opposition about an eventual transfer of power. In June de Klerk canceled the state of emergency in most of the country, asked foreign governments to end economic sanctions, and invited private firms to reinvest in the economy. And one year later he introduced laws that would "remove the remnants of racially discriminatory legislation which have become known as the cornerstones of apartheid."[89]

Although de Klerk in 1990 initiated the process of constitutional reform and democratization, which in South Africa meant a transition to black majority rule, it would take another four years to complete. During the long negotiations about constitutional reform, conducted through the Conference for a Democratic South Africa (Codesa), the regime held a number of important advantages. It retained control of the government, its security forces, and the country's economic assets. It also used a whites-only referendum to shore up its political base and negotiate as a representative of a united white community. Further, it was able to exploit differences within the black majority and win the support of some colored groups fearful of black majority rule.[90] Economic control was extremely important because a revival of the South African economy *now* depended on a favorable business climate that only *whites* could provide. That is, economic recovery would occur only if the white minority endorsed the constitutional reforms adopted by Codesa. This economic power gave the National Party government an effective political veto during negotiations.

For its part, the ANC negotiated effectively, but its position was weakened by Mandela's differences with Buthelezi, who tried to sabotage the process and threatened to boycott the general election, as well as by the violence associated with black competition for power in a post-apartheid state.[91] Between 1990 and 1992 eight thousand people died in violent clashes between ANC supporters and Buthelezi's Inkatha, which were frequently aided by de Klerk's security forces.[92] This violence made it difficult for the ANC to establish itself as a politically "responsible" party, weakening its numerical advantages.

When de Klerk initiated the process of constitutional reform and democratization in 1990, he told one diplomat, "Don't expect me to negotiate myself out of power."[93] By effectively managing the devolutionary process, de Klerk found a way to negotiate himself out of office without fully surrendering his power. The interim constitution that was adopted by the twenty-one-member negotiating council on November 17, 1993, "effectively ended white minority rule after 341 years" and provided for the country's first nonracial general election on April 26–28, 1994.[94] In the election the ANC captured almost 63 percent of the vote and 252 seats in the new National Assembly, and Nelson Mandela became South Africa's first black president.[95] When Mandela was inaugurated on May 10, 1994, joyous black crowds chanted, "*Amandla! Ngawethu!*" ("Power! It is ours!").

Although constitutional reform and general elections led to black majority rule, the constitution gave minority parties an important say in political change. The new government needed to secure a two-thirds majority in the parliament to revise the constitution and a 60 percent majority to pass normal legislation. Until 1996 representatives of minority parties won seats in the twenty-seven-member cabinet with just 5 percent of the vote.[96] As a result, the ANC and its supporters, who constituted a large majority, were forced to share power with minority political parties.[97] One observer argued that de Klerk's National Party negotiated "a kind of swap where it [gave] up the right to run the country its way in exchange for the right to stop blacks from running it their own way."[98]

Democratization resulted in political power for the black majority. But the Mandela government has done little to wrest economic power from the white minority. Indeed, foreign investment and reinvestment in part depends on the Mandela government's economic inaction. Although democratization and an end to the political violence associated with apartheid reduced economic risk for foreign investors, any attempt by the Mandela government to seize, transfer, or share the economic resources of the white minority and its allied foreign investors could trigger divestment by South African whites and deter foreign businesses from reinvesting in the country. The problem for the government is that economic resources are tightly held—only five South African superconglomerates control nearly 80 percent of the country's private industry and 75 percent of the capital represented on the Johannesburg stock exchange.[99] The majority of land remains in the hands of white owners, and the government still owes $17 billion on foreign debts incurred during the 1970s and 1980s.[100] As a result, democratization in South Africa has transferred considerable, but not unqualified, political power to the black majority, without transferring commensurate economic wealth.

Democratization in Africa?

During the early 1990s, when South Africa dismantled apartheid and moved toward majority rule, other states in sub-Saharan Africa also democratized. Some scholars in 1991 argued that as many as one-half of the forty-eight states in sub-Saharan Africa could be "classified as either democratic or moderately to strongly committed to democratic change." They described Africa as a "workshop of democracy" and maintained that "not a single country in Africa is now untouched by the spirit of change which has made itself felt since 1989–90."[101] But other scholars argued that democratization applied only to a limited number of states, mostly extremely small countries like Benin, Cape Verde, Mauritius, São-Tomé and Príncipe, and Madagascar, and a few large states such as Namibia, Angola, and Zambia. Elsewhere, they argued, there has been some "political liberalization," the legalization of opposition parties and holding of multiparty elections, but they maintained that "the partial liberalization of authoritarian regimes does not amount to a transition to democracy."[102]

The limited and qualified character of democratization in the African states outside of South Africa is curious because sub-Saharan Africa, like Latin America, faced a serious debt crisis during the 1980s. Between 1970 and 1992 the foreign debt of African states climbed from $6.0 billion to more than $183.4 billion, a development that triggered chronic balance of payments deficits, currency devaluations, hard currency shortages, hyperinflation, declining production, and budget deficits.[103] Debt crisis, declining production in agriculture and industry, and falling commodity prices for export commodities—"by 1986, average real commodity prices were the lowest recorded in this century with the exception of 1932, the trough of the Great Depression"—reduced real incomes 25 percent during the 1980s, increasing the number of people in "absolute poverty" to one-half of the total population.[104]

Although debt crisis contributed to political change in Latin America and in South Africa, a similar economic crisis did not produce dramatic political change throughout Africa. It did not for a variety of reasons. First, the independent states created by decolonization in the 1950s, 1960s, and 1970s were captured by dictators and individual political parties who monopolized important economic sectors and used patronage to create extensive social networks—organized either along familial or ethnic tribal lines—that supported the regime and resisted change. By providing public sector employment and jobs in the government bureaucracy—"levels of public employment [were] substantially higher than in Asia or even Latin America" throughout Africa—dictators and one-party regimes created a large social and economic clientele that defended the regime and often co-opted potential political opposition.[105] In Ghana, for example, between 1972 and 1980 the government's bureaucracy increased eightfold and Tanzania's grew threefold during the same period.[106]

Although widespread corruption and debt crisis discredited regimes and their clientele support networks, few were forced to transfer or share economic or political power with opposition political forces. Because the industrial sector in Africa was small and mostly state-controlled, the independent bourgeoisie and organized working classes were economically weak, politically divided, and either unwilling or unable to mobilize the rural farmers or the urban poor, which represented the large majority in most African states.[107] When debt crisis struck, these large, mostly rural populations retreated from both the market and the state, returning to subsistence agriculture and informal black markets to produce and distribute goods.[108] Because state authority was weak and the services it provided inadequate, communities in rural areas began "to organize their own schools and clinics . . . to enunciate an ethic of self-reliance."[109] Although the retreat of the rural poor reduced political pressure for democratization, they contributed to a kind of democratization at the grass roots. Naomi Chazan noted that "Africa's potential for democracy is more convincingly revealed by the creation of small collectives established and controlled by rural or urban groups than by parliaments and parties."[110]

There were, of course, exceptions to this general pattern. In Zambia, where the large copper-mining industry had given rise to a well-organized trade union movement, effective political opposition emerged. Like Lech Walesa, Frederick Chiluba, head of the trade union and leader of the Movement for Multiparty Democracy, created an effective alliance between industrial workers and urban-rural groups who had seen their standard of living decline as a result of the government's debt-related austerity programs.[111] With urban inhabitants making up 42 percent of the population, the support of Zambia's urban workers was crucial to Chiluba's success. Because his party was able to attract the support of these urban workers, Zambia's "Solidarity" was able to wrest power from President Kenneth Kaunda's one-party socialist regime in 1991 in the country's first multiparty elections.[112] But the emergence of African *minjungs*, like those that emerged in South Africa and in Zambia, were rare.

Second, political change did not come about in many African dictatorships due to their dependence on foreign armies to maintain their power. Dictatorships in Gabon, the Ivory Coast, Cameroon, Senegal, the Central African Republic, Chad, Djibouti, and the Indian Ocean islands of Réunion and Mayotte relied on French troops based in these countries to protect them, while governments in Mauritania, Mali, Burkina Faso, Benin, Togo, Equatorial Guinea, Congo, Zaire, Rwanda, and Burundi have military cooperation agreements with the French.[113] As Howard French observed, since 1964 "France has intervened militarily on the continent every other year on average. Paris has repeatedly sent troops into action in Chad . . . and used its forces to replace political leaders in the Central Africa Republic."[114] Like the Soviet army in Eastern Europe, the French armies in Africa provide reliable troops for regimes that cannot depend on the loyalty or strength of indigenous armies to protect them from opposition movements. In this context, postcolonial states continue to depend on postimperial power.

Finally, the United States and global lending agencies began promoting democratization in Africa in the 1990s, often attaching new political conditions linking multiparty elections to financial aid and loan agreements. But their efforts to promote democratization were undermined by their increasing disinterest in Africa. The end of the Cold War shifted their attention to the emergence of new problems in Eastern Europe and the Soviet Union and reduced U.S. and European political interest in Africa. At the same time, Africa's continuing debt crisis and sharp economic decline in the 1980s reduced U.S. and European economic interest in African states. As a consequence, external pressure for democratization in Africa is now weaker than it might have been. In Africa these developments have disconnected the relation between economic crisis and political change. So despite a ubiquitous debt crisis, most African regimes have not been compelled to transfer or share political power.

eleven

DEMOCRACY AND DEVELOPMENT

Political relations in states around the world were transformed between 1974 and 1994. Although different developments contributed to change in different settings, economic crisis everywhere played a central role. And although economic crisis and political change were linked, their relation was contingent, leading in some but not all cases to democratization. At the global level democratization did not create a "new" world order. Rather, by expanding the number of democratic republics and creating a more homogeneous interstate system, democratization consolidated a world order that was created during World War II but long deferred by the Cold War. For individual states, democratization meant that political participation was extended, in some states more than in others, to social groups who had been excluded from power. But nowhere did political participation become fully inclusive. Accordingly, it is more accurate to speak of political change resulting in democratization, not necessarily in the creation of democracy.

As we have seen, economic crisis played a central role in the fall of dictatorships and the rise of civilian democrats. Of course, the character of economic crisis differed from region to region and from state to state within these regions. In Southern Europe the 1973 oil embargo triggered economic crises for dictatorships in Portugal, Spain, and Greece. For Latin American countries and the Philippines, the debt crisis of the late 1970s and early 1980s wrecked the developmentalist projects of dictators, though the severity and timing of crisis differed from one country to the next. In East Asia problems associated with rapid economic growth and increased competition with neighboring states created economic crisis in the mid-1980s for regimes in South Korea and Taiwan, as they also did in China. For the Soviet Union, heavy military spending and declining productivity in industry and agriculture led to economic stagnation, while debt-burdened Eastern European regimes, which had organized their economies along Soviet lines, were similarly affected. In South Africa debt and divestment created serious economic problems for the white regime.

Although regional economic crises created serious economic problems for dictatorships, in most cases economic crisis alone did not induce political change. Economic crises were compounded by a variety of political developments. For many regimes the death or illness of dictators created crises of succession. The death of Admiral Blanco and then of Franco in Spain left the regime without leaders of equal stature to replace them, resulting in the transfer of power to a royalist king who became a republican. The reconfiguration of military juntas in Greece and Argentina brought leaders to power who initiated disastrous military adventures. The illness and ouster of South Africa's Botha brought to power a white supremacist who eventually dismantled apartheid. And in the Soviet Union the deaths, in rapid succession, of aging leaders in the early 1980s brought a reformer to the helm who triggered a battle for power among the younger generation of Communist leaders, a struggle that is, to some extent, still under way in Russia.

Military defeat also created serious problems for dictators. The Portuguese regime's inability to defeat insurgents in its African colonies led to a revolt by its own armed forces. For the Greek colonels, their decision to support a coup in Cyprus led to a political debacle and a humiliating military confrontation with Turkey. The rapid defeat of the Argentine army by Great Britain in the Falklands War was a disaster for the Argentine junta. The defeat of Soviet armed forces in Afghanistan forced the Soviet Union to withdraw its forces from that country and initiate a general military retreat from Eastern Europe, with important consequences for dictators there. And South Africa's defeat by allied Communist armies in Angola forced it to withdraw both from Angola and neighboring Namibia.

Defeat in war had serious immediate consequences for the regimes that had initiated war. But it also contributed to problems for dictatorships elsewhere because defeat sometimes revealed or triggered changes in superpower policy toward dictators. The Greek-sponsored coup in Cyprus and the Argentine invasion of the Falklands forced the United States to reassess its relation with putative allies and side with their opponents, Turkey in Cyprus and Great Britain in the Falklands. By abandoning their Greek and Argentine allies, U.S. officials not only crippled their diplomatic and military positions, but also indicated that unqualified U.S. support for other dictators might not be forthcoming. Changing U.S. policy toward Somoza during the 1978–79 civil war and toward Marcos during the 1986 election campaign likewise crippled the Nicaraguan and Filipino regimes and compromised U.S. relations with dictatorships in Latin America. In less dramatic circumstances, changing U.S. military and economic policy toward the East Asian frontline states of South Korea and Taiwan forced them to reevaluate their domestic and foreign policies, while changing European and U.S. policies toward South Africa in the mid-1980s put significant pressure on the white regime.

Changed superpower policy probably had its most dramatic impact on regimes in Eastern Europe. The unilateral Soviet decision to abrogate its long-standing military guarantees to allied regimes and to begin withdrawing its military forces from the region proved fatal for regimes that could muster little domestic political support. Of course, changed superpower policy was less a product of any explicit U.S. or Soviet policy to promote democratization than it was a result of a determination to pursue their own idiosyncratic domestic and foreign policy agendas. Although U.S. and Soviet leaders congratulated themselves for having contributed to democratization, they typically abandoned client regimes for expedient reasons, not because they wanted to advance global democratization as a general foreign policy principle. For a brief period the Carter administration argued that U.S. support for allied dictatorships was under review and insisted that its policy toward Somoza reflected this new general policy. But the revolution in Iran and the ascension of the Sandinistas in Nicaragua forced the United States to reassess a global condemnation of dictatorship. After Reagan took office, the administration sometimes abandoned dictators and championed democrats, as it did in the Philippines. But U.S. policy in the Philippines was designed less to promote democracy than it was to avoid another Iran, where radical opponents of the United States came to power. In this instance U.S. policy toward allied dictatorships was defensive rather than proactive.

Much the same could be said of Soviet policy. Gorbachev never advocated democratization in Afghanistan or Eastern Europe. Instead, he urged allied dictators to adopt the kind of reforms that he was introducing in the Soviet Union. Like his predecessors, Gorbachev believed that Soviet domestic policy should be adopted as a blueprint for Warsaw Pact allies to emulate. Whereas Lenin, Stalin, and Brezhnev had *insisted* on this policy transfer, Gorbachev indicated that its adoption was, for the first time, *voluntary*, insisting that the Eastern European regimes could choose their own paths. This signaled an important change in Soviet foreign policy, but it would be hard to characterize it as a proactive policy of democratization within the Soviet sphere. Instead, the Soviets were prepared to live with the results of political change. In Afghanistan they were glad to see the Communist regime survive the Soviet military withdrawal, but they were also resigned to its eventual collapse. For the Soviet Union as for the United States, changed foreign policy was more a product of necessity than of inclination.

In some countries opponents of regimes organized social movements to compete for political power. In Portugal radical dissidents within the armed forces organized a military coup that toppled the dictatorship and opened the door to multiparty elections. In Nicaragua and El Salvador opponents of the regime took up arms and waged guerrilla wars to obtain power, successfully in Nicaragua and unsuccessfully in El Salvador. The creation of a *minjung* alliance between urban intellectuals and workers in South Korea and also in China presented a serious political challenge to these regimes. In Poland and in South Africa *minjung* movements waged long, determined, and ultimately successful campaigns against the regime. But although opposition movements played important roles in these countries, they were relatively rare. Dictators often surrendered power *before* opposition movements became an important political factor, though newly organized movements often played crucial roles during the transition periods that followed the departure of dictators. Opposition movements in some few countries served as important warnings to governments in other countries where such groups had not yet emerged. Leaders in Spain were quite aware of events in neighboring Portugal, and they may have acted in part to forestall the emergence of similar movements in Spain. Dictators throughout Latin America watched rebellions in Nicaragua and El Salvador with alarm and could imagine "People Power" demonstrators filling their streets, as they did in Manila. Eastern European regimes regarded the protests and massacre in Tiananmen Square with alarm. Dictators generally understood that the conditions leading to the emergence of opposition movements were present in some form in their own countries. Because political conditions were widely shared, opposition movements in a few countries became "virtual realities" for regimes in other countries. Dictators were forced to include these virtual realities in their calculations, even if these groups had not yet assumed organizational forms.

Opposition movements were not the only virtual realities that impacted upon political events. The civil wars in Spain and Greece loomed large in transition-period deliberations. Fearing a revival of civil war, politicians of the right and left acted with some caution. In Latin America and the Philippines revolutionary guerrilla wars and state-sponsored "dirty" wars helped shape political decisions, affecting decisions even in countries where such events had not occurred. Massacres of opposition groups in South Korea (1980) and Taiwan (1948) still resonate in contemporary politics, just as the Tiananmen Square massacre (1989) does in China. In Eastern Europe the traumas inflicted by domestic uprisings and postwar Soviet invasions shaped politics in Poland (1980) and throughout Eastern Europe during the fall of 1989.

The prosecution of former dictators for political and economic crimes in Greece, Argentina, the Philippines, South Korea, and East Germany, and the summary execution of Ceausescu in Romania also became important realities for dictators throughout the world. Although the individuals responsible for crimes were not everywhere vigorously prosecuted and although many escaped punishment altogether, the prosecution of some made others fear for their lives and assets and insist that immunity from prosecution be included in agreements transferring political power.

Although past and present virtual realities—civil wars, social movements, and public prosecutions—played some part in democratization, the extent of their role is difficult to ascertain, and few scholars have investigated them in any detail. Generally, scholars have focused on the "transmission" of these realities, usually by electronic media, from one setting to another, and numerous articles have been written about the role of facsimile machines and television in the democratization process. But less has been written about why some historical and contemporary events—past wars, modern revolutions—became salient political realities.

Unorganized social movements also played a role in democratization. As we have seen, individual and mass migrations have been important, though often neglected, components of change. The migrations of workers from Portugal, Spain, Greece, and Yugoslavia acted first as a way to vent dissent and earn remittance income for dictators in the 1960s and 1970s. But the return of migrant workers from Western Europe proved troublesome. Whereas migration out of East Germany contributed directly to democratization there, migration from Cuba and El Salvador probably helped dictators or conservatives retain power. The role of migration, not only of workers but also of tourists, has also been neglected by scholars of political change.

Finally, when economic and political crises emerged, dictators frequently miscalculated, taking steps that sharpened the crisis and strengthened their adversaries. The decisions by Marcos and later Pinochet to call elections as a way to rally support for the regime actually provided opponents with an opportunity to organize successfully against the dictatorship. But this was not the only way that dictators undermined their own legitimacy. The assassination of prominent political opponents had the same effect. The assassinations of Chamorro in Nicaragua, Romero in El Salvador, Spadafora in Panama, and Aquino in the Philippines decisively undermined the credibility of regimes and pushed elites into the opposition.

Economic Crisis, Political Change, and Democratization

Although the character of economic crisis differed from region to region and combined in different ways with political, military, and social developments, there is nonetheless an important relation between economic crisis and political change. Generally, economic crisis has contributed to democratization and peaceful social change. This contemporary experience contrasts sharply with the interwar experience, when economic crises related to World War I and the Great Depression led to dictatorship and sometimes to violent revolution and civil war in many countries. This suggests that the relation between economic crisis and political change is *contingent* and historically shaped, not automatically linked, as many postwar scholars of the left and right have often assumed. This perhaps explains their surprise at the events of the last twenty years. Because they associated economic crisis with the onset of dictatorship or revolution, they did not expect contemporary dictatorships to fall as a result of economic crisis.

Not only is the relation between economic crisis and political change contingent in the general historical sense, it is also contingent in individual countries. The account of democratization presented here does not support a new determinism or supposition that economic crisis inevitably leads to democratization. Instead, the findings here suggest that economic crisis frequently produces democratic change but does not always do so.

There are important exceptions to the general rule in the present period. The ability of the non-Communist regime in Mexico and of Communist regimes in Cuba, China, Vietnam, and North Korea to survive economic crisis (at least for a time) and to resist political change at a time when neighboring dictatorships plagued by similar economic problems collapsed indicates that the relation between economic crisis and political change in individual countries is contingent, not concatenated.

One explanation for this contingency is that dictatorships have different capacities to survive crisis and resist change. Of course, it is difficult to determine the strength of regimes prior to the onset of crisis, although scholars have attempted to identify strengths and weaknesses and evaluate capacities in comparative terms. Jeane Kirkpatrick's famous typology, which classified regimes as authoritarian or totalitarian, was developed in part to distinguish between those regimes that might change in the face of domestic pressure (authoritarian) and those that would be impervious to such pressure (totalitarian). Other political scientists developed more complex typologies to assess the relative strengths of regimes. But these typologies proved to be of little value in assessing political systems in the contemporary period, when strong and weak and capitalist and Communist regimes alike collapsed.

By contrast, the analysis here—particularly of regimes that survived in Mexico, Cuba, China, Vietnam, and North Korea—suggests that the "strength" of these states could be attributed to several developments. First, regimes in these states all possessed a "revolutionary" tradition, whether nationalist or Communist or both. They all fought revolutionary wars against domestic and foreign opponents, a tradition that helped forge collective contemporary identities. Second, they derived considerable legitimacy from their political success and, most importantly, from their military success, particularly against foreign powers. Cuban, Chinese, Vietnamese, and North Korean military victories against foreign invaders and superpower opponents was crucial to their continued legitimacy. Third, these regimes provided tangible economic and social benefits to at least some important groups in their countries, typically rural peasants. All these regimes used land reform and other mechanisms to provide real benefits to the peasantry, an important social group in predominantly agrarian societies. The Mexican government also provided important benefits to economic elites. Conversely, they provided few benefits to urban workers, intellectuals, or professionals, many of whom fled in large numbers or formed the basis of the foreign or domestic opposition. When economic crisis struck, these regimes could draw on their revolutionary histories, military experiences, and bases of popular support to weather crisis and resist change, at least for a time. In this context the "strength" of regimes depended less on their formal, institutional attributes and more on their historical and political experiences.

Reviving the World Order

In global terms, economic and political crisis produced civilian democratic governments in republican states. This development did not create a new world order. It revived a world order that had long been deferred by the Cold War. The interstate system developed by the United States and the Soviet Union during World War II was designed to expand the number of republican states and extend self-determination and democracy to people around the world. The subsequent decolonization of European and Asian empires expanded the number of republican states in the interstate system. But U.S.-Soviet conflict over the political and economic character of some of these states, the division of the world into U.S. and Soviet spheres of influence, and the emergence of dictatorships in many republics within these spheres deferred the development of a new interstate system based on republican *and* democratic values.

The collapse of anti-republican dictatorships that survived war in Spain and Portugal, the fall of dictatorships in the U.S. sphere in Latin America and East Asia, and the collapse of dictators in the Soviet sphere in Eastern Europe and in the Soviet Union itself established both republican and democratic states in dozens of countries around the world. By recovering the democratic promise of the postwar interstate system and by subjugating the dictators who supported U.S. and Soviet spheres of influence, democratization weakened Cold War political structures and contributed to its demise. Indeed, it was democratization in both the U.S. and Soviet spheres that brought the Cold War to a conclusion. Without dictators, it became impossible for either superpower to maintain credible and exclusive spheres of influence. When dictators left the fold, the Cold War teams assembled by the superpowers to compete in global political competition disbanded, and the

Cold War then lost its meaning and relevance. The Cold War ended not because one side won but because participants on both sides withdrew. This process was first initiated by participants in the nonaligned movement. The decision by a few countries not to join the superpower spheres and by civilian democrats to withdraw brought an end to the competition. Today the interstate system looks like one that might have emerged after World War II, but did not because of the Cold War.

Shifting from a global perspective to individual states, economic crisis and political change have resulted in democratization, though not necessarily *democracy*. In most cases democratization has resulted in the extension of political power to people who had been excluded from participation in government by dictators. When dictators surrendered, political power was extended to other social groups. But it was not universally distributed. So, for example, Communists were denied a significant role in democratic governments in Portugal, Spain, and Greece, and Basques were excluded from participation in Spain. In Latin America the socialist and Communist left was generally excluded, and participation by the rural and urban poor has been discouraged. In South Korea and Taiwan radical dissidents and socialist and Communist groups were excluded. In the Soviet Union and Eastern Europe ethnic minorities and recent immigrants are frequently excluded, and former Communists are sometimes barred from participation altogether, as they have been in East Germany and the Czech Republic. In South Africa, by contrast, most groups participate in government, though the rural and urban poor lack an effective voice in the political parties that control the state.

The exclusion of some social groups from political power in democratic states is not uncommon. After all, even the Western democracies exclude *some* social groups from participation as citizens. Although they now extend the rights and duties of citizenship to *most* residents—a development that took nearly two hundred years to achieve in the United States, for example—they do not extend them to minors, felons, legal or illegal immigrants, residents handicapped by certain physical or mental illnesses, or, in some cases, American Indians or people living in residual colonies or territories. To some extent even these "democracies" are still democratizing. The same is true of contemporary democratizing states.

Not only has the social meaning of democracy been qualified in newly democratizing states, but the extent of political change has also varied considerably. In Southern Europe the political landscape was dramatically altered by democratization. The change from royalist and anti-republican dictatorships to socialist governments in republican states was significant and far-reaching. In South Africa the end of exclusive white-minority rule and Nationalist Party government and the introduction of black majority rule and ANC government resulted in profound political change.

But democratization elsewhere resulted in more modest change. A remodeled dictatorship in South Korea retained considerable power by allying with the moderate opposition, and the ruling party in Taiwan opened the political process to other groups without ever surrendering power. In Latin America Christian Democrats or Peronist parties that had held power before dictators forced them from office frequently returned to power as a result of democratization. In some cases elections returned former dictators to power or, as in Chile, allowed the dictator to retain considerable power in the democratized state. Democratization in Latin America produced important but modest change. The end of one-party Communist rule in Eastern Europe and the Soviet Union resulted, for a time, in the rise of anti-Communist dissidents in some countries. But this fairly dramatic change was followed in most of these states by the return of reformed or revived Communist parties, a "retreat" that has limited the extent of political change. In most former Soviet republics and in Bulgaria and Romania Communist Party leaders never really surrendered power at all.

Democratization everywhere produced significant political change. The fall of dictators who harassed, imprisoned, and often murdered their political opponents was a momentous and welcome occasion. But democratization produced *moderate* political change in most countries and *dramatic* political change only in a few.

Of course, democratization is a relatively recent phenomenon. It may take some time for more dramatic change to occur. But if democratization is to expand, deepen, or consolidate, civilian democrats must successfully address the economic problems that first helped bring them to power. If they do not address these issues, the political gains they have already made—whether modest or dramatic—may be lost.

Democratization and Economic Policy

After taking power, most civilian democrats adopted the *same* economic solutions to their separate economic problems. They typically opened their economies to foreign investment and trade, sold state assets to foreign and domestic entrepreneurs, and cut government spending, particularly reducing defense expenditures. Although these measures assisted some states, they caused problems in others, undermining the ability of civilian authorities to defend, consolidate, or extend democratic government. Because continued democratization is contingent on effective solutions to economic problems, these common economic policies may in some cases contribute to crises that force democrats from power.

Before analyzing these economic programs and the problems associated with them, it is important to ask why so many governments adopted the *same* economic policies. First, they did so because the global economic institutions created during World War II—the World Bank and the International Monetary Fund—and signatories to the General Agreement on Tariffs and Trade insisted that a uniform set of policies be adopted as a condition for receiving new government loans, private foreign investment, access to foreign markets, or membership in global or regional trade groups such as GATT, the European Community, or the North America Free Trade Agreement (NAFTA). As the World Bank's chief economist Lawrence Summers argued in 1991, "The laws of economics, it's often forgotten, are like laws of engineering. There's only one set of laws, and they work everywhere."[1]

With many of the newly democratizing states burdened by large foreign debts, trade deficits, or investment deficiencies, the World Bank and other global economic institutions and powerful states were in a position to insist that democratizing states adopt the same set of laws.[2] Some governments, particularly heavily indebted ones in Latin America, adopted these policies because they had little choice and few alternatives.

But many governments also adopted these policies because they shared the developmentalist assumptions implicit in them. Just as postwar republican assumptions remained strong among dissident and opposition movements around the world, developmentalist economic assumptions remained strong on both sides of the Cold War divide. They were kept alive by economists in Western universities, by the Nobel Prize committee, which regularly awarded prizes to economists who codified the global set of laws, and by indigenous groups who saw them as an alternative to the failed developmentalist projects of capitalist or Communist dictatorships. Where capitalist or Communist states practiced mercantilist and import substitution economic policies to promote development, domestic groups opposed to these programs adopted the new developmentalist paradigm as an alternative. So when the opportunity to adopt a new strategy presented itself, they applied it with enthusiasm.

One of the first voluntary applications took place in Chile after Pinochet took power, under the direction of economists trained at the University of Chicago.[3] But it was subsequently adopted by many governments in democratizing states, in some with particular enthusiasm. Vaclav Klaus, for example, was a champion of this approach in Czechoslovakia, and adherents could be found in the economic ministries of many democratizing states around the world. These policies have also been adopted by some regimes that did *not* democratize. Regimes in Mexico and China have embraced these economic programs while spurning the political reforms sometimes associated with them. Only a few democratizing states, such as South Korea and Taiwan, have not adopted them, probably because they have not been required or inclined to do so. Indeed, their particular export-oriented but neo-mercantilist and monopolist economic programs have often been cited as models in their own right. Russia and many of the republics in the former Soviet Union have adopted them only slowly, if at all, because their implementation would jeopardize democratization.

Whether the adoption of these programs was compulsory or voluntary, most democratizing states have applied them in one form or another. Of course, governments in individual states implemented different versions of these programs, and economists debate the timing, sequence, and merits of implementing component parts. But most of the packages adopted in different settings contain the same essential features, and the problems associated with each are widely shared.

Civilian democrats around the world commonly adopted a three-part economic strategy to solve their separate economic problems. First, they began to open their economies to foreign investment and trade. Second, they sold state assets and reduced government participation in the economy. Third, they cut government spending, particularly military spending, and reduced the size of their armed forces. They took these steps to eliminate the economic legacies of previous dictators and to set the stage for what they hoped would be renewed economic growth.

Opening Domestic Economies

After taking power, civilian democrats opened their economies to foreign investment and trade. They relaxed restrictions on private investment flows, making it easier for foreign businesses to invest in domestic industries and stock markets and to liquidate assets and withdraw their capital. They encouraged investment because they needed foreign capital to spur economic growth and because they expected foreign investors to introduce new technologies and management techniques into industry, boosting productivity and increasing the competitiveness of firms in domestic and export markets.

Of course, democratizing states desperately needed foreign investment.[4] In 1991 the IMF announced that $100 billion was needed immediately to address the new demands of German reunification and reform in Eastern Europe and the Soviet Union.[5] This estimate was probably much too low, given that a $120 billion figure was cited as the amount required just to bring Russia's phone service up to the level of Spain's.[6]

Not only did democratizing states have huge new investment needs, but many also had to repay large foreign debts. Understandably, foreign investors were reluctant to invest in heavily indebted countries. As a result, financial flows to the developing world in 1990 were just over half their early 1980s level.[7]

Of course, institutional and private investors in Western Europe, the United States, and Japan have recognized that investment is economically essential and potentially profitable in democratizing states. Accordingly, they have provided both debt relief and new investment to some democratizing states. In 1991, for example, Western European creditors canceled half of the $33 billion that Poland owed to Paris Club members, while Japan provided $10 billion in debt relief to Latin American countries, though 20 percent of this went to nondemocratizing Mexico.[8] In the same year foreign businesses also invested nearly $3 billion in Eastern Europe and the Soviet Union.[9] But foreign investment flows have either been insufficient or unevenly distributed. In 1989 creditors disbursed $92 billion to Third World debtors, most of this to democratizing states in Latin America. But Latin American states returned $142 billion to creditors, "leaving a net transfer of $50 billion from poor countries to rich ones."[10]

In Eastern Europe, where investment was stronger and debts were smaller than in Latin America, overall investment flows have often exceeded debt repayments. But foreign investment has been allocated unevenly to the region. Between 1990 and 1994 the $5.5 billion invested in Hungary alone was greater than the combined amount invested in Poland, the Czech Republic, Romania, Bulgaria, Slovenia, and Slovakia.[11] Even Russia saw less investment—just $4 billion—than Hungary during this same period.[12] Still, Hungary's relatively heavy investment rate failed to spur growth or slow rising unemployment, which reached 12.6 percent in 1994.[13] East Germany was the main recipient of foreign investment in Eastern Europe. The unified German government poured more than $200 billion into the east after the country was reunited.[14] Private businesses in Europe's largest economy likewise invested heavily in eastern Germany. As a result, little capital was made available to other democratizing states.[15]

Despite taking steps to open their economies to foreign investment, democratizing states did not always see this foreign investment materialize. The demand in democratizing states exceeded the supply of available capital, making investment resources scarce, and debt-ridden economies did not offer many benefits to investors. But investment was also in short supply because investors concentrated their efforts in just a few countries—Romania, with 22 million inhabitants, received investment totaling $760 million between 1990 and 1994, while eastern Germany, with only 16 million inhabitants, received $200 billion in the same period. Of course, foreign governments and businesses were also reluctant for different reasons to invest in democratizing states. As *New York Times* columnist Leslie Gelb said of Russia in 1993, "Throwing money at a trillion dollar economy that is sinking in political anarchy, waste and corruption is not a brilliant idea."[16] The IMF and the World Bank evidently reached the same conclusion, promising $17 billion to Russia in 1993, but delivering only $2 billion, and tied subsequent financial deliveries to Russian economic reform.[17]

In South Africa, by contrast, investor disinterest is a result of a different set of circumstances. Foreign investors have been reluctant to reinvest in the post-apartheid state because frequent strikes have raised wages. South African employers now pay about $5 an hour in the heavily unionized manufacturing sector, twice the wage in Mexico or Brazil and eight times that of China, and productivity is comparatively low.[18] Democratization in South Africa eliminated apartheid, which for many years was the major obstacle to foreign investment. But by improving the conditions of long-suffering black workers, democratization has given foreign businesses a new reason to withhold investment. Despite their adoption of open investment policies, then, many democratizing countries have yet to see substantial inflows of foreign investment.[19]

Not only did democratizing states open their economies to foreign *investment*, they also opened their economies to foreign *goods*, reducing tariffs to provide imported goods at lower prices for domestic consumers and to make domestic industries competitive.[20] Democratizing states unilaterally cut tariffs and eliminated quotas and import restrictions and many joined GATT, committing themselves to tariff reduction with all member countries, or joined regional free trade agreements with neighboring states.[21]

But tariff reduction has led to two different problems. In many countries the reduction of taxes on imported goods led to buying binges, particularly in countries where imports had previously been difficult to obtain. In Latin America tariffs were reduced across the continent between 1989 and 1992—in Argentina the average tariff fell from 39 percent to 15 percent, in Colombia from 44 percent to 12 percent, and in Peru from 66 percent to 18 percent.[22] But tariff reduction then "unleashed a consumer boom, as Latin Americans . . . flocked to snap up imported goods at bargain prices."[23] Because consumers binged on imported goods, trade deficits increased and "Latin America's regional trade balance swung into the red in 1992, and by 1994 was heading for a $18 billion trade deficit."[24]

Countries in Southern and Eastern Europe experienced similar problems after tariffs were cut, and their trade deficits also grew.[25] But this process had the most dramatic effects in Mexico. When Mexico reduced tariffs to comply with NAFTA, consumers binged on imported goods, creating a $23 billion trade deficit in 1994. The trade deficit forced the government to deplete its foreign currency reserves and then to devalue its currency, which was designed to increase the real cost of imports and slow consumer purchases of imported goods. But the devaluation triggered massive capital flight, which further lowered the value of the peso and threatened the government with collapse. The regime was saved from defaulting on government bonds (it had no foreign currency reserves to pay bondholders in dollars) only because the United States and international lenders provided a $50 billion rescue package.[26]

A second problem related to tariff reduction was that it exposed domestic industries to foreign competition. Sometimes this competition forced domestic industries to increase productivity and deliver higher quality goods at lower prices. But it also forced many of them out of business, a plight that was particularly evident in the domestic auto industries of some democratizing states. In Spain, Eastern Europe, and South Africa, tariff reductions meant that Western European and Japanese cars could be imported more cheaply, and domestic consumers responded by purchasing foreign cars in increasing numbers. But the purchase of imported cars has since crippled the domestic auto industries. "We were seduced into believing we were in the major league," said business consultant Jaime Mariategui of the Spanish auto industry. "But when you are racing a Spanish SEAT [car] against a Mercedes, eventually you have to face reality."[27] The reduction of tariff barriers in Eastern Europe and the Soviet Union exposed the auto industries there to foreign competition, forcing manufacturers out of business or into subsidiary arrangements with foreign auto makers.[28] Lower tariffs in South Africa, meanwhile, will make it easier to import cars, thus exposing the seven domestic companies that make cars for the "small" South African market (three hundred thousand vehicles annually) to a "drastic shakeout."[29] Another consequence of the demise of the domestic car industries in these countries has been the loss of high-paying jobs, particularly among workers who have supported democratization.

While democratizing states opened their economies to foreign investment and imported goods, they also tried to increase the export of domestic products. They often did this by devaluing their currencies, which made their goods cheaper in export markets and imported goods more expensive at home. Currency devaluations thus served a dual purpose, discouraging consumers from purchasing imported goods in the absence of tariff barriers and creating trade surpluses that could be used to repay debt (as in most countries) or to invest in the domestic economy. All three democratizing states in Southern Europe, half of the countries in Latin America and the Philippines, South Korea, and virtually every country in Eastern Europe and the former Soviet Union devalued their currencies.[30]

But the widespread use of currency devaluations to promote exports and discourage imports encountered several difficulties. Because currency devaluations increased the cost of foreign imports, countries paid more for essential goods like oil and technology, a particular problem for countries without domestic energy resources. Currency devaluations were also supposed to make it easier for countries to sell their goods in export markets. But in Latin America, where debt crisis and devaluations reduced the ability of states to buy imported goods, regional export markets for producers collapsed, and it became more difficult for Latin American producers to sell goods to their neighbors. Likewise, the collapse of the Communist common market in Eastern Europe and the breakup of the Soviet Union made it extremely difficult for producers to sell goods to their traditional customers in Eastern Europe and the Soviet Union.[31] The collapse of economies in Africa makes it difficult for South African producers to sell goods in continental markets. Overall it has been difficult for democratizing states to promote their exports through currency devaluations, especially given their traditional ties to weak export markets. When every country tries to devalue its currency to gain export advantages, the net effect is to make currency devaluations relatively ineffective.

Currency devaluations have not produced the expected results for another reason. As Marx said of the capitalist countries in the last century, "The cheap prices of [their] commodities are the heavy artillery with which [the bourgeoisie] batters down all Chinese walls."[32] But today price is not the only consideration. For consumers, quality is also important. "Quality" need not mean superior craftsmanship or durability—it may simply mean the "quality" associated with a particular brand—Nike shoes, Marlboro cigarettes, Coca-Cola—and the attributes shaped by advertising campaigns in global media. Because many consumers now believe that quality is as important as price, they sometimes act in ways that economists, who use price as their central variable in determining consumer behavior, cannot predict. So, for example, when the U.S. government devalued the dollar in 1971 and again in 1985, consumers did not stop buying more expensive imports and purchase cheaper domestic products in their place. Instead, they continued buying the more expensive Japanese and German cars because they had been persuaded of their higher quality. Economists introduced the concept of "hysteresis," or "resistance to change," to explain why successive dollar devaluations did *not* change consumer behavior, increase U.S. exports, or reduce U.S. trade deficits.[33]

The use of currency devaluations to promote the export of cheap goods is no longer effective due to a change in consumer behavior. Consumers often prefer expensive, brand-name goods that they associate with particular qualities, an association formed through exposure to advertising, an industry that was in its infancy when Marx wrote. Consumers purchase expensive foreign commodities rather than similar domestic goods that are less expensive, often shunning these goods *because* they are cheap. Because democratizing states do not, for the most part, make "quality" merchandise for export markets, currency devaluations have done less to deter consumers from purchasing expensive imports and less to encourage exports than economists in democratizing states expected. The salience of price for consumers and economists is changing in ways that have made some economic strategies unrewarding or irrelevant.

Privatization

Democratizing states adopted a second set of policies. They sold, transferred, or returned state assets to foreign investors and domestic entrepreneurs. The "privatization" of state assets was designed to enable governments to repay debts, balance budgets, or finance new investment, while also increasing the efficiency of businesses that had languished under state control. By delivering assets to domestic owners, governments hoped to create the economic base for a new or reinvigorated social class of entrepreneurs who could revitalize the economy and become the vanguard of economic development for the country as a whole.

The privatization process differed substantially from one region to the next. In Southern Europe democratizing states typically increased domestic and foreign participation in state-run companies but did not entirely relinquish government ownership or control.[34] Democratizing states in Latin America sold off state-owned businesses and para-statal firms to raise money for debt repayment, a strategy that had been used during previous debt crises in the nineteenth and early twentieth centuries.[35] Privatization was much less extensive in East Asia—South Korea sold only seven firms by 1990—because both South Korea and Taiwan had few state-owned industrial assets compared with countries elsewhere and instead provided significant state support to large private monopolies, or *chaebols,* which they were unwilling to break up. In Eastern Europe and the former Soviet Union democratizing states sometimes returned property to owners who had been expropriated by Communist governments after World War II and transferred assets to tenants, farmers, workers, or managers who occupied, used, or controlled assets. Assets were also sold to foreign and domestic firms, and voucher systems were used to distribute shares of assets throughout the general population.[36] Privatization was most rapid and extensive in East Germany and in Czechoslovakia and slowest and most limited in the former Soviet Union, where the privatization and sale of agricultural land was permitted only in 1996.[37] In South Africa the transfer of state assets has been limited, primarily because most of the country's assets had previously been distributed by the state to private, white owners.

The sweeping privatization of state assets, particularly in Latin America and Eastern Europe, was similar in some respects to the great privatization of public land and natural resources in the United States during the nineteenth century. The 1862 Homestead Act, 1902 Reclamation Act, railroad right-of-way legislation, and subsurface mining laws transferred ownership and control of public assets to create a large class of farm owner-operators and spur agricultural, industrial, and mining development in the West. Unlike contemporary privatization, the U.S. government did not attempt to raise much money by selling public real estate and resources but instead transferred them at minimal cost to private owners. The aim of privatization in the United States was to use public resources to create entrepreneurial social classes. Contemporary privatization does much the same thing.

Although the privatization process differed in democratizing states around the world, the result was a huge sale or transfer of public assets.

The sale of national banks, airlines, telephone companies, shipping lines, cement factories, and port facilities was common in Latin America.[38] By the end of 1992 Brazil had sold 92 firms and a port authority for a total of $52 billion, and the two "keenest privatizers," Argentina and Mexico, sold off 173 companies for $32.5 billion from 1989 to 1992.[39] In Eastern Europe and the former Soviet Union assets worth hundreds of billions of dollars were offered for sale.[40]

But privatization by democratizing states did not produce the expected results. The widespread sale of public assets led to a glut of businesses on the investment market, resulting in fewer sales at lower prices than governments had anticipated. Only 58 of the 123 firms put on the market in the Philippines were sold, for a total of $228 million, considerably less than their book value.[41] In East Germany the government agency responsible for privatization was able to sell only 6,500 of the 11,000 large firms offered for sale.[42] And many countries in Eastern Europe decided not to sell their large firms because they could not find ready buyers at any price.

Part of the problem was the lack of domestic capital. In Poland the state in 1990 offered firms worth $100 billion for sale, but the total savings of the Polish population amounted to only $8 billion.[43] As one World Bank official observed, "[The Poles] naturally assume that these huge plants with all that heavy machinery have to be worth millions of dollars. [But they] have no concept of depreciation. [They don't understand] that something is worth a lot [of money] only if someone is willing to buy it."[44] Foreign investors were reluctant to purchase assets in Poland given estimates that "about a third of the industrial sector is not likely to be viable at all," and another third would not produce a "positive return."[45]

Where the sale of large firms was accompanied by currency devaluations, as it was in many countries, the assets prized as potentially profitable were often sold to foreigners at fire-sale prices. Currency devaluations made domestic goods—commodities, natural resources, and corporate assets—cheaper for foreigners but not for domestic buyers. As the economist Andre Gunder Frank noted, "The real market value of their properties and goods is suffering a classical and severe deflation in terms of . . . world currencies, [so that] property and land . . . in the East can be and is bought by Westerners 'for a song.'"[46]

In social terms privatization has helped create the economic base for new or transformed social classes, particularly in Eastern Europe and the Soviet Union. The sale of small-scale businesses has been more successful than the sale of large industrial firms because they could be purchased by domestic investors with limited capital. Privatization of these assets has provided economic resources to new social groups.[47] In Poland, for example, "362,000 new private businesses were set up and survived in 1990, while some 35,000 state and cooperative stores were either leased or sold to private individuals that same year."[48]

Some of the entrepreneurs who obtained these assets were new to business, having used their savings to purchase small shops and other productive assets. But many were the managers, bureaucrats, and state officials, the *nomenklatura* who controlled economic assets in Communist regimes.[49] And many more were "black market money changers, swindlers and higher-ranking Communist Party members who could exploit various connections."[50] One Czech official recognized that the new entrepreneurs often purchased state assets with money obtained through unscrupulous or illegal activities: "It's sure, there is dirty money here. But the best method of cleansing the money is to let them invest it."[51] Although new and old entrepreneurs might be expected to play a progressive economic role in democratizing states, the widespread perception that privatization was a form of *prikhvatizatsiia* (piratization), simply an opportunity "to steal what was stolen" resulting in the "enfranchisement of the nomenklatura," has been an ongoing problem in democratizing states.[52]

The corruption associated with privatization should not be surprising given the U.S. experience in the last century, where the transfer of public resources often resulted in the accumulation of large private fortunes. But it is nonetheless a problem because widespread corruption and the unequal distribution of public assets to foreigners and some domestic social groups raises issues of fairness and undermines the economic legitimacy of democratizing states. Moreover, even if privatization creates the economic base for a new or transformed class of entrepreneurs and even if it gives them an opportunity to "cleanse their money," they may not play the progressive role assigned to them. Whereas Communist regimes had long assigned the role of the economic "vanguard" to the proletariat, democratizing states, particularly in Eastern Europe, designated entrepreneurs as the key agents of economic and social change.

But the new entrepreneurs have not always performed their assigned roles. Many have used their wealth and savings on consumption rather than on investment.[53] In Poland, for example, purchases of Western European cars by nouveau entrepreneurs increased from 106,000 in 1990 to 500,000 in 1991, a form of binge buying that contributed both to Polish trade deficits and to the collapse of the domestic auto industry.[54] Entrepreneurs in Latin America, Eastern Europe, and South Africa invested savings and profits abroad, a flight of capital that starved domestic economies of scarce investment supplies. Capital flight has been particularly damaging for Russia, where it has been estimated that between $4 billion and $15 billion left the country in 1992 alone.[55] When entrepreneurs did invest domestically, they often engaged in currency trading, speculation, and other kinds of "unproductive" activities.

The economist John Maynard Keynes argued long ago that asset-holders would be more likely to save or consume their wealth than to risk it in productive investment. Only if governments were to offer incentives, such as low interest-rate policies, would the wealthy classes become inclined to invest in productive activity.[56] But although this absence of incentive is evident in the economies of democratizing states, particularly in Eastern Europe and the former Soviet Union, neoconservative economists, many of them anti-Keynesian, and global economic institutions deny the extent of the problem or oppose the policy prescriptions associated with it. They do so because they are reacting against the efforts by Communist states to channel, direct, or shape investments decisions, and they want democratizing states to reduce state intervention in the economy. As a spokesman for Czechoslovakia's Prime Minister Vaclav Klaus explained, "For us, Keynes is the father of western socialism, of state intervention. Keynesian economic interventions cause problems, so he is not a good model for us."[57]

Demilitarization

Finally, democratizing states adopted a third set of policies. Most tried to cut government spending and create budget surpluses that could be used to repay debt or finance domestic economic development. The sale of unprofitable public assets helped cut spending, as did the reduction of price subsidies for essential consumer goods and social services. Military spending was also reduced to balance budgets. These spending cuts were usually accompanied by tax increases, which were typically regressive. General spending cuts and tax increases helped democratizing states balance their budgets, but reduced government spending had different social and economic consequences for each country.

Where governments eliminated or cut subsidies for essential consumer goods such as food, oil, transportation, and rent, the prices of these goods rose dramatically. In economic terms, the rising price of essential goods fueled discriminatory inflation. In social terms, higher prices forced the poor to spend a greater percentage of their income on essentials and to reduce their consumption of these goods.[58] These developments were most evident in Latin America and in Eastern Europe and parts of the former Soviet Union, though democratizing states in some regions chose not to eliminate consumer subsidies entirely. Russia's determination to retain many subsidies was one reason why the IMF and World Bank refused to release funds they had earmarked for the country. By contrast, cuts in military spending generally had beneficial economic and political consequences, though there were some problems associated with reduced defense spending.

Democratizing states generally cut military spending for three related reasons. First, they wanted to reduce government expenditures. Second, they recognized that heavy defense spending inhibited rather than encouraged economic development and contributed to debt. Some scholars estimated that arms imports were responsible for 20–30 percent of total developing country debt.[59] Many civilian democrats agreed with the findings of scholars like A. F. Mullins, who concluded that "in general, those states that did best in GNP growth . . . paid less attention to military capability than others. This relation holds right across the range from poor states to rich states and from weak states to powerful. Those that did poorly in GNP growth . . . paid more attention to military capability."[60] Third, civilian democrats also wanted to reduce the ability of conservative militaries to use their positions in the military-industrial complexes to threaten nascent democracies.[61]

The most dramatic cuts in military spending were made in Latin America, Eastern Europe, and the Soviet Union. In Latin America successive Argentine presidents cut military spending in half, scaled back the draft, and cut the army to one-half its size during the Falklands War.[62] States across the continent also cut spending. Annual military spending in Argentina, Brazil, and Chile, where armies were large, dropped by 25 percent, from $4.9 billion in 1985 to $3.7 billion in 1992.[63] Julio Maria Sanguinetti, Uruguay's president in the late 1980s, described the changed political climate: "If you get a group of Latin American politicians together in a room and ask, 'Who wants to be foreign minister?' everyone will wave his or her hand in the air. But if you ask, 'Who wants to be defense minister?' everyone stares at the floor."[64]

Cuts in military spending have been even more dramatic in Eastern Europe and in the successor states of the Soviet Union. Gorbachev began the process, withdrawing from Afghanistan and cutting troop levels in Eastern Europe, which contributed to democratization there. Democrats in Eastern Europe promptly slashed military spending, reduced troop levels, disbanded party militias, and withdrew from the Warsaw Pact, causing its demise in 1991.[65] After the 1991 coup in the Soviet Union failed and the country democratized and divided, military spending fell drastically. Whereas in 1987 the Soviet Union had 5.1 million troops under arms and spent $356 billion on defense, by 1994, the Russian government kept only 1.5 million troops under arms and spend only $29 billion on defense, one-tenth as much.[66]

The large-scale defense cuts in democratizing states and around the world helped reduce overall military expenditures 14 percent between 1987 and 1991.[67] Of course, not all states cut their military spending. In Southern Europe democratizing states joined or rejoined NATO. They did not substantially reduce the size of their armed forces, but the move into NATO helped "professionalize" their armies, and their integration with military forces from northern Europe and the United States was designed, in part, to depoliticize conservative armies in Spain and Greece and an extremely radical army in Portugal. Because the United States assumed many of the costs associated with NATO, these governments were able to shift the burden of defense costs to others.[68]

The democratizing states of South Korea, Taiwan, and the Philippines have actually increased military spending. All three have done so in response to domestic or foreign threats and in response to the withdrawal of U.S. troops, bases, and military aid, which began in 1972 in Taiwan and has occurred more recently in South Korea and the Philippines.[69]

Post-Marcos governments in the Philippines have continued to battle radical domestic guerrillas, while in South Korea and Taiwan ongoing military threats related to partition have kept spending levels high. Chinese military spending, which increased sharply after Tiananmen Square, doubled between 1989 and 1994 (thereby reversing a substantial decline of previous years). China's renewed threats prior to Taiwan's 1996 presidential election forced Taiwan to respond in kind.[70] Taiwan increased military spending from $6.5 billion to $9.7 billion between 1987 and 1991 and increased its troop levels by 25 percent.[71] At the same time, troop levels increased in both North and South Korea and renewed North Korean belligerence in 1996 helped maintain high levels of defense spending. Unless or until these divided states resolve the conflicts related to partition or—in the cases of China and North Korea—democratize, military spending will remain high.

Although defense spending cuts have no doubt been a positive economic and social development for the world and for democratizing states, there are, nonetheless, some important problems related to them. For countries that had sold arms in export markets—Brazil, Czechoslovakia, and the Soviet Union—cuts in military spending have slowed production and crippled sales, depriving them of important export earnings. In Czechoslovakia, for example, the government reversed its 1990 decision to ban arms exports and renewed arms production because the impact on domestic employment and export earnings was too severe.[72] Russia is now trying to revive its moribund defense industries in an effort to reduce unemployment and increase export earnings.[73] Russian export earnings from arms sales fell from $50 billion a year in the mid-1980s to less than $3 billion a year in the 1990s.[74] In the former Soviet states other problems resulted from defense cuts. Russia and Ukraine quarreled over the division of the Black Sea fleet, and the breakup of the Soviet Union divided the nuclear arsenal between five successor states. The conversion of defense industries into consumer goods industries proved a difficult task. And the rapid demobilization of large armies also flooded labor and housing markets, increasing unemployment and raising rental prices, and produced groups of unemployed former soldiers who could be remobilized by opportunistic politicians.[75]

Prospects and Problems

Most of the democratizing states around the world adopted these common economic strategies, but only a few of them enjoyed any real and continuing success. The most successful were democratizing states in Southern Europe and East Asia.

In 1955 per capita incomes in Portugal and Greece were only 33 percent of the European Community average, while in Spain incomes were 61 percent of the EC average. By 1985, however, Portugal's per capita income had increased to 43 percent, Greece's to 51 percent, and Spain's to 74 percent.[76] Although this improvement can be attributed in part to the economic policies of dictators before 1974–75, much of it is due to the strategies of democratizing states, which made entry into the European Community a priority. Entry into the European Community brought important economic benefits for all three, though Spain in the 1990s experienced high unemployment (21.5 percent in 1993) and large trade deficits.[77] One journalist said of the Spanish experience, "The danger seems real that Spain, having made a great leap, could slip back."[78]

Both South Korea and Taiwan continued to record high rates of economic growth in the 1990s, though not at the same exceptional levels they had reached earlier.[79] Of all the democratizing states, South Korea and Taiwan began the democratization process in the best economic conditions— with rapid growth and little debt. They did not adopt the economic policies pursued elsewhere, largely because they were not forced to do so, which may account in part for their continued success. Like Southern European states, they benefited from close economic relations with a neighboring economic power, Japan, but also worked closely with the United States. Their long and beneficial economic relations with Japan differed from the relations between Southern European countries and the EC insofar as their relations with Japan were informal, whereas relations among EC members are carefully structured in formal organizations: the Common Market, the European Parliament, and NATO.

Much of the economic success of Southern European and East Asian democratizing states can be attributed to their incorporation and participation in the great-power economic spheres. Whether organized on a formal or an informal basis, these economic spheres have no doubt provided economic benefits to democratizing states. Massive economic assistance—already in the tens, if not hundreds, of billions of dollars—has accompanied East Germany's incorporation into West Germany and its subsequent inclusion into the European Union.[80] Although there have been difficult problems in East Germany—high unemployment and vast income disparities— there is little doubt that East Germans will eventually benefit from democratization in ways that their former compatriots in Eastern Europe will not. Indeed, the fact that West Germany has invested so heavily in the East means that German economic assistance will not be widely available elsewhere, thereby diminishing the economic prospects of other Eastern European states.

The story in Latin America is similar. Mexico's incorporation into the U.S. economic sphere through NAFTA provided the regime, which has not substantially democratized, with important economic and political benefits. As in East Germany, there have been serious economic problems related to incorporation—trade deficits, peso devaluation, and the near collapse of the economy in 1995. But the $50 billion in economic assistance provided by the United States and global lending agencies effectively managed these problems. U.S. aid also made it possible for the Mexican regime to avoid serious democratization. The fact that Mexico, like East Germany, is absorbing the lion's share of superpower economic assistance and attention means that democratizing states elsewhere in Latin America will not receive substantial aid.

Although incorporation into economic spheres in the European Community, the United States, and Japan is an important ingredient for economic success for democratizing and sometimes nondemocratizing states (Mexico and perhaps China), the benefits of membership in these spheres are not widely available. Eastern European countries are clamoring for admission into the European Union, Chile for entry into NAFTA, and China and Vietnam for inclusion into Japan's informal sphere. But admission will take some time, if it happens at all. The European Union, for example, is considering eventual membership for Poland, Hungary, the Czech Republic, and Slovenia. But membership for many of their neighbors—Slovakia, most former Yugoslav states, Romania, Bulgaria, Albania, and states in the former Soviet Union—is extremely unlikely. Because the incorporation of Mexico has created problems, it is unlikely that the United States will soon enroll the rest of Latin America into a *formal* economic sphere and extend NAFTA southward. In the case of South Africa, its distance from the great economic powers means that its incorporation into any great-power sphere is unlikely, and most observers think that its economic prospects depend on its ability to organize its own "mini-sphere" in southern Africa, a difficult project given its own limited resources and the economic weakness of its neighbors.

Although democratization in a few states has led to their economic development, democratization throughout most of Latin America and Eastern Europe and the former Soviet Union has not. In Latin America some democratizing states recorded modest economic growth in the 1990s: 4.2 percent in Argentina, 2.8 percent in Brazil, and 2.6 percent in Chile in 1994.[81] But debt in each country has also increased, in Argentina from $49.3 billion in 1985 to $75.0 billion, in Brazil from $105.0 to $151.5 billion, and in Chile from $20.4 to $21.5 billion in 1994.[82] Wages have also fallen in fifteen of nineteen Latin American countries surveyed in this period.[83] As the Inter-American Development Bank observed in 1994, "The resumption of [modest] economic growth has been bought at a very high social price, which includes poverty, increased unemployment and income inequality, and this is leading to social problems."[84] By the end of the century it is estimated that 192 million people in Latin America, or 46 percent of the population, will live in poverty, up from 130 million people, or 35 percent of the population, in 1980.[85] "Growth has really been on only one end of the spectrum, the wealthy. The rich are getting richer and the poor are getting poorer. And this will generate social conflict," U.N. official Peter Jensen argued.[86]

The problem for many democratizing governments is that democratization in Latin America has become associated with ongoing economic crisis. As Brazil's President Fernando Henrique Cardoso observed, "Latin America is trying to establish democracy without prosperity."[87] As a result of deep economic crisis, one democratizing state has already returned to dictatorship. Peru's president Alberto Fujimori, who was first elected in 1990, forged an alliance with the military, dissolved the congress, and adopted a new constitution that centralized political power, allowing him to create a compliant legislature. But his military success against the radical Shining Path insurgency and against Ecuador in a brief border war in 1995, a reduction of inflation from four- to two-digit figures, and renewed economic growth (8.9 percent in 1994) created a strong base of support for Fujimori among the urban middle and upper classes, enabling his reelection in 1996.[88] "Fujipopulism" was thus a response to the democratic government's failure to address Peru's ongoing economic and social crisis during the 1980s. The reemergence of dictatorship in Peru, albeit with a new political and social character, is a reminder and a warning that democratization is a contingent political development.

Many of these problems were shared by governments in Eastern Europe and the former Soviet Union. In the first few years after 1989 economic conditions worsened dramatically, with wages in industrial production falling by more than one-third and trade deficits, debt, inflation, and unemployment all rising.[89] A 1992 Harvard University study found that "the vast majority of people in Eastern Europe live in economic conditions which are demonstrably worse than those under the inefficiencies of central planning."[90]

Although the economies of the Eastern European countries have improved recently, unemployment and inflation remain in double-digit figures. The Czech Republic is an exception, however. It has lowered its unemployment rates by separating from Slovakia, where the economy was troubled and unemployment rates were high.[91] Russia's economic recovery has not been as pronounced, however. According to the Center for Economic Reform, wages have fallen 39 percent between 1990 and 1993, and 37 percent of Russia's 150 million people lived in poverty, a figure approaching poverty rates for Latin America.[92] The deepening economic crisis also lowered the life expectancy of adult men and shrank the population in 1994, a development that British demographer David Coleman described as "an incredibly clear picture of a society in crisis. A decline in life expectancy this dramatic has never happened in the postwar period. It shows the malaise of society, the lack of public health awareness, and the fatigue associated with people who have to fight a pitched battle their whole lives just to survive."[93] Under these circumstances, it should not be surprising that in a 1994 opinion poll, two-thirds of all Russians believed that things were "better" under communism than they are now. In Eastern Europe large minorities and sometimes majorities agreed with this assessment.[94]

Of course, some observers argue that these problems are associated with a "transition period" or are merely a "legacy" of communism. That may be the case. But the fact that similar problems are shared by democratizing states in Latin America, where communism was, for the most part, absent, indicates that this is not a sufficient explanation for the current crisis in Eastern Europe and the Soviet Union. Instead, it may be that the common economic solutions adopted by democratizing states in both regions have exacerbated problems that were the separate legacies of capitalist and Communist development policies. Although these policies differed in important respects, they were alike in others. For example, dictatorships in both regions adopted neomercantilist economic policies and borrowed heavily in the 1970s to promote growth.

Communist parties in many of the Soviet successor states retained power, returned to power, or, in the case of Russia, moved to the fringes of power. Of course, their ability to do so depends not only on widespread discontent with economic and political reforms, but also on their ability to create new political structures and social constituencies, as Fujimori has done in Peru. In the former Soviet Union, as in Latin America, dictatorship, if it does reappear, will differ from the dictatorships that existed prior to democratization. New forms of political rule will, no doubt, rely on different economic strategies and social constituencies and depend on new kinds of political legitimacy. If democratizing states in these regions cannot address serious economic problems, they risk the return of dictatorship in a new guise.

Global Obstacles

Democratizing states have used common economic strategies to address separate economic crises, and with different results. But whether they have enjoyed success or experienced failure, they have all had to confront another, more general set of global economic problems.

The first problem is that economic opportunities are scarce in a global economy that has been in a period of slow economic growth since the early 1970s. In contrast to the period of rapid global growth between 1945 and 1970, when the economies of capitalist *and* Communist, democratic *and* dictatorial states collectively advanced, the period since has been one of slower economic growth, in which benefits have been more narrowly distributed. During this recent period, what some economists describe as a cyclical downturn at the global level, or "B-phase" in the world economy, economic opportunities have been relatively scarce.[95] The fact that so many democratizing states have adopted the same economic strategies, which have been designed to seize the opportunities that do exist, probably reduces the chances for individual success. Although the poor economic climate at the global level may have contributed in some ways to the economic crises that undermined dictatorships and contributed to democratization in individual states, it may also prevent democratizing states from addressing their separate problems in the future.

A second, related problem is that the world's leading economic powers have adopted strategies aimed at improving their own positions in the world. These strategies may disadvantage other countries, making it more difficult for democratizing states to achieve any real economic development. The United States is one example. In an effort to improve U.S. competitiveness and reduce trade deficits with Japan, U.S. officials devalued the dollar in 1971 and again in 1985, effectively ending the system of fixed exchange rates established at Bretton Woods and affecting currency values and trade balances around the world. And by adopting high interest rates to combat inflation in the late 1970s, U.S. officials raised global interest rates and triggered a debt crisis in many countries.[96]

Although changed U.S. economic policy had important and often disruptive consequences, collective strategies adopted by the United States and other First World countries have also had disruptive consequences. Generally, First World countries have taken steps together to reduce commodity prices for the goods they import. These strategies, which have helped cut commodity prices dramatically during the 1980s and 1990s, have caused serious problems for countries that now depend on export sales to repay debt and promote economic development.

Commodity prices for raw materials, natural resources, and unfinished manufactured goods—the kind of goods most poor countries and democratizing states produce for export markets—have fallen as a result of a combination of developments. The domination of export commodity markets by small groups of multinational corporations has resulted in "monopsonies" that benefit buyers, not suppliers. Some 130 countries produce cocoa for chocolate, but just three companies—Mars, Hershey, and Nestle—control more than 80 percent of the world's cocoa trade. Their monopsony position in the market enables them to force producer prices down—by about 50 percent during the 1980s—and consumer prices up—consumers paid about 30 percent more for chocolate bars during this period.[97]

First World states and private companies have also encouraged producers to diversify and expand the production of many commodities. Japan has financed the expansion of soy estates in Brazil, international lending agencies have encouraged the expansion of coffee production in Thailand, a country that did not previously produce coffee, and First World countries have increased oil-exploration efforts in non-OPEC countries.[98] These efforts have created supplies that are less vulnerable to political or economic change in individual states, increased supplies from and competition among primary goods producers, and eroded the economic power of producer groups, such as the coffee cartel and OPEC, that organized collectively to limit supplies and support prices. By increasing the volume of supplies, First World countries have helped to lower commodity prices.

Although supplies have generally increased, First World demand for many goods has fallen. The development of new technologies by First World countries has enabled their producers to replace Third World products with their own, a new form of import substitution.[99] So, for example, First World demand for sugarcane grown in tropical countries has fallen as cane sugar has been replaced by artificial dietary sweeteners and high-fructose corn sweeteners grown in the U.S. Midwest. Tropical oils have been replaced by temperate oil seeds.[100] The use of fiber-optic cable and wireless communication and satellite technologies has reduced demand for copper mined in Chile or Zambia. The manufacture of high-mileage cars and solar engineering has reduced First World demand for oil produced in Mexico and Saudi Arabia. These technological innovations have enabled First World countries to adopt import substitution policies, effectively reducing demand for Third World goods and contributing to the downward pressure on prices.

Because supplies of many Third World goods are more ubiquitous and abundant and because First World demand for many goods has weakened as domestic substitutes are developed, First World buyers, like tourists strolling through street markets in developing countries, can buy inexpensive goods, but they can also walk away. They can be indifferent to the pitch of any single vendor because they can be certain that another vendor, even more desperate to make a sale, will offer a deal at least as good as the first. As one economist has explained, "Unlike banks, whose billions were tied up in long-term loans, most of the new [First World] investors [in the Third World] are holding debt or equity securities that trade in the open market, and they will move on when it no longer pays to stay put. . . . If [First World investors] don't like a particular [Third World] policy, they will react to it, and exert a rather severe penalty on local securities markets."[101]

This new reality has given rise to Third World fears that investors will walk away from their markets, threatening them with ruin. They engage themselves in a furious competition for First World economic attention, a competition that is advantageous to First World investors and consumers but detrimental to Third World producers.

One political result of these economic developments is what I have called "indifferent imperialism."[102] Because the old European and Asian empires had permanent territorial claims in their colonies, they had a certain stake in economic and political events there, sometimes described as a "burden." Likewise, the United States and Soviet Union made long-term investments in postcolonial states and engaged in a sometimes bitter competition for their allegiance. As a result, they paid close attention to economic and political developments in colonial and postcolonial states. But today it is easier for First World states to view economic and political developments in postcolonial and democratizing states with considerable indifference, detachment, or "complacency," to use William Pfaff's term.[103] A *New York Times* headline of an article opposing U.S. intervention in Bosnia expressed this new insouciance by reminding readers: "There's No Oil in Bosnia."[104] Or, as Salim A. Salim, secretary general of the Organization of African Unity, told policymakers in Washington, "I am not nostalgic about the Cold War," when First World interest in Africa was great. "What I am saying is that there is diminishing [First World] interest in the issues of real human concern [in Africa]."[105]

First World indifference comes at a bad time for democratizing states. In economic terms, it makes their attempts to address serious economic problems more difficult. In political terms, it makes them more vulnerable to change. Democratization was a great achievement, but it remains an ongoing struggle.

NOTES

Introduction

1. Russell Bova, "Political Dynamics of the Post-Communist Transition: A Comparative Perspective," in *Liberalization and Democratization: Change in the Soviet Union and Eastern Europe,* ed. Nancy Bermeo (Baltimore: Johns Hopkins University Press, 1992), pp. 114, 116–17; Adam Zwass, *From Failed Communism to Underdeveloped Capitalism: The Transformation of Eastern Europe, the Post-Soviet Union and China* (Armonk, N.Y.: M. E. Sharpe, 1995), p. 249; Valerie Bunce, "Should Transitologists Be Grounded?" *Slavic Review* 54, no. 1 (spring 1995): 111–27.

2. Bova, "Political Dynamics of the Post-Communist Transition," in Bermeo, 1992, p. 117.

Chapter One

1. William Roger Louis, *Imperialism at Bay: The United States and the Decolonization of the British Empire, 1941–1945* (New York: Oxford University Press, 1978), p. 226.

2. Ibid., p. 121; Ruth B. Russell, *A History of the United Nations Charter: The Role of the United States, 1940–1945* (Washington, D.C.: The Brookings Institution, 1958), p. 14.

3. Pollard argued that "the erection of closed economic blocs by fascist Germany in Eastern Europe, Japan in the Far East, and Britain in the Commonwealth countries had exacerbated economic rivalries and set the great powers on the road to war." Robert A. Pollard, *Economic Security and the Origins of the Cold War, 1945–1950* (New York: Columbia University Press, 1985), p. 8.

4. Richard N. Gardner, *Sterling-Dollar Diplomacy in Current Perspective: The Origins and the Prospects of Our International Economic Order* (New York: Columbia University Press, 1980), p. 9.

5. Ibid., p. 5.

6. Michael Howard, "The Historical Development of the U.N.'s Role in International Security," in *United Nations, Divided World: The U.N.'s Roles in International Relations,* ed. Adam Robert and Benedict Kingsbury (Oxford: Clarendon Press, 1993), p. 63.

7. Ted Robert Gurr, "War, Revolution, and the Growth of the Coercive State," in *The Elusive State: International and Comparative Perspectives,* ed. James A. Caporaso (Beverly Hills, Calif.: Sage, 1989), p. 52.

8. Russell, *A History of the United Nations Charter,* p. 83. Undersecretary of State Sumner Well's May 1942 speech outlined U.S. policy on independence for colonial peoples.

9. Theodore A. Wilson, *The First Summit: Roosevelt and Churchill at Placentia Bay, 1941* (Lawrence, Kans.: University of Kansas Press, 1991), pp. 178–79.

10. Historically, republics have been post-monarchist states. Revolutionaries in the United States, France, and the Soviet Union all fought against or overthrew monarchs and created "constitutional" forms of government, establishing congresses and assemblies as the institutional expressions of popular sovereignty. It is important to note, however, that republican states are not necessarily democratic. Many republics with constitutional forms of government have been, in fact, dictatorships as well. And although most republics have been postcolonial states—demanding independence and opposing colonialism—some have also maintained colonies of their own.

11. Ibid., pp. 147–48.

12. Peter W. Rodman, *More Precious Than Peace: The Cold War and the Struggle for the Third World* (New York: Charles Scribner's Sons, 1991), p. 42.

13. Tony Smith, *America's Mission: The United States and the Worldwide Struggle for Democracy in the Twentieth Century* (Princeton: Princeton University Press, 1994), p. 126.

14. Ibid., p. 118.

15. Robert Schaeffer, *Warpaths: The Politics of Partition* (New York: Hill and Wang, 1990), pp. 46–59, 106–119.

16. Russell, *A History of the United Nations Charter,* pp. 103, 52–54.

17. Ibid., p. 165; Peter J. Taylor, "Geopolitical World Orders," in *Political Geography of the Twentieth Century: A Global Analysis,* ed. Peter J. Taylor (New York: John Wiley and Sons, 1993), p. 51.

18. Russell, *A History of the United Nations Charter,* p. 149.

19. Ibid., p. 738.

20. Wilson, *The First Summit,* p. 175.

21. Diane S. Clemens, *Yalta* (London: Oxford University Press, 1970), p. 130; Russell, *A History of the United Nations Charter,* p. 478.

22. Akira Iriye, *The Globalizing of America, 1913–1945,* vol. 3 of *The Cambridge History of American Foreign Relations* (Cambridge: Cambridge University Press, 1993), pp. 178–79.

23. Gardner, *Sterling-Dollar Diplomacy in Current Perspective,* p. 300.

24. Eric Hobsbawm, *The Age of Extremes: A History of the World, 1914–1991* (New York: Pantheon, 1994), p. 97; John O'Loughlin and Herman van der Wusten, "Political Geography of War and Peace," in Taylor, 1993, pp. 77–81.

25. William H. Honan, "Wartime Decoding of Allies Said to Have Aided U.S. in U.N." *New York Times,* 23 April 1995.

26. John Gallagher, *The Decline, Revival and Fall of the British Empire: The Ford Lectures and Other Essays* (Cambridge: Cambridge University Press, 1982), p. 75; Ronald Robinson and John Gallagher, "The Imperialism of Free Trade," in *Imperialism: The Robinson and Gallagher Controversy,* ed. William Roger Louis (New York: New Viewpoints, 1976), p. 54; Edward Mortimer, *The World That FDR Built: Vision and Reality* (New York: Charles Scribner's Sons, 1988), p. 98.

27. The term "collective security" was not initially used, but it was implied in Article 1 of the Atlantic Charter. Michael Howard, "The Historical Development of the UN's Role in International Security," in Robert and Kingsbury, 1993, p. 64; Russell, *A History of the United Nations Charter*, p. 485.

28. Russell, *A History of the United Nations Charter*, p. 509; Richard Fenno, *The Yalta Conference* (Boston: D.C. Heath, 1955), pp. 12–13.

29. Russell, *A History of the United Nations Charter*, p. 1032.

30. Robert Divine, *Roosevelt and World War II* (Baltimore: Johns Hopkins University Press, 1969), p. 52; Clemens, *Yalta*, p. 53.

31. Robert and Kingsbury, eds., *United Nations, Divided World*, pp. 6–7.

32. Bruce D. Marshall, *The French Colonial Myth* (New Haven: Yale University Press, 1969), p. 182.

33. Clemens, *Yalta*, p. 48.

34. Mortimer, *The World That FDR Built*, p. 93.

35. Ibid., p. 90; Paul Kennedy, *The Rise and Fall of the Great Powers* (New York: Random House, 1987), p. 358.

36. Lloyd C. Gardner, *Architects of Illusion: Men and Ideas in American Foreign Policy, 1941–1949* (Chicago: Quadrangle Books, 1980), p. 78.

37. Michael Moffitt, *The World's Money: International Banking from Bretton Woods to the Brink of Insolvency* (New York: Simon and Schuster, 1983), pp. 21–22.

38. Alfred E. Eckes, Jr., *A Search for Solvency: Bretton Woods and the International Monetary System, 1941–1971* (Austin, Tex.: University of Texas Press, 1975), p. 158; Gardner, *Architects of Illusion*, pp. 74, xxii.

39. Moffitt, *The World's Money*, p. 25.

40. Mortimer, *The World That FDR Built*, p. 95.

41. Moffitt, *The World's Money*, pp. 20, 67.

42. Gardner, *Architects of Illusion*, pp. 101–102.

43. Ibid., p. xxvi.

44. Ibid., p. 13.

45. Pollard, *Economic Security and the Origins of the Cold War*, pp. 17–18.

46. Stephen J. Lee, *The European Dictatorships, 1918–1945* (London: Methuen, 1987), p. 23.

47. John Lewis Gaddis, *The Long Peace: Inquires into the History of the Cold War* (New York: Oxford University Press, 1987), p. 84.

48. The term "decolonization" was first introduced by M. J. Bonn, a German economist who emigrated to Britain during the 1930s. See Rudolf Von Albertini, *Decolonization: The Administration and Future of the Colonies, 1919–1960* (New York: Doubleday, 1971), pp. 16–17.

49. Stanley Karnow, *Vietnam: A History* (New York: Viking Press, 1983), p. 137; Von Albertini, *Decolonization*, p. 24; Louis, *Imperialism at Bay*, p. 567; John Darwin, *Britain and Decolonisation: The Retreat from Empire in the Post-War World* (New York: St. Martin's Press, 1988), p. 43.

Of course, neither the United States nor the Soviet Union were wholly anticolonial. The United States made good on its promise to grant independence to the Philippines but did not do so for Puerto Rico; the Soviet Union retained the Baltic states—Latvia, Lithuania, and Estonia—that were acquired by treaty with Nazi Germany. See Von Albertini, *Decolonization*, p. 486. But both superpowers nonetheless urged full and rapid decolonization of European empires.

50. Von Albertini, *Decolonization,* p. 24.

51. Ibid., p. 85.

52. Mortimer, *The World That FDR Built,* p. 116.

53. Schaeffer, *Warpaths,* pp. 32–33.

54. Ibid., pp. 20–22.

55. Ibid., p. 41.

56. Ibid., p. 23.

57. Gallagher discounted their role: "Colonial resistance movements, a romantic term, are not going to help us through our problems. We need have no truck with the view that the downfall of this empire was brought about by colonial freedom fighters because, except in some Pickwickian sense, these processes involved next to no fighting. . . . [There were] no Dublin Post offices [in most colonial settings]." Gallagher, *The Decline, Revival and Fall of the British Empire,* pp. 73–74. But there *were* Dublin post offices or King David Hotels in some settings, and the absence of actual rebellion in other colonies did not mean that the threat of rebellion did not loom large in the minds of colonial authorities.

58. H. V. Hodson, *The Great Divide* (Oxford: Oxford University Press, 1985), p. 166.

59. Darwin, *Britain and Decolonisation,* p. 24.

60. David Held, *Prospects for Democracy: North, South, East, West* (Stanford, Calif.: Stanford University Press, 1993), pp. 29, 34.

61. There are, of course, different varieties. Socialist republics distinguish themselves by using adjectives like "Democratic" or "People's" before "Republic" in their proper names; capitalist republics typically use the simple form, "Republic of . . . ," and Muslim states qualify "republic" with the adjective "Islamic."

Chapter Two

1. "In the end . . . the great powers had to state quite baldly that unless the Yalta formula . . . giving the permanent members of the Security Council a 'veto' right . . . was accepted, there would be no world organization," wrote U.N. historian Ruth Russell. Ruth B. Russell, *A History of the United Nations Charter: The Role of the United States, 1940–45* (Washington, D.C.: The Brookings Institution, 1958), p. 713.

2. Lloyd C. Gardner, *Architects of Illusion: Men and Ideas in American Foreign Policy, 1941–49* (Chicago: Quadrangle Books, 1970), p. 6.

3. Gaddis Smith, *The Last Years of the Monroe Doctrine, 1945–1993* (New York: Hill and Wang, 1994), p. 130.

4. T. E. Vadney, *The World Since 1945* (London: Penguin, 1992), p. 39; Warren I. Cohen, *America in the Age of Soviet Power, 1945–1991,* vol. 4 of *The Cambridge History of American Foreign Relations* (Cambridge: Cambridge University Press, 1993), p. 8.

5. Edward Mortimer, *The World That FDR Built: Vision and Reality* (New York: Charles Scribner's Sons, 1988), p. 48. "As U.S. diplomat Charles Bohlen noted in 1947, Washington's wartime agreements with Moscow clearly indicated that 'we are not attempting to deny to Russia the perquisites of a great power,' namely that she has a certain primary strategic interest in the countries that lie along her bor-

ders." Robert A. Pollard, *Economic Security and the Origins of the Cold War, 1945–1950* (New York: Columbia University Press, 1985), p. 34; John Lewis Gaddis, *The Long Peace: Inquiries into the History of the Cold War* (New York: Oxford University Press, 1987), p. 48. Gaddis also argued (p. 239) that "neither Russians nor Americans officially admit to having such 'spheres,' but in fact much of the history of the Cold War can be written in terms of the efforts both have made to consolidate and extend them."

6. "The Monroe Doctrine is not now and never was an instrument of aggression; it is and always has been a cloak of protection," U.S. diplomats insisted. "The Doctrine is not a lance; it is a shield." Smith, *The Last Years of the Monroe Doctrine*, p. 34.

7. Walter LaFeber, *America, Russia and the Cold War, 1945–1984* (New York: Alfred A. Knopf, 1985), p. 13.

8. Vadney, *The World Since 1945*, p. 40.

9. LaFeber, *America, Russia and the Cold War*, pp. 13–14.

10. Gaddis, *The Long Peace*, p. 51.

11. Cohen, *America in the Age of Soviet Power*, p. 38; LaFeber, *America, Russia and the Cold War*, p. 52.

12. Smith, *The Last Years of the Monroe Doctrine*, pp. 54–55; LaFeber, *America, Russia and the Cold War*, p. 22.

13. Smith, *The Last Years of the Monroe Doctrine*, p. 55.

14. Paul Kennedy, *The Rise and Fall of the Great Powers* (New York: Random House, 1987), p. 389; LaFeber, *America, Russia and the Cold War*, p. 67.

15. John Gerard Ruggie, "Multilateralism: The Anatomy of an Institution," *International Organization* 46, no. 3 (summer 1992): 589; LaFeber, *America, Russia and the Cold War*, p. 84.

16. Robert Schaeffer, *Warpaths: The Politics of Partition* (New York: Hill and Wang, 1990), see Chapter 8.

17. Ralph B. Levering, *The Cold War, 1945–1987* (Arlington Heights, Ill.: Harlan Davidson, 1988), p. 19. "The conflict had destroyed 1,700 [Soviet] towns, 70,000 villages, and left 25 million homeless. Twenty million died; 600,000 starved to death at the single siege of Leningrad," Walter LaFeber wrote. LaFeber, *America, Russia and the Cold War*, p. 39.

18. Levering, *The Cold War*, pp. 20–22.

19. Ibid., pp. 16, 18; LaFeber, *America, Russia and the Cold War*, pp. 16–17.

20. LaFeber, *America, Russia and the Cold War*, pp. 38–39.

21. Cohen, *America in the Age of Soviet Power*, p. 39.

22. Peter Lowe, *The Origins of the Korean War* (London: Longman, 1986), p. 14; James I. Matray, "Captive of the Cold War: Decision to Divide Korea at the 38th Parallel," *Pacific Historical Review* 5, no. 2 (May 1981): 164; John Sullivan, *Two Koreas—One Future?* (Lanham, Md.: University Press of America, 1987), p. 7; Bong-youn Choy, *A History of the Korean Unification Movement* (Peoria, Ill.: Institute of International Studies, Bradley University, 1984), p. 12.

23. Matray, "Captive of the Cold War," p. 166. Coincidentally, Russia and Japan had twice discussed dividing Korea at the thirty-eighth parallel, first in 1896 and again in 1903. Choy, *A History of the Korean Unification Movement*, p. 13.

24. John King Fairbank, *The United States and China* (Cambridge, Mass.: Harvard University Press, 1983), pp. 341–42; LaFeber, *America, Russia and the Cold*

War, pp. 30–31; Gabriel Kolko, *The Politics of War* (New York: Vintage, 1986), p. 255.

25. Kolko, *The Politics of War,* p. 255.

26. Stanley Karnow, *Vietnam: A History* (New York: Viking Press, 1983), p. 137.

27. John L. Snell, *Dilemma over Germany* (New Orleans: Phauser Press, 1959), p. 79.

28. Bruce Kuklick, *American Policy and the Division of Germany* (Ithaca: Cornell University Press, 1972), p. 25; John Lewis Gaddis, *The United States and the Origins of the Cold War* (New York: Columbia University Press, 1972), p. 120.

29. Frank Ninkovich, *Germany and the United States* (Boston: Twayne, 1988), p. 58.

30. LaFeber, *America, Russia and the Cold War,* p. 75.

31. Snell, *Dilemma over Germany,* p. 224; Ninkovich, *Germany and the United States,* p. 60.

32. Gaddis, *The Long Peace,* p. 64.

33. Ninkovich, *Germany and the United States,* p. 71.

34. Henry Ashby Turner, Jr., *The Two Germanies Since 1945* (New Haven: Yale University Press, 1987), p. 50.

35. Choy, *A History of the Korean Unification Movement,* pp. 41–42.

36. Ibid., p. 45.

37. Ibid., pp. 46–48.

38. Ibid., p. 60.

39. Ibid., p. 62.

40. Ibid., p. 63.

41. LaFeber, *America, Russia and the Cold War,* p. 99.

42. "In the coming year," Rhee promised on December 30, 1949, "we shall unanimously strive to regain lost territory . . . through our own efforts." Meanwhile, Kim Il Sung said he would use North Korea "as a democratic basis for Korean unification." Choy, *A History of the Korean Unification Movement,* p. 61.

43. According to Nikita Khrushchev, North Korean leader Kim Il Sung proposed the attack and obtained approval from Stalin and Chinese Communist leader Mao Tsetung. Lowe, *The Origins of the Korean War,* p. 156; Levering, *The Cold War,* p. 44.

44. Seymour Topping, *Journey Between Two Chinas* (New York: Harper Colophon, 1972), p. 71.

45. Lowe, *The Origins of the Korean War,* pp. 54, 108.

46. George Kennan, for instance, argued that "Formosan separatism is the only concept which has sufficient grassroots appeal to resist communism." Gaddis, *The Long Peace,* p. 81. And Secretary of State Dean Acheson hoped to satisfy "the legitimate demands of indigenous Formosans for self-determination either under a U.N. trusteeship or through independence." Bruce Cumings, *Child of Conflict: The Korean-American Relationship* (Seattle: Washington University Press, 1983), p. 47. But these schemes foundered because the Kuomintang was strong, Taiwanese independence movements were weak, and the U.S. had already agreed to return Taiwan to China. A State Department memo warned that an attempt to detach the island "would outrage *all* Chinese elements and as a resort to naked expediency would destroy our standing with the small countries of the world" (emphasis added). Gaddis, *The Long Peace,* p. 83.

47. June Grasso, *Truman's Two-China Policy* (Armonk, N.Y.: M. E. Sharpe, 1987), p. 113.

48. Mortimer, *The World That FDR Built*, p. 356.

49. Andrew J. Rotter, *The Path to Vietnam* (Ithaca: Cornell University Press, 1987), p. 96.

50. Levering, *The Cold War*, p. 84.

51. Rotter, *The Path to Vietnam*, p. 217.

52. Lowe, *The Origins of the Korean War*, p. 119; Grasso, *Truman's Two-China Policy*, p. 127; LaFeber, *America, Russia and the Cold War*, p. 92.

53. Grasso, *Truman's Two-China Policy*, pp. 128, 141.

54. Ibid., p. 177.

55. Rotter, *The Path to Vietnam*, p. 104.

56. Cumings, *Child of Conflict*, p. 187.

57. Melvin Gurtov and Byong-Moo Huang, *China Under Threat* (Baltimore: Johns Hopkins University Press, 1980), p. 54.

58. Lloyd C. Gardner, *Approaching Vietnam* (New York: W. W. Norton, 1988), p. 116.

59. R. F. Holland, *European Decolonization, 1918–1981* (New York: St. Martin's Press, 1985), p. 100; Gardner, *Approaching Vietnam*, p. 179.

60. Gardner, *Approaching Vietnam*, p. 340; Cohen, *America in the Age of Soviet Power*, p. 96.

61. Gabriel Kolko, *The Roots of American Foreign Policy* (Boston: Beacon Press, 1969), p. 111; Topping, *Journey Between Two Chinas*, p. 151.

62. Ninkovich, *Germany and the United States*, pp. 84–85.

63. Rotter, *The Path to Vietnam*, pp. 218–19; Levering, *The Cold War*, pp. 65–66.

64. Gaddis, *The Long Peace*, p. 185.

65. Audrey Kurth Cronin, *Great Power Politics and the Struggle Over Austria, 1945–1955* (Ithaca: Cornell University Press, 1986), pp. 147, 159. Soviet premier Nikita Khrushchev told the Austrian leaders at the close of negotiations, "Follow my example and turn Communist. . . . But if I really can't convince you, then for God's sake stay as you are." Cronin, pp. 150–51.

66. Gaddis, *The Long Peace*, p. 143.

67. Ibid.

68. David P. Calleo, "The U.S. in the 1960s: Hegemon in Decline?" in *The Rise and Decline of the Nation State*, ed. Michael Mann (Oxford: Basil Blackwell, 1990), pp. 156, 151.

69. Ibid., pp. 156, 151.

70. Ibid., pp. 157, 151. Of course, U.S. defense spending in constant 1982 dollars has increased, from $66.5 billion in 1985 to $850 billion in 1986. John Agnew, "The United States and American Hegemony," in *Political Geography of the Twentieth Century: A Global Analysis*, ed. Peter J. Taylor (New York: John Wiley and Sons, 1993), p. 226. The share of defense spending fell even while the total amount of spending increased. At least until the 1980s, a growing economy enabled the government to increase military budgets without contributing to budget deficits.

71. J. H. Parry, *Europe and the Wider World, 1415–1715* (London: Hutchinson University Library, 1961), pp. 50–51.

72. Ibid., p. 51.

73. Robert Schaeffer, "The Standardization of Time and Space," in *Ascent and Decline in the World-System,* ed. Edward Friedman (Beverly Hills, Calif.: Sage, 1982).

74. Parry, *Europe and the Wider World,* p. 58.

75. Ibid.

76. Gaddis, *The Long Peace,* p. 103.

77. Schaeffer, *Warpaths,* passim.

Chapter Three

1. T. E. Vadney, *The World Since 1945* (London: Penguin, 1992), pp. 52–53.

2. Ibid., p. 53; Walter LaFeber, *America, Russia and the Cold War, 1945–1984* (New York: Alfred A. Knopf, 1985), p. 76.

3. LaFeber, *America, Russia and the Cold War,* p. 76; Vadney, *The World Since 1945,* pp. 53–54.

4. John Lewis Gaddis, *The Long Peace: Inquiries into the History of the Cold War* (New York: Oxford University Press, 1987), p. 158.

5. Ibid., pp. 158–59.

6. Peter Willetts, *The Non-Aligned Movement: The Origins of a Third World Alliance* (London: Frances Pinter, 1978), p. 6.

7. Ibid., p. 7.

8. Peter W. Rodman, *More Precious Than Peace: The Cold War and the Struggle for the Third World* (New York: Charles Scribner's Sons, 1994), p. 57.

9. Ali E. Hillal Dessouki, "Nasser and the Struggle for Independence," in *Suez 1956: The Crisis and Its Consequences,* ed. William Roger Louis and Roger Owen (Oxford: Clarendon, 1989), p. 33.

10. Diane B. Kunz, *The Economic Diplomacy of the Suez Crisis* (Chapel Hill, N.C.: University of North Carolina Press, 1991), p. 40.

11. Robert Schaeffer, *Warpaths: The Politics of Partition* (New York: Hill and Wang, 1990), p. 113; Kunz, *The Economic Diplomacy of the Suez Crisis,* p. 44; William Roger Louis, "The Tragedy of the Anglo-Egyptian Settlement of 1954," in Louis and Owen, 1989, p. 49.

12. Dessouki, "Nasser and the Struggle for Independence," in Louis and Owen, 1989, p. 35.

13. Kunz, *The Economic Diplomacy of the Suez Crisis,* pp. 44–45.

14. Ibid., p. 111.

15. Ibid., p. 64.

16. Ibid.

17. Ibid., pp. 73, 75, 76.

18. LaFeber, *America, Russia and the Cold War,* p. 185.

19. Diane B. Kunz, "The Economic Diplomacy of the Suez Crisis," in Louis and Owen, 1989, p. 222.

20. John Darwin, *Britain and Decolonisation: The Retreat from Empire in the Post-War World* (New York: St. Martin's, 1988), p. 212.

21. Willetts, *The Non-Aligned Movement,* p. 22.

22. Ibid., p. 10.

23. Barbara Crossette, "The 'Third World' Is Dead, But Spirits Linger," *New York Times,* 13 November 1994; Stuart Corbridge, "Colonialism, Post-Colonialism and the Political Geography of the Third World," in *Political Geography of the Twentieth Century: A Global Analysis,* ed. Peter J. Taylor (New York: John Wiley and Sons, 1993), p. 189; Steven R. David, *Choosing Sides: Alignment and Realignment in the Third World* (Baltimore: Johns Hopkins University Press, 1991), p. 11.

24. Willetts, *The Non-Aligned Movement,* p. 3.

25. Ibid., pp. 17, 15–16.

26. Ibid., pp. 20, 18.

27. Rodman, *More Precious Than Peace,* p. 68; LaFeber, *America, Russia and the Cold War,* p. 171.

28. Gaddis, *The Long Peace,* pp. 48–49.

29. Akira Iriye, *The Globalizing of America, 1913–1945,* vol. 3 of *The Cambridge History of American Foreign Relations* (Cambridge: Cambridge University Press, 1993), pp. 21–22.

30. Audrey Kurth Cronin, *Great Power Politics and the Struggle Over Austria, 1945–1955* (Ithaca: Cornell University Press, 1986), pp. 131, 165.

31. Zbigniew K. Brzezinski, *The Soviet Bloc: Unity and Conflict* (Cambridge, Mass.: Harvard University Press, 1971), p. 153.

32. Kunz, *The Economic Diplomacy of the Suez Crisis,* p. 118; Mordechai Bar-On, "David Ben-Gurion and the Sevres Collusion," in Louis and Owen, 1989, p. 150; Keith Kyle, "Britain and the Crisis, 1955–1956," in Louis and Owen, 1989, p. 122.

33. Kunz, *The Economic Diplomacy of the Suez Crisis,* p. 4; Maurice Vaisse, "France and the Suez Crisis," in Louis and Owen, 1989, p. 137.

34. Louis and Owen, *Suez 1956,* pp. xv-xvi.

35. Kunz, *The Economic Diplomacy of the Suez Crisis,* p. 107.

36. Ibid., p. 25.

37. Yaacov Bar-Simon-Tov, *Israel, the Superpowers and the War in the Middle East* (New York: Praeger, 1987), p. 50.

38. Stephen Ambrose, *Eisenhower: The President* (New York: Simon and Schuster, 1984), p. 361.

39. Kyle, "Britain and the Crisis," in Louis and Owen, 1989, pp. 112–13; Robert R. Bowie, "Eisenhower, Dulles, and the Suez Crisis," in Louis and Owen, 1989, p. 201.

40. Kunz, "The Economic Diplomacy of the Suez Crisis," in Louis and Owen, 1989, p. 225; John C. Campbell, "The Soviet Union, the United States, and the Twin Crisis of Hungary and Suez," in Louis and Owen, 1989, p. 245.

41. Bowie, "Eisenhower, Dulles, and the Suez Crisis," in Louis and Owen, 1989, pp. 208–210.

42. Kunz, *The Economic Diplomacy of the Suez Crisis,* pp. 47, 86.

43. Ibid., pp. 120, 124.

44. Ibid., p. 116; Kunz, "The Economic Diplomacy of the Suez Crisis," in Louis and Owen, 1989, pp. 218–20; Kyle, "Britain and the Crisis," in Louis and Owen, 1989, p. 117.

45. Campbell, "The Soviet Union, the United States, and the Twin Crisis of Hungary and Suez," in Louis and Owen, 1989, p. 246.

46. Ibid., p. 248.

47. Bar-Siman-Tov, *Israel, the Superpowers and the War in the Middle East,* pp. 60–61.

48. Bowie, "Eisenhower, Dulles, and the Suez Crisis," in Louis and Owen, 1989, p. 215.

49. Kunz, *The Economic Diplomacy of the Suez Crisis,* p. 171.

50. Word of Khrushchev's attack soon spread throughout Eastern Europe, and a text of the speech was printed in the West in June. Vadney, *The World Since 1945,* pp. 195–96.

51. Ibid., p. 196.

52. Paul E. Zinner, *Revolution in Hungary* (New York: Columbia University Press, 1962), pp. 164, 170; Brzezinski, *The Soviet Bloc,* p. 251.

53. Vadney, *The World Since 1945,* p. 194; LaFeber, *America, Russia and the Cold War,* p. 185; Zinner, *Revolution in Hungary,* p. 178.

54. Vadney, *The World Since 1945,* pp. 99, 197; LaFeber, *America, Russia and the Cold War,* p. 183.

55. Vadney, *The World Since 1945,* p. 194; Zinner, *Revolution in Hungary,* p. 226.

56. Vadney, *The World Since 1945,* p. 198.

57. Brzezinski, *The Soviet Bloc,* pp. 262–63; Campbell, "The Soviet Union, the United States, and the Twin Crisis of Hungary and Suez," in Louis and Owen, 1989, p. 234; LaFeber, *America, Russia and the Cold War,* p. 187; Vadney, *The World Since 1945,* p. 197.

58. Vadney, *The World Since 1945,* p. 199; Zinner, *Revolution in Hungary,* pp. 268, 271, 286; Brzezinski, *The Soviet Bloc,* p. 231.

59. Vadney, *The World Since 1945,* p. 200.

60. Campbell, "The Soviet Union, the United States, and the Twin Crisis of Hungary and Suez," in Louis and Owen, 1989, pp. 242, 239.

61. Vadney, *The World Since 1945,* pp. 200–201; LaFeber, *America, Russia and the Cold War,* p. 188.

62. Conor Cruise O'Brien, "Conflicting Concepts of the United Nations," in *International Law and Organization: An Introductory Reader,* ed. Richard A. Falk and Wolfram F. Hanrieder (New York: J. B. Lippincott, 1968), p. 192.

63. Warren I. Cohen, *America in the Age of Soviet Power, 1945–1991,* vol. 4 of *The Cambridge History of American Foreign Relations* (Cambridge: Cambridge University Press, 1993), p. 92.

64. Gaddis, *The Long Peace,* p. 190.

65. Ibid.

66. Rodman, *More Precious Than Peace,* p. 83.

67. Darwin, *Britain and Decolonisation,* p. 223.

68. Kunz, *The Economic Diplomacy of the Suez Crisis,* p. 156.

69. Michael M. Harrison, *The Reluctant Ally: France and Atlantic Security* (Baltimore: Johns Hopkins University Press, 1981), p. 42.

70. McGeorge Bundy, *Danger and Survival* (New York: Random House, 1988), p. 475; Harrison, *The Reluctant Ally,* p. 37.

71. Harrison, *The Reluctant Ally,* pp. 6–7; Adam Watson, "The Aftermath of Suez: Consequences of the Suez Crisis in the Arab World," in Louis and Owen, 1989, p. 342; Kunz, *The Economic Diplomacy of the Suez Crisis,* pp. 177, 188.

72. Harrison, *The Reluctant Ally*, pp. 49–50.

73. Ibid., p. 97.

74. Ibid., pp. 125–26.

75. Ibid., p. 96.

76. Ibid., pp. 111, 134, 143–45.

77. Leonard S. Spector, *Going Nuclear* (Cambridge, Mass.: Ballinger, 1987), passim.

78. Rodman, *More Precious Than Peace*, p. 90; LaFeber, *America, Russia and the Cold War*, p. 91; Vadney, *The World Since 1945*, p. 180.

79. John Lewis and L. Xue, *China Builds the Bomb* (Stanford, Calif.: Stanford University Press), p. 12.

80. William Kincade and C. Bertram, *Nuclear Proliferation in the 1980s* (London: Macmillan, 1982), p. 13.

81. Rodman, *More Precious Than Peace*, p. 93.

82. Cohen, *America in the Age of Soviet Power*, p. 101.

83. Vadney, *The World Since 1945*, pp. 179–80; Brzezinski, *The Soviet Bloc*, pp. 398–403.

84. Lewis and Xue, *China Builds the Bomb*, p. 216.

85. Ibid., p. 130.

86. Peter J. Taylor, "Geopolitical World Orders," in Taylor, 1993, pp. 55–56.

87. Darwin, *Britain and Decolonisation*, p. 167. "In 1960, eleven former French colonies became independent and joined the United Nations." Louis and Owen, *Suez 1956*, p. 12.

88. R. F. Holland, *European Decolonization, 1918–1981* (New York: St. Martin's, 1985), p. 281.

89. O'Brien, "Conflicting Concepts of the United Nations," in Falk and Hanrieder, 1968, p. 195.

90. Charles H. Hession, *John Maynard Keynes: A Personal Biography of the Man Who Revolutionized Capitalism and the Way We Live* (New York: Macmillan, 1984), p. 12.

91. LaFeber, *America, Russia and the Cold War*, pp. 71–73.

92. Stephen Lee, *The European Dictatorships, 1918–1945* (London: Methuen, 1987), pp. 247–48.

93. Gaddis Smith, *The Last Years of the Monroe Doctrine, 1945–1993* (New York: Hill and Wang, 1994), pp. 73–74, 82, 89; LaFeber, *America, Russia and the Cold War*, p. 160.

94. Eric Hobsbawm, *The Age of Extremes: A History of the World, 1914–1991* (New York: Pantheon, 1994), p. 113.

95. Joel S. Migdal, *Strong Societies and Weak States: State-Society Relations and State Capabilities in the Third World* (Princeton: Princeton University Press, 1988), p. 178. Another estimate of U.S. spending is $80.1 billion between 1950 and 1979. Vadney, *The World Since 1945*, p. 98.

96. Vadney, *The World Since 1945*, p. 98. Between 1973 and 1980 the Soviet Union sold $59.6 billion in arms. Michael T. Klare, *American Arms Supermarket* (Austin, Tex.: University of Texas Press, 1984), p. 9.

97. Klare, *American Arms Supermarket*, p. 1.

98. Ibid., p. 5.

99. Ibid., p. 2.

100. Rodman, *More Precious Than Peace*, p. 47.

101. Smith, *The Last Years of the Monroe Doctrine*, p. 191.

102. Robert Jervis, "Domino Beliefs and Strategic Behavior," in *Coping With Complexity in the International System*, ed. Robert Jervis and Jack Snyder (Boulder: Westview Press, 1993), p. 20.

103. Ibid., pp. 20–21.

104. Ibid., p. 24.

105. Ibid.

106. Smith, *The Last Years of the Monroe Doctrine*, pp. 70–71, 68–69.

107. Tony Smith, *America's Mission: The United States and the Worldwide Struggle for Democracy in the Twentieth Century* (Princeton: Princeton University Press, 1994), p. 288.

108. Alain Rouquie, *The Military and the State in Latin America* (Berkeley: University of California Press, 1982), p. 138.

109. Gaddis Smith, *The Last Years of the Monroe Doctrine*, pp. 13–14.

110. Klare, *American Arms Supermarket*, pp. 219–23.

111. Rouquie, *The Military and the State in Latin America*, p. 181.

112. Immanuel Wallerstein, "The Concept of National Development, 1917–1989: Elegy and Requiem," in *Reexamining Democracy: Essays in Honor of Seymour Martin Lipset*, ed. Gary Marks and Larry Diamond (Newbury Park, Calif.: Sage, 1992), p. 83.

113. Robert Schaeffer, "The Entelechies of Mercantilism," *Scandinavian Economic History Review* 29, no. 2 (1981): 81–96.

114. Vadney, *The World Since 1945*, p. 98.

115. LaFeber, *America, Russia and the Cold War*, pp. 63–64.

116. Ibid., pp. 69–70; Marshall I. Goldman, *U.S.S.R. in Crisis: The Failure of an Economic System* (New York: W. W. Norton, 1983), p. 145; Joseph Vincent Yakowicz, *Poland's Postwar Recovery* (Hicksville, N.Y.: Exposition Press, 1979), pp. 5–6.

117. LaFeber, *America, Russia and the Cold War*, p. 105.

118. Robert W. Oliver, *George Woods and the World Bank* (Boulder: Lynne Rienner, 1995), p. 219.

119. Ibid., p. 232.

120. Migdal, *Strong Societies and Weak States*, pp. 215–24.

121. Ibid.

122. Ibid., pp. 242–43.

123. Ibid., p. 260.

124. Ibid., pp. 204, 208.

Chapter Four

1. A republican state was briefly established in Spain between 1873–74, but it was only a brief interregnum.

2. Hugh Kay, *Salazar and Modern Portugal* (New York: Hawthorn Books, 1970), p. 20.

3. Philippe C. Schmitter, "'The Regime d'Exception' That Became the Rule: Forty-Eight Years of Authoritarian Domination in Portugal," in *Contemporary Por-*

tugal: The Revolution and its Antecedents, ed. Lawrence S. Graham and Harry M. Makler (Austin, Tex.: University of Texas Press, 1979), p. 30; Neil Bruce, *Portugal: The Last Empire* (London: David and Charles, 1975), p. 28.

4. Kay, *Salazar and Modern Portugal,* p. 44.

5. Ibid., p. 30.

6. Ibid., pp. 30–31; Bruce, *Portugal,* p. 28.

7. Stephen J. Lee, *The European Dictatorships, 1918–1945* (London: Methuen, 1987), pp. 221–22.

8. Ibid., p. 22; Bruce, *Portugal,* pp. 26–27.

9. Kay, *Salazar and Modern Portugal,* p. 42.

10. Ibid., pp. 44–45.

11. Bruce, *Portugal,* pp. 36–37.

12. Kay, *Salazar and Modern Portugal,* pp. 48–49; Bruce, *Portugal,* pp. 37–38.

13. Constantine P. Danopoulos, "Democratization by Golpe: The Experience of Modern Portugal," in *Military Disengagement from Politics,* ed. Constantine P. Danopoulos (London: Routledge, 1988), p. 233.

14. Bruce, *Portugal,* pp. 32–34; Danopoulos, "Democratization by Golpe," in Danopoulos, 1988, pp. 234–35; Giovanni Arrighi, "Fascism to Democratic Socialism: Logic and Limits of a Transition," in *Semiperipheral Development: The Politics of Southern Europe in the Twentieth Century,* ed. Giovanni Arrighi (Beverly Hills, Calif.: Sage, 1985), p. 257.

15. Kay, *Salazar and Modern Portugal,* pp. 68, 70.

16. Rainer Eisfeld, "The Ambiguity of Portugal's Foreign Policy in the World," in *Portugal: Ancient Country, Young Democracy,* ed. Kenneth Maxwell and Michael H. Haltzel (Washington, D.C.: Woodrow Wilson Center Press, 1990), p. 84.

17. Kay, *Salazar and Modern Portugal,* pp. 70–71.

18. Ibid., p. 31.

19. Bruce, *Portugal,* p. 34.

20. Sheelagh Ellwood, *Franco* (London: Longman, 1994), p. 38; Raymond Carr and Juan Pablo Fusi Aizpurua, *Spain: Dictatorship to Democracy* (London: George Allen and Unwin, 1979), p. 2.

21. Lee, *The European Dictatorships,* p. 30.

22. Ibid., p. 231.

23. Ibid., pp. 231–32.

24. Ibid., p. 233; Paul Brooker, *Twentieth-Century Dictatorships: The Ideological One-Party States* (New York: New York University Press, 1995), p. 139.

25. Ibid.

26. Lee, *The European Dictatorships,* pp. 233, 241, 244–45.

27. Carr and Aizpurua, *Spain,* p. 17.

28. Paul Preston, *The Politics of Revenge: Fascism and the Military in Twentieth-Century Spain* (London: Unwin Hyman, 1990), pp. 41–42; Lee, *The European Dictatorships,* pp. 235–36.

29. Military spending fell from 30 percent of the budget in 1953 to less than 15 percent in 1968. Brooker, *Twentieth-Century Dictatorships,* p. 146.

30. Ibid., p. 142; David Gilmour, *The Transformation of Spain: From Franco to the Constitutional Monarchy* (London: Quartet Books, 1985), p. 14.

31. Ibid., pp. 54–55.

32. For many years Franco ordered the press to refer to the monarchy as little as possible. George Steiner, "Franco's Games," *The New Yorker,* 17 October 1994, p. 118; Paul Preston, *Franco: A Biography* (New York: Basic Books, 1994), p. 580.

33. Gilmour, *The Transformation of Spain,* p. 133.

34. Brooker, *Twentieth-Century Dictatorships,* p. 147.

35. Lee, *The European Dictatorships,* p. 242.

36. Gilmour, *The Transformation of Spain,* p. 10.

37. Ibid., p. 9.

38. Ibid., pp. 20, 23.

39. Ibid., p. 19.

40. George Zaharopoulos, "Politics and the Army in Postwar Greece," in *Greece Under Military Rule,* ed. Richard Clogg and George Yannopoulos (London: Secker and Warburg, 1972), p. 20.

41. Constantine Tsoucalas, *The Greek Tragedy* (Harmondsworth, United Kingdom: Penguin Books, 1969), pp. 33–34, 35, 41–42.

42. Ibid., pp. 42, 43; Lee, *The European Dictatorships,* p. 289.

43. Tsoucalas, *The Greek Tragedy,* pp. 46–47.

44. Ibid., pp. 50–51.

45. Lee, *The European Dictatorships,* p. 290; Tsoucalas, *The Greek Tragedy,* p. 55.

46. Ibid., p. 53.

47. Gilmour, *The Transformation of Spain,* p. 3.

48. Kay, *Salazar and Modern Portugal,* pp. 68–69.

49. Ibid., pp. 154–55.

50. Ellwood, *Franco,* p. 120.

51. Ibid., pp. 120–22; Kay, *Salazar and Modern Portugal,* pp. 88, 158–60.

52. Ibid., p. 157.

53. Tsoucalas, *The Greek Tragedy,* pp. 57–58; Michalis Papayannakis, "The Crisis in the Greek Left," in *Greece at the Polls: The National Elections of 1974 and 1977,* ed. Howard R. Penniman (Washington, D.C.: American Enterprise Institute, 1981), p. 138; Michalis Spourdalakis, *The Rise of the Greek Socialist Party* (London: Routledge, 1988), p. 17.

54. Steiner, "Franco's Games," p. 120; Preston, *The Politics of Revenge,* pp. 45–46; Ellwood, *Franco,* pp. 155–56.

55. Ellwood, *Franco,* p. 115.

56. Tsoucalas, *The Greek Tragedy,* p. 63.

57. Papayannakis, "The Crisis in the Greek Left," in Penniman, 1981, pp. 135, 137; Spourdalakis, *The Rise of the Greek Socialist Party,* p. 17; Tsoucalas, *The Greek Tragedy,* p. 64.

58. Steiner, "Franco's Games," p. 119. U.S. officials soon began advocating a more friendly attitude toward the dictators. Benny Pollack, *The Paradox of Spanish Foreign Policy: Spain's International Relations From Franco to Democracy* (New York: St. Martin's Press, 1987), pp. 40–44.

59. Thanos Veremis, "Greece: Veto and Impasse, 1967–74," in *The Political Dilemmas of Military Regimes,* ed. Christopher Clapham and George Philip (Totowa, N.J.: Barnes and Noble Books, 1985), p. 28; Papayannakis, "The Crisis in the Greek Left," in Penniman, 1981, p. 139; Tsoucalas, *The Greek Tragedy,* pp. 73–74, 85, 97.

60. Papayannakis, "The Crisis in the Greek Left," in Penniman, 1981, p. 140; Tsoucalas, *The Greek Tragedy,* p. 114.

61. Tsoucalas, *The Greek Tragedy,* p. 105.

62. Ibid., p. 77.

63. Ibid.

64. Ibid., pp. 110–13; Joze Pirjevec, "The Tito-Stalin Split and the End of the Civil War in Greece," in *Studies in the History of the Greek Civil War, 1945–1949,* Lars Baerentzen, John O. Iatrides, and Ole L. Smith (Copenhagen, Denmark: Museum Tusculanum Press, 1987), pp. 309–16.

65. Tsoucalas, *The Greek Tragedy,* p. 106.

66. Ibid., p. 123.

67. Robert P. Clark, *The Basques: The Franco Years and Beyond* (Reno, Nev.: University of Nevada Press, 1979), p. 94; Pollack, *The Paradox of Spanish Foreign Policy,* pp. 14–15.

68. Pollack, *The Paradox of Spanish Foreign Policy,* pp. 15–16, 22, 26, 36–37, 42–43; Preston, *Franco,* p. 574.

69. Preston, *Franco,* pp. 623, 627.

70. Ellwood, *Franco,* p. 150.

71. Preston, *Franco,* p. 542.

72. Tsoucalas, *The Greek Tragedy,* p. 67; Ellwood, *Franco,* pp. 151, 158, 163, 169; Kostis Papadantonakis, "Incorporation Is Peripheralization: Contradictions of Southern Europe's Economic Development," in Arrighi, 1985, p. 93.

73. Caglar Keyder, "The American Recovery of Southern Europe: Aid and Hegemony," in Arrighi, 1985, pp. 141–42.

74. Carr and Aizpurua, *Spain,* p. 57; Keyder, "The American Recovery of Southern Europe," in Arrighi, 1985, pp. 135, 145.

75. Maria Beatriz Rocha Trinidade, "Portugal," in *International Labor Migration in Europe,* ed. Ronald E. Krane (New York: Praeger, 1979), p. 171; David D. Gregory and J. Cazorla Perez, "Intra-European Migration and Regional Development: Spain and Portugal," in *Guests Come to Stay: The Effects of European Labor Migration on Sending and Receiving Countries,* ed. Rosmarie Rogers (Boulder: Westview Press, 1985), p. 237.

76. Collette Callier Boisvert, "Working-Class Portuguese Families in a French Provincial Town: Adaptive Strategies," in *Migrants in Europe: The Role of Family, Labor and Politics,* ed. Hans Christian Buechler and Judith-Maria Buechler (Westport, Conn.: Greenwood Press, 1987), p. 63.

77. Gregory and Perez, "Intra-European Migration and Regional Development," in Rogers, 1985, p. 234.

78. David D. Gregory and Jose Cazorla, "Family and Migration in Andalusia," in Buechler and Buechler, 1987, p. 150; Gregory and Perez, "Intra-European Migration and Regional Development," in Rogers, 1985, p. 234.

79. Tsoucalas, *The Greek Tragedy,* pp. 134, 137; George Yannopoulos, "Workers and Peasants Under Military Dictatorship," in Clogg and Yannopoulos, 1972, p. 121.

80. John Spraos, "Government and the Economy: The First Term of PASOK, 1982–84," in *Greece on the Road to Democracy: From the Junta to PASOK, 1974–1986,* ed. Speros Vryonis, Jr. (New Rochelle, N.Y.: Orpheus Publishing, 1991), p. 165; Richard Clogg, "The Ideology of the 'Revolution of 21 April 1967,'"

in Clogg and Yannopoulos, 1972, pp. 63, 66. "The cessation of German migration from the east after the erection of the Berlin Wall in 1961 was replaced by an inflow of migratory workers from Southern Europe: Italy, Greece, Spain, Turkey, Yugoslavia and Portugal." Clogg, "The Ideology of the 'Revolution of 21 April 1967,'" p. 64; Christos Lyrintzis, "PASOK in Power: From 'Change' to Disenchantment," in *Greece, 1981–89: The Populist Decade,* ed. Richard Clogg (New York: St. Martin's Press, 1993), p. 90.

81. Eric Hobsbawm, *The Age of Extremes: A History of the World, 1914–1991* (New York: Pantheon, 1994), p. 277; James F. Hollifield, *Immigrants, Markets, and States: The Political Economy of Postwar Europe* (Cambridge, Mass.: Harvard University Press, 1992), p. 61.

82. Papadantonakis, "Incorporation Is Peripheralization," in Arrighi, 1985, p. 88; Carr and Aizpurua, *Spain,* pp. 49, 71–72; Spourdalakis, *The Rise of the Greek Socialist Party,* p. 20. Arrighi argued that the decline was less dramatic, from 48 percent in all three to 28 percent in Portugal and Spain and only 40 percent in Greece. Arrighi, "Fascism to Democratic Socialism," in Arrighi, 1985, p. 274. Until 1960 most Spanish and Portuguese emigrants made their way to Latin America and most Greeks to the United States. But declining economic opportunities in Latin America in the 1960s discouraged Iberian workers from emigrating there, and the proximity of Western European countries made it easier and less expensive for workers to return home. Salustiano del Campo, "Spain," in Krane, 1979, pp. 157–58, 169; Caroline B. Brettell, "Emigration and Its Implications for the Revolution in Northern Portugal," in Graham and Makler, 1979, p. 285; Anthony Leeds, "Work, Labor, and the Recompenses: Portuguese Life Strategies Involving Migration," in Buechler and Buechler, 1987, p. 41.

83. Carr and Aizpurua, *Spain,* p. 68.

84. Boisvert, "Working-Class Portuguese Families in a French Provincial Town," in Buechler and Buechler, 1987, p. 63; Trinidade, "Portugal," in Krane, 1979, p. 167.

85. Leeds, "Work, Labor, and the Recompenses," in Buechler and Buechler, 1987, p. 37; Gregory and Perez, "Intra-European Migration and Regional Development," in Rogers, 1985, p. 237.

86. C. M. Woodhouse, *The Rise and Fall of the Greek Colonels* (London: Granada Publishers, 1985), p. 238; Arrighi, "Fascism to Democratic Socialism," in Arrighi, 1985, p. 164.

87. Arrighi, "Fascism to Democratic Socialism," in Arrighi, 1985, p. 164; Reginald Appleyard, "The Greeks of Australia: A New Diasporic Hellenism," in Vryonis, 1991, p. 51.

88. John Logan, "Democracy from Above: Limits to Change in Southern Europe," in Arrighi, 1985, p. 164; del Campo, "Spain," in Krane, 1979, p. 162.

89. Demetrios Papademetriou, "Greece," in Krane, 1979, p. 192; Tsoucalas, *The Greek Tragedy,* p. 134. They might have injected even more into the Greek economy, but many Greek workers deposited their savings in German banks, a sum amounting to DM 10 billion in 1987. Ira Emke-Poulopoulos, "Problems of Greek Migrants in West Germany Upon Their Return to Greece," in Vryonis, 1991, p. 340.

90. Hans Binnendijk, *Authoritarian Regimes in Transition,* Center for the Study of Foreign Affairs (Washington, D.C.: Department of State Publication, 1987), pp. 28, 55.

91. Alan S. Milward, *The European Rescue of the Nation-State* (Berkeley: University of California Press, 1992), p. 13; Edward Malefakis, "Spain and its Francoist Heritage," in *From Dictatorship to Democracy: Coping with the Legacies of Authoritarianism and Totalitarianism*, ed. John H. Herz (Westport, Conn.: Greenwood Press, 1982), p. 218. In 1994, 60 million tourists visited Spain, a number "one and a half times the country's native population." Daniel Samper, "The Power of Tourism," *The World Paper*, September 1994, p. 1.

92. Jaime Gama, "Foreign Policy," in Maxwell and Haltzel, 1990, p. 97.

93. Louis Turner and John Ash, *The Golden Hordes: International Tourism and the Pleasure Periphery* (London: Constable, 1975), pp. 96–98; George Young, *Tourism: Blessing or Blight?* (Harmondsworth, United Kingdom: Penguin, 1973), p. 66; Carr and Aizpurua, *Spain*, p. 57.

94. Gregory and Perez, "Intra-European Migration and Regional Development," in Rogers, 1985, p. 236; Clark, *The Basques*, p. 211; Carr and Aizpurua, *Spain*, p. 57.

95. Young, *Tourism*, p. 134.

96. In 1971 "90 percent of the mental illnesses in the province of Malaga affected young peasants who were unable to bear the change from the plow [agricultural employment] to the tray [service sector employment]. As a result, the Malaga General Hospital was forced to create a special service known as the waiter's wing." Samper, "The Power of Tourism," p. 2.

97. Joe Foweraker, *Making Democracy in Spain: Grassroots Struggle in the South, 1955–1975* (Cambridge: Cambridge University Press, 1989), p. 64.

98. Alvaro Soto Carmona, "Long Cycle of Social Conflict in Spain (1868–1986)," *Review* XVI, no. 2 (spring 1993): 179; Ellwood, *Franco*, p. 180; Gilmour, *The Transformation of Spain*, p. 44.

99. Gilmour, *The Transformation of Spain*, p. 44; Foweraker, *Making Democracy in Spain*, pp. 68, 216; Ellwood, *Franco*, p. 187; E. Ramon Arango, *Spain: From Repression to Renewal* (Boulder: Westview Press, 1985), p. 194.

100. Arango, *Spain*, pp. 121, 222.

101. Workers in Greece were more successful at obtaining higher wages during the 1960s under the conservative royalist government, the moderate republican government, and the military junta that took power in 1967. Unlike in Spain, the Greek dictatorship allowed wages to rise faster than consumer prices, hoping to secure worker loyalty. Between 1966 and 1971 wages increased 9.8 percent on average, whereas the consumer price index rose only 2.1 percent annually. Nicos Poulantzas, *The Crisis of the Dictatorships: Portugal, Greece and Spain* (London: New Left Books, 1976), p. 74; Clark, *The Basques*, p. 238; Christopher Bliss and Jorge Braga De Macedo, *Unity With Diversity in the European Economy: The Community's Southern Frontier* (Cambridge: Cambridge University Press, 1990), p. 10; Spourdalakis, *The Rise of the Greek Socialist Party*, p. 36.

102. Arrighi, "Fascism to Democratic Socialism," in Arrighi, 1985, pp. 265, 268.

103. Keyder, "The American Recovery of Southern Europe," in Arrighi, 1985, p. 145; Arango, *Spain*, p. 198.

104. Mario Murteria, "The Present Economic Situation: Its Origins and Prospects," in Graham and Makler, 1979, p. 332; Eric N. Baklanoff, "Spain's Emergence as a Middle Industrial Power: The Basis and Structure of Spanish-Latin American Economic Relations," in *The Iberian-Latin American Connection: Implications*

for U.S. Foreign Policy, ed. Howard J. Wiarda (Boulder: Westview Press, 1986), p. 134; Michael Harsgor, *Portugal in Revolution* (Washington, D.C.: The Center for Strategic and International Studies; Beverly Hills, Calif.: Sage, 1976), p. 30; Clark, *The Basques,* p. 208; Tassos Giannitsis, "Transformation and Problems of Greek Industry: The Experience During the Period 1974–85," in Vryonis, 1991, p. 1.

105. Arango, *Spain,* p. 187; Tsoucalas, *The Greek Tragedy,* p. 139; Baklanoff, "Spain's Emergence as a Middle Industrial Power," in Wiarda, 1986, p. 139.

106. Giovanni Arrighi, "World Income Inequalities and the Future of Socialism," *New Left Review,* no. 189 (September-October 1991): 45; Arrighi, "Fascism to Democratic Socialism," in Arrighi, 1985, p. 249.

107. Eusebio Mujal-Leon, "An Overview of 'Remarkable Developments,'" in Binnendijk, 1987, p. 176.

108. "Transcript of President Nixon's Address in Move to Deal With Economic Problems," *New York Times,* 16 August 1971.

109. Berch Bergeroglu, *The Legacy of Empire: Economic Decline and Class Polarization in the United States* (New York: Praeger, 1992), p. 56.

110. Arango, *Spain,* p. 201; Baklanoff, "Spain's Emergence as a Middle Industrial Power," in Wiarda, 1986, p. 140; Insight Team of the Sunday Times, *Insight on Portugal: The Year of the Captains* (London: Andre Deutsch, 1975), p. 209.

111. Constantine P. Danopoulos, *From Military to Civilian Rule* (London: Routledge, 1992), p. 44.

112. Ibid.

113. Constantine P. Danopoulos, "Beating a Hasty Retreat: The Greek Military Withdraws from Power," in *The Decline of Military Regimes: The Civilian Influence,* ed. Constantine P. Danopoulos (Boulder: Westview Press, 1988), p. 231.

114. Gregory and Cazorla, "Family and Migration in Andalusia," in Buechler and Buechler, 1987, p. 169, 170; Emke-Poulopoulos, "Problems of Greek Migrants in West Germany," in Vryonis, 1991, p. 333; Loukas Tsoukalis, "The Austerity Program: Causes, Reactions and Prospects," in Vryonis, 1991, p. 285; Lyrintzis in Clogg, 1993, p. 75.

115. Lyrintzis in Clogg, 1993, p. 176; Gregory and Perez, "Intra-European Migration and Regional Development," in Rogers, 1985, p. 241; Emke-Poulopoulos, "Problems of Greek Migrants in West Germany," in Vryonis, 1991, p. 353; Hollifield, *Immigrants, Markets, and States,* p. 89.

116. Gregory and Cazorla, "Family and Migration in Andalusia," in Buechler and Buechler, 1987, p. 167, 172, 174. West Germany's Greek migrant population increased from 42,000 in 1960 to 407,600 in 1973, and then decreased to 280,600 in 1985. Emke-Poulopoulos, "Problems of Greek Migrants in West Germany," in Vryonis, 1991, p. 330.

117. Arango, *Spain,* pp. 200–201.

118. Ibid., p. 200; Jose Maravall, *The Transition to Democracy in Spain* (New York: St. Martin's Press, 1982), p. 121.

119. Kenneth Maxwell, "The Emergence of Portuguese Democracy," in Herz, 1982, p. 235.

120. Valene L. Smith, "Privatization in the Third World: Small-Scale Tourism," in *Global Tourism: The Next Decade,* ed. William F. Theobald (Oxford: Butterworth-Heinemann, 1994), p. 2.

121. Stephen Castles and Godula Kosack, *Immigrant Workers and Class Structure in Western Europe* (Oxford: Oxford University Press, 1985), p. 221.

122. John Pesmazoglu, "The Greek Economy Since 1967," in Clogg and Yannopoulos, 1972, pp. 76, 100, 104.

123. Insight Team, *Insight on Portugal*, p. 10; Arrighi, "Fascism to Democratic Socialism," in Arrighi, 1985, p. 263.

124. Kay, *Salazar and Modern Portugal*, pp. 321–22; Insight Team, *Insight on Portugal*, p. 13.

125. Insight Team, *Insight on Portugal*, p. 15; Bruce, *Portugal*, pp. 67, 70, 72, 80, 88.

126. Neto was arrested and tortured while a medical student in Portugal, arrested, beaten, and then exiled from Angola, and then jailed in Portugal before escaping and rejoining the MPLA leadership in Africa. Kenneth Maxwell, "Portugal and Africa: The Last Empire," in *The Transfer of Power in Africa: Decolonization, 1940–1960*, ed. Gifford Prosser and Wm. Roger Louis (New Haven: Yale University Press, 1982), p. 353.

127. Kay, *Salazar and Modern Portugal*, p. 229, 258.

128. Ibid., p. 263; Bruce, *Portugal*, p. 84.

129. Maxwell in Prosser and Louis, 1982, p. 345.

130. Portugal no longer profited from its colonies as it had before 1961. Instead, war drained money out of the country, making it "Africa's only colony in Europe," editors of the *Economist* wrote in 1974. Douglas L. Wheeler, "The Military and the Portuguese Dictatorship, 1926–1974: The Hour of the Army," in Graham and Makler, 1979, p. 204; Danopoulos in Danopoulos, *Military Disengagement*, 1988, p. 238; Maxwell, "The Emergence of Portuguese Democracy," in Herz, 1982, p. 235.

131. The United Nations challenged this position after Portugal and Spain were "admitted to the United Nations as part of a package deal which brought in 16 new members, some fostered by the Western powers, others by the Soviet Union." Kay, *Salazar and Modern Portugal*, pp. 183, 193; Rodney J. Morrison, *Portugal: Revolutionary Change in an Open Economy* (Boston: Auburn House, 1981), p. 11.

132. Kay, *Salazar and Modern Portugal*, pp. 188–91.

133. Kenneth Maxwell, "Forces Moving the Transition," In Binnendijk, 1987, p. 199; Insight Team, *Insight on Portugal*, pp. 125–26.

134. Danopoulos in Danopoulos, *Military Disengagement*, 1988, pp. 239–40; Insight Team, *Insight on Portugal*, pp. 23–25.

135. Harsgor, *Portugal in Revolution*, p. 16; Enrique A. Baloyra, "Democratic Transition in Comparative Perspective," in *Comparing New Democracies: Transition and Consolidation in Mediterranean Europe and the Southern Cone*, ed. Enrique A. Baloyra (Boulder: Westview Press, 1987), p. 32.

136. Danopoulos in Danopoulos, *Military Disengagement*, 1988, p. 252.

137. Maxwell, "Portugal and Africa," in Prosser and Louis, 1982, p. 367.

138. Baloyra, "Democratic Transition in Comparative Perspective," in Baloyra, 1987, p. 32.

139. Insight Team, *Insight on Portugal*, p. 72.

140. Ibid., pp. 49–52; Robert Harvey, *Portugal: Birth of a Democracy* (New York: St. Martin's Press, 1978), p. 109; Harsgor, *Portugal in Revolution*, p. 28.

141. Harsgor, *Portugal in Revolution*, pp. 8–9.

142. Harvey, *Portugal*, p. 109; Insight Team, *Insight on Portugal*, p. 243.

143. Morrison, *Portugal*, pp. 50, 59, 70; Harvey, *Portugal*, pp. 72, 105.

144. Danopoulos in Danopoulos, *Military Disengagement*, 1988, p. 250; Harvey, *Portugal*, p. 48.

145. Maxwell, "The Emergence of Portuguese Democracy," in Herz, 1982, p. 238.

146. Tsoucalas, *The Greek Tragedy*, p. 157; Stanley Mayes, *Makarios: A Biography* (New York: St. Martin's Press, 1981), p. 37.

147. Mayes, *Makarios*, pp. 54–55.

148. Ibid., p. 159.

149. Ibid., pp. 162–63. "The Greeks would have liked to describe the new Republic as 'democratic,' but, as the neutral advisor, M. Bridel, pointed out that 'democratic' implied majority rule, the Turks managed to get this word deleted." Mayes, *Makarios*, p. 141.

150. Ibid., p. 164.

151. Ibid., p. vii.

152. Ibid., p. 176.

153. Ibid., pp. 192, 223–24.

154. Constantine Danopoulos described it as a "parliamentary dictatorship." Danopoulos in Danopoulos, *The Decline of Military Regimes*, 1988, p. 227.

155. Woodhouse, *The Rise and Fall of the Greek Colonels*, p. 2.

156. Tsoucalas, *The Greek Tragedy*, p. 186.

157. George Zaharopoulos, "Politics and the Army in Postwar Greece," in Clogg and Yannapoulos, 1972, p. 28; Tsoucalas, *The Greek Tragedy*, pp. 192–93.

158. Woodhouse, *The Rise and Fall of the Greek Colonels*, pp. 14–15; Tsoucalas, *The Greek Tragedy*, pp. 203–204.

159. Woodhouse, *The Rise and Fall of the Greek Colonels*, p. 7.

160. Ibid., p. 32.

161. Ibid., pp. 26–27.

162. Ibid., pp. 45–48.

163. Danopoulos, *From Military to Civilian Rule*, p. 46; Danopoulos in Danopoulos, *The Decline of Military Regimes*, 1988, p. 233; Veremis, "Greece: Veto and Impasse," in Clapham and Philip, 1985, pp. 36, 38; Woodhouse, *The Rise and Fall of the Greek Colonels*, p. 119.

164. A. G. Xydis, "The Military Regime's Foreign Policy," in Clogg and Yannopoulos, 1972, p. 120.

165. Woodhouse, *The Rise and Fall of the Greek Colonels*, pp. 134–40, 143–44; Danopoulos, *From Military to Civilian Rule*, p. 47; Veremis, "Greece: Veto and Impasse," in Clapham and Philip, 1985, p. 40.

166. According to Makarios, in 1964 Ioannidis had approached him with a plan to eliminate the entire Turkish population of Cyprus. Woodhouse, *The Rise and Fall of the Greek Colonels*, p. 7.

167. Ibid., pp. 154–55. In a transcript supplied by the Greek embassy to a journalist, Ioannidis and Sampson discuss Makarios's escape. "I see that the old s– has escaped. Where could he be now?" Ioannidis asked Sampson by phone the day after the coup. "On the mountains. . . . I hope to have him arrested within two or three hours," Sampson replied. At this point Ioannidis demanded, "Nicky, I want his head. You shall bring it to me yourself, OK Nicky?" Christopher Hitchens, *Cyprus* (London: Quartet Books, 1984), pp. 93–94.

168. Danopoulos in Danopoulos, *The Decline of Military Regimes,* 1988, p. 242.

169. Hitchens, *Cyprus,* pp. 97–98.

170. Woodhouse, *The Rise and Fall of the Greek Colonels,* pp. 157–58.

171. Danopoulos argued that the mobilization brought into the army many soldiers who opposed the government. Danopoulos in Danopoulos, *The Decline of Military Regimes,* 1988, p. 239.

172. Ibid.

173. Taki Tehodoracopulos, *The Greek Upheaval: Kings, Demagogues and Bayonets* (New Rochelle, N.Y.: Caratzas Brothers Publishers, 1978), p. 11; Mayes, *Makarios,* p. 248; Harry J. Psomiades, "Greece: From the Colonels' Rule to Democracy," in Herz, 1982, pp. 252–54.

174. Woodhouse, *The Rise and Fall of the Greek Colonels,* p. 171; Hitchens, *Cyprus,* pp. 107, 142; Psomiades, "Greece," in Herz, 1982, p. 256.

175. "As it turned out, this abortive coup was the fourth such undertaking since the military decided to relinquish power in July 1974." Danopoulos in Danopoulos, *The Decline of Military Regimes,* 1988, pp. 246, 247.

176. Psomiades, "Greece," in Herz, 1982, p. 261.

177. Michael M. Harrison, *The Reluctant Ally: France and Atlantic Security* (Baltimore: Johns Hopkins University Press, 1981), p. 228.

178. Psomiades, "Greece," in Herz, 1982, p. 262.

179. Ibid., p. 263.

180. Ibid., pp. 264–65.

181. Gilmour, *The Transformation of Spain,* p. 80.

182. "Franco told [U.S. General Vernon] Walters that there was no need for alarm; he had created institutions, the army would be loyal and the transition smooth." Kenneth Maxwell and Steven Spiegel, *The New Spain: From Isolation to Influence* (New York: Council on Foreign Relations Press, 1994), p. 10.

183. Carr and Aizpurua, *Spain,* p. 40.

184. Gilmour, *The Transformation of Spain,* p. 136.

185. Ibid., p. 79.

186. Ibid., p. 67.

187. Like Franco, Blanco was a fanatic opponent of Jews, "the reformation, the enlightenment, liberalism, masonry, atheism and communism," who had argued in 1968 that "it is better to be blown up by a nuclear explosion than to go on living as part of a Godless mass of slaves." Ibid., p. 68.

188. Donald Share, *The Making of Spanish Democracy* (New York: Praeger, 1986), p. 207.

189. Clark, *The Basques,* p. 153.

190. Maxwell and Spiegel, *The New Spain,* p. 12.

191. Logan, "Democracy from Above," in Arrighi, 1985, p. 167.

192. Rafael Lopez-Pintor, "Mass and Elite Perspectives in the Process of Transition to Democracy," in Baloyra, 1987, p. 82; Malefakis, "Spain and its Francoist Heritage," in Herz, 1982, p. 226; Carr and Aizpurua, *Spain,* p. 218; Logan, "Democracy from Above," in Arrighi, 1985, p. 168.

193. Lopez-Pintor, "Mass and Elite Perspectives," in Baloyra, 1987, p. 82; Patrick Camiller, "Spain: The Survival of Socialism?" in *Mapping the European Left,* ed. Perry Anderson and Patrick Camiller (London: Verso, 1994), p. 237.

194. Charles W. McCaskill, "Pasok's Third World/Nonaligned Relations," in *Greece Under Socialism: A NATO Ally Adrift*, ed. Nicholaos A. Stavrou (New Rochelle, N.Y.: Orpheus, 1988), p. 138.

195. Constantine II fled into exile in Rome after his abortive 1967 coup in Greece, and the Greek dictatorship abolished the monarchy in 1973, a decision subsequently reaffirmed by a referendum initiated by the Karamanlis government in 1974. Ellwood, *Franco*, p. 192; Psomiades noted, "The outcome [of the referendum] was not surprising: 69.2 percent of the voters were opposed to the [restoration] of the monarchy." Psiomiades, "Greece," in Herz, 1982, pp. 261–62.

196. Preston, *The Politics of Revenge*, pp. 37–38.

197. Ibid., pp. 41–42; Foweraker, *Making Democracy in Spain*, p. 171; Arango, *Spain*, p. 190.

198. Gilmour, *The Transformation of Spain*, pp. 128–30; Pollack, *The Paradox of Spanish Foreign Policy*, p. 137; Maxwell and Spiegel, *The New Spain*, p. 23.

199. Gilmour, *The Transformation of Spain*, p. 92; Eusebio Mujal-Leon, *Communism and Political Change in Spain* (Bloomington, Ind.: Indiana University Press, 1983), p. 61; Gilmour, *The Transformation of Spain*, p. 27.

200. Gilmour, *The Transformation of Spain*, p. 60; Harvey, *Portugal*, p. 6; Mujal-Leon, *Communism and Political Change in Spain*, p. 62; Maxwell and Spiegel, *The New Spain*, pp. 8–9.

201. Papademetriou, "Greece," in Krane, 1979, pp. 4, 10.

202. Carr and Aizpurua, *Spain*, p. 179; Share, *The Making of Spanish Democracy*, p. 210.

203. Ibid.

204. Ibid., p. 224.

205. Ibid., p. 233; Jose Maraval, *The Transition to Democracy in Spain* (New York: St. Martin's Press, 1982), p. 42; Lopez-Pintor, "Mass and Elite Perspectives," in Baloyra, 1987, pp. 99–100.

206. Gilmour, *The Transformation of Spain*, p. 192; Foweraker, *Making Democracy in Spain*, p. 226.

207. In 1981 the democratic process even survived a coup by young officers who seized the parliament and held the delegates hostage. The coup ended after Juan Carlos appeared on television and told the country that "the crown . . . cannot tolerate in any form actions or attitudes of persons who try to interrupt the democratic process of the Constitution." Unlike his royalist predecessors or contemporaries, Juan Carlos acted decisively to defend the republican state. Maxwell and Spiegel, *The New Spain*, p. 17; Carr and Aizpurua, *Spain*, p. 220; Gilmour, *The Transformation of Spain*, pp. 244, 248.

208. Camiller, "Spain: The Survival of Socialism?" in Anderson and Camiller, 1994, p. 248; Maxwell and Spiegel, *The New Spain*, pp. 26–27.

209. Camiller, "Spain: The Survival of Socialism?" in Anderson and Camiller, 1994, p. 239.

210. Ibid., p. 241.

211. Ibid., p. 248.

212. Ibid., p. 246.

213. Gilmour, *The Transformation of Spain*, pp. 261–62.

214. Camiller, "Spain: The Survival of Socialism?" in Anderson and Camiller, 1994, pp. 247–48; Gilmour, *The Transformation of Spain*, p. 96.

215. Stanley G. Payne, "Natural Evolution in Spanish Political Culture," in Binnendijk, 1987, p. 189.

Chapter Five

1. Howard P. Lehman, *Indebted Development: Strategic Bargaining and Economic Adjustment in the Third World* (New York: St. Martin's Press, 1993), passim.

2. "Transcript of President Nixon's Address in Move to Deal with Economic Problems," *New York Times*, 16 August 1971; Berch Berberglou, *The Legacy of Empire: Economic Decline and Class Polarization in the U.S.* (New York: Praeger, 1992), p. 56; Paul A. Volcker and Toyoo Gyohten, *Changing Fortunes: The World's Money and the Threat to American Leadership* (New York: Times Books, 1992), p. 81.

3. Daniel Yergin, *The Prize: The Epic Quest for Oil, Money and Power* (New York: Simon and Schuster, 1991), p. 625. Ernst J. Oliveri, *Latin American Debt and the Politics of International Finance* (Westport, Conn.: Praeger, 1992), p. 11.

4. Oliveri, *Latin American Debt*, p. 11.

5. Ibid., p. 13.

6. David Rock, "Military Politics in Argentina, 1973–83," in *The Latin American Left: From the Fall of Allende to Perestroika*, ed. Barry Carr and Steve Ellner (Boulder: Westview Press, 1993), p. 325; Werner Baer, *The Brazilian Economy: Growth and Development* (Westport, Conn.: Praeger, 1989), p. 96.

7. Rock, "Military Politics in Argentina," in Carr and Ellner, 1993, p. 11; Ernesto Zedillo Ponce de Leon, "The Mexican External Debt: The Last Decade," in *Politics and Economics of External Debt Crisis: The Latin American Experience*, ed. Miguel S. Wionczek (Boulder: Westview Press, 1985), p. 305; Judith Ewell, "Venezuela Since 1930," in *Latin American Since 1930, Spanish South America*, ed. Leslie Bethell, vol. 8 of *The Cambridge History of Latin America* (Cambridge: Cambridge University Press, 1991), p. 773.

8. William H. Friedland et al., *Towards a New Political Economy of Agriculture* (Boulder: Westview Press, 1991), pp. 84–85; Robert L. Paarlberg, *Food Trade and Foreign Policy: India, the Soviet Union and the United States* (Ithaca: Cornell University Press, 1985), p. 131; Nick Butler, *The International Grain Trade* (New York: St. Martin's Press, 1986), p. 55.

9. Malcolm H. Forbes and Louis J. Merrill, *Global Hunger: A Look at the Problem and Potential Solutions* (Evansville, Ind.: University of Evansville Press, 1986), p. 117; Robert E. Long, *The Farm Crisis*, vol. 49, no. 6 of *The Reference Shelf* (New York: H. W. Wilson Co., 1987), p. 14; Raymond F. Hopkins and Donald J. Puchala, "The Global Political Economy of Food," *International Organization* 32, no. 3 (summer 1978): 584; Mary Summers and Edward Tufte, "The Crisis of American Agriculture: Minding the Public's Business," (unpublished paper, January 10, 1988), p. 7.

10. Victor L. Urquidi, "The World Crisis and the Outlook for Latin America," in Wionczek, 1985, p. 38.

11. Mitchell Wallerstein, *Food for War—Food for Peace: United States Food Aid in a Global Context* (Cambridge, Mass.: MIT Press, 1980), p. 54.

12. Ibid., pp. 54, 15; Peter J. Taylor, "The Globalization of Agriculture," *Political Geography* 12, no. 3 (May 1993): 241; Hopkins and Puchala, "The Global Political Economy of Food," p. 633.

13. Long, *The Farm Crisis*, p. 68; Robert E. Wood, *From Marshall Plan to Debt Crisis: Foreign Aid and Development Choices in the World Economy* (Berkeley: University of California Press, 1986), p. 21.

14. Edmar L. Bacha and Pedro S. Malan, "Brazil's Debt: From the Miracle to the Fund," in *Democratizing Brazil: Problems of Transition and Consolidation,* ed. Alfred Stepan (New York: Oxford University Press, 1989), pp. 126–27.

15. Victor Blumer-Thomas, *The Economic History of Latin America Since Independence* (Cambridge: Cambridge University Press, 1994), p. 344; Bacha and Malan, "Brazil's Debt," in Stepan, 1989, p. 128.

16. Thomas O. Enders and Richard P. Mattione, *Latin America: The Crisis of Debt and Growth* (Washington, D.C.: Brookings Institution, 1984), p. 7.

17. Ibid.; Ronaldo Munck, *Latin America: The Transition to Democracy* (London: Zed Books, 1989), p. 54.

18. Arturo Escobar, *Encountering Development: The Making and Unmaking of the Third World* (Princeton: Princeton University Press, 1995), p. 80; David Lehman, *Democracy and Development in Latin America: Economics, Politics and Religion in the Postwar Period* (Philadelphia: Temple University Press, 1990), p. 7; Fernando Henrique Cardoso, "Associated-Dependent Development and Democratic Theory," in Stepan, 1989, p. 308.

19. Blumer-Thomas, *The Economic History of Latin America,* pp. 17–18, 264–65, 279–80.

20. Ibid., p. 309; Lehman, *Democracy and Development in Latin America,* p. 43; Howard Handelman and Werner Baer, *Paying the Costs of Austerity in Latin America* (Boulder: Westview Press, 1989), p. 1.

21. Enrique Ayala Mora, "Ecuador Since 1930," in Bethell, 1991, p. 713; James K. Boyce, *The Philippines: The Political Economy of Growth and Impoverishment in the Marcos Era* (Honolulu, Hawaii: University of Hawaii Press, 1993), p. 254.

22. Michael Moffitt, *The World's Money: International Banking from Bretton Woods to the Brink of Insolvency* (New York: Simon and Schuster, 1983), p. 46. "The term 'Eurodollar' can be misleading, for it is often used to describe any currency holding outside the issuing country. Thus a Japanese yen deposit in the Panamanian international banking center can sometimes be included, as can U.S. dollar deposits in a London financial institution." Blumer-Thomas, *The Economic History of Latin America,* p. 360.

23. Sue Branford and Bernardo Kucinski, *The Debt Squads: The U.S., the Banks and Latin America* (London: Zed Books, 1988), p. 58.

24. Ibid., p. 58. Blumer-Thomas argues that it grew from $12 billion in 1964 to $57 billion by 1970, but Oliveri says that it had grown to $160 billion before the first oil shock. Estimates vary widely because governments did not effectively track these holdings. Blumer-Thomas, *The Economic History of Latin America,* p. 360; Oliveri, *Latin American Debt,* p. 29; Eric Hobsbawm, *The Age of Extremes: A History of the World, 1914–1991* (New York: Pantheon, 1994), p. 278.

25. Barbara Stallings, *Banker to the World: U.S. Portfolio Investment in Latin America, 1900–1986* (Berkeley: University of California Press, 1987), p. 298.

26. Branford and Kucinski, *The Debt Squads,* p. 58.

27. John Walton, "Debt, Protest and the State in Latin America," in *Power and Popular Protest: Latin American Social Movements,* ed. Susan Eckstein (Berkeley: University of California Press, 1989), p. 301.

28. Richard W. Lombardi, *Debt Trap: Rethinking the Logic of Development* (New York: Praeger, 1985), pp. 90, 91.

29. Thomas E. Skidmore, "Brazil's Slow Road to Democratization: 1974–1985," in Stepan, 1989, p. 8; Dragoslav Avramovic, "External Debt of Developing Countries in Late 1983," in Wionczek, 1985, p. 27; Riordan Roett, "The Post-1964 Military Republic in Brazil," in *The Politics of Anti-Politics,* ed. Brian Loveman and Thomas M. Davies, Jr. (Lincoln, Nebr.: University of Nebraska Press, 1989), p. 396.

30. Avramovic, "External Debt of Developing Countries," in Wionczek, 1985, p. 27; Boyce, *The Philippines,* pp. 262, 365.

31. Blumer-Thomas, *The Economic History of Latin America,* p. 361.

32. Roett, "The Post-1964 Military Republic in Brazil," in Loveman and Davies, 1989, p. 396; Skidmore, "Brazil's Slow Road to Democratization," in Stepan, 1989, p. 8.

33. Howard J. Wiarda, *Latin America at the Crossroads: Debt, Development and the Future* (Boulder: Westview Press, 1987), pp. 74–76.

34. Some countries like the Philippines expanded "non-traditional" industries. The Marcos regime evidently used borrowed money to finance construction of hotels for the sex tour and pornographic film industries in the 1970s, an extreme form of the tourist-based development practiced by southern European dictatorships in the 1960s. Like those dictatorships, the Marcos regime also encouraged the export of workers both as a way to reduce possible dissent and to secure remittance income. David Wurfel, *Filipino Politics: Development and Decay* (Ithaca: Cornell University Press, 1988), p. 67; A. Lin Neumann, "Tourism Promotion and Prostitution," in *The Philippines Reader: A History of Colonialism, Neo-Colonialism, Dictatorship and Resistance,* ed. Daniel B. Schirmer and Stephen Rosskamm Shalom (Boston: South End Press, 1987), pp. 182–83; Robert S. Dohner and Ponciano Intal, Jr., "Debt Crisis and Adjustment in the Philippines," in *Developing Country Debt and the World Economy,* ed. Jeffrey D. Sachs (Chicago: University of Chicago Press, 1989), p. 184; Linda Richter, "Exploring the Political Role of Gender in Tourism Research," in *Global Tourism: The Next Decade,* ed. William F. Theobald (Oxford: Butterworth-Heinemann, 1994), p. 153.

35. Branford and Kucinski, *The Debt Squads,* p. xiv; Blumer-Thomas, *The Economic History of Latin America,* p. 361.

36. Tony Smith, *America's Mission: The United States and the Worldwide Struggle for Democracy in the Twentieth Century* (Princeton: Princeton University Press, 1994), p. 245.

37. Lombardi, *Debt Trap,* p. 83. In Argentina military spending increased 200 percent between 1972 and 1980. Peru's defense budget grew 14.05 percent annually between 1970 and 1977 and by the end of the decade amounted to "about a quarter to a third of total public expenditure." After Marcos declared martial law, the defense budget in the Philippines increased nearly tenfold between 1972 and 1977. Edward S. Herman, "Resurgent Democracies in Latin America: Rhetoric and Reality," in *Latin America: Bankers, Generals and the Struggle for Social Justice,* ed.

James F. Petras (Totowa, N.J.: Rowman and Littlefield, 1986), p. 93; Aldo C. Vacs, "Authoritarian Breakdown and Redemocratization in Argentina," in *Authoritarians and Democrats,* ed. James M. Malloy and Mitchell A. Seligson (Pittsburgh: University of Pittsburgh Press, 1987), p. 25; Juan Carlos Torre and Liliana Riz, "Argentina Since 1946," in Bethell, 1991, p. 163; Carlos A. Astiz, "A Postmortem of the Institutional Military Regime in Peru," in *The Decline of Military Regimes: The Civilian Influence,* ed. Constantine P. Danopoulos (Boulder: Westview Press, 1988), pp. 182–83, 190; Julio Colter, "Military Interventions and 'Transfer of Power to Civilians' in Peru," in *Transitions from Authoritarian Rule: Latin America,* ed. Guillermo O'Donnell, Philippe C. Schmitter, and Laurence Whitehead (Baltimore: Johns Hopkins University Press, 1986), p. 155; Wurfel, *Filipino Politics,* p. 140.

    38. Arturo R. Guillen, "Crisis, the Burden of Foreign Debt and Structural Dependence," *Latin American Perspectives* 16, no. 1 (winter 1989): 38.

    39. Ibid. General Motors, Ford, Union Carbide, Pepsi, and Volkswagen borrowed $750 million in Mexico during this period.

    40. Oliveri, *Latin American Debt,* p. 12; Edward F. Buffie and Allen Sangines Krause, "Mexico 1958–86: From Stabilizing Development to Debt Crisis," in *Developing Country Debt and the World Economy,* ed. Jeffrey D. Sachs (Chicago: University of Chicago Press, 1989), p. 162. Commodity prices varied widely. Oil and many food products increased in value, but the price of copper plummeted, from 93.4 U.S. cents a pound in 1974 to only 56.1 cents in 1975, creating major problems for the new dictatorship in Chile. Alan Angell, "Chile Since 1958," in Bethell, 1991, p. 364.

    41. Robert A. Pastor, *Whirlpool: U.S. Foreign Policy Toward Latin America and the Caribbean* (Princeton: Princeton University Press, 1986), p. 89.

    42. William C. Smith, *Authoritarianism and the Crisis of the Argentine Political Economy* (Stanford, Calif.: Stanford University Press, 1989), p. 259; Oliveri, *Latin American Debt,* pp. 8–9; Economic Commission for Latin America and the Caribbean, *External Debt in Latin America: Adjustment Policies and Re-negotiation* (Boulder: Lynne Rienner, 1985), p. 6.

    43. Michael H. Armacost, "Philippine Aspirations for Democracy," in *Authoritarian Regimes in Transition,* ed. Hans Binnendijk (Washington, D.C.: Foreign Service Institute, 1987), p. 136.

    44. Munck, *Latin America,* p. 50; Stephan Haggard and Robert R. Kaufman, *The Political Economy of Democratic Transitions* (Princeton: Princeton University Press, 1995), p. 327; Astiz, "The Institutional Military Regime in Peru," in Danopoulos, 1988, p. 179; Neumann, "Tourism Promotion and Prostitution," in Schirmer and Shalom, 1987, p. 176; Joseph Collins and John Lear, *Chile's Free-Market Miracle: A Second Look* (Oakland, Calif.: Food First, 1995), p. 7.

    45. Anthony S. Compagna, *The Economic Consequences of the Vietnam War* (New York: Praeger, 1991), p. 122.

    46. Branford and Kucinski, *The Debt Squads,* p. 59; Jacobo Schatan, *World Debt: Who is to Pay?* (London: Zed Books, 1987), p. 7.

    47. Branford and Kucisnki, *The Debt Squads,* p. 56.

    48. William Greider, *Secrets of the Temple: How the Federal Reserve Runs the Country* (New York: Touchstone, 1987), p. 114.

49. "Test of Fed's Announcement on Measures to Curb Inflation," *New York Times,* 8 October 1979; Steven Rattner, "Anti-Inflation Plan by Federal Reserve Increases Key Rate," *New York Times,* 7 October 1979.

50. Morton H. Halperin, David J. Scheffer, and Patricia L. Small, *Self-Determination in the New World Order* (Washington, D.C.: Carnegie Endowment for International Peace, 1992), p. 14; Bacha and Malan, "Brazil's Debt," in Stepan, 1989, p. 130; Greider, *Secrets of the Temple,* pp. 148–49.

51. Sachs, 1989, p. 302; Robert Devlin, *Debt and Crisis in Latin America: The Supply Side of the Story* (Princeton: Princeton University Press, 1989), p. 50.

52. Economic Commission, *External Debt in Latin America,* p. 10. Although total debt rose 195 percent during this period, interest payments rose 415 percent. U.S. economist William Cline estimated that high interest rates in the 1980s cost Third World countries, Latin American among them, $41 billion more than they would have paid had interest rates remained at their average level between 1961 and 1980. Vincent Ferraro, "Global Debt and Third World Development," in *World Security: Trends and Challenges at Century's End,* ed. Michael T. Klare and Daniel C. Thomas (New York: St. Martin's Press, 1991), p. 329. Other economists have estimated that Latin American countries paid out more than $100 billion in "excessive interest" between 1976 and 1985. Schatan, *World Debt,* p. 110.

53. Boyce, *The Philippines,* pp. 279, 317–18; Manuel Pastor, Jr., *Capital Flight and the Latin America Debt Crisis* (Washington, D.C.: Economic Policy Institute, 1989), p. 9.

54. Ibid., p. 1.

55. Boyce, *The Philippines,* p. 280; Buffie and Krause, "Mexico 1958–86," in Sachs, 1989, p. 151.

56. Bill Orr, *The Global Economy in the 90s: A User's Guide* (New York: New York University Press, 1992), p. 303.

57. Ibid., p. 287.

58. Walton, "Debt, Protest and the State in Latin America," in Eckstein, 1989, p. 306.

59. Lombardi, *Debt Trap,* p. 10; Blumer-Thomas, *The Economic History of Latin America,* p. 378; Dohner and Intal, "Debt Crisis and Adjustment in the Philippines," in Sachs, 1989, p. 180; Buffie and Krause, "Mexico 1958–86," in Sachs, 1989, p. 162.

60. Darrell Delmaide, *Debt Shock: The Full Story of the World Credit Crisis* (New York: Doubleday, 1984), p. 28; Schatan, *World Debt,* p. 41.

61. Howard J. Wiarda, *The Democratic Revolution in Latin America: History, Politics and U.S. Policy* (New York: Holmes and Meier, 1990), p. 174.

62. Enders and Mattione, *Latin America,* p. 14; Blumer-Thomas, *The Economic History of Latin America,* p. 9.

63. Wiarda, *Latin America at the Crossroads,* pp. 12–13; Harriet Friedmann, "Change in the International Division of Labor: Agri-Food Complexes and Export Agriculture," in Friedland et al., 1991, pp. 38–39, 67, 75–77; David Goodman, "Some Recent Tendencies in the Industrial Reorganization of the Agri-Food System," in Friedland et al., 1991, p. 47.

64. Barbara Dinham and Colin Hines, *Agribusiness in Africa* (London: Earth Resources, 1983), pp. 189, 193.

65. Economic Commission, *External Debt in Latin America,* p. 71.

66. Iliana Zloch-Christy, *Debt Problems of Eastern Europe* (Cambridge: Cambridge University Press, 1987), p. 29; Christopher A. Kojm, *The Problem of International Debt,* vol. 5, no. 1 of *The Reference Shelf* (New York: The H. W. Wilson Company, 1984), p. 8.

67. Zloch-Christy, *Debt Problems of Eastern Europe,* p. 34.

68. Walton, "Debt, Protest and the State in Latin America," in Eckstein, 1989, p. 301; Economic Commission, *External Debt in Latin America,* p. 58.

69. Robert Gilpin, *The Political Economy of International Relations* (Princeton: Princeton University Press, 1987), p. 317.

70. Jackie Roddick, *The Dance of the Millions: Latin America and the Debt Crisis* (London: Latin America Bureau, 1988), p. 65.

71. Gilpin, *The Political Economy of International Relations,* p. 326.

72. Branford and Kucinski, *The Debt Squads,* p. 8; Gilpin, *The Political Economy of International Relations,* p. 327; Robert A. Pastor, *Latin America's Debt Crisis: Adjusting to the Past or Planning for the Future?* (Boulder: Lynne Rienner, 1987), pp. 151–52.

73. Economic Commission, *External Debt in Latin America,* pp. 12–13, 67; Oliveri, *Latin American Debt,* p. 15.

74. Roddick, *The Dance of the Millions,* pp. 71, 110–11.

75. Sachs, 1989, p. 13.

76. Blumer-Thomas, *The Economic History of Latin America,* p. 281; Ewell, "Venezuela Since 1930," in Bethell, 1991, p. 783; Mora, "Ecuador Since 1930," in Bethell, 1991, p. 720; Gerald Sussman, David O'Connor, and Charles W. Lindsey, "Post-Assassination Crisis," in Schirmer and Shalom, 1987, p. 286; Juan Gabriel Valdes, *Pinochet's Economists: The Chicago School in Chile* (Cambridge: Cambridge University Press, 1995), p. 25; Boyce, *The Philippines,* p. 305; William C. Smith, "The Political Transition in Brazil: From Authoritarian Liberalization and Elite Conciliation to Democratization," in *Comparing New Democracies: Transition and Consolidation in Mediterranean Europe and the Southern Cone,* ed. Enrique A. Baloyra (Boulder: Westview Press, 1987), p. 213; Handelman and Baer, *Paying the Costs of Austerity,* p. 4; Henry Finch, "Uruguay Since 1930," in Bethell, 1991, p. 222; Karen L. Remmer, "Democratization in Latin America," in *Global Transformation and the Third World,* ed. Robert O. Slater, Barry M. Schutz, and Steven R. Dorr (Boulder: Lynne Rienner, 1993), p. 100.

77. Blumer-Thomas, *The Economic History of Latin America,* p. 380.

78. Branford and Kucinski, *The Debt Squads,* p. 5; Blumer-Thomas, *The Economic History of Latin America,* p. 386.

79. Blumer-Thomas, *The Economic History of Latin America,* p. 372.

80. Clyde H. Farnsworth, "Latin America Records Some Economic Gains," *New York Times,* 11 September 1989; Economic Commission, *External Debt in Latin America,* pp. 26, 113.

81. Pastor, *Capital Flight,* p. 36. "Between 1982 and 1989, the Third World had an annual average surplus of $26 billion. . . . These trade surpluses were achieved mainly by the use of austerity programs to squeeze imports; attempts to increase exports were diminished by protectionism and slow growth in the North." Michael

Dolan, "Global Economic Transformation and Less Developed Countries," in Slater, Schutz, and Dorr, 1993, p. 264.

82. Miquel D. Ramirez, *Mexico's Economic Crisis: Its Origins and Consequences* (Westport, Conn.: Praeger, 1989), p. 108.

83. Lehman, *Indebted Development,* pp. 44–45.

84. Stephany Griffith-Jones and Osvaldo Sunkel, *Debt and Development Crises in Latin America: The End of an Illusion* (Oxford: Clarendon Press, 1986), p. 6.

85. Handelman and Baer, *Paying the Costs of Austerity,* p. 14; Blumer-Thomas, *The Economic History of Latin America,* p. 399; Munck, *Latin America,* p. 53.

86. Branford and Kucinski, *The Debt Squads,* p. 24.

87. Blumer-Thomas, *The Economic History of Latin America,* p. 388.

88. Baer, *The Brazilian Economy,* pp. 136, 151.

89. Smith, *The Crisis of the Argentine Political Economy,* p. 271

90. Ferraro, "Global Debt and Third World Development," in Klare and Thomas, 1991, p. 335.

91. Walton, "Debt, Protest and the State in Latin America," in Eckstein, 1989, passim.

92. Ibid., p. 299.

93. Herman, "Resurgent Democracies in Latin America," in Petras, 1986, pp. 90–91; Oliveri, *Latin American Debt,* p. 165.

94. Smith, "The Political Transition in Brazil," in Baloyra, 1987, p. 215.

Chapter Six

1. Laurence Whitehead, "The Alternatives to 'Liberal Democracy': A Latin American Perspective," in *Prospects for Democracy: North, South, East, West,* ed. David Held (Stanford, Calif.: Stanford University Press, 1993), p. 316.

2. Edmundo Campos Coehlo, "Back to the Barracks: The Brazilian Military Style," in *The Decline of Military Regimes: The Civilian Influence,* ed. Constantine Danopoulos (Boulder: Westview Press, 1988), p. 164.

3. Brian Loveman and Thomas M. Davies, Jr., *The Politics of Anti-Politics* (Lincoln, Nebr.: University of Nebraska Press, 1989), p. 244.

4. Ibid., p. 249.

5. Leslie Bethell, *The Cambridge History of Latin America: Latin America Since 1930, Spanish South America* (Cambridge: Cambridge University Press, 1991), p. 714.

6. Juan Rial, "Political Parties and Elections in the Process of Transition in Uruguay," in *Comparing New Democracies: Transition and Consolidation in Mediterranean Europe and the Southern Cone,* ed. Enrique A. Baloyra (Boulder: Westview Press, 1987), p. 275.

7. Mark R. Thompson, "Democracy After Sultanism: The Troubled Transition in the Philippines," in *Politics, Society and Democracy: Comparative Studies,* ed. H. E. Chebai and Alfred Stepan (Boulder: Westview Press, 1995), p. 329.

8. Frank Moya Pons, "The Dominican Republic Since 1930," in Bethell, 1991, p. 532.

9. Ibid., p. 537.

10. Ibid.

11. Howard J. Wiarda, *The Democratic Revolution in Latin America: History, Politics and U.S. Policy* (New York: Holmes and Meier, 1990), p. 77.

12. Ibid., pp. 77–78; Pons, "The Dominican Republic," in Bethell, 1991, pp. 533–34.

13. Ibid., p. 542.

14. Ibid., pp. 542–43.

15. Howard H. Lentner, *State Formation in Central America: The Struggle for Autonomy, Development and Democracy* (Westport, Conn.: Greenwood Press, 1993), p. 154.

16. Richard Stahler-Sholk, "Foreign Debt and Economic Stabilization," in *The Political Economy of Revolutionary Nicaragua,* ed. Rose J. Spalding (Boston: Allen and Unwin, 1987), p. 153.

17. Nigel Haworth, "Peru," in *Latin America Between the Second World War and the Cold War, 1944–1948,* ed. Leslie Bethell and Ian Roxborough (Cambridge: Cambridge University Press, 1992), pp. 153, 156.

18. Stahler-Sholk, "Foreign Debt and Economic Stabilization," in Spalding, 1987, p. 153.

19. Tony Smith, *America's Mission: The United States and the Worldwide Struggle for Democracy in the Twentieth Century* (Princeton: Princeton University Press, 1994), p. 248; Stahler-Sholk, "Foreign Debt and Economic Stabilization," in Spalding, 1987, pp. 62–63.

20. Smith, *America's Mission,* p. 249.

21. Richard Stahler-Sholk, "Building Democracy in Nicaragua," in *Liberalization and Re-Democratization in Latin America,* ed. George A. Lopez and Michael Stohl (Westport, Conn.: Greenwood Press, 1987), p. 73.

22. Ibid., p. 74.

23. Ibid, pp. 73–74.

24. Smith, *America's Mission,* p. 249.

25. Stahler-Sholk, "Building Democracy in Nicaragua," in Lopez and Stohl, 1987, p. 72.

26. Ibid.

27. Ibid.; Stahler-Sholk, "Foreign Debt and Economic Stabilization," in Spalding, 1987, p. 352.

28. Stahler-Sholk, "Building Democracy in Nicaragua," in Lopez and Stohl, 1987, pp. 75–76; Smith, *America's Mission,* p. 251.

29. Stahler-Sholk, "Building Democracy in Nicaragua," in Lopez and Stohl, 1987, p. 76.

30. Ibid., pp. 80–81; Stahler-Sholk, "Foreign Debt and Economic Stabilization," in Spalding, 1987, p. 357.

31. Stahler-Sholk, "Foreign Debt and Economic Stabilization," in Spalding, 1987, p. 361.

32. Ibid., pp. 364–65.

33. Thomas Carothers, *In the Name of Democracy: U.S. Policy Toward Latin America in the Reagan Years* (Berkeley: University of California Press, 1991), pp. 47–48.

34. Victor Blumer-Thomas, "Honduras Since 1930," in *Latin America Since 1930, Mexico, Central America and the Caribbean,* ed. Leslie Bethell, vol. 7 of *The Cambridge History of Latin America* (Cambridge: Cambridge University Press, 1990), p. 310.

35. Ibid., pp. 310–11.

36. Carothers, *In the Name of Democracy,* pp. 53, 55.

37. Blumer-Thomas, "Honduras Since 1930," in Bethell, 1990, pp. 314–15.

38. Carothers, *In the Name of Democracy,* p. 57.

39. Enrique Ayala Mora, "Ecuador Since 1930," in Bethell, 1991, p. 711.

40. Ibid., p. 713.

41. Ibid., p. 716.

42. Baloyra, 1987, p. 28.

43. Ibid, pp. 29, 31.

44. Ibid., p. 31; Mora, "Ecuador Since 1930," in Bethell, 1991, p. 717.

45. Julio Colter, "Peru Since 1930," in Bethell, 1991, p. 475.

46. Ibid., pp. 475–76.

47. Carlos A. Astiz, "A Postmortem of the Institutional Military Regime in Peru," in Danopoulos, 1988, p. 185; Stephen M. Gorman, "Antipolitics in Peru," in Loveman and Davies, 1989, p. 478.

48. Gorman, "Antipolitics in Peru," in Loveman and Davies, 1989, p. 479.

49. Colter, "Peru Since 1930," in Bethell, 1991, p. 487; Julio Colter, "Military Interventions and 'Transfer of Power to Civilians' in Peru," in *Transitions from Authoritarian Rule: Latin America,* ed. Guillermo O'Donnell, Philippe C. Schmitter, and Laurence Whitehead (Baltimore: Johns Hopkins University Press, 1986), p. 149.

50. James F. Petras, *Latin America: Bankers, Generals and the Struggle for Social Justice* (Totowa, N.J.: Rowman and Littlefield, 1986), p. 158.

51. Cynthia McClintock, "Communal Strife in Peru: A Case of Absence of Spillover into the International Arena," in *The Internationalization of Communal Strife,* ed. Manus I. Midlarsky (London: Routledge, 1992), p. 209.

52. Laurence Whitehead, "Bolivia Since 1930," in Bethell, 1991, pp. 576, 578.

53. Ibid., pp. 575–76.

54. James M. Malloy and Eduardo Gamarra, "The Transition to Democracy in Bolivia," in *Authoritarians and Democrats,* ed. James M. Malloy and Mitchell A. Seligson (Pittsburgh: University of Pittsburgh Press, 1987), p. 108.

55. Ibid., p. 110.

56. Ibid., pp. 111–12.

57. Ibid., p. 113.

58. Ibid., p. 114.

59. Ibid.

60. Whitehead, "Bolivia Since 1930," in Bethell, 1991, pp. 577–78.

61. Karen L. Remmer, "Democratization in Latin America," in *Global Transformation and the Third World,* ed. Robert O. Slater, Barry M. Schutz, and Steven R. Dorr (Boulder: Lynne Rienner, 1993), p. 92.

62. Malloy and Gamarra, "The Transition to Democracy in Bolivia," in Malloy and Seligson, 1987, p. 93.

63. Juan Carlos Torre and Liliana Riz, "Argentina Since 1946," in Bethell, 1991, pp. 165, 171; Gary W. Wynia, *Argentina: Illusions and Realities* (New York:

Holmes and Meier, 1986), p. 136; William C. Smith, *Authoritarianism and the Crisis of the Argentine Political Economy* (Stanford, Calif.: Stanford University Press, 1989), p. 249.

64. Baloyra, 1987, p. 20; Smith, *The Crisis of the Argentine Political Economy*, p. 242; James W. McGuire, "Interim Government and Democratic Consolidation: Argentina in Comparative Perspective," in *Between States: Interim Governments and Democratic Transitions*, ed. Yossi Shaim and Juan J. Linz (Cambridge: Cambridge University Press, 1995), p. 186.

65. Jack S. Levy and Lily I. Vakili, "Diversionary Action by Authoritarian Regimes: Argentina in the Falklands/Malvinas Case," in Midlarsky, 1992, p. 129; Torre and Riz, "Argentina Since 1946," in Bethell, 1991, pp. 166–67.

66. Baloyra, 1987, p. 19.

67. Joseph S. Tulchin, *Argentina and the United States: A Conflicted Relationship* (Boston: Twayne, 1990), p. 154.

68. Lawrence Freedman, *Britain and the Falklands War* (London: Basil Blackwell, 1988), p. 19; Dennis R. Gordon, "Withdrawal in Disgrace: Decline of the Argentine Military, 1976–1983," in Danopoulos, 1988, p. 214.

69. Aldo C. Vacs, "Authoritarian Breakdown and Redemocratization in Argentina," in Malloy and Seligson, 1987, p. 28; Smith, *The Crisis of the Argentine Political Economy*, p. 256; Wynia, *Argentina*, p. 12.

70. Tulchin, *Argentina and the United States*, p. 155.

71. McGuire, "Interim Government and Democratic Consolidation," in Shaim and Linz, 1995, p. 188; Smith, *The Crisis of the Argentine Political Economy*, p. 256; Gordon, "Withdrawal in Disgrace," in Danopoulos, 1988, p. 213; Levy and Vakili, "Diversionary Action by Authoritarian Regimes," in Midlarsky, 1992, p. 130.

72. Wynia, *Argentina*, p. 3.

73. Ibid., p. 96; David Pion-Berlin, "Military Breakdown and Redemocratization in Argentina," in Lopez and Stohl, 1987, p. 221.

74. Gaddis Smith, *The Last Years of the Monroe Doctrine, 1945–1993* (New York: Hill and Wang, 1994), p. 174.

75. Paul G. Buchanan, "Democratization Top-Down and Bottom-Up," in *Authoritarian Regimes in Transition*, ed. Hans Binnendijk (Washington, D.C.: Foreign Service Institute, 1987), p. 239; Wynia, *Argentina*, pp. 24, 99; Freedman, *Britain and the Falklands War*, p. 72.

76. Freedman, *Britain and the Falklands War*, p. 1.

77. Ibid., p. 84.

78. Ibid., pp. 61, 65; Wynia, *Argentina*, p. 100.

79. Levy and Vakili, "Diversionary Action by Authoritarian Regimes," in Midlarsky, 1992, p. 135.

80. Ronaldo Munck, *Latin America: The Transition to Democracy* (London: Zed Books, 1989), p. 95; Gordon, "Withdrawal in Disgrace," in Danopoulos, 1988, p. 218; Vacs, "Authoritarian Breakdown," in Malloy and Seligson, 1987, p. 31; Baloyra, 1987, p. 24.

81. Edward C. Epstein, "What Difference Does Regime Type Make? Economic Austerity Programs in Argentina," in *Paying the Costs of Austerity Programs in Latin America*, ed. Howard Handelman and Werner Baer (Boulder: Westview Press, 1989), p. 67.

82. Tulchin, *Argentina and the United States,* p. 156.

83. Smith, *The Last Years of the Monroe Doctrine,* pp. 75–76.

84. Buchanan, "Democratization Top-Down and Bottom-Up," in Binnendijk, 1987, p. 225; Guillermo O'Donnell, "Transitions to Democracy: Some Navigational Instruments," in *Democracy in the Americas: Stopping the Pendulum,* ed. Robert A. Pastor (New York: Holmes and Meier, 1989), p. 63; Torre and Riz, "Argentina Since 1946," in Bethell, 1991, p. 169.

85. Torre and Riz, "Argentina Since 1946," in Bethell, 1991, p. 158; Wynia, *Argentina,* p. 171.

86. McGuire, "Interim Government and Democratic Consolidation," in Shaim and Linz, 1995, p. 183. General Luciano Menendez calculated, "We are going to have to kill 50,000 people: 25,000 subversives, 20,000 sympathizers, and we will make 5,000 mistakes." Tulchin, *Argentina and the United States,* p. 144; Gordon, "Withdrawal in Disgrace," in Danopoulos, 1988, p. 209.

87. Torre and Riz, "Argentina Since 1946," in Bethell, 1991, p. 175; Wynia, *Argentina,* p. 170.

88. Torre and Riz, "Argentina Since 1946," in Bethell, 1991, p. 185.

89. McGuire, "Interim Government and Democratic Consolidation," in Shaim and Linz, 1995, p. 206.

90. Charles G. Gillespie, "Uruguay's Transition from Collegial Military-Technocratic Rule," in O'Donnell, Schmitter, and Whitehead, 1986, pp. 179–80.

91. Ibid., p. 180.

92. Ibid., p. 181; Munck, *Latin America,* p. 96.

93. Munck, *Latin America,* p. 96.

94. Gillespie, "Uruguay's Transition," in O'Donnell, Schmitter, and Whitehead, 1986, p. 187.

95. Ibid., pp. 189–90; Henry Finch, "Uruguay Since 1930," in Bethell, 1991, pp. 225, 229.

96. Ibid., p. 225.

97. Ibid., p. 226.

98. Buchanan, "Democratization Top-Down and Bottom-Up," in Binnendijk, 1987, pp. 230, 250.

99. Scott Mainwaring, "The Transition to Democracy in Brazil," in Loveman and Davies, 1989, p. 237; Luciano Martins, "The 'Liberalization' of Authoritarian Rule in Brazil," in O'Donnell, Schmitter, and Whitehead, 1986, p. 84.

100. Martins, "The 'Liberalization' of Authoritarian Rule in Brazil," in O'Donnell, Schmitter, and Whitehead, 1986, p. 87; Coehlo, "Back to the Barracks," in Danopoulos, 1988, p. 163.

101. Scott Mainwaring, "The Transition to Democracy in Brazil," in Loveman and Davies, 1989, p. 423.

102. Ibid., pp. 415, 423; Albert Fishlow, "A Tale of Two Presidents: The Political Economy of Crisis Management," in *Democratizing Brazil: Problems of Transition and Consolidation,* ed. Alfred Stepan (New York: Oxford University Press, 1989), p. 83.

103. Mainwaring, "The Transition to Democracy in Brazil," in Loveman and Davies, 1989, p. 421.

104. Ibid., p. 416.

105. Larry Diamond, Juan J. Linz, and Seymour Martin Lipset, *Politics in Developing Countries: Comparing Experiences with Democracy* (Boulder: Lynne Rienner, 1990), p. 87; Wilfred A. Bacchus, "Controlled Political Transition in Brazil: *Abertura* as a Process for a Gradual Sharing of Political Power," in Lopez and Stohl, 1987, p. 166; Mainwaring, "The Transition to Democracy in Brazil," in Loveman and Davies, 1989, p. 419.

106. Bacchus, "Controlled Political Transition in Brazil," in Lopez and Stohl, 1987, p. 166.

107. Thomas E. Skidmore, "Brazil's Slow Road to Democratization: 1974–1985," in Stepan, 1989, p. 31.

108. Belinda A. Aquino, "The Philippines: End of an Era," *Current History,* April 1986, p. 158.

109. James K. Boyce, *The Philippines: The Political Economy of Growth and Impoverishment in the Marcos Era* (Honolulu, Hawaii: University of Hawaii Press, 1993), p. 28.

110. Benedict Anderson, "Cacique Democracy in the Philippines: Origins and Dreams," *New Left Review* 169 (May-June 1986): 17.

111. Boyce, *The Philippines,* pp. 14–15.

112. John Bresnan, *Crisis in the Philippines: The Marcos Era and Beyond* (Princeton: Princeton University Press, 1986), p. 145.

113. Edward F. Buffie and Allen Sangines Krause, "Mexico 1958–86: From Stabilizing Development to Debt Crisis," in *Developing Country Debt and the World Economy,* ed. Jeffrey D. Sachs (Chicago: University of Chicago Press, 1989), p. 169; David Wurfel, *Filipino Politics: Development and Decay* (Ithaca: Cornell University Press, 1988), p. 291.

114. Anderson, "Cacique Democracy in the Philippines," p. 158.

115. Daniel B. Schirmer and Stephen Rosskamm Shalom, eds., *The Philippines Reader: A History of Colonialism, Neo-colonialism, Dictatorship and Resistance* (Boston: South End Press, 1987), p. 316.

116. Ibid., pp. 69–70, 74.

117. David Joel Steinberg, "Philippine Collaboration in World War II," in Schirmer and Shalom, 1987, p. 76; Wurfel, *Filipino Politics,* pp. 12, 224.

118. Schirmer and Shalom, *The Philippines Reader,* p. 105; Stephen R. Shalom, "Counter-Insurgency in the Philippines," in Schirmer and Shalom, 1987, pp. 111–17.

119. A rebellion by the Muslim minority, or "Moros," also emerged after the 1972 imposition of martial law, though negotiations brought an end to this conflict by the end of the decade. Lela Noble, "The Muslim Insurgency," in Schirmer and Shalom, 1987, pp. 94–98.

120. Wurfel, *Filipino Politics,* p. 266.

121. Walden Bello, *U.S. Sponsored Low-Intensity Conflict in the Philippines,* Food First Development Report, no. 2, San Francisco: Institute for Food and Development Policy (December 1987): 49; Wurfel, *Filipino Politics,* p. 292.

122. Bello, *U.S. Sponsored Low-Intensity Conflict,* pp. 31–32.

123. Ibid., p. 32.

124. Ibid., p. 39.

125. Wurfel, *Filipino Politics,* p. 268.

126. Bello, *U.S. Sponsored Low-Intensity Conflict,* p. 49.

127. Boyce, *The Philippines,* p. 1.

128. Wurfel, *Filipino Politics,* pp. 116–129.

129. Ibid., pp. 233, 247–48.

130. Ibid., pp. 274–76.

131. John Bresnan, *Crisis in the Philippines: The Marcos Era and Beyond* (Princeton: Princeton University Press, 1986), p. 121.

132. Miriani C. Dimaranan, "Increasing Terror," in Schirmer and Shalom, 1987, pp. 322–23.

133. Schirmer and Shalom, *The Philippines Reader,* p. 278; Bello, *U.S. Sponsored Low-Intensity Conflict,* p. 63.

134. Schirmer and Shalom, *The Philippines Reader,* p. 279; John F. Maisto, "Reform: The Bedrock of U.S. Policy," in Binnendijk, 1987, pp. 318–19.

135. Bello, *U.S. Sponsored Low-Intensity Conflict,* pp. 64–65; Wurfel, *Filipino Politics,* pp. 297–300.

136. Wurfel, *Filipino Politics,* p. 300.

137. Bello, *U.S. Sponsored Low-Intensity Conflict,* p. 66; Wurfel, *Filipino Politics,* pp. 304–305.

138. Wurfel, *Filipino Politics,* pp. 314, 318–20.

139. Thompson, "Democracy After Sultanism," in Chebai and Stepan, 1995, p. 341; Wurfel, *Filipino Politics,* p. 317.

140. Louis Hecht Oppenheim, *Politics in Chile: Democracy, Authoritarianism and the Search for Development* (Boulder: Westview Press, 1993), pp. 129, 132.

141. Remmer, "Democratization in Latin America," in Slater, Schutz, and Dorr, 1993, p. 94; Silvia T. Borzutsky, "The Pinochet Regime: Crisis and Consolidation," in Malloy and Seligson, 1987, p. 70; Oppenheim, *Politics in Chile,* p. 130; Joseph Collins and John Lear, *Chile's Free-Market Miracle: A Second Look* (Oakland, Calif.: Food First, 1995), p. 32.

142. Oppenheim, *Politics in Chile,* p. 152; Collins and Lear, *Chile's Free-Market Miracle,* pp. 34, 61.

143. Oppenheim, *Politics in Chile,* p. 152.

144. Juan Gabriel Valdes, *Pinochet's Economists: The Chicago School in Chile* (Cambridge: Cambridge University Press, 1995), p. 266.

145. Collins and Lear, *Chile's Free-Market Miracle,* p. 30; Alan Angell, "Chile Since 1958," in Bethell, 1991, pp. 372–73; Oppenheim, *Politics in Chile,* p. 137.

146. Oppenheim, *Politics in Chile,* pp. 172, 186.

147. Ibid., pp. 185, 188–89.

148. Carothers, *In the Name of Democracy,* pp. 135–36.

149. Ibid., pp. 57–58, 153–55.

150. Oppenheim, *Politics in Chile,* p. 191.

151. Ibid., p. 190.

152. Ibid., p. 192; Arturo Valenzuela and Pamela Constable, "The Chilean Plebiscite: Defeat of a Dictator," *Current History,* March 1989, p. 129.

153. Oppenheim, *Politics in Chile,* pp. 141, 192–93; Angell, "Chile Since 1958," in Bethell, 1991, p. 378; Arturo Valenzuela and Pamela Constable, "Democracy in Chile," *Current History,* February 1991, pp. 54–55.

154. Oppenheim, *Politics in Chile,* p. 192; Valenzuela and Constable, "Democracy in Chile," p. 53.

155. Angell, "Chile Since 1958," in Bethell, 1991, p. 379.

156. Oppenheim, *Politics in Chile,* pp. 125, 217–18, 222.

157. Steve C. Ropp, "Things Fall Apart: Panama After Noriega," *Current History,* March 1993, p. 104.

158. Yoichi Funabashi, *Managing the Dollar: From the Plaza to the Louvre* (Washington, D.C.: Institute for International Economics, 1989), p. 263.

159. Paul A. Volcker and Toyoo Gyohten, *Changing Fortunes: The World's Money and the Threat to American Leadership* (New York: Times Books, 1992), p. 142.

160. Steve C. Ropp, "Military Retrenchment and Decay in Panama," *Current History,* January 1990, p. 39.

161. Carothers, *In the Name of Democracy,* pp. 173–75.

162. Steve C. Ropp, "Panama: The U.S. Invasion and Its Aftermath," *Current History,* March 1991, p. 116.

163. Carothers, *In the Name of Democracy,* p. 169.

164. Ibid.

165. Ibid., p. 180.

166. Ropp, "Things Fall Apart," p. 105.

167. Ibid., p. 103.

168. Paul H. Lewis, "Paraguay Since 1930," in Bethell, 1991, pp. 263, 265; Carothers, *In the Name of Democracy,* pp. 165–66.

169. Lewis, "Paraguay Since 1930," in Bethell, 1991, p. 262.

170. Ibid., p. 266.

171. James Dunkerly, "El Salvador Since 1930," in Bethell, 1990, pp. 271–72.

172. Ibid., pp. 266, 272–73.

173. Ibid., pp. 267–68.

174. Ibid., p. 275.

175. Ibid., pp. 275–76.

176. Ibid., p. 278.

177. Ibid., pp. 279–80; Carothers, *In the Name of Democracy,* pp. 22–23.

178. Pamela Constable, "At War's End in El Salvador," *Current History,* March 1993, p. 106.

179. Lentner, *State Formation in Central America,* p. 69.

180. Ibid.; Constable, "At War's End in El Salvador," p. 106.

181. Lentner, *State Formation in Central America,* pp. 142–43.

182. Constable, "At War's End in El Salvador," p. 107.

183. Ibid., pp. 108–11.

184. David Nicholls, "Haiti Since 1930," in Bethell, 1990, p. 564.

185. Ibid., p. 565.

186. Carothers, *In the Name of Democracy,* pp. 183, 185.

187. Nicholls, "Haiti Since 1930," in Bethell, 1990, p. 567.

188. Ibid., pp. 567–68.

189. Ibid., pp. 572, 574.

190. Ibid., pp. 572–74.

191. Ibid., pp. 574, 576.

192. Ibid., p. 576.

193. Ibid., pp. 576–77.

194. Pamela Constable, "Haiti: A Nation in Despair, A Policy Adrift," *Current History*, March 1994, p. 111.

195. Ibid., pp. 108, 111; Anthony P. Maingot, "Haiti: The Political Rot Within," *Current History*, February 1995, p. 63.

196. Anthony T. Bryan, "Haiti: Kick Starting the Economy," *Current History*, February 1995, pp. 65–66.

197. Constable, "Haiti: A Nation in Despair," p. 108.

198. Gaddis Smith, "Haiti: From Intervention to Invasion," *Current History*, February 1995, p. 54.

199. Michelle Faul, "Crowds in Haiti Everywhere But the Polling Stations," *San Francisco Chronicle,* 18 December 1995.

200. Bethell and Roxborough, *Latin America Between the Second World War and the Cold War,* pp. 3, 5.

201. U.S. diplomats, for example, warned in March 1948 that radical republicans in Costa Rica could make it "the Czechoslovakia of the Western Hemisphere," and argued that "the most favorable solution, obviously, from our point of view, would be a constitutional succession acceptable to a majority of the people that would include the elimination of the communist influence in the government." Ibid., p. 28.

202. Ibid., p. 22.

203. In Brazil, for example, the 1946 constitution "denied the vote to illiterates (more than half the population) and distributed seats in Congress in such a way as seriously to underrepresent the more densely populated, urban, and developed [radical] regions of the country." Ibid., pp. 16–17, 18, 28.

204. Ibid., pp. 329–30; Andrew Barnard, "Chile," in Bethell and Roxborough, 1992, pp. 76, 91.

205. Bethell and Roxborough, *Latin America Between the Second World War and the Cold War,* pp. 18–19.

206. Charles Bergquist, Ricardo Penaranda, and Gonzolo Sanchez, *Violence in Colombia: The Contemporary Crisis in Historical Perspective* (Wilmington, Del.: Scholarly Resources Books, 1992), pp. xi-xii; Rodolfo Cedras Cruz, "Costa Rica," in Bethell and Roxborough, 1992, pp. 280–299.

207. James Dunkerly, "Guatemala," in Bethell and Roxborough, 1992, pp. 300–326; Bethell and Roxborough, *Latin America Between the Second World War and the Cold War,* p. 30.

208. Bethell and Roxborough, *Latin America Between the Second World War and the Cold War,* p. 2.

209. Timothy P. Wickham-Crowley, "Winners, Losers and Also-Rans: Toward a Comparative Sociology of Latin American Guerilla Movements," in Eckstein, 1989, pp. 133–38; George Philip, "Military Rule in South America: The Dilemmas of Authoritarianism," in *The Political Dilemmas of Military Regimes,* ed. Christopher Clapham and George Philip (Totowa, N.J.: Barnes and Noble, 1985), pp. 133–34.

210. Brian Loveman, "The Political Left in Chile, 1973–1990," in *The Latin American Left: From the Fall of Allende to Perestroika,* ed. Barry Carr and Steve Ellner (Boulder: Westview Press, 1993), p. 23; Wickham-Crowley, "Winners, Losers and Also-Rans," in Eckstein, 1989, passim.

211. James Dunkerly, "The Military and Bolivian Politics," in Loveman and Davies, 1989, p. 163.

212. Jon Lee Anderson, "Where is Che Guevara Buried? A Bolivian Tells," *New York Times*, 21 November 1995.

213. Bethell and Roxborough, *Latin America Between the Second World War and the Cold War,* p. 332; Ronald H. Chilcote, "Left Political Ideology and Practice," in Carr and Ellner, 1993, p. 173.

214. Peter B. Smith, "Mexico Since 1946," in Bethell, 1990, pp. 87, 141; Werner Baer, *The Brazilian Economy: Growth and Development* (Westport, Conn.: Praeger, 1989), pp. 16, 82, 84, 90.

215. Paul Brooker, *Twentieth Century Dictatorships: The Ideological One-Party States* (New York: New York University Press, 1995), pp. 222–23, 229.

216. Laura Nuzz O'Shaughnessy, "Redemocratization in Mexico: The Unique Challenge," in Lopez and Stohl, 1987, p. 28; Daniel C. Levy, "Mexico: Sustained Civilian Rule Without Democracy," in Diamond, Linz, and Lipset, 1990, p. 140; Miguel D. Ramirez, *Mexico's Economic Crisis: Its Origins and Consequences* (Westport, Conn.: Praeger, 1989), p. 29.

217. Paul Gordon Lauren, *Diplomacy: New Approaches in History, Theory and Policy* (New York: Free Press, 1979), p. 220; Ramirez, *Mexico's Economic Crisis,* pp. 27–28.

218. Brooker, *Twentieth Century Dictatorships,* p. 219; Baer, *The Brazilian Economy,* p. 7; Levy, "Mexico," in Diamond, Linz, and Lipset, 1990, p. 149.

219. Ramirez, *Mexico's Economic Crisis,* p. 31.

220. Ibid., p. 33; Alan Knight, "Mexico, c. 1930–46," in Bethell, 1990, pp. 16–17.

221. Ramirez, *Mexico's Economic Crisis,* p. 34; Julie A. Erfani, *The Paradox of the Mexican State: Rereading Sovereignty from Independence to NAFTA* (Boulder: Lynne Rienner, 1995), pp. 50, 64, 70, 73.

222. Erfani, *The Paradox of the Mexican State,* p. 73.

223. Knight, "Mexico, c. 1930–46," in Bethell, 1990, p. 44.

224. Erfani, *The Paradox of the Mexican State,* pp. 52–53.

225. Knight, "Mexico, c. 1930–46," in Bethell, 1990, pp. 44–45; Ramirez, *Mexico's Economic Crisis,* p. 36.

226. Erfani, *The Paradox of the Mexican State,* pp. 57, 63, 68, 89–90.

227. Ramirez, *Mexico's Economic Crisis,* pp. 86–88.

228. Ibid., p. 1; Smith, "Mexico Since 1946," in Bethell, 1990, p. 150.

229. O'Shaughnessy, "Redemocratization in Mexico," in Lopez and Stohl, 1987, p. 21; Smith, "Mexico Since 1946," in Bethell, 1990, pp. 121–22, 149–50.

230. Baer, *The Brazilian Economy,* p. 57.

231. Levy, "Mexico," in Diamond, Linz, and Lipset, 1990, p. 137.

232. Ian Roxborough, "Mexico," in Bethell and Roxborough, 1992, p. 195. During the economic crisis of the 1980s, for example, between three hundred thousand and five hundred thousand Mexicans annually emigrated to the United States, and some 3 million Mexicans resided in the United States on a permanent basis. Smith, "Mexico Since 1946," in Bethell, 1990, p. 148.

233. Ramirez, *Mexico's Economic Crisis,* p. 99; Smith, "Mexico Since 1946," in Bethell, 1990, p. 151.

234. Jorge Dominguez, "Cuba Since 1959," in Bethell, 1990, p. 457.

235. Susan Eva Eckstein, *Back From the Future: Cuba Under Castro* (Princeton: Princeton University Press, 1994), pp. 52–53.

236. Ibid., pp. 52, 222.

237. Ibid., p. 107.

238. Ibid., p. 220.

239. Dominguez, "Cuba Since 1959," in Bethell, 1990, p. 462.

240. Ibid., pp. 462–63.

241. Ibid., pp. 463–64.

242. Ibid., pp. 464–65.

243. Eckstein, *Back From the Future*, p. 181.

244. Ibid., p. 172.

245. Ibid., p. 173.

246. Ibid., pp. 175–77, 189–90.

247. Ibid., pp. 129, 224–25, 228, 232.

248. Ibid., p. 226.

249. Ibid., pp. 69, 121; Jorge I. Dominguez, "The Caribbean Question: Why has Liberal Democracy (Surprisingly) Flourished?" in *Democracy in the Caribbean: Political, Economic and Social Perspectives*, ed. Jorge I. Dominguez, Robert A. Pastor, and R. Delisle Worrell (Baltimore: Johns Hopkins University Press, 1993), p. 18.

250. Eckstein, *Back From the Future*, p. 125.

251. Ibid., p. 69.

252. Ibid., p. 73.

Chapter Seven

1. Nicholas D. Kristof, "China Sees 'Market-Leninism' as Way to Future," *New York Times*, 6 September 1993.

2. Walden Bello and Stephanie Rosenfeld, *Dragons in Distress: Asia's Miracle Economies in Crisis* (San Francisco: Food First Books, 1990), p. 58; James K. Boyce, *The Philippines: The Political Economy of Growth and Impoverishment in the Marcos Era* (Honolulu, Hawaii: University of Hawaii Press, 1993), p. 4.

3. Il Sakong, *Korea in the World Economy* (Washington, D.C.: Institute for International Economics, 1993), p. xv; Steve Chan and Cal Clark, *Flexibility, Foresight and Fortuna in Taiwan's Development: Navigating Between Scylla and Charybdis* (London: Routledge, 1992), p. 34; Hung-Mao Tien, "Taiwan's Evolution Toward Democracy: A Historical Perspective," in *Taiwan: Beyond the Economic Miracle*, ed. Denis Fred Simon and Michael Y. M. Kau (Armonk, N.Y.: M. E. Sharpe, 1992), p. 16.

4. Chalmers Johnson, "Political Institutions and Economic Performance: The Government-Business Relationship in Japan, South Korea and Taiwan," in *The Political Economy of the New Asian Industrialism*, ed. Frederic C. Deyo (Ithaca: Cornell University Press, 1987), p. 136; John F. Cooper, "Taiwan: A Nation in Transition," *Current History*, April 1989, p. 173.

5. Carter J. Eckert, *Offspring of Empire: the Koch 'ang Kims and the Colonial Origins of Korean Capitalism, 1876–1945* (Seattle: University of Washington Press, 1991), p. 41.

6. Kyong-Dong Kim, "The Mixed Role of Intellectuals and Higher Education in Building Democratic Culture in the Republic of Korea," in *Political Culture and Democracy in Developing Countries,* ed. Larry Diamond (Boulder: Lynne Rienner, 1993), p. 210; Eckert, *Offspring of Empire,* pp. 42–44.

7. Gary Hawes, *The Philippine State and the Marcos Regime: The Politics of Export* (Ithaca: Cornell University Press, 1987), p. 30; Bruce Cumings, "The Origins and Development of the Northeast Asian Political Economy: Industrial Sectors, Product Cycles and Political Consequences," in Deyo, 1987, p. 55.

8. Cumings, "The Northeast Asian Political Economy," pp. 55–56.

9. Ibid., p. 45; Sakong, *Korea in the World Economy,* p. 1.

10. Eckert, *Offspring of Empire,* p. 6.

11. Cumings, "The Northeast Asian Political Economy," in Deyo, 1987, p. 56.

12. Robert Schaeffer, *Warpaths: The Politics of Partition* (New York: Hill and Wang, 1990), passim.

13. Giovanni Arrighi, Satoshi Ikeda, and Alex Irwan, "The Rise of East Asia: One Miracle or Many?" in *Pacific-Asia and the Future of the World-System,* ed. Ravi Arvind Palat (Westport, Conn.: Greenwood Press, 1993), p. 60; Cumings, "The Northeast Asian Political Economy," in Deyo, 1987, pp. 77–78, 80.

14. As Arrighi, Ikeda, and Irwan argued, "We suggest that the competitiveness and profitability of the regionally expanded Japanese multilayered subcontracting system has constituted the main foundation of the East Asian economic miracle of the 1970s and 1980s." Arrighi, Ikeda, and Irwan, "The Rise of East Asia," in Palat, 1993, p. 61.

15. Peter Lowe, *The Origins of the Korean War* (London: Longman, 1986), p. 119.

16. Schaeffer, *Warpaths,* pp. 137–39.

17. June M. Grasso, *Truman's Two-China Policy* (Armonk, N.Y.: M. E. Sharpe, 1987), p. 113.

18. Seymour Topping, *Journey Between Two Chinas* (New York: Harper Colophon, 1972), p. 53.

19. Grasso, *Truman's Two-China Policy,* pp. 128, 141.

20. Melvin Gurtov and Byong-Moo Huang, *China Under Threat* (Baltimore: Johns Hopkins University Press, 1980), p. 49.

21. Chan and Clark, *Taiwan's Development,* pp. 137–38.

22. Cumings, "The Northeast Asian Political Economy," in Deyo, 1987, p. 67.

23. Ibid.; Tien, "Taiwan's Evolution Toward Democracy," in Simon and Kau, 1992, pp. 3, 67; Sakong, *Korea in the World Economy,* p. 96; C. I. Eugene Kim, "After the Coup: South Korea Creates a New Political Order," in *The Decline of Military Regimes: The Civilian Influence,* ed. Constantine Danopoulos (Boulder: Westview Press, 1988), p. 47; Bello and Rosenfeld, *Dragons in Distress,* p. 4; Chan and Clark, *Taiwan's Development,* p. 141; Richard Halloran, "U.S. Considers the Once Unthinkable on Korea," *New York Times,* 13 July 1989.

24. Young Whan Kihl, *Politics and Policies in Divided Korea: Regimes in Contest* (Boulder: Westview Press, 1984), p. 155.

25. Bello and Rosenfeld, *Dragons in Distress,* p. 5.

26. Chan and Clark, *Taiwan's Development,* pp. 100, 110.

27. Cumings, "The Northeast Asian Political Economy," in Deyo, 1987, p. 76; Meredith Woo-Cumings, "East Asia's America Problem," in *Past as Prelude: His-*

tory in the Making of a New World Order, ed. Meredith Woo-Cumings and Michael Loriaux (Boulder: Westview Press, 1993), p. 147.

28. Sakong, *Korea in the World Economy,* p. 65; Frank Gibney, *Korea's Quiet Revolution: From Garrison State to Democracy* (New York: Walker and Company, 1992), p. 57.

29. Gibney, *Korea's Quiet Revolution,* p. 61; Cumings, "The Northeast Asian Political Economy," in Deyo, 1987, p. 76.

30. Cumings, "The Northeast Asian Political Economy," p. 77.

31. Chan and Clark, *Taiwan's Development,* p. 99.

32. Ibid., pp. 137, 141.

33. Ibid., p. 99.

34. Bello and Rosenfeld, *Dragons in Distress,* p. 183; Douglas Mendel, *The Politics of Formosan Nationalism* (Berkeley: University of California Press, 1970), p. 69; Jaushieh Joseph Wu, *Taiwan's Democratization: Forces Behind the New Momentum* (Hong Kong: Oxford University Press, 1995), p. 58.

35. Chan and Clark, *Taiwan's Development,* p. 80.

36. Ibid., p. 106.

37. Ibid., pp. 44–45; Mark Selden, *The Political Economy of Chinese Development* (Armonk, N.Y.: M. E. Sharpe, 1983), p. 117.

38. Selden, *The Political Economy of Chinese Development,* p. 113.

39. Ambrose Y. C. King, "A Nonparadigmatic Search for Democracy in a Post-Confucian Culture: The Case of Taiwan, R.O.C.," in Diamond, 1993, p. 144.

40. Selden, *The Political Economy of Chinese Development,* p. 131.

41. Ibid., pp. 119–21, 127–131; Bello and Rosenfeld, *Dragons in Distress,* pp. 184–85.

42. Melvin Gurtov, *Global Politics in the Human Interest* (Boulder: Lynne Rienner, 1994), p. 119.

43. Bello and Rosenfeld, *Dragons in Distress,* pp. 23, 186.

44. Grasso, *Truman's Two-China Policy,* p. 54; Cumings, "The Northeast Asian Political Economy," in Deyo, 1987, p. 67.

45. Chan and Clark, *Taiwan's Development,* p. 49.

46. Ibid., p. 105; Robert Wader, "The Visible Hand: The State and East Asia's Economic Growth," *Current History,* September 1995, p. 431.

47. Bello and Rosenfeld, *Dragons in Distress,* p. 47; Hagen Koo, "The Interplay of State, Social Class, and World System in East Asian Development: The Cases of South Korea and Taiwan," in Deyo, 1987, pp. 176–77.

48. Chan and Clark, *Taiwan's Development,* p. 146; Koo, "State, Social Class, and World System in East Asian Development," in Deyo, 1987, p. 177.

49. Bello and Rosenfeld, *Dragons in Distress,* p. 219.

50. Chan and Clark, *Taiwan's Development,* p. 83; Susan M. Collins and Won-Am Park, "External Debt and Macroeconomic Performance in South Korea," in *Developing Country Debt and the World Economy,* ed. Jeffrey D. Sachs (Chicago: University of Chicago Press, 1989), p. 133; Cumings, "The Northeast Asian Political Economy," in Deyo, 1987, pp. 68, 69.

51. Wader, "The Visible Hand," p. 434; Bruce Cumings, "The Abortive Abertura: South Korea in the Light of the Latin American Experience," *New Left Review* (January-February 1989): 13.

52. King, "A Nonparadigmatic Search for Democracy," in Diamond, 1993, p. 139; Chan and Clark, *Taiwan's Development*, p. 40.

53. Tien, "Taiwan's Evolution Toward Democracy," in Simon and Kau, 1992, p. 4.

54. Nicholas D. Kristof, "Adrift, Taiwan Loses Urge for Firmer Footing," *New York Times*, 25 December 1992, p. A5; Nicholas D. Kristof, "Taiwan's Desire for Mainland is Dwindling," *New York Times*, 5 February 1989.

55. Wu, *Taiwan's Democratization*, p. 150.

56. Robert G. Sutter, "Taiwan Rising," *Current History*, September 1994, p. 281.

57. Peter Evans, "Class, State and Dependence in East Asia: Lessons for Latin America," in Deyo, 1987, p. 76.

58. Sutter, "Taiwan Rising," p. 281.

59. Jan S. Prybyla, *Reform in China and Other Socialist Economies* (Washington, D.C.: American Enterprise Institute Press, 1990), p. 265.

60. Schaeffer, *Warpaths*, p. 229.

61. Berch Berberoglu, *The Legacy of Empire: Economic Decline and Class Polarization in the U.S.* (New York: Praeger, 1992), p. 56.

62. Prybyla, *Reform in China and Other Socialist Economies*, p. 267; Jan S. Prybyla, "Economic Developments in the Republic of China," in *Democracy and Development in East Asia: Taiwan, South Korea and the Philippines*, ed. Thomas W. Robinson (Washington, D.C.: American Enterprise Institute Press, 1991), p. 65.

63. Stephan Haggard, Richard N. Cooper, and Susan Collins, "The Political Economy of Adjustment in the 1980s," in *Macroeconomic Policy and Adjustment in Korea, 1970–1990*, ed. Stephan Haggard et al. (Cambridge, Mass.: Harvard University Press, 1994), p. 98.

64. Yoichi Funabashi, *Managing the Dollar: From the Plaza to the Louvre* (Washington, D.C.: Institute for International Economics, 1989), p. 263; Daniel Burstein, *Yen! Japan's New Financial Empire and Its Threat to America* (New York: Simon and Schuster, 1988), p. 142.

65. Bello and Rosenfeld, *Dragons in Distress*, p. 256; Prybyla, "Economic Developments in the Republic of China," in Robinson, 1991, p. 69; Chan and Clark, *Taiwan's Development*, pp. 36, 154, 160.

66. Prybyla, "Economic Developments in the Republic of China," in Robinson, 1991, p. 70; Chan and Clark, *Taiwan's Development*, p. 34.

67. Mark L. Clifford, *Troubled Tiger: Businessmen, Bureaucrats and Generals in South Korea* (Armonk, N.Y.: M. E. Sharpe, 1994), p. 239; Haggard, Cooper, and Collins, "The Political Economy of Adjustment," in Haggard et al., 1994, pp. 78, 97; Collins and Park, "External Debt and Macroeconomic Performance in South Korea," in Sachs, 1989, pp. 126–27.

68. Haggard, Cooper, and Collins, "The Political Economy of Adjustment," in Haggard et al., 1994, p. 98.

69. Bello and Rosenfeld, *Dragons in Distress*, p. 2.

70. Haggard, Cooper, and Collins, "The Political Economy of Adjustment," in Haggard et al., 1994, p. 98.

71. Bello and Rosenfeld, *Dragons in Distress*, p. 7.

72. Robert Schaeffer, "Free Trade Agreements: Their Impact on Agriculture and the Environment," in *Food and Agrarian Orders in the World-Economy*, ed. Philip McMichael (Westport, Conn.: Praeger, 1995), passim.

73. Bello and Rosenfeld, *Dragons in Distress,* pp. 88–89, 166, 191–92.

74. Ibid. p. 178.

75. Ibid., p. 91.

76. Sakong, *Korea in the World Economy,* pp. 131–32.

77. Bello and Rosenfeld, *Dragons in Distress,* p. 14.

78. Ibid., p. 14.

79. Ibid., pp. 122–23.

80. Ibid., p. 123.

81. Sakong, *Korea in the World Economy,* p. 113; Prybyla, "Economic Developments in the Republic of China," in Robinson, 1991, p. 70.

82. Bello and Rosenfeld, *Dragons in Distress,* pp. 168, 180.

83. Chan and Clark, *Taiwan's Development,* p. 56. Robinson, 1991, p. 5.

84. Bello and Rosenfeld, *Dragons in Distress,* p. 246.

85. Robert G. Wesson, *State Systems: International Pluralism, Politics and Culture* (New York: The Free Press, 1978), p. 180; Jonathan Spence, "The Other China," *New York Review of Books,* 22 October 1992, p. 13.

86. Clifford, *Troubled Tiger,* pp. 138–39.

87. Ibid., p. 143.

88. Ibid., p. 157.

89. Ibid., p. 80.

90. Kihl, *Politics and Policies in Divided Korea,* p. 80; Clifford, *Troubled Tiger,* pp. 159–60.

91. Hagen Koo, "The State, *Minjung,* and the Working Class in South Korea," in *State and Society in Contemporary Korea,* ed. Hagen Koo (Ithaca: Cornell University Press, 1993), pp. 148–49.

92. Ibid., p. 131.

93. Ibid., pp. 142–43.

94. Ibid., p. 132.

95. Manwoo Lee, *The Odyssey of Korean Democracy: Korean Politics, 1987–1990* (New York: Praeger, 1990), p. 3; Gurtov, *Global Politics in the Human Interest,* p. 119.

96. Bello and Rosenfeld, *Dragons in Distress,* pp. 24–25, 217.

97. Lee, *The Odyssey of Korean Democracy,* p. 4.

98. Bello and Rosenfeld, *Dragons in Distress,* p. 39.

99. Tun-jen Cheng and Eun Mee Kim, "Making Democracy: Generalizing the South Korean Case," in *The Politics of Democratization: Generalizing the East Asian Experiences,* ed. Edward Friedman (Boulder: Westview Press, 1994), p. 144; Bello and Rosenfeld, *Dragons in Distress,* pp. 39–40.

100. Koo, "The State, *Minjung,* and the Working Class," in Koo, 1993, p. 149.

101. Clifford, *Troubled Tiger,* p. 279; Gurtov, *Global Politics in the Human Interest,* p. 120; Heng Lee, "Uncertain Promise: Democratic Consolidation in South Korea," in Friedman, 1994, p. 152.

102. Clifford, *Troubled Tiger,* p. 276.

103. Koo, "The State, *Minjung,* and the Working Class," in Koo, 1993, p. 157.

104. Bello and Rosenfeld, *Dragons in Distress,* pp. 224, 227; Wu, *Taiwan's Democratization,* p. 60.

105. Stephan Haggard and Robert R. Kaufman, *The Political Economy of Democratic Transitions* (Princeton: Princeton University Press, 1995), p. 95.

106. Ibid.

107. Wesson, *State Systems,* p. 179.

108. Wu, *Taiwan's Democratization,* p. 30; Ya-Li Lu, "Political Developments in the Republic of China," in Robinson, 1991, p. 38; King, "A Nonparadigmatic Search for Democracy," in Diamond, 1993, pp. 147–48.

109. Ray E. Johnston, *The Politics of Division, Partition and Unification* (New York: Praeger, 1976), p. 794; Wu, *Taiwan's Democratization,* p. 30; Wesson, *State Systems,* p. 184.

110. Lu, "Political Developments in the Republic of China," in Robinson, 1991, p. 38; John F. Cooper, "Taiwan: A Nation in Transition," *Current History,* April 1989, p. 175; Wu, *Taiwan's Democratization,* p. 35; Tien, "Taiwan's Evolution Toward Democracy," in Simon and Kau, 1992, p. 10.

111. Cooper, "Taiwan: A Nation in Transition," p. 173.

112. Bruce Cumings, "South Korea: Trouble Ahead?" *Current History,* April 1986, p. 162; John F. Cooper, "Taiwan: New Challenge to Development," *Current History*, April 1986, p. 168.

113. Eckert, *Offspring of Empire,* pp. 169–70; Sung-Joo Han, "South Korea: Politics in Transition," in Diamond, Linz, and Lipset, 1990, p. 335.

114. Gibney, *Korea's Quiet Revolution,* pp. 94–95.

115. Ibid., p. 90.

116. Ibid., pp. 93–94.

117. Bello and Rosenfeld, *Dragons in Distress,* p. 20.

118. Ibid., pp. 20–21; Clyde Haberman, "Fury and Turmoil: Days That Shook Korea," *New York Times,* 23 January 1990.

119. Gibney, *Korea's Quiet Revolution,* p. 87; Tim Shorrock, "South Korea: Chun, the Kims and the Constitutional Struggle," *Third World Quarterly* 10, no. 1 (January 1988): 108.

120. Haggard and Kaufman, *The Political Economy of Democratic Transition,* p. 95.

121. Bello and Rosenfeld, *Dragons in Distress,* p. 45; Mark Clifford, "Pre-emptive Strike," *Far Eastern Economic Review,* 19 April 1990, pp. 74–75.

122. "Two Parties Merge With Ruling Party in South Korea," *New York Times,* 23 January 1990; Han, "South Korea: Politics in Transition," in Diamond, 1990, p. 336.

123. Cheng and Kim, "Making Democracy," in Friedman, 1994, pp. 139–40; Gurtov, *Global Politics in the Human Interest,* p. 123.

124. Gibney, *Korea's Quiet Revolution,* p. 94.

125. Hung-mao Tien, "Taiwan's Evolution Toward Democracy: A Historical Perspective," in Simon and Kau, 1992, p. 6. "By the early 1970s, the younger Chiang had already risen to the second, most powerful position in the regime's hierarchy, surpassed only by his father." Ibid.

126. Andrew J. Nathan, "Is China Ready for Democracy?" in Diamond, 1990, p. 286.

127. Wu, *Taiwan's Democratization,* pp. 41–42; King, "A Nonparadigmatic Search for Democracy," in Diamond, 1993, p. 150.

128. Wu, *Taiwan's Democratization*, p. 37; Cooper, "Taiwan: A Nation in Transition," p. 175; King, "A Nonparadigmatic Search for Democracy," in Diamond, 1993, p. 150.

129. Lu, "Political Developments in the Republic of China," in Robinson, 1991, p. 37.

130. Wu, *Taiwan's Democratization*, p. 44.

131. Ibid., p. 124; Chan and Clark, *Taiwan's Development*, p. 93.

132. Nicholas D. Kristof, "Taiwan's Parties Test Limits of a New Political Freedom," *New York Times*, 17 December 1992.

133. Wu, *Taiwan's Democratization*, p. 1.

134. Sheryl WuDunn, "South Korean Goes on Trial on Charges of Bribery," *New York Times*, 18 December 1995.

135. Paul Brooker, *Twentieth-Century Dictatorships: The Ideological One-Party States* (New York: New York University Press, 1994), pp. 197–98; King, "A Nonparadigmatic Search for Democracy," in Diamond, 1993, p. 143; Wu, *Taiwan's Democratization*, p. 12.

136. Tony Saich, "The Reform Decade in China: The Limits to Revolution from Above," in *The Reform Decade in China: From Hope to Dismay,* ed. Marta Dassu and Tony Saich (London: Kegan Paul, 1992), pp. 14, 18; Selden, *The Political Economy of Chinese Development,* p. 25.

137. Saich, "The Reform Decade in China," in Dassu and Saich, 1992, p. 15.

138. Richard Baum, *Burying Mao: Chinese Politics in the Age of Deng Xiaoping* (Princeton: Princeton University Press, 1994), p. 1.

139. Ibid., p. 4; Yves Chevrier, "NEP and Beyond: The Transition to 'Modernization' in China (1978–85)," in *Reform in China and Other Socialist Economies,* ed. Jan S. Prybyla (Washington, D.C.: American Enterprise Institute Press, 1990), p. 7.

140. Ibid.

141. Thomas Bernstein, "Democratization in China," in *Global Transformation and the Third World,* ed. Robert O. Slater, Barry M. Schutz, and Steven R. Dorr (Boulder: Lynne Rienner, 1993), p. 144.

142. Saich, "The Reform Decade in China," in Dassu and Saich, 1992, p. 25.

143. Baum, *Burying Mao,* p. 17.

144. Ian Jeffries, *Socialist Economies and the Transition to the Market: A Guide* (London: Routledge, 1993), p. 142; Claude Aubert, "China's Food-Takeoff?" in *The Rural Sector, Welfare and Employment,* ed. Stephan Feuchtwang, Athar Hussain, and Thierry Pairault, vol. 1 of *Transforming China's Economy in the Eighties* (London: Zed Books, 1988), p. 103; Susan L. Shirk, *The Political Logic of Economic Reform in China* (Berkeley: University of California Press, 1993), pp. 38–39.

145. Aubert, "China's Food-Takeoff?" in Feuchtwang, Hussain, and Pairault, 1988, pp. 107–108; Kathleen Hartford, "No Way Out? Rural Reforms and Food Policy in China," in Dessu and Saich, 1992, p. 77; Selden, *The Political Economy of Chinese Development,* p. 31.

146. Hartford, "No Way Out?" in Dassu and Saich, 1992, pp. 81–82.

147. Selden, *The Political Economy of Chinese Development,* p. 19.

148. Athar Hussain and Stephan Feuchtwang, "The Peoples' Livelihood and the Incidence of Poverty," in Feuchtwang, Hussain, and Pairault, 1988, p. 42; Hartford,

"No Way Out?" in Dassu and Saich, 1992, p. 97; Prybyla, *Reform in China and Other Socialist Economies,* p. 174.

149. Jeffries, 1993, p. 140; Elisabeth J. Croll, "The New Peasant Economy," in Feuchtwang, Hussain, and Pairault, 1988, p. 101; Hussain and Feuchtwang, "The Peoples' Livelihood," in Feuchtwang, Hussain, and Pairault, 1988, p. 51.

150. Jeffries, *Socialist Economies and the Transition to the Market,* p. 159.

151. Gerald Segal, "The Challenges to Chinese Foreign Policy," in Dassu and Saich, 1992, p. 183; Renssalaer W. Lee III, "Issues in Chinese Economic Reform," in *Economic Reform in the Three Giants,* ed. John Echeverri-Gent and Friedemann Muller (Washington, D.C.: Overseas Development Council, 1990), p. 86.

152. Jeffries, *Socialist Economies and the Transition to the Market,* p. 162.

153. Shirk, *The Political Logic of Economic Reform in China,* p. 49; Jeffries, *Socialist Economies and the Transition to the Market,* pp. 161, 167.

154. Shirk, *The Political Logic of Economic Reform in China,* p. 48; Lee, "Issues in Chinese Economic Reform," in Echeverri-Gent and Muller, 1990, p. 86; Prybyla, *Reform in China and Other Socialist Economies,* p. 241.

155. Susumu Yabuki, *China's New Political Economy: The Giant Awakes* (Boulder: Westview Press, 1995), pp. 111–12.

156. Jeffries, *Socialist Economies and the Transition to the Market,* p. 154.

157. Saich, "The Reform Decade in China," in Dassu and Saich, 1992, pp. 29–30; Harlan W. Jencks, "The Military in China," *Current History,* September 1989, p. 265.

158. Yabuki, *China's New Political Economy,* p. 43.

159. Ibid., p. 17.

160. Fox Butterfield, "The Same Old Response, but Not the Same Old China," *New York Times,* 28 May 1989.

161. Gordon White, *The Chinese State in the Era of Economic Reform: The Road to Crisis* (Armonk, N.Y.: M. E. Sharpe, 1991), p. 1; Yves Chevrier, "From Modernization to Involution: Failed Pragmatism and Lost Opportunities in Deng Xiaoping's China," in Dassu and Saich, 1992, p. 116.

162. Hartford, "No Way Out?" in Dassu and Saich, 1992, p. 98; Selden, *The Political Economy of Chinese Development,* p. 37; Prybyla, *Reform in China and Other Socialist Economies,* p. 180; Louise do Rosario, "Coming a Cropper," *Far Eastern Economic Review,* 3 July 1989, p. 71.

163. Yabuki, *China's New Political Economy,* p. 91; Vaclav Smil, "Feeding China," *Current History,* September 1995, pp. 280–81.

164. Mark Selden, "The Social and Political Consequences of Chinese Reform: The Road to Tiananmen," in Palat, 1993, p. 153; Lee, "Issues in Chinese Economic Reform," in Echeverri-Gent and Muller, 1990, p. 79; Shirk, *The Political Logic of Economic Reform in China,* p. 17.

165. Nan Lin, *The Struggle for Tiananmen: Anatomy of the 1989 Mass Movement* (Westport, Conn.: Praeger, 1992), p. 36; Shirk, *The Political Logic of Economic Reform in China,* p. 39.

166. Barry Naughton, "Inflation and Economic Reform in China," *Current History,* September 1989, p. 270; Nicholas Kristof, "China Erupts," *New York Times Magazine,* 4 June 1989; Lin, *The Struggle for Tiananmen,* p. 33; Yabuki, *China's*

New Political Economy, p. 125; Selden, "The Social and Political Consequences of Chinese Reform," in Palat, 1993, p. 158.

167. Prybyla, *Reform in China and Other Socialist Economies,* p. 178.

168. Naughton, "Inflation and Economic Reform in China," pp. 270–71.

169. Selden, "The Social and Political Consequences of Chinese Reform," in Palat, 1993, p. 158; Lena H. Sun, "Chinese Grow Cautious on Reform, CIA Says," *Washington Post,* 2 May 1988; Naughton, "Inflation and Economic Reform in China," p. 269; Prybyla, *Reform in China and Other Socialist Economies,* p. 177.

170. Lee, "Issues in Chinese Economic Reform," in Echeverri-Gent and Muller, 1990, p. 80.

171. Dorothy J. Solinger, "China's Economy: Reform and State Control," *Current History,* September 1986, p. 264; Jeffries, *Socialist Economies and the Transition to the Market,* pp. 152, 166; Chevrier, "From Modernization to Involution," in Dassu and Saich, 1992, p. 127.

172. Jeffries, *Socialist Economies and the Transition to the Market,* p. 150.

173. Lee, "Issues in Chinese Economic Reform," in Echeverri-Gent and Muller, 1990, p. 82.

174. Marie-Clair Bergere, "Tiananmen 1989: Background and Consequences," in Dassu and Saich, 1992, p. 134.

175. Baum, *Burying Mao,* p. 192.

176. Bergere, "Tiananmen 1989," in Dassu and Saich, 1992, p. 137.

177. Selden, "The Social and Political Consequences of Chinese Reform," in Palat, 1993, p. 161.

178. Selden, *The Political Economy of Chinese Development,* pp. 206, 215, 217, 219–20.

179. Ibid., p. 225.

180. Baum, *Burying Mao,* pp. 263–64.

181. Ibid., pp. 264–65.

182. Ibid., p. 276.

183. "Deng's June 9 Speech: 'We Faced a Rebellious Clique' and 'Dregs of Society,'" *New York Times,* 30 June 1989.

184. Baum, *Burying Mao,* pp. 19–20.

185. Jialin Zhang, "Guiding China's Market Economy," *Current History,* September 1994, p. 280.

186. Selden, *The Political Economy of Chinese Development,* pp. 14, 32; Michel Bonnin and Michel Cartier, "Urban Employment in Post-Mao China," in Feuchtwang, Hussain, and Pairault, 1988, p. 198.

187. Friedman, 1994, p. 20.

188. Nicholas D. Kristof, "Riddle of China: Repression Soars as Standard of Living Soars," *New York Times,* 7 September 1993.

189. Selden, *The Political Economy of Chinese Development,* p. 5; Yabuki, *China's New Political Economy,* p. 73.

190. Selden, *The Political Economy of Chinese Development,* p. 228; Selden, "The Social and Political Consequences of Chinese Reform," in Palat, 1993, pp. 167–68.

191. June Teufel Dreyer, "The People's Army: Serving Whose Interest?" *Current History,* September 1994, p. 267.

192. Jan S. Prybyla, "All that Glitters: The Foreign Investment Boom," *Current History*, September 1995, p. 275; Yabuki, *China's New Political Economy*, p. 56.

193. Prybyla, "All that Glitters," p. 275.

194. David Arase, "Japan's Foreign Policy and Asian Democratization," in Friedman, 1994, pp. 88–91.

195. Woo-Cumings, "East Asia's America Problem," in Woo-Cumings and Loriaux, 1993, p. 155; Jeffries, *Socialist Economies and the Transition to the Market*, p. 170; Sutter, "Taiwan Rising," p. 283; Hung-Mao Tien, "Toward Peaceful Resolution of Mainland-Taiwan Conflicts: The Promise of Democratization," in Friedman, 1994, pp. 185–86.

196. Selden, *The Political Economy of Chinese Development*, p. 8; Jeffries, *Socialist Economies and the Transition to the Market*, pp. 171–72; Kristof, "China Sees 'Market-Leninism' as Way to Future," p. A1.

197. Barry Gills, "The Crisis of Socialism in North Korea," in *Regimes in Crisis: The Post-Soviet Era and the Implications for Development*, ed. Barry Gills and Shalid Qadir (London: Zed Books, 1995), p. 189.

198. Ibid., p. 201; Jeffries, *Socialist Economies and the Transition to the Market*, pp. 201–203; Kihl, *Politics and Policies in Divided Korea*, p. 189.

199. Jeffries, *Socialist Economies and the Transition to the Market*, pp. 201–202.

200. Kihl, *Politics and Policies in Divided Korea*, p. 56.

201. Ibid., pp. 154–55.

202. Gills, "The Crisis of Socialism in North Korea," in Gills and Qadir, 1995, pp. 179, 206.

203. Jeffries, *Socialist Economies and the Transition to the Market*, pp. 197–98; Kihl, *Politics and Policies in Divided Korea*, p. 133.

204. Kihl, *Politics and Policies in Divided Korea*, pp. 99, 138.

205. Gills, "The Crisis of Socialism in North Korea," in Gills and Qadir, 1995, p. 205.

206. Jeffries, *Socialist Economies and the Transition to the Market*, p. 203; Gills, "The Crisis of Socialism in North Korea," in Gills and Qadir, 1995, pp. 190, 203; Kihl, *Politics and Policies in Divided Korea*, pp. 197–98; Michael Breen, "North Korea's Ruler Maintains a Firm Grip," *San Francisco Chronicle*, 8 April 1991.

207. Gills, "The Crisis of Socialism in North Korea," in Gills and Qadir, 1995, p. 195.

208. Bruce Cumings, "The Corporate State in North Korea," in Koo, 1993, pp. 212, 218–19.

209. Kihl, *Politics and Policies in Divided Korea*, p. 91; Cumings, "The Corporate State in North Korea," in Koo, 1993, passim.

210. Cumings, "The Corporate State in North Korea," p. 214.

211. Jeffries, *Socialist Economies and the Transition to the Market*, p. 205.

212. Ibid.

213. Douglas Pike, "Vietnam in 1990: The Last Picture Show," *Asia Survey* 21, no. 1 (January 1991): 84.

214. Chan and Clark, *Taiwan's Development*, p. 211.

215. James Elliott, "Socialism in Vietnam: Crisis, Reform, Crisis," in Gills and Qadir, 1995, p. 211.

216. David W. P. Elliott, "Vietnam Faces the Future," *Current History,* December 1995, p. 414.

217. Ibid.

218. Elliott, "Socialism in Vietnam," in Gills and Qadir, 1995, p. 213.

219. Ibid., p. 217; Douglas Pike, "Change and Continuity in Vietnam," *Current History*, March 1990, p. 177.

220. William J. Duiker, "Vietnam: The Challenge of Reform," *Current History,* April 1989, pp. 177–79; Elliott, "Socialism in Vietnam," in Gills and Qadir, 1995, p. 212.

221. Pike, "Vietnam in 1990," p. 82; Elliott, "Socialism in Vietnam," in Gills and Qadir, 1995, p. 212.

222. Elliott, "Socialism in Vietnam," in Gills and Qadir, 1995, p. 213.

223. Elliott, "Vietnam Faces the Future," p. 414.

224. Pike, "Change and Continuity in Vietnam," p. 132.

225. Frederick Z. Brown, "The United States and South East Asia Enter a New Era," *Current History*, December 1995, p. 403.

226. Elliott, "Socialism in Vietnam," in Gills and Qadir, 1995, p. 223.

227. Ibid., p. 213.

Chapter Eight

1. John Sallnow, *Reform in the Soviet Union: Glasnost and the Future* (New York: St. Martin's Press, 1989), pp. 11–13; Adam Zwass, *From Failed Communism to Underdeveloped Capitalism: Transformation of Eastern Europe, the Soviet Union and China* (Armonk, N.Y.: M. E. Sharpe, 1995), p. 62.

2. Richard Sakwa, *Gorbachev and His Reforms, 1985–1990* (New York: Prentice Hall, 1990), p. 22.

3. Ibid., p. 22; Marshall I. Goldman, *Gorbachev's Challenge: Economic Reform in the Age of High Technology* (New York: W. W. Norton, 1987), p. 15; William Moskoff, *Hard Times: Impoverishment and Protest in the Perestroika Years: The Soviet Union, 1985–1991* (Armonk, N.Y.: M. E. Sharpe, 1993), p. 9.

4. Marshall I. Goldman, "The Future of Soviet Economic Reform," *Current History*, October 1989, p. 329.

5. Zwass, *From Failed Communism to Underdeveloped Capitalism,* p. 76.

6. Sakwa, *Gorbachev and His Reforms,* pp. 282–83.

7. Robert Schaeffer, *Warpaths: The Politics of Partition* (New York: Hill and Wang, 1990), pp. 81, 128–29.

8. Zwass, *From Failed Communism to Underdeveloped Capitalism,* p. 12.

9. Marshall I. Goldman, *U.S.S.R. in Crisis: The Failure of an Economic System* (New York: W. W. Norton, 1983), p. 145.

10. Ibid., p. 149.

11. Ibid., pp. 149–50.

12. Peter W. Rodman, *More Precious Than Peace: The Cold War and the Struggle for the Third World* (New York: Charles Scribner's Sons, 1994), pp. 313–14; Sakwa, *Gorbachev and His Reforms,* p. 283.

13. Rodman, *More Precious Than Peace,* pp. 297–98.

14. Zhores A. Medvedev, *Gorbachev* (New York: W. W. Norton, 1986), p. 230; Zwass, *From Failed Communism to Underdeveloped Capitalism*, p. 4.

15. Goldman, *Gorbachev's Challenge*, p. 4.

16. Goldman, *U.S.S.R. in Crisis*, p. 65; Goldman, *Gorbachev's Challenge*, pp. 32–33.

17. Bjorn Hettne, *Development Theory and the Three Worlds* (New York: John Wiley and Sons, 1990), p. 45; Moshe Lewin, *Russia/USSR/Russia: The Drive and Drift of a Superstate* (New York: The New Press, 1995), pp. 13, 85.

18. Goldman, *U.S.S.R. in Crisis*, p. 73.

19. Zwass, *From Failed Communism to Underdeveloped Capitalism*, p. 6.

20. Goldman, *Gorbachev's Challenge*, p. 32; Sakwa, *Gorbachev and His Reforms*, p. 286; Goldman, *U.S.S.R. in Crisis*, p. 76.

21. Goldman, *Gorbachev's Challenge*, pp. 32–33; Goldman, *U.S.S.R. in Crisis*, p. 76.

22. Edward C. Cook, "Agriculture's Role in the Soviet Economic Crisis," in *The Disintegration of the Soviet Economic System*, ed. Michael Ellman and Vladimir Kontorovich (London: Routledge, 1992), p. 199.

23. Goldman, *U.S.S.R. in Crisis*, p. 65; Goldman, *Gorbachev's Challenge*, p. 65.

24. Cook, "Agriculture's Role in the Soviet Economic Crisis," in Ellman and Kontorovich, 1992, p. 196.

25. David A. Dyker, *Restructuring the Soviet Economy* (London: Routledge, 1992), p. 103; Silviu Brucan, *The Post-Brezhnev Era: An Insider's View* (New York: Praeger, 1983), p. 83.

26. Goldman, *U.S.S.R. in Crisis*, p. 77; Sallnow, *Reform in the Soviet Union*, p. 19; John Walton and David Seddon, *Free Markets and Food Riots: The Politics of Global Adjustment* (Oxford: Blackwell, 1994), p. 295; Goldman, *Gorbachev's Challenge*, p. 35.

27. Cook, "Agriculture's Role in the Soviet Economic Crisis," in Ellman and Kontorovich, 1992, p. 203.

28. Ibid., p. 210.

29. Moskoff, *Hard Times*, p. 45.

30. Ibid., p. 42.

31. Ruth Sivard, *World Military and Social Expenditures, 1987–88* (Washington, D.C.: World Priorities, 1987), pp. 5, 54–55; Somnath Sen, "The Economics of Conversion: Transforming Swords into Plowshares," in *Economic Reform in Eastern Europe*, ed. Graham Bird (Brookfield, Vt.: Edward Elgar Publishing, 1992), p. 26; Sallnow, *Reform in the Soviet Union*, p. 85.

32. Sakwa, *Gorbachev and His Reforms*, p. 335; Henry S. Rowen and Charles Wolf, eds., *The Impoverished Superpower: Perestroika and the Soviet Military Burden* (San Francisco: Institute for Contemporary Studies Press, 1990), p. 7. David F. Epstein, "The Economic Cost of Soviet Security and Empire," in Rowen and Wolf, 1990, p. 153.

33. D. Derek Swain, "The Soviet Military Sector," in Rowen and Wolf, 1990, pp. 103, 105; Sen, "The Economics of Conversion," in Bird, 1992, p. 25.

34. Alan Smith, *Russia and the World Economy: Problems of Integration* (London: Routledge, 1993), p. 89.

35. Ibid., pp. 74, 88–89, 90–93; Michael T. Klare, *American Arms Supermarket* (Austin, Tex.: University of Texas Press, 1984), p. 312.

36. Roger E. Kanet, "The Politics and Economics of Soviet Arms Exports," in *Economics and Politics in the Soviet Union: Problems of Interdependence,* ed. Hans-Herman Hohmann, Alec Nove, and Heinrich Vogel (Boulder: Westview Press, 1986), p. 282.

37. Smith, *Russia and the World Economy,* pp. 94, 98; Kanet, "The Politics and Economics of Soviet Arms Exports," in Hohmann, Nove, and Vogel, 1986, pp. 274–75, 294.

38. David Gold, "Conversion and Industrial Policy," in *Economic Conversion,* ed. Suzanne Gordon and Dave McFadden (Cambridge, Mass.: Ballinger, 1984), p. 195.

39. Serge Schmemann, "The Sun Has Trouble Setting on the Soviet Empire," *New York Times,* 10 March 1991.

40. Mark Kramer, "Soviet Military Policy," *Current History,* October 1989, p. 351.

41. Christopher Davis, "Economic and Political Aspects of the Military-Industrial Crisis in the USSR," in Hohmann, Nove, and Vogel, 1986, p. 113.

42. Barnett R. Rubin, *The Search for Peace in Afghanistan: From Buffer State to Failed State* (New Haven: Yale University Press, 1995), pp. 65, 67; Rodman, *More Precious Than Peace,* pp. 339–40.

43. Sakwa, *Gorbachev and His Reforms,* p. 332.

44. James Blitz, "Gloom for the Russians in Gulf Weapons Toll," *Times* (London), Sunday, 3 March 1991.

45. Ibid.

46. Rubin, *The Search for Peace in Afghanistan,* pp. 21, 25.

47. Ibid., p. 22.

48. Ibid., p. 25; Stephen White, *After Gorbachev* (Cambridge: Cambridge University Press, 1993), p. 211.

49. Rubin, *The Search for Peace in Afghanistan,* p. 25; White, *After Gorbachev,* p. 211.

50. T. E. Vadney, *The World Since 1945* (London: Penguin, 1992), p. 515; Rodman, *More Precious Than Peace,* p. 210.

51. Rodman, *More Precious Than Peace,* p. 212.

52. White, *After Gorbachev,* p. 211.

53. Rodman, *More Precious Than Peace,* p. 208; White, *After Gorbachev,* p. 211.

54. Rodman, *More Precious Than Peace,* p. 210.

55. Rubin, *The Search for Peace in Afghanistan,* pp. 29, 63; Rodman, *More Precious Than Peace,* p. 206.

56. Rubin, *The Search for Peace in Afghanistan,* p. 29; White, *After Gorbachev,* p. 212.

57. Rubin, *The Search for Peace in Afghanistan,* p. 63.

58. The number of Soviet casualties ranges from 13,000 to 15,000 dead and 35,000 to 37,000 wounded. Rodman, *More Precious Than Peace,* p. 315; White, *After Gorbachev,* p. 212; Vadney, *The World Since 1945,* p. 516.

59. Rodman, *More Precious Than Peace,* p. 315.

60. Rubin, *The Search for Peace in Afghanistan,* p. 30.

61. Rodman, *More Precious Than Peace,* p. 218.

62. White, *After Gorbachev,* p. 212.

63. Smith, *Russia and the World Economy,* pp. 167–68; Goldman, *U.S.S.R. in Crisis,* p. 130.

64. Goldman, *U.S.S.R. in Crisis,* p. 136–37.

65. Ibid., p. 138; Grigorii Khanin, "Economic Growth in the 1980s," in Ellman and Kontorovich, 1992, p. 77.

66. Goldman, *U.S.S.R. in Crisis,* p. 137.

67. Sakwa, *Gorbachev and His Reforms,* p. 284; Michael Kaser and Michael Maltby, "Foreign Trade," in *Gorbachev and Perestroika,* ed. Martin McCauley (New York: St. Martin's Press, 1990), p. 97. Estimates on the size of the debt in 1984 vary widely; one estimate is as low as $10.2 billion, whereas another gives a range of $23.0 billion to $25.5 billion. Smith, *Russia and the World Economy,* pp. 121, 158.

68. Smith, *Russia and the World Economy,* pp. 138, 140, 144; Kaser and Maltby, "Foreign Trade," in McCauley, 1990, p. 98.

69. Anders Aslund, *Gorbachev's Struggle for Economic Reform* (Ithaca: Cornell University Press, 1991), p. 197; Smith, *Russia and the World Economy,* p. 151; Andre Gunder Frank, "Soviet and Eastern European 'Socialism': What Went Wrong?" in *Regimes in Crisis: The Post-Soviet Era and the Implications for Development,* ed. Barry Gills and Shalid Qadir (London: Zed Books, 1995), p. 98; Sakwa, *Gorbachev and His Reforms,* p. 284; Moskoff, *Hard Times,* p. 17.

70. Smith, *Russia and the World Economy,* p. 148; Rodman, *More Precious Than Peace,* p. 313.

71. Smith, *Russia and the World Economy,* pp. 153–54.

72. Sakwa, *Gorbachev and His Reforms,* pp. 272–73; Gregory Grossman, "Inflationary, Political and Social Implications of Current Economic Slowdown," in Hohmann, Nove, and Vogel, 1986, p. 182; Michael Ellman, "Money in the 1980s: From Disequilibrium to Collapse," in Ellman and Kontorovich, 1992, p. 117.

73. Other sources argue that it ran small budget deficits prior to this time. Sakwa, *Gorbachev and His Reforms,* p. 272; Ellman, "Money in the 1980s," in Ellman and Kontorovich, 1992, p. 113.

74. Aslund, 1991, p. 192; Ellman and Kontorovich, 1992, p. 25; Sen in Bird, 1992, p. 27. Some scholars estimate it might have been as much as 120 billion rubles in 1989. Moskoff, *Hard Times,* p. 16.

75. Ellman in Ellman and Kontorovich, 1992, p. 120. Mel Gurtov argued that it reached nearly 500 billion rubles by 1989. Melvin Gurtov, *Global Politics in the Human Interest* (Boulder: Lynne Rienner, 1994), p. 160.

76. Moskoff, *Hard Times,* p. 65.

77. Ibid., p. 55.

78. Aslund, 1991, p. 19.

79. Ibid., p. 189.

80. David A. Dyker, *Restructuring the Soviet Economy* (London: Routledge, 1992), p. 182; Smith, *Russia and the World Economy,* p. 110.

81. Sakwa, *Gorbachev and His Reforms,* p. 275; Goldman, *U.S.S.R. in Crisis,* p. 55.

82. Moskoff, *Hard Times,* pp. 67–69.

83. Ibid., p. 89.

84. White, *After Gorbachev,* p. 4.

85. Ibid., p. 5.

86. Ibid., p. 7.

87. Ibid., pp. 7–8

88. Ed A. Hewett, *Reforming the Soviet Economy: Equality Versus Efficiency* (Washington, D.C.: Brookings Institution, 1988), p. 257; Zwass, *From Failed Communism to Underdeveloped Capitalism,* pp. 15–16.

89. Frank in Gills and Qadir, 1995, p. 100; Aslund, 1991, pp. 15–17, 23, 28; Hewett, 1988, p. 303.

90. Aslund, 1991, p. 28.

91. Ibid., p. 34.

92. Susan L. Shirk, *The Political Logic of Economic Reform in China* (Berkeley: University of California Press, 1993), p. 11.

93. White, *After Gorbachev,* p. 29.

94. Ibid.; Shirk, 1993, pp. 11–12; John Dunlop, *The Rise of Russia and the Fall of the Soviet Empire* (Princeton: Princeton University Press, 1993), p. 9.

95. Aslund, 1991, p. 31; Sakwa, *Gorbachev and His Reforms,* p. 290.

96. Aslund, 1991, p. 71: Dunlop, 1993, p. 5; Zwass, *From Failed Communism to Underdeveloped Capitalism,* p. 64.

97. Sakwa, *Gorbachev and His Reforms,* p. 290.

98. Gertrude E. Schroeder, "Soviet Consumption in the 1980s: A Tale of Woe," in Ellman and Kontorovich, 1992, pp. 98–99.

99. Rodman, *More Precious Than Peace,* p. 305.

100. Karen Dawisha, *Eastern Europe, Gorbachev and Reform: The Great Challenge* (Cambridge: Cambridge University Press, 1990), p. 211; Rodman, *More Precious Than Peace,* p. 307.

101. Rubin, *The Search for Peace in Afghanistan,* pp. 59–60.

102. Ibid., pp. 8, 68, 74–75.

103. Rodman, *More Precious Than Peace,* pp. 327–28.

104. Jonathan Steele, *Eternal Russia: Yeltsin, Gorbachev and the Mirage of Democracy* (Cambridge, Mass.: Harvard University Press, 1994), pp. 168–69; Sakwa, *Gorbachev and His Reforms,* p. 349; Rodman, *More Precious Than Peace,* p. 315.

105. Rubin, *The Search for Peace in Afghanistan,* pp. 7, 84, 91.

106. Eric Hobsbawm, *The Age of Extremes: A History of the World, 1914–1991* (New York: Pantheon, 1994), p. 459.

107. Rubin, *The Search for Peace in Afghanistan,* pp. 122–23, 127–28.

108. Rodman, *More Precious Than Peace,* p. 325.

109. Sallnow, *Reform in the Soviet Union,* pp. 97, 100.

110. Nan Lin, *The Struggle for Tiananmen: Anatomy of the 1989 Mass Movement* (Westport, Conn.: Praeger, 1992), p. 70. Meredith Woo-Cumings, "East Asia's America Problem," in *Past as Prelude: History in the Making of a New World Order,* ed. Meredith Woo-Cumings and Michael Loriaux (Boulder: Westview Press, 1993), p. 156.

111. Sallnow, *Reform in the Soviet Union,* p. 102; Sakwa, *Gorbachev and His Reforms,* p. 344; White, *After Gorbachev,* p. 209.

112. Kanet in Hohmann, Nove and Vogel, 1986, p. 25.

113. Sakwa, *Gorbachev and His Reforms,* p. 335.

114. Ibid.

115. Sen in Bird, 1992, pp. 30–33, 40.

116. Sakwa, *Gorbachev and His Reforms,* pp. 322, 324–25.

117. Sallnow, *Reform in the Soviet Union,* p. 91.

118. White, *After Gorbachev,* p. 202.

119. Ibid., p. 203; Thomas W. Simons Jr., *Eastern Europe in the Postwar World* (New York: St. Martin's Press, 1991), p. 184.

120. White, *After Gorbachev,* p. 203; Sallnow, *Reform in the Soviet Union,* p. 94.

121. Zwass, *From Failed Communism to Underdeveloped Capitalism,* pp. 89–90; Sallnow, *Reform in the Soviet Union,* pp. 94–95.

122. Ibid., p. 91; Sakwa, *Gorbachev and His Reforms,* p. 343; Moskoff, *Hard Times,* p. 23; Russell Bova, "The Soviet Economy and International Politics," in Ellman and Kontorovich, 1992, p. 50; Vadney, *The World Since 1945,* p. 486.

123. White, *After Gorbachev,* p. 206; Gale Stokes, *From Stalinism to Pluralism: A Documentary History of Eastern Europe Since 1945* (New York: Oxford University Press, 1993), pp. 132–34.

124. White, *After Gorbachev,* p. 207.

125. Ibid.

126. Dawisha, 1990, p. 210.

127. Ibid., p. 214.

128. Walton and Seddon, 1994, p. 301; Sakwa, *Gorbachev and His Reforms,* p. 326.

129. "Sinatra's song was actually a sad little piece about an old man's 'final curtain' when 'the end is near,' but never mind," wrote Ralf Dahrendorf. Ralf Dahrendorf, *Reflections on the Revolution in Europe* (New York: Times Books, 1990), p. 16. Dawisha, 1990, p. 220.

130. Steele, 1994, p. 185.

131. Ibid., p. 186.

132. Nancy Bermeo, "Surprise, Surprise: Lessons from 1989 and 1991," in ed., *Liberalization and Democratization: Change in the Soviet Union and Eastern Europe,* ed. Nancy Bermeo (Baltimore: Johns Hopkins University Press, 1992), p. 180.

Chapter Nine

1. Although a Polish encyclopedia asserted that "crisis is a phenomena solely connected with the capitalist economies and does not occur in other socio-economic systems," Eastern European dictators were not immune from social crisis. Bjorn Hettne, *Development Theory and the Three Worlds* (New York: John Wiley and Sons, 1990), p. 12.

2. Michael H. Bernhard, *The Origins of Democratization in Poland: Workers, Intellectuals, and Oppositional Politics, 1976–1980* (New York: Columbia University Press, 1993), p. 39.

3. Ibid., p. 41; Robin Alison Remington, "Polish Soldiers in Politics: The Party in Uniform?" in *The Decline of Military Regimes: The Civilian Influence,* ed. Constantine P. Danopoulos (Boulder: Westview Press, 1988), p. 84.

4. John Walton and David Seddon, eds., *Free Markets and Food Riots: The Politics of Global Adjustment* (Oxford: Blackwell, 1994), p. 292.

5. Bernhard, *The Origins of Democratization in Poland*, p. 41; Remington, "Polish Soldiers in Politics," in Danopoulos, 1988, p. 84; Thomas W. Simons, Jr., *Eastern Europe in the Postwar World* (New York: St. Martin's Press, 1991), p. 156.

6. Bernhard, *The Origins of Democratization in Poland*, pp. 36–37.

7. J. F. Brown, *Surge to Freedom: The End of Communist Rule in Eastern Europe* (Durham, N.C.: Duke University Press, 1991), p. 29.

8. Bernhard, *The Origins of Democratization in Poland*, p. 42; Andre Gunder Frank, "Soviet and Eastern European 'Socialism': What Went Wrong?" in *Regimes in Crisis: The Post-Soviet Era and the Implications for Development*, ed. Barry Gills and Shahid Qadir (London: Zed Books, 1995), p. 95.

9. Frank, "Soviet and Eastern European 'Socialism,'" in Gills and Qadir, 1995, p. 94.

10. Ibid., p. 95.

11. Marshall I. Goldman, *U.S.S.R. in Crisis: The Failure of an Economic System* (New York: W. W. Norton, 1983), p. 157.

12. Ibid.; Simons, *Eastern Europe in the Postwar World*, p. 162.

13. Karen Dawisha, *Eastern Europe, Gorbachev and Reform: The Great Challenge* (Cambridge: Cambridge University Press, 1990), p. 188.

14. Simons, *Eastern Europe in the Postwar World*, p. 162.

15. Brown, *Surge to Freedom*, p. 103.

16. Adam Zwass, *From Failed Communism to Underdeveloped Capitalism: The Transformation of Eastern Europe, the Post-Soviet Union and China* (Armonk, N.Y.: M. E. Sharpe, 1995), p. 147; Simons, *Eastern Europe in the Postwar World*, p. 160.

17. John Sallnow, *Reform in the Soviet Union: Glasnost and the Future* (New York: St. Martin's Press, 1989), p. 85.

18. Simons, *Eastern Europe in the Postwar World*, pp. 157, 173; Goldman, *U.S.S.R. in Crisis*, p. 166.

19. Dawisha, *Eastern Europe, Gorbachev and Reform*, pp. 169–70, 179.

20. Simons, *Eastern Europe in the Postwar World*, p. 159.

21. Ibid.; Dawisha, *Eastern Europe, Gorbachev and Reform*, p. 179.

22. Simons, *Eastern Europe in the Postwar World*, p. 160.

23. Ben Slay, "Poland and the International Economy in the 1980s: The Failure of Reforming Socialist Foreign Trade and Prospects for the Future," in *The Polish Road From Socialism: The Economics, Sociology and Politics of Transition*, ed. Walter D. Connor and Piotr Ploszajski (Armonk, N.Y.: M. E. Sharpe, 1992), p. 43.

24. David Turnock, *Eastern Europe: An Economic and Political Geography* (London: Routledge, 1989), p. 239.

25. Edward C. Cook, "Agriculture's Role in the Soviet Economic Crisis," in *The Disintegration of the Soviet Economic System*, ed. Michael Ellman and Vladimir Kontorovich (London: Routledge, 1992), p. 9.

26. Simons, *Eastern Europe in the Postwar World*, p. 161.

27. Ibid.

28. Bernhard, *The Origins of Democratization in Poland*, pp. 46–47, 50.

29. Ibid., p. 76.

30. Ibid.

31. Ibid., p. 100.

32. Ibid., pp. 83, 94.

33. Ibid., p. 49.

34. Ibid., p. 154; Simons, *Eastern Europe in the Postwar World*, p. 169.

35. Bernhard, *The Origins of Democratization in Poland*, pp. 113, 116–17, 121.

36. Ibid., p. 169.

37. Ibid., p. 202.

38. Ibid., pp. 204–208.

39. Walton and Seddon, *Free Markets and Food Riots*, p. 293.

40. Gale Stokes, *From Stalinism to Pluralism: A Documentary History of Eastern Europe Since 1945* (New York: Oxford University Press, 1991), pp. 204, 212–13; Walton and Seddon, *Free Markets and Food Riots*, p. 293.

41. Andrzej Kondratowicz and Marek Okolski, "The Polish Economy on the Eve of the Solidarity Take-Over," in *Stabilization and Structural Adjustment in Poland*, ed. Henryk Kierzkowski, Marek Okolski, and Stanislaw Willisz (London: Routledge, 1993), p. 10.

42. Remington, "Polish Soldiers in Politics," in Danopoulos, 1988, p. 86.

43. Zwass, *From Failed Communism to Underdeveloped Capitalism*, p. 143; Remington, "Polish Soldiers in Politics," in Danopoulos, 1988, pp. 86–87.

44. Stokes, *From Stalinism to Pluralism*, pp. 214–15.

45. Raphael Shen, *The Polish Economy: Legacies from the Past, Prospects for the Future* (New York: Praeger, 1992), p. 73; Kondratowicz and Okolski, "The Polish Economy," in Kierzkowski, Okolski, and Willisz, 1993, pp. 15–16; Dawisha, *Eastern Europe, Gorbachev and Reform*, p. 180.

46. Kondratowicz and Okolski, "The Polish Economy," in Kierzkowski, Okolski, and Willisz, 1993, p. 14.

47. Remington, "Polish Soldiers in Politics," in Danopoulos, 1988, pp. 93–94.

48. Shen, *The Polish Economy*, p. 86.

49. Ibid., pp. 86–87.

50. Ibid., pp. 74, 75–79.

51. Brown, *Surge to Freedom*, p. 81.

52. Ibid., p. 87; Walton and Seddon, *Free Markets and Food Riots*, p. 294.

53. Brown, *Surge to Freedom*, p. 88.

54. Simons, *Eastern Europe in the Postwar World*, p. 197; Timothy Garton Ash, *The Magic Lantern* (New York: Random House, 1990), p. 25.

55. Simons, *Eastern Europe in the Postwar World*, p. 205.

56. Ibid.; Ash, *The Magic Lantern*, p. 205.

57. Simons, *Eastern Europe in the Postwar World*, pp. 205–206; Stokes, *From Stalinism to Pluralism*, pp. 240–42.

58. Dawisha, *Eastern Europe, Gorbachev and Reform*, p. 177.

59. Nigel Swain, *Hungary: The Rise and Fall of Feasible Socialism* (London: Verso, 1992), p. 10.

60. Ibid.; Dawisha, *Eastern Europe, Gorbachev and Reform*, p. 177; Walton and Seddon, *Free Markets and Food Riots*, p. 298.

61. Brown, *Surge to Freedom*, p. 108.

62. Ash, *The Magic Lantern*, p. 14.

63. Ibid.

64. Dawisha, *Eastern Europe, Gorbachev and Reform,* p. 286.

65. Ibid., p. 155.

66. Ibid., p. 287.

67. Joseph Held, "Hungary: 1956 to the Present," in *The Columbia History of Eastern Europe in the Twentieth Century,* ed. Joseph Held (New York: Columbia University Press, 1992), p. 226.

68. Konrad H. Jarausch, *The Rush to German Unity* (Oxford: Oxford University Press, 1994), p. 15.

69. Ibid., p. 8; Robert Schaeffer, *Warpaths: The Politics of Partition* (New York: Hill and Wang, 1990), see cover, p. 155; Gregory Henderson, R. N. Lebow, and J. G. Stroessinger, *Divided Nations in a Divided World* (New York: David McKay, 1974), p. 28.

70. Jarausch, *The Rush to German Unity,* p. 17.

71. Ibid.; Brown, *Surge to Freedom,* p. 136.

72. Melvin Croan, "Germany and Eastern Europe," in Held, 1992, p. 380.

73. Jarausch, *The Rush to German Unity,* p. 24.

74. Simons, *Eastern Europe in the Postwar World,* p. 209.

75. Jarausch, *The Rush to German Unity,* p. 99; Walton and Seddon, *Free Markets and Food Riots,* p. 300.

76. Jarausch, *The Rush to German Unity,* p. 61.

77. Ibid., p. 33.

78. Ibid., pp. 34, 47.

79. Ibid., pp. 53–54.

80. Ibid., p. 34; Edward Friedman, *The Politics of Democratization: Generalizing the East Asian Experiences* (Boulder: Westview Press, 1994), pp. 23–24.

81. Jarausch, *The Rush to German Unity,* p. 54.

82. Ibid., p. 22.

83. Simons, *Eastern Europe in the Postwar World,* p. 209.

84. Jarausch, *The Rush to German Unity,* p. 3.

85. Ibid., p. 23.

86. Ibid., p. 64.

87. Ibid., p. 40.

88. Croan, "Germany and Eastern Europe," in Held, 1992, p. 386.

89. Ibid.; Jarausch, *The Rush to German Unity,* p. 116.

90. Jarausch, *The Rush to German Unity,* p. 173.

91. Ibid., pp. 175, 177.

92. Croan, "Germany and Eastern Europe," in Held, 1992, p. 387.

93. Ibid.; Jarausch, *The Rush to German Unity,* p. 158.

94. Jarausch, *The Rush to German Unity,* pp. 138–39.

95. Ibid., p. 137.

96. Ibid., p. 177.

97. Croan, "Germany and Eastern Europe," in Held, 1992, p. 388.

98. Sharon L. Wolchik, "Czechoslovakia," in Held, 1992, pp. 145, 150–51; Christine Sadowski, "Autonomous Groups as Agents of Democratic Change in Communist and Post-Communist Eastern Europe," in *Political Culture and*

Democracy in Developing Countries, ed. Larry Diamond (Boulder: Lynne Rienner, 1993), p. 188; Dawisha, *Eastern Europe, Gorbachev and Reform,* p. 287.

99. Sadowski, "Autonomous Groups as Agents of Democratic Change," in Diamond, 1990, p. 188.

100. Maria Pundeff, "Bulgaria," in Held, 1992, pp. 110–11.

101. Sadowski, "Autonomous Groups as Agents of Democratic Change," in Diamond, 1990, p. 189.

102. Dawisha, *Eastern Europe, Gorbachev and Reform,* p. 287.

103. Ibid., p. 288.

104. Zwass, *From Failed Communism to Underdeveloped Capitalism,* p. 19.

105. Eric Hobsbawm, *The Age of Extremes: A History of the World, 1914–1991* (New York: Pantheon, 1994), pp. 165, 168.

106. Bogdan Denitch, *Ethnic Nationalism: The Tragic Death of Yugoslavia* (Minneapolis: University of Minnesota Press, 1994), p. 58.

107. Christopher Bennett, *Yugoslavia's Bloody Collapse: Causes, Course, and Consequences* (New York: New York University Press, 1995), p. 68. Remittances to Yugoslavia equaled one-third of the foreign exchange earnings from commodity exports. Turnock, *Eastern Europe,* pp. 131–32.

108. Turnock, *Eastern Europe,* pp. 131–32, Table 8.1.

109. Bennett, *Yugoslavia's Bloody Collapse,* p. 68.

110. Ibid., p. 69.

111. Ibid., p. 68.

112. Ibid., p. 69.

113. Ibid., p. 53.

114. Dimitrije Djordjevic, "The Yugoslav Phenomenon," in Held, 1992, p. 332.

115. Bennett, *Yugoslavia's Bloody Collapse,* p. 70; Djordjevic, "The Yugoslav Phenomenon," in Held, 1992, p. 334.

116. Brown, *Surge to Freedom,* p. 234.

117. Djordjevic, "The Yugoslav Phenomenon," in Held, 1992, p. 338; Brown, *Surge to Freedom,* p. 236.

118. Bennett, *Yugoslavia's Bloody Collapse,* pp. 94–96.

119. Ibid., p. 117.

120. Ibid., p. 110.

121. Ibid., pp. 110–11.

122. Ibid., p. 119.

123. Ibid., p. 120.

124. Geoffrey Pridham and Tatu Vanhanen, *Democratization in Eastern Europe: Domestic and International Perspectives* (London: Routledge, 1994), pp. 128–29; Bennett, *Yugoslavia's Bloody Collapse,* p. 119.

125. Bennett, *Yugoslavia's Bloody Collapse,* p. 121.

126. Ibid.

127. Ibid., p. 133.

128. Ibid., p. 139.

129. Ibid., p. 137.

130. Ibid., pp. 137–38.

131. Ibid., p. 77.

132. Ibid., pp. 140–41.

133. Milica Z. Bookman, "War and Peace: The Divergent Breakups of Yugoslavia and Czechoslovakia," *Journal of Peace Research* 31, no. 2 (1994): 176.

134. Milan Svec, "Czechoslovakia's Velvet Divorce," *Current History*, November 1992, pp. 377–78.

135. Ibid., pp. 378–79; Peter Passell, "Economic Scene: The Czechs Are Doing Well, With Luck and Without Slovakia," *New York Times*, 23 May 1996.

136. Carol Skalnik Leff, "The Czechoslovak Divorce," *Current History*, March 1996, p. 131.

137. John Dunlop, *The Rise of Russia and the Fall of the Soviet Empire* (Princeton: Princeton University Press, 1993), pp. 21–22.

138. Anatol Lieven, *The Baltic Revolution: Estonia, Latvia, Lithuania and the Path to Independence* (New Haven: Yale University Press, 1993), p. 228.

139. Jonathan Steele, *Eternal Russia: Yeltsin, Gorbachev and the Mirage of Democracy* (Cambridge, Mass.: Harvard University Press, 1994), p. 206.

140. Lieven, *The Baltic Revolution*, pp. 225, 227.

141. Ibid., p. 219.

142. Ibid., p. 223.

143. Steele, *Eternal Russia*, p. 13; David R. Marples, *Ukraine Under Perestroika: Ecology, Economics and the Worker's Revolt* (New York: St. Martin's Press, 1991), p. 26.

144. Mark R. Beissinger, "Demise of an Empire-State: Identity, Legitimacy and the Deconstruction of Soviet Politics," in *The Rising Tide of Cultural Pluralism: The Nation-State at Bay*, ed. Crawford Young (Madison, Wisc.: University of Wisconsin Press, 1993), p. 106.

145. Zwass, *From Failed Communism to Underdeveloped Capitalism*, p. 102.

146. Dunlop, *The Rise of Russia and the Fall of the Soviet Empire*, p. 19.

147. Ibid., p. 18.

148. Ibid., p. 59.

149. Ibid., pp. 23–27.

150. Ibid., p. 35.

151. William Moskoff, *Hard Times: Impoverishment and Protest in the Perestroika Years: The Soviet Union 1985–1991* (Armonk, N.Y.: M. E. Sharpe, 1993), p. 133.

152. Seweryn Bialer, "The Yeltsin Affair: The Dilemma of the Left in Gorbachev's Revolution," in *Politics, Society, and Nationality Inside Gorbachev's Russia*, ed. Seweryn Bialer (Boulder: Westview Press, 1989), p. 98.

153. Ellman and Kontorovich, 1992, p. 2; Moskoff, *Hard Times*, pp. 72–74.

154. Richard Sakwa, *Gorbachev and His Reforms, 1985–1990* (New York: Prentice-Hall, 1990), p. 276.

155. Moskoff, *Hard Times*, p. 183.

156. Ibid., p. 190.

157. Ibid., p. 194.

158. Ibid., p. 211.

159. Zwass, *From Failed Communism to Underdeveloped Capitalism*, p. 66.

160. Moskoff, *Hard Times*, p. 94; Zwass, *From Failed Communism to Underdeveloped Capitalism*, p. 68.

161. Zwass, *From Failed Communism to Underdeveloped Capitalism*, p. 22; Anders Aslund, *Gorbachev's Struggle for Economic Reform* (Ithaca: Cornell Univer-

sity Press, 1991), p. 184; Melvin Gurtov, *Global Politics in the Human Interest* (Boulder: Lynne Rienner, 1994), p. 162; Stephen White, *After Gorbachev* (Cambridge: Cambridge University Press, 1993), p. 272.

162. Moskoff, *Hard Times,* p. 15.

163. Walton and Seddon, *Free Markets and Food Riots,* pp. 310–11.

164. Zwass, *From Failed Communism to Underdeveloped Capitalism,* p. 20.

165. Ibid.

166. Walton and Seddon, *Free Markets and Food Riots,* p. 322.

167. Ibid.

168. Zwass, *From Failed Communism to Underdeveloped Capitalism,* p. 100.

169. Ibid.

170. Ibid., p. 101.

171. David Remmich, "Gorbachev's Last Hurrah," *The New Yorker,* 11 March 1996, pp. 72–77.

172. John Coldrusso, "Chechnya: The War Without Winners," *Current History,* October 1995, pp. 334–35.

Chapter Ten

1. Michael K. Gavin, "The High Cost of Reform," in *Apartheid in Crisis,* ed. Mark A. Uhlig (New York: Vintage Books, 1986), p. 225.

2. Martin J. Murray, *South Africa: Time of Agony, Time of Destiny* (London: Verso, 1987), p. 23.

3. Stephen R. Lewis Jr., *The Economics of Apartheid* (New York: Council on Foreign Relations Press, 1990), pp. 37, 39; Gavin, "The High Cost of Reform," in Uhlig, 1986, p. 233; James DeFronzo, *Revolutions and Revolutionary Movements* (Boulder: Westview Press, 1991), p. 273.

4. Fuad Cassim, "Growth, Crisis and Change in the South African Economy," in *After Apartheid: Renewal of the South African Economy,* ed. John Suckling and Landeg White (Trenton, N.J.: Africa World Press, 1988), p. 6.

5. Ibid.

6. Ibid., p. 3.

7. Lewis, *The Economics of Apartheid,* pp. 16, 64.

8. Gavin, "The High Cost of Reform," in Uhlig, 1986, p. 221.

9. Lewis, *The Economics of Apartheid,* p. 103.

10. Ibid.

11. Martin J. Murray, *Revolution Deferred: The Painful Birth of Post-Apartheid South Africa* (London: Verso, 1994), p. 30.

12. Lewis, *The Economics of Apartheid,* p. 37.

13. Ibid., pp. 36–37, 39; Merle Lipton, "Reform: Destruction or Modernization of Apartheid?" in *South Africa in Crisis,* ed. Jesmond Blumenfeld (London: Croom Helm, 1987), pp. 39–40.

14. Lewis, *The Economics of Apartheid,* pp. 30, 64.

15. Murray, *South Africa,* pp. 26, 328.

16. Ibid., p. 275.

17. T. C. Moll, "'Probably the Best Laager in the World': The Record and Prospects of the South African Economy," in *Can South Africa Survive? Five Minutes to Midnight,* ed. John D. Brewer (New York: St. Martin's Press, 1989), p. 143.

18. Lewis, *The Economics of Apartheid,* p. 64; Cassim, "Growth, Crisis and Change in the South African Economy," in Suckling and White, 1988, p. 7.

19. Lewis, *The Economics of Apartheid,* p. 66; Cassim, "Growth, Crisis and Change in the South African Economy," in Suckling and White, 1988, pp. 8, 18; Jesmond Blumenfeld, "Economy Under Siege," in Blumenfeld, 1987, p. 26.

20. Murray, *South Africa,* p. 275; Guy Arnold, *South Africa: Crossing the Rubicon* (New York: St. Martin's Press, 1992), p. 130.

21. Lewis, *The Economics of Apartheid,* p. 67; Murray, *South Africa,* p. 359.

22. Murray, *South Africa,* p. 275.

23. Ibid.

24. Lewis, *The Economics of Apartheid,* p. 28; Murray, *South Africa,* pp. 357–58.

25. Cassim, "Growth, Crisis and Change in the South African Economy," in Suckling and White, 1988, p. 8.

26. Lipton, "Reform: Destruction or Modernization of Apartheid?" in Blumenfeld, 1987, pp. 17, 20.

27. Blumenfeld, "Economy Under Siege," in Blumenfeld, 1987, pp. 20–21.

28. Lewis, *The Economics of Apartheid,* pp. 28, 113; Blumenfeld, "Economy Under Siege," in Blumenfeld, 1987, p. 26; Murray, *South Africa,* pp. 361–62.

29. Arnold, *South Africa,* p. 132.

30. Ibid., p. 133.

31. Murray, *Revolution Deferred,* p. 29.

32. Ibid.

33. Chester A. Crocker, *High Noon in Southern Africa: Making Peace in a Rough Neighborhood* (New York: W. W. Norton, 1992), p. 326.

34. "How Do South African Sanctions Work?" *The Economist,* 14 October 1989, p. 45.

35. T. E. Vadney, *The World Since 1945* (London: Penguin, 1992), p. 497.

36. Arnold, *South Africa,* p. 4.

37. Ibid., p. 12.

38. Vadney, *The World Since 1945,* p. 497.

39. Ibid., pp. 497–98.

40. Ibid., p. 498.

41. Arnold, *South Africa,* p. 10.

42. Ibid., pp. 10–11.

43. Murray, *South Africa,* pp. 14, 42; Robert Davies, Dan O'Meara, and Sipho Damini, *The Struggle for South Africa: A Reference Guide to Movements, Organizations, and Institutions,* vol. 1 (London: Zed Books, 1984), p. 183.

44. Davies, O'Meara, and Damini, *The Struggle for South Africa,* pp. 179, 181–82; Paul L. Moorcraft, *African Nemesis: War and Revolution in Southern Africa* (London: Brassey's, 1990), p. 47; Moll, "'Probably the Best Laager in the World,'" in Brewer, 1989, p. 154; Murray, *South Africa,* p. 54.

45. Murray, *South Africa,* p. 55; Arnold, *South Africa,* p. 61; William Finnigan, *A Complicated War: The Harrowing of Mozambique* (Berkeley: University of California Press, 1992), pp. 4–5.

46. Arnold, *South Africa,* pp. 17–19.

47. Ibid., p. 19.

48. Moorcraft, *African Nemesis,* p. 208.

49. Vadney, *The World Since 1945,* p. 499; Arnold, *South Africa,* pp. 21, 30–31.

50. "A Dismantler's Guide to Apartheid," *The Economist,* 10 February 1990, p. 38; Christopher S. Wren, "Freer Expression May Unlock Deeper Changes," *New York Times,* 23 June 1991; Vadney, *The World Since 1945,* p. 501.

51. Murray, *South Africa,* pp. 21, 81; Jacques Derrida, "Racism's Last Word," *Harper's,* February 1986, p. 22.

52. Davies, O'Meara, and Damini, *The Struggle for South Africa,* pp. 171–72; Murray, *South Africa,* pp. 65, 99; Vadney, *The World Since 1945,* p. 503.

53. Murray, *South Africa,* pp. 5, 91, 101.

54. Ibid., p. 80.

55. Lewis, *The Economics of Apartheid,* p. 25.

56. Murray, *South Africa,* p. 77.

57. Ibid.

58. "A Dismantler's Guide to Apartheid," p. 38; Derrida, "Racism's Last Word," p. 22; Davies, O'Meara, and Damini, *The Struggle for South Africa,* p. 176; DeFronzo, *Revolutions and Revolutionary Movements,* p. 281.

59. DeFronzo, *Revolutions and Revolutionary Movements,* p. 290.

60. Ibid., pp. 286, 289.

61. Ibid., pp. 292–93; John Saul, *Recolonization and Resistance: Southern Africa in the 1990s* (Trenton, N.J.: Africa World Press, 1993), p. 7.

62. DeFronzo, *Revolutions and Revolutionary Movements,* p. 293.

63. Ibid.; Heidi Holland, *The Struggle: A History of the African National Congress* (New York: George Braziller, 1990), pp. 178–79.

64. Saul, *Recolonization and Resistance,* p. 183.

65. Murray, *South Africa,* p. 200.

66. Ibid., pp. 129, 144.

67. Ibid., pp. 146–47.

68. Ibid., p. 159.

69. Graham Leach, *South Africa: No Easy Path to Peace* (London: Routledge and Kegan Paul, 1986), pp. 128–29.

70. Murray, *South Africa,* pp. 247–48, 251–52, 272.

71. Ibid., pp. 248, 304.

72. Ibid., p. 303.

73. Ibid., pp. 130, 166–67, 170, 188; DeFronzo, *Revolutions and Revolutionary Movements,* p. 295.

74. DeFronzo, *Revolutions and Revolutionary Movements,* p. 164.

75. Ibid., pp. 191, 414.

76. Ibid., p. 417.

77. Ibid., pp. 258, 420.

78. Murray, *Revolution Deferred,* p. 73; Murray, *South Africa,* p. 239.

79. DeFronzo, *Revolutions and Revolutionary Movements,* pp. 296–97; Murray, *Revolution Deferred,* p. 108.

80. DeFronzo, *Revolutions and Revolutionary Movements,* pp. 296–98.

81. Murray, *Revolution Deferred,* p. 100.

82. Murray, *South Africa,* pp. 367, 369.

83. Lewis, *The Economics of Apartheid,* p. 44.

84. Allister Sparks, "The Secret Revolution," *The New Yorker,* 11 April 1994, p. 68; Murray, *Revolution Deferred,* p. 9; Arnold, *South Africa,* pp. 44–45.

85. Sparks, "The Secret Revolution," pp. 68–69.

86. Ibid., p. 72.

87. Arnold, *South Africa,* p. 1.

88. Pauline H. Baker, "South Africa on the Move," *Current History,* May 1990, p. 197.

89. Wren, "Freer Expression May Unlock Deeper Changes"; Baker, "South Africa on the Move," p. 197; DeFronzo, *Revolutions and Revolutionary Movements,* p. 304.

90. Murray, *Revolution Deferred,* p. 189.

91. Ibid., pp. 184–85, 205.

92. Kenneth W. Grundy, "South Africa's Tortuous Transition," *Current History,* May 1993, p. 230; Melvin Gurtov, *Global Politics in the Human Interest* (Boulder: Lynne Rienner, 1994), p. 117.

93. Sparks, "The Secret Revolution," p. 59.

94. Murray, *Revolution Deferred,* pp. vii, 192.

95. Ibid., p. 210.

96. Ibid., pp. 192–95.

97. Ibid., p. 210.

98. Ibid., p. 12.

99. Donald G. McNeil Jr., "Keeping Corporate Score," *New York Times,* 2 March 1996.

100. Murray, *Revolution Deferred,* p. 213.

101. Richard Joseph, "Africa: The Rebirth of Political Freedom," in *The Global Resurgence of Democracy,* ed. Larry Diamond and Marc F. Plattner (Baltimore: Johns Hopkins University Press, 1993), pp. 307–308, 314; Jennifer A. Widner, ed., *Economic Change and Political Liberalization in Sub-Saharan Africa* (Baltimore: Johns Hopkins University Press, 1994), p. 1; John Walton and David Seddon, "Debt Crisis and Democratic Transition," in *Free Markets and Food Riots: The Politics of Global Adjustment,* ed. John Walton and David Seddon (Oxford: Blackwell, 1994), p. 333; Stephen P. Riley and Trevor W. Parfitt, "Economic Adjustment and Democratization in Africa," in Walton and Seddon, 1994, p. 136.

102. Naomi Chazan and Donald Rothchild, "The Political Repercussions of Economic Malaise," in *Hemmed In: Responses to Africa's Economic Decline,* ed. Thomas M. Callaghy and John Ravenhill (New York: Columbia University Press, 1993), p. 203; Richard Sandbrook, *The Politics of Africa's Economic Recovery* (Cambridge: Cambridge University Press, 1993), pp. 88–90; Widner, *Economic Change and Political Liberalization,* p. 8; "The State of Government in Black Africa," *San Francisco Chronicle,* 19 August 1991; Hohn Darnton, "Africa Tries Democracy, Finding Peril and Hope," *New York Times,* 21 June 1994.

103. Riley and Parfitt, "Economic Adjustment and Democratization in Africa," in Walton and Seddon, 1994, p. 137; Thomas M. Callaghy, "Africa: Falling Off the Map," *Current History,* January 1994, p. 32; John Ravenhill, "A Second Decade of Adjustment: Greater Complexity, Greater Uncertainty," in Callaghy and Ravenhill, 1993, p. 28.

104. Sandbrook, *The Politics of Africa's Economic Recovery,* pp. 5, 15; David Simon, "Debt, Democracy and Development: Sub-Saharan Africa in the 1990s," in *Structurally Adjusted Africa,* ed. David Simon et al. (London: Pluto Press, 1995), pp. 22, 25; Ravenhill, "A Second Decade of Adjustment," in Callaghy and Ravenhill, 1993, pp. 32, 37.

105. Robert H. Jackson and Carl G. Rosberg, "The Political Economy of African Personal Rule," in *Political Development and the New Realism in Sub-Saharan Africa,* ed. David E. Apter and Carl G. Rosberg (Charlottesville, Va.: University Press of Virginia, 1994), p. 301; Naomi Chazan, "Between Liberalism and Statism: African Political Cultures and Democracy," in *Political Culture and Democracy in Developing Countries,* ed. Larry Diamond (Boulder: Lynne Rienner, 1993), p. 72.

106. Jackson and Rosberg, "The Political Economy of African Personal Rule," in Apter and Rosberg, 1994, pp. 301–302.

107. Chazan, "Between Liberalism and Statism," in Diamond, 1993, p. 80; Robert H. Bates, "The Impulse to Reform in Africa," in Uhlig, 1986, p. 21; Sandbrook, *The Politics of Africa's Economic Recovery,* p. 98.

108. Chazan, "Between Liberalism and Statism," in Diamond, 1993, p. 89.

109. Ibid.; Chazan and Rothchild, "The Political Repercussions of Economic Malaise," in Callaghy and Ravenhill, 1993, p. 189.

110. Chazan, "Between Liberalism and Statism," in Diamond, 1993, p. 92.

111. Michael Bratton, "Economic Crisis and Political Realignment in Zambia," in Widner, 1994, pp. 102, 104.

112. Ibid., pp. 104, 110.

113. Howard W. French, "France's Army Keeps Grip in African Ex-Colonies," *New York Times,* 22 May 1996.

114. Ibid.

Chapter Eleven

1. Duncan Green, *Silent Revolution: The Rise of Market Economies in Latin America* (London: Cassell, 1995), p. 27.

2. Ibid., pp. 35–36.

3. Lois Hecht Oppenheim, *Politics in Chile: Democracy, Authoritarianism and the Search for Development* (Boulder: Westview Press, 1993), passim; Juan Gabriel Valdes, *Pinochet's Economists: The Chicago School in Chile* (Cambridge: Cambridge University Press, 1995), passim; Adam Zwass, *From Failed Communism to Underdeveloped Capitalism: Transformation of Eastern Europe, the Post-Soviet Union and China* (Armonk, N.Y.: M. E. Sharpe, 1995), pp. 24–26.

4. Zwass, *From Failed Communism to Underdeveloped Capitalism,* p. 159.

5. Thomas R. Callaghy, "Vision and Politics in the Transformation of the Global Political Economy: Lessons from the Second and Third Worlds," in *Global Transformation and the Third World,* ed. Robert O. Slater, Barry M. Schutz, and Steven R. Dorr (Boulder: Lynne Rienner, 1993), p. 174.

6. Richard W. Stevenson, "Russia Seeks Help to Fix its Phones," *New York Times,* 9 May 1995.

7. Callaghy, "Vision and Politics," in Slater, Schutz, and Dorr, 1993, p. 174.

8. John Walton and David Seddon, "The Politics of Economic Reform in Central and Eastern Europe," in *Free Markets and Food Riots: The Politics of Adjustment,* ed. John Walton and David Seddon (Oxford: Blackwell, 1994), p. 307; Zwass, *From Failed Communism to Underdeveloped Capitalism,* p. 158.

9. Anders Aslund, *Post-Communist Economic Revolutions: How Big a Bang?* (Washington, D.C.: Center for Strategic and International Studies, 1992), p. 56.

10. Clyde H. Farnsworth, "For Developing Countries, Debt Payments Outstrip Aid," *New York Times*, 18 September 1989.

11. Jane Perlez, "Hungarians Grow Cool to Foreign Investment," *New York Times*, 3 May 1994.

12. Lynn D. Nelson and Irina Y. Kuzes, *Property to the People: The Struggle for Radical Economic Reform in Russia* (Armonk, N.Y.: M. E. Sharpe, 1994), p. 118.

13. Perlez, "Hungarians Grow Cool to Foreign Investment," p. A3.

14. Nelson and Kuzes, *Property to the People*, p. 96.

15. Zwass, *From Failed Communism to Underdeveloped Capitalism*, p. 191.

16. George W. Breslauer, "Aid to Russia: What Difference Can Western Policy Make?" in *The New Russia: Troubled Transformation*, ed. Gail W. Lapidus (Boulder: Westview Press, 1995), p. 224.

17. Jeffrey Sachs, "The Reformer's Tragedy," *New York Times*, 23 January 1994; Alan Smith, *Russia and the World Economy: Problems of Integration* (London: Routledge, 1993), p. 235; Zwass, *From Failed Communism to Underdeveloped Capitalism*, p. 78; Nelson and Kuzes, *Property to the People*, pp. 96–97.

18. Bill Keller, "In Mandela's South Africa, Foreign Investors are Few," *New York Times*, 3 August 1994.

19. Zwass, *From Failed Communism to Underdeveloped Capitalism*, p. 160.

20. Green, *Silent Revolution*, pp. 45–46.

21. Ibid., pp. 80–81.

22. Ibid., p. 138.

23. Ibid., p. 139.

24. Ibid.

25. Zwass, *From Failed Communism to Underdeveloped Capitalism*, p. 180.

26. Green, *Silent Revolution*, pp. 85–87.

27. Roger Cohen, "Spain's Progress Turns to Pain," *New York Times*, 17 November 1992.

28. Matthew Brzezinski, "East Europe's Car Makers Feel Sting of Capitalism," *New York Times*, 28 April 1994.

29. Keller, "In Mandela's South Africa," p. C2.

30. Bill Orr, *The Global Economy in the 90s: A User's Guide* (New York: New York University Press, 1992), pp. 168, 170, 174.

31. Stephen Engelberg, "Eastern Europe's Hardships Grow as Trade With Soviets Dries Up," *New York Times*, 6 May 1991.

32. Karl Marx, *The Communist Manifesto* (Harmondsworth, United Kingdom: Penguin, 1967), p. 84.

33. Paul Volcker and Toyoo Gyohten, *Changing Fortunes: The World's Money and the Threat to American Leadership* (New York: Times Books, 1992), p. 270; Dilip K. Das, *The Yen Appreciation and the International Economy* (New York: New York University Press, 1993), pp. 25–28.

34. Artur Santos Silva, "Continuity and Change: A Banker's View," in *Portugal: Ancient Country, Young Democracy*, ed. Kenneth Maxwell and Michael H. Haltzel (Washington, D.C.: Woodrow Wilson Center Press, 1990), p. 69; Ronald H. Chilcote, "Portugal: From Popular Power to Bourgeois Democracy," in *Mediter-*

ranean Paradoxes: Politics and Social Structure in Southern Europe, ed. James Kurth and James Petras (Providence, R.I.: Berg, 1993), p. 138.

35. Carlos Marichal, *A Century of Debt Crises in Latin America: From Independence to the Great Depression, 1820–1930* (Princeton: Princeton University Press, 1989), passim.

36. John Tagliabue, "Germany Returning Property in East to Pre-War Owners," *New York Times,* 2 February 1991; Richard E. Ericson, "The Russian Economy Since Independence," in Lapidus, 1995, pp. 56–57; Ivan T. Berend, "Hungary: Eastern Europe's Hope?" *Current History,* November 1992, p. 382; Nelson and Kuzes, *Property to the People,* p. 146; Green, *Silent Revolution,* pp. 149–50.

37. Jane Perlez, "Unlike Neighbors, Czechs Are Quick to Privatize," *New York Times,* 23 December 1993; Michael Specter, "With Land Sale Edict, Yeltsin Opens Way to Longed-For Era," *New York Times,* 17 March 1996; Peter Passell, "A Capitalist Free-for-All in Czechoslovakia," *New York Times,* 12 April 1992.

38. Nathaniel Nash, "Argentina Races to Sell Oil Stake," *New York Times,* 16 April 1993.

39. Eul-Soo Pang and Laura Jarnagin, "Brazil's Catatonic Lambada," *Current History,* February 1991, p. 75; Green, *Silent Revolution,* p. 72. In Peru the government even granted Peruvian passports to foreigners who invested $25,000 in the economy. James Brooke, "Privatization to Reshape Peru Market," *New York Times,* 18 April 1993.

40. Steven Greenhouse, "East Europe's Sale of the Century," *New York Times,* 22 May 1990; Zwass, *From Failed Communism to Underdeveloped Capitalism,* p. 83.

41. Jose Marte A. Abueg, "Selling of Marcos Legacy Proves Difficult in Manila," *The World Paper,* April 1991, p. 7.

42. Zwass, *From Failed Communism to Underdeveloped Capitalism,* p. 154; Ferdinand Protzman, "Privatization is Floundering in Eastern Germany," *New York Times,* 12 March 1991.

43. Zwass, *From Failed Communism to Underdeveloped Capitalism,* p. 153.

44. John Darnton, "Polish Parliament Rejects Bill to Privatize Industries," *New York Times,* 19 March 1993.

45. Roger Manser, *Failed Transitions: The Eastern European Economy and Environment Since the Fall of Communism* (New York: New Press, 1993), p. 62.

46. Andre Gunder Frank, "Soviet and Eastern European 'Socialism': What Went Wrong?" in *Regimes in Crisis: The Post-Soviet Era and the Implications for Development,* ed. Barry Gills and Shahid Qadir (London: Zed Books, 1995), p. 105.

47. Zwass, *From Failed Communism to Underdeveloped Capitalism,* p. 156.

48. Brooke, "Privatization to Reshape Peru Market," p. C1.

49. James Leftwich Curry, "The Puzzle of Poland," *Current History,* November 1992, p. 387.

50. Perlez, "Hungarians Grow Cool to Foreign Investment," p. A4.

51. "Czechoslovakia Auctions Stores to Private Buyers," *New York Times,* 27 January 1991.

52. Nelson and Kuzes, *Property to the People,* pp. 62, 78; "Enter Comrade Capitalist," *The Economist,* 26 August 1989, p. 36; Curry, "The Puzzle of Poland," p. 387.

53. Zwass, *From Failed Communism to Underdeveloped Capitalism,* p. 151.

54. Ibid.

55. Celestine Bohlen, "Russia is Bleeding Billions in Wealth As Cash and Goods are Sent Abroad," *New York Times*, 1 February 1993.

56. Robert Schaeffer, "The Entelechies of Mercantilism," *Scandinavian Economic History Review* 29, no. 2 (1981): 89–91; John M. Keynes, *The General Theory of Employment, Interest and Money* (London: MacMillan, 1936), p. 350.

57. Fajom Hynek, information officer for Obcansk Demokraticka Stramn, interview by author, June 1992.

58. Walton and Seddon, *Free Markets and Food Riots,* passim; Steven Greenhouse, "Year of Economic Tumult Looms for Eastern Europe," *New York Times*, 31 December 1990.

59. Robert E. Looney and Robert L. West, *Third World Military Expenditures and Arms Production* (New York: St. Martin's Press, 1988), p. 21.

60. A. F. Mullins, Jr., *Born Arming: Development and Military Power in New States* (Stanford, Calif.: Stanford University Press, 1987), p. 103.

61. John Otis, "Hondurans Rethink Role of Military," *San Francisco Chronicle*, 10 April 1991. As Costa Rican president and Nobel Peace prize recipient Oscar Arias Sanchez argued, "It is necessary to have the courage to ban the army as a permanent institution . . . not only in Costa Rica but in Panama and throughout Latin America, with its shameful history of repression." Oscar Arias Sanchez, "Panama Without an Army," *New York Times, 9* January 1990.

62. Gary W. Wynia, "Argentina's Economic Reform," *Current History*, February 1991, pp. 59–60.

63. James Brooke, "The New South Americans: Friends and Partners," *New York Times*, 8 April 1994.

64. James Brooke, "Latin American Armies Are Looking for Work," *New York Times*, 24 March 1991.

65. Daniel N. Nelson, "What End of Warsaw Pact Means," *San Francisco Chronicle*, 24 April 1991.

66. "The World's Shrinking Armies," *New York Times*, 30 May 1994; Stephen M. Meyer, "The Devolution of Russian Military Power," *Current History*, October 1995, p. 324.

67. "The World's Shrinking Armies," p. A16.

68. Kenneth Maxwell and Steven Spiegel, *The New Spain: From Isolation to Influence* (New York: Council on Foreign Relations Press, 1994), p. 31; Benny Pollack, *The Paradox of Spanish Foreign Policy: Spain's International Relations From Franco to Democracy* (New York: St. Martin's Press, 1987), p. 121. In Spain the paramilitary civil guard has shifted its attention from attacking radical republicans to fighting drug traffickers and criminals who trade in endangered animal species. "Spain's Turned Civil Guard: Friend of Wildlife," *New York Times*, 28 April 1990.

69. Sheila Coronel, "With Hope and Tears, U.S. Closes Philippine Base," *New York Times*, 25 November 1992.

70. June Teufel Dreyer, "The People's Army: Serving Whose Interest?" *Current History*, September 1994, p. 267; Nicholas D. Kristof, "China Builds Its Military Muscle, Making Some Neighbors Nervous," *New York Times*, 11 January 1993; Patrick E. Tyler, "China's Military's Business Profits Being Put Back into Business, Not Arms," *New York Times, 24* May 1994; Nicholas D. Kristof, "China Raises Military Budget Despite Deficit," *New York Times, 17* March 1993.

71. "The World's Shrinking Armies," p. A16; Stephan Haggard and Robert R. Kaufman, *The Political Economy of Democratic Transitions* (Princeton: Princeton University Press, 1995), p. 115.

72. Jonathan C. Randal, "Czechoslovakia's New Age: A Farewell to Arms?" *New York Times*, 11 February 1990; Stephen Engelberg, "New Nation, Imperiled Economy," *New York Times*, 9 January 1990; "Hard-Pressed Czechs Retain Arms Trade," *New York Times*, 3 May 1991.

73. Steven Erlanger, "Russia's Workers Pay Price as Military Industries Fade," *New York Times*, 3 December 1993.

74. David Holloway and Michael McFaul, "Demilitarization and Defense Conversion," in Lapidus, 1995, p. 212.

75. Meyer, "The Devolution of Russian Military Power," pp. 326–27; Andrew Rosenthal, "For Soviets, Military Cuts May Not Feed the Economy," *New York Times*, 18 December 1988; Vaclav Havel, "New Democracies for Old Europe," *New York Times*, 17 October 1993.

76. Jeffrey Sachs, *Poland's Jump to the Market Economy* (Cambridge, Mass.: MIT Press, 1993), p. 97.

77. Craig R. Whitney, "Western Europe's Dreams Turning to Nightmares," *New York Times*, 8 August 1993; James Petras, "Spanish Socialism: The Politics of Neoliberalism," in Kurth and Petras, 1993, p. 122.

78. Cohen, "Spain's Progress Turns to Pain," p. C1; Maxwell and Spiegel, *The New Spain*, p. 73.

79. Robert Wader, "The Visible Hand: The State and East Asia's Economic Growth," *Current History*, September 1995, p. 434.

80. David B. Walker, "Germany: Confronting the Aftermath of Reunification," *Current History*, November 1992, pp. 360–61.

81. Green, *Silent Revolution*, pp. 212, 215, 217.

82. Ibid.

83. Ibid., pp. 211–243.

84. Nathaniel C. Nash, "Latin Economic Speedup Leaves Poor in the Dust," *New York Times*, 7 September 1994.

85. Ibid.; Samuel A. Morley, "Structural Adjustment and Determinants of Poverty in Latin America," in *Coping With Austerity: Poverty and Inequality in Latin America*, ed. Nora Lustig (Washington, D.C.: Brookings Institution, 1995), p. 42; Green, *Silent Revolution*, pp. 91, 202.

86. Nash, "Latin Economic Speedup Leaves Poor in the Dust," p. A1.

87. James Brooke, "Debt and Democracy," *New York Times*, 5 December 1990.

88. David Scott Palmer, "'Fujipopulism' and Peru's Progress," *Current History*, February 1996, pp. 70–75; Green, *Silent Revolution*, p. 238.

89. Silviu Brucan, "Shock Therapy Mauls Those Who Unleashed It in Eastern Europe," *The World Paper*, June 1994, p. 3; Zwass, *From Failed Communism to Underdeveloped Capitalism*, pp. 242–43; Stanislaw Wellisz, Henryk Kierzkowski, and Marek Okolski, "The Polish Economy, 1989–1991," in *Stabilization and Structural Adjustment in Poland*, ed. Henryk Kierzkowski, Marek Okolski, and Stanislaw Wellisz (London: Routledge, 1993), p. 41; Sachs, *Poland's Jump to the Market Economy*, p. 76.

90. Brucan, "Shock Therapy Mauls Those Who Unleashed It," p. 3.

91. Sabrina P. Ramet, "Eastern Europe's Painful Transition," *Current History*, March 1996, p. 99.

92. Celestine Bohlen, "Russians Find Harsh Realities in the Post-Communist Order," *New York Times*, 13 November 1993.

93. Michael Specter, "Climb in Russia's Death Rate Sets Off Population Implosion," *New York Times*, 6 March 1994.

94. Michael Burawoy, "Reply," *Contemporary Sociology*, 23 (January 1994): 166.

95. Stephen D. Krasner, *Structural Conflict: The Third World Against Global Liberalism* (Berkeley: University of California Press, 1985), passim; Giovanni Arrighi, *Semiperipheral Development: The Politics of Southern Europe in the Twentieth Century* (Beverly Hills, Calif.: Sage, 1985), passim; Immanuel Wallerstein, *The Politics of the World-Economy* (Cambridge: Cambridge University Press, 1984), passim.

96. Robert Schaeffer, *Understanding Globalization: The Social Consequences of Political, Economic and Environmental Change* (Lanham, Md.: Rowman and Littlefield, 1997), see Chapter 4.

97. Barbara Dinham and Colin Hines, *Agribusiness in Africa* (Birmingham, United Kingdom: Earth Resources Research, 1983), pp. 34, 198.

98. John M. Talbot, "The Regulation of the World Coffee Market: Tropical Commodities and the Limits of Globalization," in *Food and Agrarian Orders in the World-Economy*, ed. Philip McMichael (Westport, Conn.: Greenwood Press, 1995), p. 159; Stephen G. Bunker and Denis O'Hearn, "Strategies of Economic Ascendants for Access to Raw Materials: A Comparison of the United States and Japan," in *Pacific-Asia and the Future of the World-System*, ed. Ravi A. Palat (Westport, Conn.: Greenwood Press, 1993), passim.

99. Harriet Friedmann, "Changes in the International Division of Labor: Agrifood Complexes and Export Agriculture," in *Towards a New Political Economy of Agriculture*, ed. William H. Friedland et al. (Boulder: Westview Press, 1991), p. 67.

100. Friedland et al., *Towards a New Political Economy of Agriculture*, p. 77.

101. Kenneth N. Gilpin, "New Third World Fear: Investors Could Walk Away," *New York Times*, 24 April 1994.

102. Robert Schaeffer, "Free Trade Agreements: Their Impact on Agriculture and the Environment," in McMichael, 1995, pp. 266–67.

103. "There are certain complacencies by which the democracies justify their aversion to sacrifice," Pfaff argued. William Pfaff, "The Complacent Democracies," *New York Review of Books*, 15 July 1993, p. 17.

104. Dimitri K. Simes, "There's No Oil in Bosnia," *New York Times*, 24 April 1994.

105. Steven A. Holmes, "Africa, From Cold War to Cold Shoulders," *New York Times*, 7 March 1993.

ABOUT THE BOOK AND AUTHOR

Since 1974 more than thirty countries around the world have democratized. The fall of dictators on both sides of the Cold War divide was triggered by regional economic crises and compounded by different political problems: the death of a dictator, defeat in war, or popular protest. The civilians who replaced dictators, juntas, and one-party regimes extended power to people who had long been excluded from politics. They also set about restoring civil society and reviving moribund economies.

After documenting the emergence of a new interstate system and the Cold War that divided it in the postwar period, *Power to the People* examines the factors that led to the process of democratization in countries around the world, including regimes in southern European countries in the 1970s and those in Latin America and the Philippines during the 1980s. Schaeffer documents how Communist regimes in the former Soviet Union and Eastern Europe struggled with stagnant economies, inflation, and mounting debt during the late 1980s. Soviet efforts to reform the economy triggered a crisis first for dictators in Eastern Europe and then a crisis in the former Soviet Union itself, developments that in 1989 led to rapid democratization throughout the region. In South Africa, meanwhile, economic problems related to debt and divestment, as well as the political turmoil caused by black protest, created a crisis for apartheid, leading to black majority rule by 1994.

Although economic crises contributed to political change in many cases, they did not bring about democratization everywhere. *Power to the People* explains why regimes in Mexico, Cuba, China, Vietnam, and North Korea survived despite shared economic crises and why democratization in the former Yugoslavia, Czechoslovakia, and the former Soviet Union led also to division. Although democratic leaders around the world rewrote constitutions, held multiparty elections to restore civil society, and reformed their economies after they took power, Schaeffer contends that these solutions may not solve problems that had different regional origins. He concludes this fascinating and readable book by looking ahead to the future and assessing the prospects and problems of democratizing states.

Robert K. Schaeffer is a professor of global sociology at San Jose State University. He is the author of *Warpaths: The Politics of Partition* (1990) and *Understanding Globalization: The Social Consequences of Political, Economic, and Environmental Change* (1997).

INDEX

Robert K. Schaeffer is professor of global sociology at San Jose State University. He is the author of *War-paths: The Politics of Partition* (1990).